THE COMPLETE MUSLIM

Mustafa Styer

The Complete Muslim:
The LIFE Manual of Primary Education

Copyright © 2025CE/1446 AH

Living Insights Foundation for Education (LIFE)

Published by: Living Insights Foundation for Education (LIFE)
20 PLYMOUTH CLOSE
CAMBRIDGE, CB3 0UG
United Kingdom

Website: www.livinginsights.org.uk/

All rights reserved. No part of this publication may be reproduced, stored in any retrieval system or transmitted in any form or by any means, electronic, mechanical, photocopying, recording or otherwise without the prior permission of the publishers.

Author: Mustafa Steven Styer

Edited by: Justin Poe

Typesetting by: Muhammad Ameen Franklin

Cover design by: Muhammad Ameen Franklin

A catalogue record of this book is available from the British Library.

ISBN-13: 978-0-9560161-7-1 (paperback)

In the name of Allah,
the Beneficent,
the Merciful

ABOUT THE AUTHOR

Dr. Mustafa Steven Styer is the founder and principal researcher and curriculum developer of LIFE (Living Insights Foundation for Education.) LIFE's mission is to produce and serve an integrated and holistic K-12 curriculum drawing on the traditional classification of the sciences, which includes the liberal arts, speculative and practical sciences, and the productive sciences embodied in the art and craft guilds. Dr. Styer currently trains teachers and develops teaching materials for the Grand Imam of al-Azhar in Cairo. He previously served as a researcher on the Tabah Classification of the Sciences project and as the Albukhary Foundation Fellow at the Oxford Centre for Islamic Studies and a lecturer in the Faculty of Theology and Religion at Oxford University. Specializing in curriculum development from the University of London, Dr. Styer's MA research focussed on working with British educators to develop an integrated Islamic K-12 curriculum on a voluntary-aided school model. He has devoted the years since then to improving and completing this curriculum. He has worked as head-teacher, deputy head, curriculum coordinator, and a teacher trainer in tarbiya for the Association of Muslim Schools (AMS-UK). As a curriculum developer at the AMS, Dr. Styer produced curriculum in Islamic music (Quran recitation and *nashid*), citizenship, and PSHE (Personal, Social, Health Education) at the primary level as well as a 99-Names resource for teaching character at the secondary level.

THE
COMPLETE MUSLIM

The LIFE Manual
of Primary Education

Mustafa Styer

PGCE, MA (IOE), DPhil (Oxon.)

LIVING INSIGHTS
Foundation for Education

CONTENTS

Transliteration Key for Readers i

1 INTRODUCTION

1.1 WHO IS THIS MANUAL FOR? 1
1.2 *THE COMPLETE MUSLIM* CURRICULUM IN CONTEXT 2
   1.2.1 Problem 2
   1.2.2 Urgency 3
   1.2.3 Aspirations 4
1.3 CONCEPTS 7
   1.3.1 Individual Obligation (*fard al-'ayn*) & Communal Obligation (*fard al-kifayah*) 8
   1.3.2 General Education 9
   1.3.3 Liberal Education 10
   1.3.4 Classification of the Sciences 11
   1.3.5 True Integration of Knowledge & the Curriculum 12
   1.3.6 Training Students to Negotiate the 'Maps' of Knowledge: Modern & Traditional 13
   1.3.7 Modernity, Ultra-Modernity, Post-Modernity, & Tradition 14
   1.3.8 Social Vision 15
   1.3.9 Overview 16
1.4 HOW TO USE THIS MANUAL 16
   1.4.1 Notes for Home Schoolers 18
   1.4.2 Notes for Schools 19
1.5 CURRICULUM ARCHITECTURE 20

2 THE THEORETICAL MODEL

2.1 THE PRINCIPLES OF EDUCATION 23
   2.1.1 The Psychology of the Complete Muslim (*al-insan al-kamil*) 24
   2.1.2 What is Tarbiyah? 25
   2.1.3 Cognitive Dissonance & 'True Happiness' 27
   2.1.4 Aims of Education & Levels of Perfection 28
   2.1.5 The Culture of Education 30

2.1.6	An Integrative Approach	33
2.1.7	Our Model	37
2.2	**THE QURAN AS A CENTRAL PILLAR**	**46**
2.2.1	Learning	46
2.2.2	Understanding	47
2.2.3	Embodying	48
2.3	**THE SPECULATIVE SCIENCES**	**49**
2.3.1	Mathematics	49
2.3.2	The Natural Sciences	51
2.3.3	The Productive Sciences	53
2.4	**THE AUXILIARY SCIENCES**	**54**
2.4.1	Grammar	54
2.4.2	The Liberal Arts	56
2.5	**THE PRACTICAL BRANCHES**	**58**
2.6	**ANSWERS TO OBJECTIONS**	**59**
2.6.1	How can one teach classical texts to young people?	59
2.6.2	Should we Teach Grammar to Young Students?	62
2.6.3	Should we not use Simple, Modern Texts that Teach the Skills we Want to Teach?	64
2.6.4	If Schooling is Bad, Should we Adopt Unschooling?	65
2.6.5	How can Parents & Teachers Teach Classical Texts if They are not Trained?	67

3 THE PRACTICAL PRE-ELEMENTARY CURRICULUM

3.1	**FROM NOW TO CONCEPTION**	**69**
3.1.1	Rectify your State with Allah	69
3.1.2	Learn your Obligatory Religious Matters	70
3.1.3	Begin Learning Arabic	70
3.1.4	Choosing a Spouse	71
3.2	**BETWEEN CONCEPTION & BIRTH**	**71**
3.3	**AGES 0 TO 3**	**72**
3.3.1	Screens	73
3.3.2	Seeing Nature	75
3.3.3	Language Learning	75
3.3.4	Seeing Parents & Family Practice	75
3.3.5	Books & Toys that Work: Birth to three	76
3.3.6	Read-aloud Books for the Very Young	78

3.4	AGES 3 TO KINDERGARTEN/PRESCHOOL	79
3.4.1	The Preschool Curriculum at a Glance	79
3.4.3	Language Learning: Arabic & English	83
3.4.4	Transforming the Self & Home	85
3.4.5	Laying the Foundations (*Mabadi'*) of Their Islamic Personality	86
3.4.6	An Outline of the Preschool Subjects	86
3.4.7	Minimalist Approach	87
3.4.8	A Maximalist Approach	90
3.4.9	Mean Approach	91
3.5	THE PRESCHOOL SUBJECTS	95
3.6	RECEPTION/KINDERGARTEN SUBJECTS - OUTLINE	132
	Subject by Subject in Detail	133

4 THE PRACTICAL ELEMENTARY CURRICULUM

4.1	DAILY SUBJECTS	143
4.1.1	Religious Instruction	143
4.1.2	Quran	172
4.1.3	The Trivium & English Literature	180
4.1.4	Arabic Liberal Arts & Literature	198
4.1.5	Mathematics	218
4.2	WEEKLY SUBJECTS	225
4.2.1	The Study of Nature	226
4.2.2	Art, Craft & Design	251
4.2.3	Digital Design & Information Technology	261
4.2.5	Physical Education	274
4.2.6	History & Cultural Studies	278
4.3	CURRICULUM SUMMARY	299

5 CONCLUDING WORD

5.1	THE COMPLETE MUSLIM MANUAL & ITS MODEL	309
5.2	FREQUENTLY ASKED QUESTIONS	313

TRANSLITERATION

KEY FOR READERS

As most English-speakers are not fluent in Arabic, it is crucial to learn to transliterate correctly. However, we recommend all educators take the time to accustom themselves to reading in Arabic. When it is something to be read, we provide voweling (*harakat*). When it comes to this manual mentioning matters such as how to pray and which *dhikrs* to recite in the morning and evening, we make Arabic primary, listing these elements in it.

We only transliterate the most elementary of steps to avoid discouraging beginners. While some cultures transliterate Arabic along the lines of their own language, there is a right way to transliterate Arabic in English. We include this, plus a couple alterations we make for matters that are to be recited (so that what is recited reads more like it is pronounced).

The letters which may need explanation are:

VOWELS

a	́ (fatha) and ا so: اَ	
i	ِ (kasra) and ي so: يِ	
u	ُ (damma) and و so: وُ	

DIPHTHONGS

aw	وَ
ay	يَ
ayy[1]	يَّ

CONSONANTS

'[2]	ء	ʿ	ع	d	د
d	ض	gh	غ	h	ح
h	ه	j	ج	kh	خ
t	ت	q	ق	th	ث
t	ط	s	س	z	ز
t[3]	ة	s	ص	z	ظ

[1] (as in *ayyam*, *sayyid*, and *Qusayy*)
[2] (*hamza*) in the middle of a word
[3] In some cases (see *Conventions* below)

Transliteration Key

CONVENTIONS

ash-hab	A hyphen is placed between s, t, and other letters and h when needed.
ard	Initial *hamzas* do not need an apostrophe.
li-Llahi	The *hamzat al-wasl* is dropped from beginning of words when preceded by a vowel.
wa-Llahi	Two words written in Arabic as one are separated by a short dash.
Misriyya	مصرية
salla Allahu	Final vowels are retained, except in pause.
hamzat al-wasl	The *ta' marbutah* is transliterated as 't' when in *idafah* or used adverbially ('*tan*' as in '*rahmatan*').
Allah الله	bi-Llahi بالله
bi-Llahi بالله	li-Llahi لله

Some join these into one word, but this appears disrespectful and unnecessary. Separating also allows retention of the capital.

PRONUNCIATION GUIDE

The following Arabic terms are used frequently, and therefore not italicised in this book. Their proper pronunciation is explained here with diacritical marks.

a-dab	a-dhān	adh-kār	ā-khi-rah
'a-qī-dah	bas-ma-lah	dun-yā	farḍ 'ayn
fiqh	fiṭ-rah	ḥa-dīth	ḥa-lāl
Ḥa-na-fī	Ḥan-ba-lī	ḥa-rām	iḥ-sān
ī-mān	i-qā-mah	Is-lām	juz'
Mā-li-kī	makh-raj	na-shīd	qa-ṣā-'id
qa-ṣī-dah	Qur-'ān	ṣa-lāt	se-pā-ra
Shā-fi'ī	sīr-ah	taj-wīd	taq-wā
tar-bi-yah	taw-ḥīd	taz-ki-yah	wu-ḍū'
za-kāt			

1

INTRODUCTION

Many parents, Muslim and otherwise, are deeply concerned about the youth culture present in the local government schools. Others are concerned that the curriculum taught in modern schools does not represent their religion and culture, so they send their children to part-time or extra-curriculum education, often in mosques. Others yet have noticed that it is not enough to merely add subjects and topics to the existing curriculum: the modern curriculum itself has apparent benefits—it allows many to enter a successful career—but it is not neutral. Upon examination, critics have noted that it has abandoned true education of the human being—opting for mere instruction, and that it presents a particular implicit worldview. The Living Insights Foundation for Education (LIFE) has responded by researching and developing a curriculum designed to connect students' hearts to Allah, gain a true education of the humanity that unites them, and only then prepare them carefully to be productive community members.

1.1 Who Is This Manual For?

The present manual is a primary education practical guide for use by schools and home schoolers alike.[1] The LIFE curriculum manual, *The Complete Muslim*, is designed to truly educate every child in a general education *before* they specialise. As such, it has been optimised equally to equip children for three graduate outcomes that are almost comprehensive:

a) entry into a competitive university;

b) entry into practical work, either a trade, a craft, or entrepreneurship; or

c) completion of their studies as a traditional scholar.

In each case, they will have great advantages over others entering those fields who have not attended the LIFE curriculum. As with other single-

---

1 This primary curriculum is part of a research programme into the full K-12 range, and the secondary curriculum is forthcoming.

volume educational manuals for primary and secondary education, *The Complete Muslim* offers thorough guidance on the materials and activities needed to oversee the proper education it advises. For further details on how this manual presents this guidance, the reader will find Section 1.4 in this introduction which is titled, 'How to use this manual'.

The following introduction gives the very basics needed to understand the LIFE curriculum and how to use it (Part 1). After reading it, educators are encouraged to acquaint themselves with the theoretical model (Part 2) as much as possible before turning to the practical curriculum (Part 3). Part 3 offers the findings at the end of a long learning journey. Parts 1 & 2 reveal some of the steps of that journey and give educators stepping stones to partake in part of it. While the reader does not necessarily need to follow those steps, one should know enough to stay motivated. The minimum required is to know what is on offer in traditional education and to know that it is missing in modern education, including in nearly all 'Islamic schools'. The first stepping stones are presented in the Part 1.

It is recognised that successful education requires commitment to the right model. Many parents merely wish to avoid the more extreme problems they see in schools, but they do not know what to advise, and so many of them merely replicate school learning at home, not knowing the shortcomings of this model.[2] The LIFE learning journey started with a review of the WCIE findings, as well as working as a curriculum developer for one of the institutions produced in the wake of the WCIE (the World Conferences on Islamic Education): the AMS-UK (Association of Muslim Schools), founded by Yusuf Islam. While one educating a student does not have the luxury of going on a learning journey of years, the present introduction allows one to get a taste for the right model in the space of a few pages. This will be essential for educators to be motivated to give the education that young souls and all humanity deserves, and it will serve to make the mass model unpalatable for them.

1.2 THE COMPLETE MUSLIM CURRICULUM IN CONTEXT

1.2.1 PROBLEM

Schools do a better job of transmitting youth culture than they do of transmitting true educational ideals, much the same for Muslim schools. The school culture is not the only problem: the curriculum itself conveys the

---

[2] Such parents also effect schools, not appreciating that they are offering something precious, and often intervening for a more mainstream curriculum.

message that only hard science and technology are serious, true knowledge, and deserve attention. While a common critique states that students lack the 'lost tools of learning', this critique does not sufficiently spell out what those tools are tools for. Tools should be to obtain true learning, and true learning is wisdom, theoretical and practical. It is the hidden worldview itself behind the modern curriculum which not only lacks wisdom, but actively undermines it. This is a shortcoming of another well-known critique: the dumbing down argument, which is that modern education is watered down to produce a maleable yet reliable workforce for industry. We explain under 'concepts' below how the worldview of the modern curriculum undermines wisdom, and hence turns education into instruction.

1.2.2 Urgency

Serious critics of modern education such as Mortimer Adler hold that modern education conveys that morals are purely subjective, a mere preference one asserts. While a common argument states that moral relativism leads to the 'closing of the American mind', Adler could go further and state that the worldview behind the modern curriculum is skeptical not only of practical wisdom, but of theoretical wisdom. Modern thinkers—with a few exceptions listed below—hold that the universe is mechanical and that our ideas do not accord with how things are, so the wisdom previous wisdom traditions including religion and philosophy aimed at was a pipe dream. But this leads to an absence of true education and wisdom. And the skepticism leads to a vacuum filled in two ways. Popular and false notions of 'the good' and related notions of who and what are worthy of respect fill the void and what goods and actions lead to satisfaction and happiness. Virtue is a type of habit, and it can only be obtained by repeatedly willing the good and acting upon it. Second, the vacuum is filled by a negative freedom in which modern people cherish their lifestyle choices, hold them dear to their identity and self-esteem, and even push them into the political arena.[3] This negative freedom runs counter in practice to basing choices on principled moral reasoning. Thus, the rational faculty does not perform its role required to gain virtues and good character, and it does not control caprice. The result is moral emotivism, or what we prefer to call sentimentalism. Such a person is termed a 'modern subject', subject because such identities are in fact shaped by the modern worldview that stamps us, even while making us feel free. We believe that modern education makes the modern subject.

This skepticism leads to individualism that prevents those individuals from developing virtues, and it makes society atomised—incapable of

---

3 Those shaped by identity politics are willing to cancel anyone who does not vociferously support their personal choices and feelings.

collective action, hollow, and leading to loneliness, depression, and the breakdown of the family and community. Muslims often project onto the material success absolute success, adopting the standards of the late, capitalist, post-industrial West. Nonetheless, Muslims brought up in the wider system often question their own morals and beliefs. They do not find their questions answered, even in Islamic schools. Parents and teachers brought up overseas do not understand the West, and those brought up in the West are only able to teach students to be like themselves: semi-cultured in both their Islamic tradition and the West.[4] Islamic schools tack on poorly taught religious subjects that do not resolve the core problem: that students inhabit two worlds, switching unconsciously between them based on the company in which they find themselves.

1.2.3 Aspirations

The LIFE curriculum aspires to a real education, addressed here in terms of its vision, aims, and outcomes, and a list of the resultant unique features of our curriculum.

The vision of the LIFE curriculum centres around delivering a real education aimed to produce the complete Muslim. Producing the complete Muslim in our time necessarily involves three matters:

a) The complete Muslim strives for 'completing' the mind and character (or heart),

b) The complete Muslim needs a full social vision and a calling, not just a 'job', and

c) The complete Muslim needs the right maps to negotiate between two worlds: the modern and the classical/traditional.

We argue that if they understand how to relate these two maps, they will easily understand how to negotiate other maps, such as the false dichotomies of the sciences and humanities, the secular and religious, and the colonial and the indigenous. This capacity to negotiate two maps is crucial, as it allows graduates to later focus on areas such as science and medicine without making serious methodological mistakes that harm them personally and undermine the grander civilisational scheme set out

---

4   One may ask, how can they be semi-literate in Western culture, when many of them have degrees or are scientists or engineers? The answer is that even university education trains students in the sciences, humanities, and social sciences to be experts embodying specific methods. But, that method in actual fact rests upon a methodology, and that methodology rests upon a philosophy, and even the few of the students who continue to undertake doctoral work are aware of the philosophy and epistemology that underlies the discipline they are trained in. Much less are they capable of critically assessing that epistemology. So, we remain cultural consumers rather than producers. We are shaped by the implicit and silent philosophy.

by thinkers such as Allama Muhammad Iqbal, Syed Naquib al-Attas, or Shaykh al-Azhar 'Abd al-Halim Mahmud.

The aim of education is a topic we at LIFE have studied for decades, and we firmly believe our statement actually translates best into successful educational practice:

a) establishing a connection (*silah*) with Allah, Most High,

b) becoming someone who is not only a functional citizen, but a contributor to a real society and community, and

c) gaining a liberal education.

A few initial words are necessary on what a liberal education is and is not. It is NOT:

a) a secular humanist education,

b) merely the liberal arts, nor

c) at odds with Islamic education.

It is an education which liberates the human being in terms of the faculties most closely related to our species: the theoretical intellect and the practical intellect. The practical intellect is where character resides, and removal of vices is coterminous with purification of the heart. Together, these are termed wisdom: *He gives wisdom unto whom He wills, and whoever is given wisdom, he truly has received abundant good. But none remember except men of understanding* (Quran 2:269).[5]

The LIFE curriculum brings out two other elements of a liberal education: a profound social vision and an understanding of the sciences and their methodologies in a way that transcends various dichotomies and specialisms. If one uses the K-12 period of a student's life to obtain a general education, the result is that it is possible to combine between a liberal education and STEM or other career pathways. They are not intrinsically at odds with each other. It is for this this reason that Mortimer Adler puts forward the notion of general education as the only alternative to the solution of the 'closing of the American mind' and Allan Bloom's 'faulty diagnosis and prescriptive, narrow remedy'.[6]

---

5   From Pickthall with modification. The manner in which wisdom is both these subjects and the Sharia is spelled out beautifully by Sa'd al-Din al-Taftazani in his theological summa which remains one of the two most important summas in Islamic theology: *Sharh al-Maqasid*. This passage is part of our Introduction to Islamic Education training course, as well as the forthcoming theoretical companion.

6   Mortimer Adler and Geraldine Van Doren (eds.), *Reforming Education*, Macmillan Publishing Company (New York: 1988), xix.

This wisdom is then poured into a new container that allows students to flourish in the world as it is, while being empowered to make it better than it is. This requires that our K-12 curriculum looks forward to where students will go and what they will do. Because our model is to offer a general education before specialising, it gives the individual soul what it needs, while keeping a careful eye on what is required for students to then specialise. The outcomes are practically comprehensive. The curriculum shape allows three outcomes:

a) Entrance into a competitive university;

b) Entrance into a practical field, be that a trade, craft or entrepreneurship; and

c) Completion of religious education to become a religious scholar.

Having researched for decades, we are aware that students who gain a liberal education alongside science excel in their capacity to write and produce a portfolio for competitive universities. Also, for Islamic seminaries in the West to thrive, they must have a feeder stream of students that have a background in Arabic and Islamic subjects.[7] Thus, *The Complete Muslim* is, with little exaggeration, a curriculum everyone needs.

The features of the LIFE curriculum that allow these high aspirations and that offer added value include that it:

- teaches the individually obligatory knowledge (*fard al-ʿayn*) not as a rote list, but as a seed that leads to further human development and that needs to be watered through K-12, and then throughout life.

- is designed with the correct methods for developing firm mental habits that allow students to obtain wisdom and firm character traits required to obtain true virtues. The modern curriculum, on the other hand, spreads children too thin to master either topics or their own character, and it trains them to swiftly acquire knowledge to regurgitate in exams.

- includes the teaching of a social vision which leads to flouring not only for the individual, but for one's dependents and society so that the atomisation of contemporary society does not lead to a breakdown of the family, loneliness, and depression. This also transforms meaningless jobs into a calling and includes thinking strategically about matters that govern the modern world such as the economy.

- teaches the subjects that are intrinsically integrated towards completing

---

[7] Currently, Islamic seminaries in the West often start at the graduate level. So, students come pre-formed, but with little Arabic or background in the Islamic subjects. As such, there is a challenge for such institutions to produce quality scholars from the twenty-year-old students who come to them with only a general exposure to a secular curriculum.

the person and producing ultimate flourishing.

- engages with modern knowledge to gain critical mastery, not blind imitation.
- plants seeds in the holistic primary curriculum to bear fruits in its secondary curriculum[8] and in life-long learning.[9]

These features channel the subjects so that they contribute towards achieving our overall aspirations. In many curricula, subjects are put on the curriculum merely to get through externally imposed texts. These subjects weigh on the mind of students, deplete their innate curiosity, and spread their mind thin such that they fail to master important topics and acquire wisdom. We have explored the different approaches not only to teaching subjects, but to the subjects themselves for decades. In each subject, educators will find a section titled simply 'Why?' which focusses on explaining how that subject contributes towards producing the complete Muslim. The 'How?' section explains how to deliver the said subject to achieve those high aims. The 'Why?' part of our curriculum keeps clear before our eyes what habits the curriculum produces. These habits must build on each other systematically. In Part 2, we set out theoretical principles that form the foundation of a curriculum that promotes theoretical and practical wisdom. We then turn directly to these wisdoms in Part 3 and detail a program for students to gain and maintain their wisdom as they competitively enter the professions or a practical route.

1.3 CONCEPTS

Our curriculum represents intense practical research and a critical learning journey. While other educators do not need to know or follow the order that our journey took, it is necessary that they take something of a learning journey. This is crucial for motivation, and generally there is more impact in deriving conclusions rather than being handed them. Be that is it may, there is a principle of education which says that we much remove the false and vain from our souls *before* we learn and acquire truth and virtue. *Before planting new seeds, one must remove the weeds.* We have seen when offering our course 'Introduction to Islamic Education' that educators who grasp what it is and how to do it simply do not want to go back to their previous practice. Here, we share the basic concepts of our learning journey

---

[8] Forthcoming in *The Complete Muslim: The LIFE Manual of Secondary Education.*

[9] This curriculum was developed as part of an MA thesis including full-time curriculum development for the AMS-UK. After an additional fifteen-year engagement with the curriculum subjects, it is being modified for publication.

which may empower educators to understand and deliver a real education.

1.3.1 INDIVIDUAL OBLIGATION (*FARD AL-'AYN*) & COMMUNAL OBLIGATION (*FARD AL-KIFAYAH*)

Individual obligation is the amount of knowledge considered obligatory for each Muslim individual; it relates to the particular soul and their core faculties and what is required of them individually. Communal obligation, by contrast, is the knowledge which is obligatory for a specific community or city: it is the knowledge that each society requires to be healthy and to know Allah's will for it. Hence, everyone within a given city sins if this obligation is not met.

Influential educationalists have argued that individual obligation relates not only to one's individual need to pray, make ablution, and read Quran, but also relates to what one is engaged with. For example, if one engages in certain financial transactions, one must know if they are permissible. Similarly, if one attends university, one must know the truth or falsity of what one is taught and any implication it has for one's core religious beliefs. As such, the said influential educators speak of an 'expanded individual obligation' that occurs due to living in the modern world; this seems surely to be the case if one attends university, for one is engaging with one or more subjects at a relatively deep level.[10]

All we shall say regarding communal obligation is that it requires a form of thinking which has become rather foreign to the average 'respectable Muslim' who merely seeks professions based on pay package, such as becoming a doctor or engineer.[11] The argument often goes that they are then in a position to financially support Islamic institutions. The truth is that they do not know how to think strategically about what institutions are needed and what they require to function efficiently, and unfortunately

10 We noted above the relevant statement of Mortimer Adler about the closing of the American mind; these causes are deeply entrenched in the various departments of the modern university, with exceptions we mention under the concepts 'Modernism and post-modernism' below.

11 If one meets with Muslim students in a university system, the majority are content to be attending the Friday prayer, but they have little knowledge of how to think as an *umma*, and even appear to have little interest. How their degree might have been selected to fulfil a communal obligation is the furthest thing from their mind. The result is that we live in a dysfunctional *umma*: we are unable to react productively when one part of our 'body' feels pain. We do not build the institutions we need, and actually do not know what institutions are needed. Many accept whatever the government provides as sufficient, as they do with government education. We have accepted a modern communal form of life and would feel awkward knocking on our neighbour's door to ask if those in the neighbourhood have considered their communal obligations, or even to offer them something we cooked or picked in our garden.

many do not give even zakat. Due to this sad reality, education on how to think as an *umma* is the first step to guiding the production of communities conducive to the flourishing of ourselves and our children.

1.3.2 GENERAL EDUCATION

A general education may be defined as teaching and training what students share: their humanity. It is opposed on the face of it to teaching and training what they differ in: their future specialisation. In reality, it is not an opposition, because it is effectively an organisational insight into the curriculum, according to which the K-12 years be used mostly for general education such that when students do specialise, they do not do so at the expense of their own humanity. A pedagogical insight behind general education is that it avoids making 90% of the curriculum a missed opportunity, or even a waste of the child's time. Imagine I have ten curriculum subjects, and the child can only specialise in adulthood in a field related to one of these subjects. Nonetheless, I teach each ten subjects by drawing from them what will lay the seeds for their future (but unlikely) specialisation. I do this rather than draw from it what they need to perfect their humanity.[12] The result of that flawed approach is that 90% of the curriculum time will turn out to have been misused. One may argue that the great scientists of the past were shaped by just such as structure: general education *before* specialisation.[13]

Mortimer Adler holds that a general education is the only real solution to the malaise in American education, other solutions being quick fixes that have repetitively shown themselves to be ineffective. He conceives it not only as a chance to give students a real education, but as a response to two deep misunderstandings deeply entrenched in Western education and its universities. The first is that only science is worthy of being termed education. The second related misunderstanding is that morality is relative, and therefore it would be folly to teach moral education: to learn to think about right and wrong carefully and based on principles. These misunderstandings are, for Adler, the true cause of 'the closing of the American mind'.[14]

---

12 Each 'Why?' section inside the curriculum in Part 3 addresses how the subject being addressed contributes towards the complete Muslim.

13 This general education before specialisation is not an ancient artefact found only museums: Sir Isaac Newton is a representative, and less than one-hundred years ago, scientists such as Michael Faraday received a general liberal education or gentlemen's education before they specialised as scientists. This is a win-win situation.

14 See Mortimer J. Adler, "Liberalism and Liberal Education," in *Reforming Education: The Opening of the American Mind*, ed. Van Doren. We believe Adler's critique falls short in two ways. First, he corrects Allan Bloom, showing that moral relativism starts earlier than he

General education is highly related to the expanded *fard al-'ayn* (individual obligation) notion of S. N. al-Attas, but this and other crucial matters must be left to Part 2. These include how this general education must teach wisdom and the lost tools of learning. But to do so, one must know what subjects both practical and theoretical wisdom consists in, and what is the best approach to the tools of learning we term the instrumental sciences. Then, to be successful, one must order these elements in the curriculum, and leave time to prepare students to enter the wider world through various examinations, expertise, and portfolios. The latter has been carefully crafted in the secondary part of the LIFE curriculum so that the usage of time in the primary and secondary are optimised.

1.3.3 Liberal Education

Liberal education in the most complete sense of the word is that which liberates and completes or perfects the core human capacities that distinguish us from animals: the theoretical and practical intellects. These are the main two branches of liberal wisdom. The late classical Islamic education and liberal education in its full sense—not merely as the liberal arts—accord with each other.[15] The subjects that comprise theoretical and practical wisdom cannot be approached directly; students must first acquire firm dispositions (*malakat*) in the so-called 'lost tools of learning', the trivium. In the hands of certain classical thinkers, the trivium alongside the quadrivium are referred to as 'liberal arts'. These liberal arts should not be confused with the broader notion of liberal education as we have defined it. In late, classical Islamic education, the larger madrasas taught not only religious subjects, but also the rational sciences. Most importantly, they integrated them in a way that the LIFE curriculum mirrors. In fact, this approach of integration is why LIFE chose to take the late classical madrasa curriculum as a model: they represent the maturity of Islamic learning in which all branches of knowledge were integrated with the Islamic revelation. They also represent the sophistication of catering for a wide, global community. It allows us to teach a coherent worldview and address all the subjects in a

---

thought: the 1930s, not the 1960s. And he shows the cause to be widespread in the university, not limited to the influence of reading the books of Friedrich Nietzsche. Adler states that moral relativism was taught by positivistic philosophers such as Carnap, and also in the social science departments of sociology and cultural anthropology. We note that this trend in philosophy and the social sciences is a development primarily of the thought of Kant. As such, it is rooted in the general epistemological trends of modern philosophy. See the entry on the concept, 'Modernism and post-modernism, and tradition', below.

15 See, Mustafa Styer, *The Vision of Islamic Education*, in the festschrift to Sayyid Ali Ashraf edited by Shaykh Mabud, forthcoming. Further elaboration is to be found in the forthcoming theoretical manual accompanying the present practical manual based on material prepared for presentation for Tabah Foundation.

way authentic to Islamic learning and provide a rigorous basis of wisdom from which to engage with modern sciences.[16]

1.3.4 CLASSIFICATION OF THE SCIENCES

The classification of the sciences is the categorisation of subject disciplines. The classification of subjects, or sciences, is not just a list, nor is it merely one, subjective manner of dividing the subjects. It is an objective classification of things as they are in themselves.[17]

Awareness of the full classification allows graduates to negotiate the complicated divisions of the modern university and give the grounds to begin to inform ourselves in confusing decisions such as what discipline or field to specialise in. 'What is the real nature of these classes I am taking?' 'What is a social science, a humanities subject, a natural science (or simply "science") and why was there no such term "science" 200 years ago?' 'Where do these fit on the objective map?' Negotiating modern and traditional subject maps is part of training graduates of our K-12 curriculum.

To mention only a few benefits of a genuine classification, first, one needs to know the basic classification as a methodology which guides one to the right science and hence the right books that will contain the answers to a question, and even which scholar to whom one should take a question. If one takes a natural science question to a jurist, the results can be embarrassing or harmful. Many ignore this to their own detriment, and much contemporary Islamic education never mentions this. In fact, a new generation of Muslim academics investigates modern issues with no reference to where—and

---

16 An important aside is that British Muslim educators in the 2000s had a rallying call: 'We need to derive inspiration from the Islamic learning at a time that it covered not only the Sharia sciences, but all sciences'. It turned out that this curriculum took its form primarily at the hands of 'Adud al-Din al-Iji (d. 1355) and Sa'd al-Din al-Taftazani (d. 1390)— two immense scholars who follow al-Ghazali and al-Razi, the books of al-Taftazani reaching Ibn Khaldun being of signal importance to him. Historical irony has determined that a form of amnesia of the Muslim past has set in such that scholarship on this period was sorely lacking up to the last approximately twenty years. Reflect on how projects such as the 1001 Inventions give the impression that Muslim genius is limited to Abbasid thinkers. Two problems plague this view. First, it gives the impression that there is such a gap between us and the Abbasid Age that there is no living tradition that connects us. Secondly, many of the thinkers that made this era notable show little capacity to integrate their thinking and research with revelation, and many merely imitate Greek materials that reached them. Fortunately, by the 2010s, a number of research groups were reviving knowledge of this era, including one at Oxford where I was completing my DPhil. Not only was the curriculum that took shape in the late, classical Islamic period broad, but it was deeply integrated, a matter we refer to in the two following entries.

17 See the following entry on 'True Integration', including the note that the full subject was added to the graduate exam for potential scholars at al-Azhar to effectively teach this classification.

therefore how—a science is addressed by scholars.

But it is also a necessary ingredient of pedagogy: Ibn Khaldun states that organising disciplines around a subject and having this logical limit is required to develop firm dispositions of knowledge. With this limit in place, one circles methodically around the attributes of one's subject, carefully studying and proving that the subject has these attributes and states. Otherwise, knowledge is not organised and one merely collects facts, not knowing how they relate to each other, which are most important, and where they end.

1.3.5 True Integration of Knowledge & the Curriculum

Integration has been a buzzword for decades in educational writing and practice, as has the related term 'inter-disciplinary' education or studies. True integration, hardly mentioned if at all in mainstream educational writings, is the relationality of the subjects discussed above. Namely, it is both the logical and ontological relation of disciplines, one to another, as they are in themselves and not merely as we perceive it, and not merely due to us drawing connections or making associations between one subject and another.

From the ontological integration, two other types of real integration emerge: epistemological and pedagogical integration. Proper study of a subject requires that in seeking knowledge of it, one finds the right principles that lead to the knowledge of that subject. It turns out that subjects generally derive principles from each other, so the sciences are integrated at an epistemological level.[18] An even more derivative yet important type of integration is the pedagogical: when we as humans comprehend this true integration and apply it in our lives, it results in an integration *in us*, or rather an integration *of us*. How? One sees how science, maths, ethics, politics, religion, and the humanities are related to each other in themselves. They are a unity and cannot be extricated completely from each other. Our thought becomes integrated, and even our actions. All the practical sciences derive their principles from the theoretical sciences. Knowing the basic proof for this helps one escape

---

[18] The outstanding Shaykh al-Azhar, Shams al-Din al-Anbabi (d. 1896) added a new subject to the graduate examination: the principles of the sciences. Why? Because he understood the classification of the sciences has a serious implication for seeking knowledge: that some subjects contain principles required to unlock other subjects. Without the map provided by the classification, one lacks the notion that subjects cannot be learned without their principles. We may give two examples returned to later in this book: without identifying the principles of biology, one may dissect 1000 frogs and learn next to nothing. And without identifying the principles of astronomy, one may look into or even study the night sky for a whole lifetime without learning anything significant in the science of astronomy.

the moral relativism rife in the universities. Then, one can build one's thought free of relativism and free from ideology, important with the rise of populism.[19] Another element of pedagogical integration is clarity regarding the unity of the disciplines and having a map to guide one. Contemporary Western culture is shaped by false dichotomies that must be healed not just to heal oneself, but also to heal society: secular versus religious and sciences versus arts and humanities. People cannot be whole persons if they do not take from each to complete themselves.

1.3.6 Training Students to Negotiate the 'Maps' of Knowledge: Modern & Traditional

The complete Muslim needs the right maps to negotiate between two worlds that we all inhabit without any choice in the matter: the modern and the traditional worlds. This ability to negotiate between the two is something not found in traditional education, but was developed by LIFE, the last years of this research coming to fruition in collaboration with Tabah Foundation and al-Azhar. Based on years of research, we teach students not only the modern map of knowledge and the traditional one, but the relationship between the two. The modern map is what is encountered at university, and this map is mirrored in society. The traditional map is based on how the subjects relate to and connect to one another in a logical manner that mirrors the unity of created being, and ultimately Divine knowledge.

We teach maps that are integrated with the sharia, made by scholars who were masters of both religious and natural sciences. Without teaching these two maps and how to relate them, a series of challenges plague students. They do not know how to navigate the university and are confused when choosing what to study. They must shift identity when inhabiting the secular world.[20] And there is a real danger of a bubble bursting outside the home if they are not practiced in relating the maps of wisdom needed for themselves and the modern world needed to navigate it and make a living.

---

19 This clear ethical and practical thinking is the best basis for action, and repeated good actions is the best way to build strong, virtuous habits and praiseworthy character, purifying the heart of vice.

20 Studies show that Muslim students typically shift between three hats they must wear: one in the school, one in the mosque, and one in the home.

1.3.7 Modernity, Ultra-Modernity, Post-Modernity, & Tradition

Throughout its publications, LIFE uses 'contemporary' to refer to the period of time we live in and 'modern' to refer to a specific approach, philosophy, or school of thought. Modernity, the abstract noun for the modern, refers to the material and social conditions of the contemporary world, many historians stating it started among a small number of people in 1452 (or 1453 or 1500). We argue that contemporary institutions are almost entirely an expression of modernity. The political and social institutions that shape contemporary life are guided by the social sciences: politics, education, and sociology are all social sciences. Being guided by the dominant schools of thought in the university, they thus adopt modern philosophy. Modern philosophy famously began with the rationalism of Descartes, progressed to the more skeptical radical empiricism of Locke and Hume, and to the yet more skeptical idealism of Kant. It can be shown that all three—rationalism, empiricism, and idealism—are highly skeptical as to whether our ideas and impressions accurately represent the outside world. For this and other reasons, many have argued that what unites the schools of thought often considered to be opposites is more than what divides them. They set out on a praiseworthy path of methodological skepticism; but the positions they took landed them in proper skepticism. Skepticism is the denial of realism. Realism is the belief that things have realities and that they are knowable, potentially at least. This skepticism is especially the case in morality and ethics, as noted by Adler, but Adler could have easily made the case that this matter began with the beginnings of modern philosophy, not so late as the 1930s.

In fact, the skepticism of the 1930s is nothing more than modernity following its principles to their logical end. While many speak of post-modernity beginning either in 1914 or 1930, LIFE crucially distinguishes between two senses of post-modernity. If it refers to a school of thought taking the skeptical principles of modernity to their logical ends, it makes more sense to refer to it as ultra-modernism. Because it is an extension of modernity, it makes little sense to refer to it as post-modernity, even if there is a grain of truth: modernity sought certain knowledge, post-modernity abandons this. A significant minority of philosophers hold that modern philosophy is a dead-end and strive to remove the traces of Descartes, such as Cartesian dualism. This heterogenous group is best termed post-modern, as they depart from modern ideas such as the claim that we only know our own ideas, not the things of the world. Mainstream philosophers in this vain include the American C. S. Peirce and the German Husserl and his teacher, Franz Brentano, and his renegade student, Martin Heidegger. But also include are notable hosts of realists such as the contemporary giants Alisdair MacIntyre and Charles Taylor and other Catholics and Neo-Thomists, Neo-Aristotelians, perennialists, and radical conservatives such as Pugin, William Cobbett, and John Ruskin; and groups such as the Southern Agrarians (including Richard Weaver), the Inklings (including Tolkien and C. S. Lewis), and writers for the Criterion such as T. S. Eliot. A common tread amongst these thinkers is to identify the beginning of modernity with the nominalism of William Ockham, and later thinkers who held that the meanings we use in speech and thought do not exist in the world, and that the world is only composed of individual particulars.

The said names should be household names and have inspired countless Muslims who are attempting to understand modernity. Unfortunately, a majority of Muslim thinkers still prefer to imitate modernity, not knowing its principles, and yet emboldened to use it to 'tell their fathers how they should rearrange their houses'. Muslims of the past who have strove to understand modernity from its principles include Mustafa Sabri Efendi—the last shaykh al-Islam of the Ottoman Empire, Shaykh 'Ali Ashraf al-Thanvi, and René Guénon ('Abd al-Wahid Yahya). Our contemporaries in this category include S. N. al-Attas and S. H. Nasr, both of whom were instrumental in the WCIE, attended by luminaries such as al-Thanvi and Titus Burkhardt. And we we believe we should add Pr. Recep Şentürk, Dr. Karim Lahham and Shaykh Hasan Spiker, to name but a few in each category.

1.3.8 SOCIAL VISION

A holistic and even holy vision of society and community is the icing on the cake of a complete education. It directs all races and 'classes' to one end: completing the human and knowing and worshipping Allah. This provides a spiritual unity which appears to be missing from modernised countries. The vision of the social promotes a unity in which one hand washes another. It is unified by its end—perfection and knowledge. This end can be used to distinguish between political leaders aiming for this perfection, and those for whom politics is merely answering to powerful funders in order to stay in office. This helps graduates immunise themselves from the power of ideology and populism.

An element we add to the traditional curriculum is how to find good work. Collectively, this makes their work a 'calling', not just a 'job'. And the spiritual unity of society we teach overcomes the fractures that exist in modern society based on class, culture, and race. There must be a view of mankind and society as one body which works together towards human development—not just economic development—and pleasing Allah, Most High.

1.3.9 Overview

The LIFE curriculum culls traditional wisdom to perfect the individual soul, before children specialise. This is the only solution to modern educational woes. In addition to packaging this wisdom to be delivered to work towards the aims you have for your student or child, it addresses the woes of Islamic education such as the additive model which leads to confusions in modernity and difficulty in navigating the modern world. It has been researched carefully from entrance into schooling to primary school (and before) to the exit realities that students face after graduation. The powerful training to think and purify the soul and gain a grounded piety make other forms of education a missed opportunity for students or your child.

1.4 How to Use This Manual

Ideally, the education recommended in the present manual begins from birth, and parents prepare for their children's education even before birth, and even if they plan to send them to school.[21]

We have organised subjects in this manual to respond to the main questions of what, why, and how. 'How?' explains the approach taken, the resources needed, and sometimes the pedagogy of delivery. We do our best in this section to cater to two audiences: those who have certain resources, and those who do not. Also, for those lacking certain resources or struggling with a matter, we offer a consultation service. Moreover, you may share thoughts with the community of people using *The Complete Muslim* through a LIFE online community that is in the pipeline.

As noted, *The Complete Muslim* subjects are ten. These divide neatly into subjects like Maths and Quran that need to be taught daily, and subjects like art and history that are taught weekly. We term these 'daily' and 'weekly' subjects, respectively. The daily schedule is merely to teach the five daily subjects, plus one weekly subject, for a total of six daily lessons. The weekly subject is arrived at through distributing the five weekly subjects across the days of the week, one subject per day. When the final element of breaks is added in—a morning break and an afternoon break for lunch and *zuhr* prayer, the following two tables emerge:

---

21 For reasons why this is important, see Section 3.1, 'Prior to Elementary', especially 3.1.1 and 3.1.2.

HOW TO USE THIS MANUAL

TABLE 1: GENERAL WEEKLY TIMETABLE

Mon	Daily Lesson 1	Daily Lesson 2	Break	Daily Lesson 3	Daily Lesson 4	Lunch & Prayer	Daily Lesson 5	Weekly Lesson 1
Tues	" "	" "	" "	" "	" "	" "	" "	Weekly Lesson 2
Wed	" "	" "	" "	" "	" "	" "	" "	Weekly Lesson 3
Thurs	" "	" "	" "	" "	" "	" "	" "	Weekly Lesson 4
Fri	" "	" "	" "	" "	" "	" "	" "	Weekly Lesson 5

TABLE 2: PARTICULAR WEEKLY TIMETABLE

Day	Daily Lesson 1	Daily Lesson 2	Break	Daily Lesson 3	Daily Lesson 4	Lunch & Prayer	Daily Lesson 5	Weekly Lesson
Mon	Quran	Maths	Break	Liberal arts	Religion	Lunch & Prayer	Arabic	Natural science
Tues	" "	" "	" "	" "	" "	" "	" "	Physical *futuwwah* disciplines
Wed	" "	" "	" "	" "	" "	" "	" "	IT and digital design
Thurs	" "	" "	" "	" "	" "	" "	" "	Art and craft
Fri	" "	" "	" "	" "	" "	" "	" "	6. History & cultural studies

Table 2 lists an order that puts Quran and maths early in the morning, but you are free to organise the day as you like. Part 3 of *The Complete Muslim* includes several pointers and alternative approaches to certain subjects that may help cater for your home or school, and student or child, or to reduce the load or break up the day.

In Part 3 of the manual, you will find a section for each subject. Within each subject, you will *consistently* find: What? Why? How? And *sometimes* you will find: How, for those without needed resources?

General resources (or LIFE resources such as: booklists and poem lists). By general resources, I mean resources which may be important in general, but which are not part and parcel of the 'How?' section above.

Extra advice: This section is sometimes needed for specific topics or situations where particular challenges are anticipated, or extra information is needed.

You may term 1 and 2 above ('What?' and 'Why?') as 'the LIFE approach', and 3 and 4 ('How?' and 'How, for those without needed resources?') as 'the LIFE curriculum'. As such, 3 and 4 of the LIFE curriculum includes matters such as timetable, chosen resources, and how to put them together to confidently cover the subject at hand.

Matters such as pedagogy are also addressed in the 'How?' section, as are occasional notes on how to handle challenges to do with motivation and finding tutors, if needed.

Whether you are a school or a home-schooler, leave ample time to find, purchase, and start to digest the learning materials for each subject. This is more a matter of months than weeks. First impressions only come once, and they literally shape learners' attitudes. So, be over-prepared for the first day, not under-prepared.

1.4.1 NOTES FOR HOME SCHOOLERS

Home schoolers have three manners to deliver the curriculum:

a) by themselves—with the help of taking additional courses,

b) through hiring a tutor—for some or all subjects, and

c) through establishing a co-op—again, for all or some subjects.

Many people imagine that home-schooling is necessarily you teaching the whole curriculum. This is wrong: historically many people were educated in their *homes* by tutors their parents arranged. In fact, if you read the biographies of historical elites, you will find how common this was. It allows you to have the best teacher in each subject teach your child. This shows how important it is *where* you live. The tutors you find in Oxford are not like the tutors you find in Detroit, Michigan. And the tutors you find in Cairo are not like the tutors you find in Jordan, which had no well-known scholars in the pre-modern era.

As we note elsewhere in this manual, parents may learn as they teach to a surprising degree. But there are subjects in which you will need to take a course, and there are subjects you must outsource if you are unable to correct your own learning, such as pronunciation of the Quran. We believe this may help you handle the challenge of performing two roles in your child's eyes: parent and teacher.

Home schoolers have the luxury to start when they wish and to choose which year of curriculum materials best suit their child's readiness, ability, and interest. You may either advance or delay a whole year, or in some cases doing so with certain subjects is possible and may suit your child. You should have an outside eye on your teaching to ensure quality, and that you do not procrastinate in beginning certain subjects or fall behind in all subjects. While a more learned and experienced person is best, any other home-schooler will help. As they say, the eye cannot see itself, and it is common to be so wrapped in teaching and preparing that it is difficult to step outside that thought process and quickly assess where you are and how you are doing.

If you are starting in the middle of the primary stage, determining how to fill any gaps your child has may be a complicated matter. Address our consultancy service if things get complicated.

1.4.2 NOTES FOR SCHOOLS

Ideally, your school would start from our preschool curriculum. The exposure to Arabic is perhaps the most important element of the preschool. If your school does not, you may be able to advance with our curriculum if you start at reception/kindergarten. If opening a new school, we recommend you start with preschool and add a new year group each year.

School teachers will also need to learn to deliver the subjects of the LIFE curriculum, either through learning as they teach or through taking courses. In some cases, schools may also wish to use tutors supplied by LIFE, whether in-person or to teach virtually—with a classroom teacher on hand in the class.

Confident educators, including home schoolers, may develop units to teach certain topics, and share or upload these to the LIFE community. In the future, LIFE intends to offer quality assurance on such exchanges and encourage people to upload, in order to receive a free subscription to the materials in the LIFE community. This may assist in the delivery of certain topics for certain educational contexts or allow us to cater to cultural alternatives based on your home country.

1.5 Curriculum Architecture

The theoretical and practical capacities of the child are developed in parallel and age-appropriately. Children must start with preliminary learning that serves as a basis for true knowledge and virtue when they are mature. The strands needed to weave these elements into the developing student may be visualised as per Table 1.5 (and in greater detail in Section 2.1.2, below).

THEORETICAL	PRACTICAL
1. Basic spoken-language acquisition	1. Pre-virtues of orderliness
2. Pre-grammar and penmanship	2. Virtue by imagination: Fables, stories of the virtuous and prophetic character
3. Grammar and Basic Islamic beliefs	3. Basic Islamic practice and *Finding True Happiness*
4. Pre-logic (and preparation to learn theoretical sciences via Euclid's *Elements* and child-friendly introduction to modernity)	4. A practical manual on the Islamic vices and virtues

ONGOING DISCIPLINES (*RIYADIYYA*)

The following require ongoing practice (*riyada*) on the model of apprenticeship seeking mastery: Quran (including learning stories and later *tafsir*), Mathematics, Arts & Crafts, and Physical Education (Sunnah or *futuwwa* disciplines).

Table 1.5

While classical learning in English relied on Greek, Roman, and European-language texts translated into English, gaining a true education in English raises 'the language issue'. Further, to understand these sciences even in English requires understanding discussions of grammar and what are called the instrumental sciences. This should not wait till secondary stage.

Rather, the primary stage has less exam pressure and years in which to learn proper language skills. The best approach is to allow children to concentrate on a few essentials and ensure they start strong in language, both Arabic and English. Proper study of any language necessarily includes grammar and literature, just as the Dars-i Nizami in the past taught Persian through texts exemplifying the highest Persian language (called the Panj Ketab). There are currently no texts that have any classical quality in English. An educational text should be age-appropriate, but it should nonetheless use august language and exemplify the tools of the scholar such as eloquence and the use of technical definitions and gently introduce the terminology of the discipline.[22] If students are able to read Arabic texts, they may read and research on their own. They would not be boxed in by the few quality, reliable materials available in English. The only acceptable alternative in English is for texts to be written with carefully translated terminology. This terminology should be chosen so that either: a) it conveys the same meaning as the Arabic or b) it is defined through to the same meaning given to the Arabic original by reliable scholars.

---

22 Classical child-friendly texts of the past were like this, such as *Mukhtasar al-Akhḍari* of the Maliki school or *al-Risalah al-jami'ah* of the Shafi'i school.

2

THE THEORETICAL MODEL

This section offers further reasoning and explanation for the curriculum and approaches to the subjects treated in Part 3. Part 2 is placed here to identify its optional, but recommended, status. As noted, being rooted in a rationale helps solidify commitment which is crucial for regular delivery of quality educational experiences. However, if one seeks nothing further than the introduction, or struggles with the new concepts, feel free to turn directly to Part 3. Some readers will need to attend a LIFE course to absorb notions which are unfortunately not part of mainstream education.

Modern teachers were deprofessionalised over the last decades, especially since the decision of what and how to teach was taken out of their hands in the 1990s in many Western parts of the world. Previously, teachers had the knowledge of the principles needed to arrive at the justification and basis of their own practice. This section aims to partially fill this gap. It covers the main topics but leaves a full treatment to the theoretical companion manual of the present manual. Many of the topics it takes up differ from that manual in that here there is greater emphasis on justifying certain practices adopted in certain sciences that are part of the integral curriculum: *The Complete Muslim*.

2.1 THE PRINCIPLES OF EDUCATION

By principles of education is meant the premises by which one knows what education is, including its method and content. A principle is a cause: these are the basic notions which lead one to understand education such that one's practice is arrived at through principles, not mere preference nor happenstance. Psychology is a foundational discipline, for the educated in question is a human soul with its various epistemological and practical faculties (or cognitive and motor, with needed caveats). The sciences which follow are what the educator learns in education. As our curriculum aims to teach wisdom before the world, it conveys traditional disciplines. These disciplines are integrated in a manner which means they cannot be taught as either unrelated facts or skills. These disciplines have a necessary logical and pedagogical order which must be observed. When done so, they operate in the soul as principles: like seeds which unfold to lead to practical and theoretical perfections operational in the world.

2.1.1 THE PSYCHOLOGY OF THE COMPLETE MUSLIM (AL-INSAN AL-KAMIL)

The Complete Muslim is a manual presenting a classical approach to education which aims to do what education worthy of the word should do: a) perfect the human being, namely to make the perfect human being (*al-insan al-kamil*) in the model of the Prophet Muhammad ﷺ and b) raise a person who can function in the world (via university, work, or to whatever role their life should direct them). In other words, the ultimate aim of education is determined by the human species: perfecting the highest faculty. Education and pedagogy should facilitate this by organising science intrinsically, i.e., through their subjects which are based on the natures of things in the world. This is the conceptualisation of education to which the LIFE curriculum is committed, not only because of its root in the Islamic tradition, but also because of its timeless relevance to the human being in the world and society. In what follows, I will first explain what I mean by 'perfect human being' and how Muslim authorities understood its implication on education.

The human soul has a) a speculative faculty whose perfection results in knowledge of the realities of things as they are and b) a practical faculty whose perfection is the performance of matters in the way they should be (i.e., virtuously) in order to obtain felicity in both worlds, this world and the Hereafter. Religions and philosophies have throughout history agreed on the concern for perfecting the two faculties of human souls and facilitating the ways of arriving at both ends. These Muslim authorities asked the essential question: what are the sciences which perfect the human speculative and practical faculties? Muslim scholars organised the science of theology and the sciences of Sharia in such a way to answer this question. Their answer was guided by reason and revelation and how the perfect human ﷺ integrated them in his person and character. The end of Part 1 presented a diagram of the main curriculum subjects based on this framework, Part 3 offers the details of the subject, and the end of Part 3 contains tables which present the curriculum at a glance.

Perfect does not mean absolutely without blemish or beyond mistake. It indicates that the human being is created in need of nurture: it has intrinsic possibilities in terms of cognitive and character development that start imperfect and require being brought to their perfection.

Perfecting the human requires two matters: a) fulfilling religious obligations (and aiming as much as possible thereafter to obtain spiritual excellence (ihsan, the third pillar of religion) and b) using timeless educational approaches designed to perfect the two major faculties which make us a human being, the theoretical and practical parts of our soul. In both cases, the proper liberal arts are the necessary gateway. The curriculum set out in 'Curricular Architecture' above is our best attempt to embody these necessary steps to producing the perfect person.

2.1.2 What is Tarbiyah?

Note that tarbiyah overlaps with the curriculum, so what relates to curriculum subjects is treated below. Let us say there was or is a science—Islamic or otherwise—which addresses character (*akhlaq*). There are two aspects to character and purifying the heart. One is knowing right from wrong. Two is repeatedly doing the right and leaving the wrong until a virtuous habit forms in the soul and all the vicious character traits leave the heart. Both are important, but knowing the right without one's soul inclining towards it causes a battle within the soul, or cognitive dissonance. In this section (under 'Educational Principles'), we address all besides the actual books and sciences which are treated below. By principle of tarbiyah we mean for instance that 'If you do not believe it is possible to change character, then you will not be able to change it'. Then tarbiyah will be impossible. If you believe it is possible, then you have to know how and think through the practical steps to purifying the soul of the child under your care who is a trust (*amanah*) from Allah.

So, let us set out the principles of tarbiyah that a parent or teacher needs to oversee tarbiyah. Tarbiyah may be used in a wide sense which includes education as a part of it. In this sense, it means something like 'upbringing'. Here, on the other hand, we will use tarbiyah in opposition to teaching (*ta'lim*): it relates to character, whereas 'teaching' relates to theoretical knowledge. Tarbiyah on this meaning may include spiritual training, but in the case of educating children includes etiquette (adab), orderliness, religious practice, and virtues, at least as much as possible for a youth. Thus, tarbiyah roughly aligns with the practical intellect, while 'teaching' relates to the theoretical intellect. It also relates to practical sciences, whereas teaching relates to theoretical sciences. It is important to avoid a fallacy here, though. Practical sciences are sciences. They are sciences formed of truth claims and proofs. A student needs the instrumental sciences—including logic, the science of proof—in order to really know the sciences, not just memorise them. The difference as set out in the opening pages of the *Ihya' 'ulum al-din* is that theoretical sciences are known as an end in themselves: knowing is the perfection sought from them. Think of contemplation and knowing

God in order to worship Him. But practical sciences are known in order to do the right act. Further, right acts are done not merely because a right act is an act which embodies justice. Rather, right acts, if acted on repeatedly, lead to a habit. These habits are virtues. Virtues are the fruits indicating the heart is purified. Because vice and virtue are a spectrum surrounding the same 'act', such as spending money, the only way to remove a vice is to gain a virtue. One must eat, spend money, etc. So, if one does so according to Quran, Sunnah, wisdom, intellect, and the mean, this is an act leading to virtue. If not, repeated acts lead to vice.

The Quran and Sunnah and Sharia are not a law code. Rather, they are a system of beliefs and acts which lead to justice, purification of the soul, and keeping a covenant with God. The acts they prescribe or advise are medicines designed ultimately to perfect character and purify the heart. In an especially important tradition, the Prophet Muhammad ﷺ stated, 'I was only sent to perfect noble character'. Ideally, these medicines designed to perfect character should be prescribed by someone who understands how the medicine effects the heart; this is the reason for choosing classical texts for purifying the heart in as early as primary education. Of course, many prophetic traditions themselves explain the proper and improper uses of acts of worship and the Sunnah itself. For this reason, one will find texts such as *al-Arba'in* and *Riyad al-salihin* in the primary curriculum, texts which are not merely 'collections' of sayings.[22]

There is a thousand-year-old tradition of Islamic ethics which both teaches what acts are good and the basic method for purifying the soul. In an independent resource, LIFE has produced a 'Tarbiyah Policy'. This policy is meant to replace the behaviour policy typical of schools. It includes a survey of prophetic and Islamic 'techniques' of tarbiyah or changing character. We think of this as a motor of change. Once we know how to change, we need to identify a direction and a set of steps or a track to travel on. This is the virtues in order of how they should be obtained in order to make a stable character. For instance, if a person has tremendous reliance on Allah and abstinence from the pleasures of this world but does not know how to take turns or speak to people, they will not be able to function in the world. These matters are thought through carefully in this pack, including by drawing on classical educators such as Charlotte Mason who identify pre-virtues needed by children on their way to true virtue. The same applies to other

---

22 In a well-known story, a group of Companions erred in continuously fasting, not marrying, or praying the entire night. Though the acts they did were acts of Quran and Sunna, they deviated from the Sunna through misapplication. This danger always exists. The Sunna itself includes a set of regulatory principles governing how to use it. Thus, one almost arrives at what a physician of the heart would know. For instance, one is advised not to pile on works beyond one's capacity. One is advised that performing small amounts of worship consistently over long periods of time is far superior to worshipping in a manner one cannot maintain.

domains of learning: one must learn coarse motor skills before learning fine motor skills. One must embody virtue in habits from a young age, lest one have cognitive dissonance later when one's head says one thing, but one's body and desires say another. Rather than merely learning about ethics and other sources of ethical teachings such as the Prophet's ﷺ biography, upon him be peace and blessings, one should use the educational setting (home or classroom) as a workshop. Here one has the ingredients (interaction with Allah and other people), tools (oneself and one's psychological faculties), and the supervisor (parent or teacher) and one may begin practicing. In our resource, we encourage individualisation—knowing where individual children are on a 'track'—but also education all students in all character virtues. They are, after all, the branches of belief (*shu'ab al-iman*). One's belief is not perfected until the attributes are rooted in the heart, and they should all be prioritised in education.

Character can be changed. Otherwise, one cannot believe in the efficacy or point of tarbiyah. While we all have a nature, we may acquire a second nature. Clearly, the Sharia commands us to have good character and work to get it. If it were impossible, we would not be ordered to do so.

Character is a habit which forms at the interface between the intellect and the lower parts of the soul. The part of the intellect which orders the lower parts to act is called the practical intellect. All character virtues and many spiritual states emerge here.

While modern science and contemporary culture discount the higher and lower faculties of the soul, one can see the parts of the soul in action. An example given by an Islamic scholar is that one sees a glass of water and has not drunk any water for three days. One knows with certainty that there is poison in the water. There will be a part of the soul which thirsts for the water and tries to push one to drink it, while another will be absolutely repelled by the thought.

2.1.3 Cognitive Dissonance & 'True Happiness'

A virtuous city (polis or city-state) is one where the wider culture encourages, by and large, true happiness. In a culture like ours which calls to matters that will not lead to true happiness, one is in danger of cognitive dissonance. In this case, this means that if one studies ethics and religion, one knows the truth and what one ought to do. But the irrational parts of the soul are directed towards other pursuits. One's head is in one place, and one's desires are in another. Such a person experiences this as a dissonance which clouds their heart and breaks their resolve and lowers their motivation.

We aim to complete a resource identifying the matters that are attractive and draw respect and other means by which a false vision of happiness makes their way into the heart and head. Then we address these through powerful antidotes and reflections on matters such as peer pressure and how to take charge of one's heart and head. Not only does our culture direct us towards a false vision of happiness, but it denies certain principles that are part of tarbiyah. These include the idea that our emotions and desires, sexual and otherwise, are precious parts of our identity and personality. This identity becomes political, and rather than question whether something is right or wrong, I am willing to fight and destroy others who do not hold my feelings, desires, and identity as sacred.

This is not a classical resource but draws on them. And without it, there is a great fear that like so many in Islamic and other religious educations, a hidden curriculum will grip students.

2.1.4 AIMS OF EDUCATION & LEVELS OF PERFECTION

The primary curriculum presented in this manual is a part of a coherent K-12 curriculum optimised to reach towards the three aims of education set out in the introduction. Though we believe these aims are more practical than many listed by other Islamic educational efforts, there are a set of challenges no one can presently ignore. The first is that the traditional aim of achieving the individual obligation is not a sufficient guide to learning, as it can be achieved in a few months. As stated in the introduction, some have entertained the notion of the expanded individual obligation, considering that every new act we enter requires the knowledge of Allah's ruling on that matter. This is especially important due to our virtual swimming in the flood of modernity, and high university attendance. Further, one may include matters such as removing all the vices from the heart. But when we look for another curricular aim beyond the individual obligation, then the pendulum swings the other way, and this is too ambitious for a K-12 curriculum, as the ability to purify the heart often requires an age range beyond this curriculum. Also, purification of the heart is ultimately in the hands of Allah. And other aims one may entertain such as becoming a full scholar are also beyond the K-12 age range. So, we have investigated a set of aims that should be kept before educators, and to complement the 'Tarbiyah Policy' mentioned above and its track of perfections. Note that all the perfections listed are effectively fulfilling the possibilities of Islamic psychology, specifically those that pertain to the practical or theoretical parts of the human.[23]

As stated in the introduction, the two levels aimed for in religious

---

23 Every educator and person should strive for perfection, even if others around one do not. Anything else is a form of spiritual sloth.

instruction are: (a) individual obligation (*fard al-'ayn*): in knowledge and practice, and (b) an extended individual obligation, covering contemporary issues and matters of belief and practice and ensuring impermissible matters of the tongue and limbs and adab with Allah are covered (such as the adab of supplication). Mind that a certain amount of Arabic language is an individual obligation. Beyond these are the category of praiseworthy (*mahmud*) supererogatory levels.

While these levels are not technically an individual obligation, the following should be born in mind.

- The Prophet ﷺ indicated that his Sunnah should be followed: 'Every (believer) enters *Jannah* except those who refuse'. His Companions asked, 'And who refuses?' He replied, 'Those who refuse my Sunnah'.

- Shaytan attacks the outer ring of one's religion. So, he will start with encouraging one to leave the Sunnah, then the obligatory (*fard*), then to encourage innovations in belief (*bid'ah*), then encourage outright unbelief (or incorrect beliefs in core points of creed).

- Practicing the Sunnah: in one's speech and actions.

- General enrichment: Being familiar with forms of supererogatory worship and having an enriched cosmology and awareness of levels of existence and the Islamic sacred calendar.

- Specialised enrichment: Praiseworthy knowledge well beyond the individual obligation in subjects such as fiqh, the Quran, and purification of the heart. If these matters are known to be in danger of loss or lack in a given area, their learning becomes an obligation upon the community (*fard al-kifayah*) and an individual obligation on the one who embarks on fulfilling them.

- Enculturation (*tathqif*): This important level refers to those who learn Islamic subjects. These subjects contain methodologies which protect one from corrupt methodologies which have seeped into the Muslim community and from corrupt epistemologies which have seeped into so-called secular subjects. 'Wherever one is ignorant of a subject, vain imagining fills in gaps in one's knowledge'. For this reason, it is praiseworthy to learn as many Sharia subjects as possible. The difference between enculturation and scholarship is that the encultured understands the subject but may make mistakes when asked specific questions.[24]

---

24 The scholar must master the given subject, requiring a level of strain not required from the encultured. It may be that the encultured therefore has time to pursue topics via research, understand the relationship between the topic and modern approaches, and explore aspects of methodology which are neglected in many seminaries, so it is a good option for someone not intending to present themselves to the community as a scholar. This rank opens the door to

- Scholarship (*'alimiyyah*): Obtaining this level requires competence in a traditional set of Sharia sciences which encompass much of the tools of the liberal arts (*'ulum al-alah*). Obtaining this level by the age of seventeen or eighteen is possible in specific contexts, but LIFE recommends a general track in which students get a rounded education first, then those choosing a scholarship track to carry on at undergraduate and postgraduate level.

Scholarship is meant to lay a sound basis not only for interpreting scripture but for the theoretical perfection of the human being. If this is completed, and augmented by practical perfection, one removes vices that distance one from Allah and draws close to Allah. Closeness (*wilaya*) to Allah, including perfection of the theoretical intellect, constitutes the complete Muslim. Although not obtainable in the K-12 period, it is the aim to which our curriculum is ordered.

2.1.5 THE CULTURE OF EDUCATION

It is widely recognised that culture is a major factor in education. Many contemporary educators would argue that culture is what is taught, and that the teacher's role is merely to facilitate this learning. But this assumes a particular view of culture: that culture is a purely active human construct and that all knowledge is culturally relative. Culture may be defined as both the embodied symbolic realities of a group of people and the immaterial ideals held by that group. These embodied realities include printed and other forms of language, and also art and architecture. On this definition, culture is a mirror of the humans that make up a social group, especially their learning: theoretical, practical, and productive. The science which treats culture as a whole is politics; at least this is the case in the Islamic tradition,[25] as well as the Greek and other traditions. Political philosophy should be about identifying how to establish a society and culture that leads to perfecting and completing humanity, in part through education.

Politics and political philosophy have become modern university disciplines; they no longer perform the wider role they once did. What is needed is a wide science which sets out a social vision that addresses and includes all different types of people. Such a science is a principle of education in that it drives education and guides the proper embodiment

---

work with scholars to solve problems and 'Islamize' subjects and professions from the inside, by working in those areas.

25 Ibn Khaldun (*al-Muqaddimah*) but also Abu Yusuf, al-Raghib al-Isfahani (*al-Dhari'ah ila makarim al-Shari'ah*), al-Mawardi (*Adab al-din wa-l-dunya*), al-Ghazali (*Ihya' 'ulum al-din*), Shah Wali Allah al-Dihlawi (*Hujjat Allah al-balighah*), and also Malek Bennabi wrote extensively in this vein.

of education in a culture. From one point of view, education should seek to perfect culture. From another, culture impacts education as students eventually integrate with a culture and impact it. Educators must know how students will navigate their host culture. If that culture has a false notion of the good and is not a virtuous state or a city of God, certain hazards exist. This includes the development of cognitive dissonance or a bubble being popped when one enters into the wider culture.

Christians who saw the changes occurring to their civilisation have thought deeply on this topic. These include those listed above as a 'second Europe'. T. S. Eliot, Jacques Maritain, Christopher Dawson, and Jacques Barzun[26] and others have written specifically on the topic of culture. What may be said in this practical manual is the following. First, culture does not exist in a relativist vacuum. Rather, its realities and ideals are reflected in a true mirror which is the realities of those symbols, institutions and ideals. As such, culture and society are either true or false, good or bad. While a modernist may argue that the social contract allows an arbitrary production (institution) of social institution, the human being is a reality, and social institution have a role: they are intrinsically to fulfil a need of the human, and they are good in as much as they facilitate the perfection of the human. The Shari'ah and practical sciences reveal these realities and make explicit these goals which are otherwise written only in Preserved Tablet.

Second, the concepts of a culture are adopted as habits in our thought. This must be addressed actively. A perfect example is the word 'perfect'. Modern people have a hang-up with this word. Even if a educator redefines the word, it is difficult to get rid of the baggage one associates with the word as a cultural symbol. But what do you do when you are surrounded with words that need to be reworked to have a sound culture? Words like subjective and objective have been inverted from their original meaning, but few people know this. Not only re-education is required, but a sensitivity to the impact of culture.

Third, a healthy culture requires a healthy social vision. Students must be ready to serve and rectify institutions such as the family and marriage. They must learn how to navigate the reticence that accrues in atomised neighbourhoods or apartment complexes in which neighbours avoid even going into the hallway or elevator at the same time. Students cannot be passively shaped by the existing social vision without great damage occurring. This is mostly addressed in the secondary stage of the curriculum, but the seeds are found here in the primary: the view of 'the good' transmitted in

---

26 One thinks of Barzun's *The Culture We Deserve*. It is not an accident that Barzun was a student of Mortimer Adler. Another important work of Barzun which assesses the state of modern culture is *From Dawn to Decadence: 1500 to the Present: 500 Years of Western Cultural Life*, (New York: Harper Collins Publishers, 2000).

our culture is addressed in the work studied across several primary years: *Finding True Happiness*.[27]

The healthy social vision mostly taught in the secondary stage clarifies that the various goods managed in a practical setting are hierarchically organised, so corruption becomes clear. Ideology used to mask corruption and self-interest also becomes clear. Thus, to free one's mind and heart, a degree of ethical and political philosophy is necessary.[28] Students should know enough of the sciences of ethics, economics, and politics to understand the structures and policies in front of them potentially or in case studies, even if they do not know the intricacies, for instance, of modern economics. Just as the meaning of liberal arts is to free the human faculties, one experiences a great sense of freedom being able to root oneself and escape the shadows and caves of polarised party politics in which everyone clamours that they alone are offering freedom, liberty, or egalitarianism and social, economic, and racial justice. Tradition becomes next to impossible without community. Modern economies militate against community, solidarity, and even family. As such, it is paramount that would-be adults can distinguish a virtuous community or family from otherwise and have a sophisticated and flexible (not fluid) view of sensitive topics such as gender relations and roles.

A social vision explains what communities should look like, as they are microcosms of the universe and macrocosms of the human. Worship is embodied in mosques, knowledge is embodied in madrasas and other institutions of learning, spirituality is embodied in *zawiya*s, and the marketplace and craft workshops relate to the body. While there is a hierarchy, they are all serving the same purpose. And, without the body, there is no mind or spirit. From another perspective, the communal obligations for knowledge as set out in *Kitab al-'ilm* need to be embodied in individuals in each town. This sets out a vision for collaboration and moving beyond the selfish and single-minded pursuit of the ultimate pay package.

The LIFE curriculum addresses the wider social issues through reading Ibn Khaldun and those who may be seen as extending his thought. This occurs in the secondary curriculum, but the primary curriculum contains readings of John Ruskin and others who wrote against the changes we now live in before they became the default position embodied in our society. These writings on culture and social vision are being included in the subject 'History and cultural studies'.[29] Further reading appears in other subjects,

---

27 This is mostly taught under the subject religious instruction.

28 Al-Ghazali also states in *Mizan al-'amal* that one must know something of the soul and its faculties to purify it and reach felicity.

29 Note that the link between history and culture is one forged deeply by Ibn Khaldun himself.

such as Islamic instruction, but also arts and craft.

Finally, we note in passing that the classification of sciences itself is needed for a healthy culture. The modern university is shaped like a conveyer belt driving everything on it towards a positive form of secularism. Harvard University was once a seminary. The mode that departments are divided practically precludes any major impact of the theology department on the other departments. This is not a surprise: Christopher Dawson saw that so long as the liberal arts no longer serve to connect the university disciplines, no amount of theology can resuscitate Western spirituality. Theology merely becomes a silo, a distinct speciality that most people never encounter after leaving secondary education.

The LIFE curriculum teaches the full classification as a traditional map and teaches how to understand and navigate the modern map. This is done in the history and cultural studies curriculum. But this topic has profound implications in all the curriculum subjects, implications educators reinforce for students in the other lessons.

2.1.6 AN INTEGRATIVE APPROACH

One last principle upon which education and our curriculum is built is integration. As per the introduction, there are various types of true integration. Islam is an integrated religion. This is exemplified in the Jibril hadith which sets out three integrated sciences—or four in reality: iman (belief), Islam (Islam), ihsan (spiritual excellence), and *amarat al-sa'ah* (signs of the end times). Iman is creedal belief, but in a wider sense it addresses the theoretical part of knowledge related to what is often termed 'worldview' (though this word has additional connotations). Islam is practice, being much wider than the notion of 'religious practice' and covering the entire realm of the practical part of knowledge. Ihsan is purification of the heart and spirituality. *Amarat al-sa'ah* are the signs of the end times; but in a wider sense, it is the devolution and corruption occurring in knowable stages. They work together like a tree in a loose metaphor. The roots are belief, practice is the trunk, and purification and spirituality are the branches and flowers or fruits.

Two matters now raise their heads. First, the sciences taught in al-Azhar were classically twelve. How do we understand the relation between three or four Sharia sciences and twelve? The first is that iman consists of theoretical principles (*usul nazariyyah*). Islam relates to actions and thus guides to practical wisdom of all sorts. In classical terms, it relates to derivative practical rulings. Thus, these two Sharia subjects cover the same ground as the theoretical and practical sciences. The twelve sciences taught at al-Azhar are nearly all practical, theoretical, or what are called instrumental sciences, such as grammar, logic, and rhetoric. So, whether we discuss the Sharia model of the Jibril hadith, the madrasa model, or even the full model of liberal education (not merely the liberal arts), we have a set of sciences designed to guide to the two main types of practical wisdom. When those sciences are being taught in a technical manner, one must also master the instrumental sciences, which are arguably necessary tools of learning which any education should have. As set out in our curriculum architecture and in Part 3, our curriculum is designed to give these three divisions of knowledge their due: practical wisdom, theoretical wisdom, and the instrumental sciences. That is because they are the sciences which perfect the human *as* human.

A second matter raised its head as follows: certain teachers have realised that a mere 'additive model' in which 'Islamic studies' (not a classical term) is sprinkled on top of a modern, secular curriculum leads to something that cannot be integrated. Those who pursued the question furthest began to note that the madrasa at certain times taught all the sciences. Not only did polymaths write on all the subjects at that time, they also worked to remove contradictions between reason and revelation. This is the first type of real integration: the consistency of truth claims.

Another matter is more technical. Imam al-Ghazali and later theologians saw that theology should be a universal science, similar to metaphysics. What this means is that all theoretical matters are addressed in it, then each science takes a portion of being as its subject. Quantity is the subject of maths, natural beings are the subject of natural sciences, and fiqh studies the actions of those who are religiously responsible. This same form of unity was once present in the high Middle Ages, when it was said that theology was the queen of the sciences and philosophy was her handmaiden. In our context, we might say logic—or even all of the trivium sciences—is her handmaiden. When organised this way, certain sciences become the principles of others. Certain other sciences become the trunk for other sciences which are its branches. One example of a science being the principle of another is *usul al-fiqh*, which can literally be translated as the 'principles of fiqh'. An example of the latter was already given: kalam theology studies all being, and the rulings of that portion of being are studied in sciences like mathematics. Traditionally, Azharis took an examination on the ten principles of the sciences. As noted by a key writer in the genre of the ten principles, 'To seek knowledge of a science, one has to know its principles'.

This is real or true integration. False integration is to make links between sciences, without ever knowing the definition of the subject of a science and hence not knowing logical boundaries governing what that science should and should not address.[30] If one draws links between sciences

---

30 Think of Richard Dawkins making pronouncements on the existence of God as a scientist

before defining their subjects, the links one makes are likely to be mere associations and purely subjective unless on is very lucky or has a great innate capacity. For instance, one may 'see' the link between geography and business, but what is the proper subject-matter of each? What is the logical notion that one speaks about in each of these two sciences, just as one speaks about 'the word' in grammar and 'actions of the religiously responsible human' in fiqh, such that in fiqh one says, 'This action of the religiously responsible human is permissible', and, 'This action...is impermissible'. The logical subject is not merely a notion, but a slice of reality or what is called ontology. Once you identify the logical/ontological subject, only then can you see the relationality between subjects. This ontological relationality is crucial, as it yields sciences which distinguish in order to unite. The sciences divide, but they come together to form a stained-glass ascending into the vault of heaven through which the Divine light shines through so many related pieces to form a single image or map. This integrated unity is taught in the history and cultural studies curriculum, but the rest of the curriculum deploys individual pieces shaped by this methodology. Even in Year 1 when we introduce the classic, but simple text *al-Risalah al-jami'ah*, the student is told about the subject of the science at hand, and how it relates to other sciences.

Sharia sciences required for a perfect human (*insan kamil*)

1. Jibril Hadith Division
2. Sciences required for *insan kamil* (general):
   - Theoretical realities (iman, covered by 'aqidah)
   - Practical guidance (Islam, covered by fiqh)
   - Spiritual purification (ihsan, covered by *tasawwuf*)
   - The Signs of the end of time

Detailed Division represented in the late, classical curriculum

3. Theoretical sciences
   - Theology (God and angels, etc.)
   - Mathematics
4. Natural science (the natural world)
   - Practical sciences (integrated with fiqh and Sharia)
   - Politics (& economics)

dabbling in theology.

- Home management (& what we would call life skills and crafts, but mind that home economics is about management, not production itself which needs management)
- Ethics (i.e., *akhlaq* and character, purification of the heart, including how to engage with people and work ethically, and in line with the prophetic character and with confidence)

Integration is found in the primary stage but is more manifest in the secondary stage. One might expect primary education to be completely dominated by the tools of learning. But in reality, the LIFE curriculum offers natural science, but through nature study, not only suitable for children, but necessary to lay a bedrock of experience before turning to abstractions such as 'friction' and 'force'. And it teaches mathematics which is a discipline requiring gradual and continual practice master. It also teaches the basics of fiqh and 'aqidah which are like seeds that must be planted early and watered with practice throughout youth. It also includes ethics—including the tension with the wider cultural view of 'the good'—and the basics of how to understand the classification, as these matters are needed to prevent corruption of the child's character or start to relate the two maps they must negotiate without confusion.

One benefit of integration is that the daily and weekly subjects are designed to develop concentration in your child through limiting the number of subjects demanding focus at any one time and integrating their content when they do become numerous. One of the biggest detriments of modern education is that it never allows your child to focus on developmental subjects such as language (including the ability to write and reason) and maths (the language of numbers).[31] By the terms 'integrated' and 'holistic', we mean a number of things. First, each subject relates to others because they each contribute to perfecting the intrinsic aspects of human nature. In each subject in *The Complete Muslim*, you will find a 'Why?' section explaining how it contributes to producing the perfect person. Second, they fit together on a classical map of the realities of the world which contains an implicit statement of how to take care of the world. This not only empowers them to be leaders of tomorrow and stewards for nature and culture, but it offers them crucial guidance for the various subjects on offer at university, where the relationship between subjects is confusing for students.

---

31 The central argument of Anthony Bryk, Valerie Lee, and Peter Holland, *Catholic Schools and the Common Good* (Cambridge: Harvard University Press, 2009) is that the lack of funding for science labs and other equipment needed to expand significantly beyond language and maths has the unexpected result of improvement in language and maths. Further, this book argues that these core sciences turn out to be more determinative of future success and achieving the 'common good' than branch sciences such as science and the arts.

SUMMARY: EDUCATIONAL PRINCIPLES

Human psychology and notions of education, tarbiyah, culture, and integration must be clear as starting points to build a curriculum that strives towards human perfection. Education pertains to the theoretical sciences and their corresponding human faculties; tarbiyah to the practical of each. This psychology and the education based on it are the basis for true integration, and one may see that this integration is already present in the Sharia sciences. However, humans do not live in a vacuum, and hence this true integration must somehow integrate with the modern. The LIFE curriculum is woven on the warp of these principles, moving through the years in a developmentally appropriate manner, and fulfilling various requirements and prerequisites along the way. This involves the instrumental sciences and other manners set out below in 'Our Model'.

2.1.7 OUR MODEL

In the most direct terms, our curriculum is a holistic and broad, integrated curriculum. This description is so general as to be meaningless, so I add that it offers true integration as set out in the introduction, going further to integrate with the modern world we live in. In more expansive terms, our curriculum model is to take traditional learning from the madrasa and beyond and pour it into a new container which requires a) engaging two sets of truth claims, b) engaging with two sets of maps of knowledge, and c) preparing students for exit examinations.

In terms which allow us to see visually in the coming diagramme how this curriculum takes shape in its ten subjects, we go further and say, it is a curriculum devoted to a general education before specialisation. It does not accomplish general education merely with *tools* of learning—like people dressed up with nowhere to go nor by opting for an applied trivium structured through treating these subjects in part as stages. This we consider a form of neo-traditionalism in a negative sense: compromising traditional principles through characteristically modern application.[32] A truly traditional general

---

32 I critically define 'neo-traditional' to mean imagining and inventing tradition at a remove from an actual living tradition and its mechanisms for dealing with problems and change. This imagining and inventing is often different from what a living tradition itself would arrive at. The point requires elaboration beyond the present remit, but it appears that Dorothy Sayers is neo-traditional in this sense. She starts with the names of sciences which are traditional and extends them into stages which are her own invention. There is a vague truth that information needs to be memorised, then logically organised, then rhetorically and effectively expressed, and that this is sometimes lacking in modern education. But this does not make her stages the best way to organise a true classical or traditional education. Rather, something closer to real traditional curricula is far more beneficial and rooted in deep principles she does not address.

A positive definition of neo-traditionalism is a tradition that has responded to new circumstances and arrived at new solutions or even practices. The problem with this definition

education which is contextualised, not compromised, is precisely the model which the human soul itself needs. Those who know these subjects have experience that contradicts these neo-traditionalisms. Traditional madrasas can teach morphology, grammar, and logic in surprisingly early years.[33]

Were we forced to summarise first the heart of traditional education underlying the LIFE model and second the contextualisation, we would say: offer a thorough classification of the sciences which conveys wisdom and is none other than the perfection of the faculties of human psychology, practical and theoretical. Do this largely after teaching the instrumental sciences. Teach students how this model gives a unity to all knowledge, including the Sharia. The mode of instruction aims to convey firm dispositions, not mere sparky associations and hyper-links. This is done through the subjects having a logical structure allowing their core topics to be comprehended properly. Study these topics through active disputation, applying the rules of traditional logic which are not just about thinking and entailment, but are about forms of proof which lead to certainty. Similarly, in tarbiyah, do not shift the student from one task to another in such a fluid manner that they never master anything, including themselves. Rather, teach them to imagine virtue (through stories they remember for the rest of their lives), know virtue with their mind, and to apply it in the 'classroom' and society (through service), like a laboratory. Follow their development, give them opportunities, and encourage consolidation of certain traits. This is the education they deserve.

Second, give this education the contextualisation it requires to stay with students in the 'real' world. At the primary level, we add a resource: *Finding True Happiness*. In late primary and secondary levels, we teach students how to negotiate two different maps of the subject: the modern subject taught critically will prove essential for their successful choice of a university degree. The ability to navigate these maps was said above to be essential in avoiding a confused identity. A significant matter we may only allude to

is that it appears to entail that traditions do not respond and grow, while neo-traditions do. That is not the case.

33 We do not advocate teaching logic proper until the age of ten or eleven, based on the student, and presupposing that grammar and pre-logic have been taught before this.

While rhetoric is taught later in Arabic, in English pre-rhetoric has a long tradition of being taught alongside grammar. This is merely the practical activities of the progymnasmata: these include developing flexibility in reordering the same sentence in as many ways as possible, identifying and explaining metaphors in simple terms, and other similar activities that are not purely abstract.

While the phrase, 'Play with the child till seven', has become a commonplace amongst Muslim educators, the LIFE curriculum notes that many biographies show that actual practice does not support this maxim. Also, children in Western schools will learn by play to the age of seven. See William Smail, trans., "The Method of Primary Instruction," in *Quintilian on Education*, which contains a debate of this very issue, including evidence of who said or disagreed with the point in ancient times.

is the integration required by language issues. Our curriculum encourages learning Arabic texts in religious instruction but discussing those texts in English. We scaffold the second language (Arabic) off of the local language (in this case English) to expedite firm learning.

The most important principles behind our curriculum may be visualised as such:

Sciences according to the four levels of ontology	Age focus
1. Sciences of written existence: script	3-6
2. Science of verbal existence: pronunciation, lexicon, grammar, rhetoric	6-10
3. Sciences of mental existence: logic, debate, and rhetoric	11-15
4. Sciences of real existence: theoretical and practical sciences[34]	12-up (many students complete *'alim* courses at 17-18)

Instrumental sciences	Practical sciences	Theoretical sciences
1. Sciences of script and spoken language	1. Pre-virtues and stories, and the resource *Finding True Happiness*	1. Applied mathematics: Arithmetic and nature study
2. Grammar	2. Religious practice	2. (cont. from above)
3. Logic and debate and research methodology	3. Practical manual of virtues and purification of the heart	3. Geometry: *Euclid's Elements*

Ongoing productive and physical disciplines

Arts and crafts, physical education (*futuwwa* disciplines), and IT and digital design (optional after obtaining confidence in at least one script)

---

34 Though many students begin with Euclid at age 10.

Curriculum in terms of developmental focus

Ages	Instrumental	Theoretical	Practical
3-6	Basic language acquisition	Memorise creed	Memorise rituals and invocations and prayers
6-8	Pre-grammar and pre-rhetoric	Learn creed	Pre-virtues and stories (the resource *Finding True Happiness*)
8-11	Grammar, pre-rhetoric, and pre-logic	Basic theology with simple proofs	
11-12	Logical fallacies		Practical manual of virtues and introduction to psychology of purification of the soul

Many educationalists think that a K-12 curriculum must aim to produce professionals because that is what is required to function in society, and any curriculum catering for a wider audience that religious scholars must produce functional members of society. On this basis, they believe education for the majority—whether by tutoring, schooling, or homeschooling—should not be or imitate a madrasa. Some would go further and argue it should not be based on a madrasa. We presently argue that while the prior is true, the latter is not. If you wish to produce the perfect person or to have an integrated curriculum (see 1. and 2. above), you need something based on the madrasa curriculum, so long as you see that it really is a liberal education curriculum. While many confuse liberal education and the liberal arts, the liberal arts vary in the hands of different writers, but refer either to the trivium—grammar, logic, and rhetoric—or to these plus the quadrivium—four branches of mathematics: arithmetic, geometry, astronomy, and music (conceived of as number in the duration of time). But a liberal education liberates the human soul in its essential faculty: the intellect. The intellect is divided into the practical—perfected by removing vice and gaining virtue—and the theoretical—perfected through learning the theoretical sciences which are subjects that study the basic parts of the map of being: natural science, mathematics, and metaphysical theology (*kalam*). Additionally, the instrumental sciences which are roughly equivalent to the trivium must be learned as a prerequisite of properly learning any science. This is a full liberal education designed to perfect the human being, and the late madrasa curriculum covered this, integrated with God's final dispensation: the revelation of Islam, primarily divided into true beliefs, good practices, and purification of the heart and adornment with virtues.

A MODERN WORLDVIEW

In the opening paragraphs of this manual, we promised to return to the modern worldview which shapes us as modern subjects. In our estimation, this is different from the argument that contemporary schooling is dumbed down as a result of mass education being designed to produce compliant and reliable workers. This narrative does not reveal the assumptions that underlie the subject disciplines studied in school and university. We argue that without addressing these assumptions, they are so deep that they guide us and make us who we are, yet we generally struggle to understand and challenge the very assumptions that are basic to our modern identity. A principle of Islamic tarbiyah is that one must remove the false and bad first, then acquire truth and virtue: the 'negative' process here is termed divestment (*takhliyah*); the 'positive' process is termed adornment (*tahliyah*). We also argue that if one learns to see these modern assumptions in one vision, as it were, one can remove their influence over one's thinking. It is as if one can then see them and remove them as one single piece from one's mind. If this is not done, they make us incline to certain conclusions and block our heart and intellect from functioning and arriving at wisdom. They also reduce the pleasure that comes from worship and contemplation, such that we do not find the same satisfaction in our relationship with God as our predecessors. Here we present such a vision in a thumbnail sketch, and direct readers to our course Introduction to Islamic Education and the forthcoming theoretical manual accompanying this practical manual for a more extensive and explanative sketch.

First note that while there is a historical tension between realism and nominalism, we prefer to speak of realism versus scepticism. We define realism as the belief that things have realities and that they are potentially knowable to a degree fit for human beings and wisdom.[35] Scepticism should include any empirical philosophy which claims we can only know the appearances of things, called 'phenomena'. And it should include any idealism which holds we only know our ideas, not how things really are in themselves. What is termed the crisis of modernity is that when one's knowledge is limited to the appearance of things, then one cannot know values, but only scientific facts. This leads to a society and political order that 'literally does not know what it wants'.[36] this is termed the crisis of modernity. In practice, greed or hedonism naturally fill this ethical vacuum.

---

35 Realism is necessary to have any 'knowledge', even religious knowledge of basic beliefs. We simply need to be able to respond to the zeitgeist that says in contradistinction: 'things do not have realities, and even if they do, they are unknowable to us'.

36 See Leo Strauss, "The Three Waves of Modernity" in Leo Strauss (and Hilail Gildin, ed. and author of introduction), *An Introduction to Political Philosophy: Ten Essays by Leo Strauss*, Detroit: Wayne State University Press, 1989: 81-98.

Second, note that idealism often expresses itself in the contemporary university as a form of constructivism. Constructivists may rightly ask, 'How do you claim that marriage, ownership, or laws or the institutions and roles—such as courts and police officers—that enforce them are "real"? In the real world, there are only people and buildings, and perhaps the clothes that the police officer wears'. This truth should be acknowledged by a realist, but the said roles and institutions should be said to be socially constituted, not socially constructed. People agree on marriage and laws, and then they take on a certain reality. Break a law, and you may lose your freedom or your life. But this does not mean that laws have zero reality. Rather, they have a mind-dependent reality. And, they have a context which determines that they are right or wrong, good or bad. Most of the matters mentioned are social: they are part of the network by which people interact with each other. When these roles and institutions are just and lead to people thriving and perfecting themselves, they are good and true. After all, the aim of human individuals and collectivities is to strive for perfection. So, laws and roles and institutions which facilitate this are good.

Because modernity is not one coherent thing, the only unity it has is historical, though one will see certain patterns and principles in it. Here is a thumbnail sketch, or what is termed a potted, yet highly useful history. Descartes aimed to be critical through rationalism: he started knowledge anew through what he considered rational principles. But English empiricists came to think his principles were baseless, that truly critical knowledge had to be empirical. Then, German idealists, such as Kant, claimed that we do not know 'empirical' objects of knowledge except through our concepts that we project onto the world: there are no basic facts. Rather, even facts are built on categories and values which we take for granted. Kant wrote the immanently famous essay, 'What is the Enlightenment?' Being enlightened is to be critical: this requires one to 'realise', he argues, that the mind projects its concepts onto the world. The result, to simplify matters, we only know our own concepts. Later Idealist thinkers held that concepts the mind projects are relative to one's historical period, what others claimed was relative to one's language, culture, or even one's individual identify. A certain German philosopher came to hold that Kant's idealist theories were wasting the German youth, and in reaction, positivism was born. Nothing was permitted to be studied but the correlation of sensible phenomena moving over time, largely expressed in mathematical equations. Here, we see the impact of these strands of thought on natural science. It too cannot get into the nature of things and analyse causality. These theories allow for certain knowledge; hence, they are not absolute scepticism. However, they are scepticism regarding what matters most: values and realities. Remove realities and you remove the value of contemplation, except for a purely subjective value which is often mocked by pragmatic business and politics or scientific culture. It is this scepticism that is the real cause for concern in the modern curriculum. A few more pages could show in outline how these theories inform the various research methodologies in the university divisions and their departments. Then, a few more could describe how they descend into the modern school subjects and indirectly shape modern society and the common features of modern identities. This is somewhat scary. But perhaps scarier is realising that we live asleep in an unquestioned life.

ONE OF THE EXIT OUTCOMES OF 'LIFE' CURRICULUM: ENTREPRENEURSHIP AND THE GUILDS

Could a curriculum serve as a feeder to 'the guilds' in general, as opposed to a single one? A curriculum from eleven to sixteen or eighteen which prepared students for the guilds might well offer them a religious liberal arts curriculum with a touch more time devoted to crafts than our does. This still does not answer the question of how those graduates would fair in finding a guild that deserves the name. We live in a technological society, and even Middle Eastern countries that lack infrastructure have generally disbanded their guilds. Many guilds remain in the UK and France, while as noted Germany in general has a healthier culture surrounding practical work and even its technology has a vague guild spirit to it. A technological society means that guilds do not produce the true virtue of *techne*, but mere proficiency in minding standards. One is generally a part in some sort of assembly line, even if not literally being a factory worker on a real assembly line. This has been well-documented, including by those who support the 'modern project' such as Hans Gadamer, who notes that modern medicine would not qualify as inculcating productive virtues in its practitioners. I have left aside the heavy accusations that modern schooling fails to prepare people for work, that it is a failed social experiment, and that it forces healthy boys into rebellion—to avoid being labelled a failure—or going against their nature.

Were we to accept the modern school as some form of vocational preparation for professional employment, how would we describe it? Historically, the hours of mandatory education were extended. While schooling was seen as a right, it was made mandatory. As the demographics of Europe and the US changed, it became more secular, losing its religious emphasis, and also lost its emphasis on the liberal arts. Thus, liberal arts became English. Mathematics became a central subject to serve the scientific disciplines needed to run Post-World War II countries. Science entered the curriculum, and labs became more common. Eventually, science went from a weekly subject to nearly a daily subject in some contexts, and information technology joined the curriculum often also as a more than weekly subject. Art was joined with design. Personal, social, and health education was joined with citizenship, which is tempted to incline towards statecraft.

INSIGHTS FROM THE GUILDS

Is one merely to accept this model and attempt to effect true integration through accepting a specific model with a specific history and disentangling skills from culture in order to represent one's culture? What about skills? Can skills be replaced with true virtuous dispositions? Even if you wished to accept the general curriculum as being vocational or aimed at the professions (in a more creative sense thought through from the ground up), how much change to the modern school curriculum would be needed to design it for its purposes. The professions should be a calling. Their craft should be imbibed with *futuwwah*, spirituality, and symbolism. Their practice should embody true practical virtue, not mere technological proficiency.

Whichever model one takes on, there are insights from a guild model, or from what should be termed a social vision or political philosophy. It is an insight whose absence in one's culture and educational culture is a permeating darkness. This is that the city is a microcosm, and the guilds and sciences work together towards a single goal and thus form a unity. This unity is a spiritual unity capable of transcending class barriers. Everyone not only worships one God but is part of one organism. Even the critic of modern culture, communitarianism, lacks this. A community must be a metaphysical community: one sharing a metaphysics to a significant degree which unites them, not merely one which is a group of bodies. Merely being in the same classroom and shopping at the same mall does not make everyone part of a real community.

Another such insight is to overcome the prejudice that thought occurs only when the hands are free, and one is not involved with work and toil. True, recreation may be holy, and leisure may facilitate contemplation, but there is a whole tradition of the crafts in which metaphysics is taught best while the hands are busy. There, the dictum is turned on its head: 'True thought only occurs when the hands are busy'. Keep the hands busy so that one can think. Matters such as knitting are well-known, but workers in the past used wood- and stone-carving as opportunities to convey the metaphysics behind the craft and its proportions, beauty, and symbolism. A glance at lost history shows that every part of the world had a trade or set of trades, and they not only whistled while they worked, but they sang significant songs and conveyed oral wisdom doctrines. While it seems unimaginable in many contexts in the UK and North America, schools in many parts of the world paid their expenses through weaving and other crafts. This is not a sign of being down and out, but rather may be a measure leading to a sense of pride and earning independence from certain funders such as the state or corporate world.

In sum, our model draws from both the madrasa and the guilds, but not them exclusively. It would be wrong to term the madrasa a seminary, as it was a full education in the branches of wisdom, aside from productive wisdom. Productive science or wisdom was embodied in the guilds which we draw on to offer a complete education mirroring both the faculties of the human being and the needs of society.

A noteworthy model exists which combines the practical and the theoretical in a single person: the Southern Agrarian movement. Here we find a history of integration of the liberal arts while simultaneously practicing agriculture or farming or other productive manners of living off the land. Participants in the agrarian movements across the south of the United States commonly wrote poetry or manuals in rhetoric or other liberal arts, and they commonly split their day between farming and such study of the liberal arts. This model brings the practical and theoretical perfections together in each person and answers the question of income and independence.

Two further viable possibilities remain. First, one may shift the focus more towards the fiqh that would inform the professions, or towards the guilds. Second, one may extract certain topics needed by all from theology and the full classification of the sciences, apply it to modern issues, and present it in place of certain disciplines that take considerable time to master. This material could be presented as modules that would leave room for one of the said specialisms in the curriculum and cherry-pick the most important insights for students. This model has its limitations. Note that graduates from different specialisms may form a community after graduation and mutually support each other to fulfil communal obligations. Here, the important notions of social vision and communal obligation overlap.

Note in closing that a guild is imbued with a sacred ethos and symbolism both in its products and in its regalia and customs which, similar to liberal arts learning, render it beyond a mere job and mere work. They are rather more of a profession or calling. They relate to a performance of a human need, but are not merely transactional, but contain meaning which involves a unity of the human community transcending class and relating one to the ultimate aims of human existence and the creation: knowing God in His creation and in our participation in transcendent meanings. What we now know as trades should be given more respect than they are—as they are in countries such as Germany which have a healthier notion of production, but this is not the point. The point is, does the training involve an ethos which purifies the soul through matters such as *futuwwah*, symbolism, and etiquette, or does it not?

2.2 THE QURAN AS A CENTRAL PILLAR

Teaching the Noble Quran in the *kuttab* was so central that they are sometimes referred to as *al-katatib al-Quraniyyah* (elementary Quran schools). There was a debate amongst early scholars as to whether the Quran should be taught as the first subject, or whether students should learn other (developmental) sciences first in order to receive the Quran with some maturity and understanding. These discussions indicate a) the central role of learning to read the Quran and then memorising from the Quran and b) the importance of understanding the Quran. A third crucial matter is to embody the Quran and its adab. A word is due on all three; but let us first say that the LIFE approach is to focus holistically in the early years on religion, language (including maths as it is the language of quantity), and memorisation, balancing this with grounding oneself in the body through developmental activities (and arts and disciplines).

The best way to learn Arabic is in parallel with the same liberal language skills in English (or in one's local language). The Quran cannot be truly accessed through mere communicative Arabic, so we teach the liberal arts of Arabic and English. Thus, the Quran being memorised is understood.

This understanding is actually a crucial part of embodying the Quran: there is no doubt that the Quran has a sonoral quality which effects the body, but there is also no doubt that the superior embodiment is a) to embody the character praised in the Quran such that it manifests on one's limbs and b) to be affected by the meanings such that one's body is like a container for the awe before Allah and His signs and majesty and for one's skin to manifest goosebumps caused by the words eliciting meanings and those meanings being realised in the mind and heart. The connection to Allah and His Names is almost identical to the overall aim of education: to produce the perfect human. The Prophet's ﷺ character was said to be the Quran in part because Allah gave him ﷺ tarbiyah and *ta'dib* via the Quran itself, which was sometimes revealed regarding the Prophet's ﷺ own actions or otherwise, called Islamic virtues; and the Prophet ﷺ was the first, of course, to embody them. Even the revelation itself was a tremendous force on his purest of souls ﷺ.

2.2.1 LEARNING

Three important authors give us a window into the historical role of the Quran in the *kuttab*, the equivalent of primary school (starting at the age of 5-6 and ending at the age of 10-11 according to many authors). Ibn Sahnun indicates that the highest priority in the *kuttab* is the Quran. The matter is not solely of memorisation; but rather students should learn good recitation, to write the Quran beautifully, and should not move from one *sura* to another without knowing how to parse (*i'rab*) the verses learned. They should learn the sciences and literature needed to support their grasping the meanings of Allah's book. The teacher must teach etiquette and character, giving the students advice and looking after them (in their religion and character). The Andalusian scholar, Imam Abu Bakr Ibn al-'Arabi criticised beginning with the Quran, stating his dismay at studying something which is not understood. Thus, he proposed learning Arabic (likely meaning not only grammar, but other related disciplines) and Arab poetry—because poetry is the register of the Arabs (*diwan al-'Arab*) and their culture, then arithmetic—practicing it until one learns from it rules and principles—then the Quran. Thereafter, he set out four Sharia sciences to be learned in order which looks like the steps of a scholar: the principles of religion (*usul al-din*, i.e., 'aqidah and *kalam*), the principle of jurisprudence, debate (*jadal*), and hadith and its ancillary sciences. Ibn Khaldun in turn praises this pathway, indicating that it strengthens the dispositions (*malakat*) and ability to understand—but says that typical circumstances and realities do not support implementing this and that there is merit in teaching the Quran while children are young. Thereafter, the storms of youth may overtake them, casting them on the 'shores of laziness'. Many before Ibn al-'Arabi had a similar approach, encouraging certain learning which would enable children to understand the Quran when they reached it. These include well-known grammarian and scholar of letters, Abu 'Abdallah Ibn al-A'rabi. Note the similarity between this advice to learn poetry early and the advice of Sayyiduna 'Umar (may Allah be pleased with him) for Muslim settlers in the cities outside the Hijaz: 'Teach your children swimming and to ride on horseback and transmit to them common maxims and goodly poetry'.

2.2.2 UNDERSTANDING

Because early Muslims spoke in an integral manner about this related set of topics, the topic of understanding was already addressed presently. The upshot is that understanding was taught, even in places where Arabic was not the primary language. There are several reports which indicate the importance of this, one of which links to Sayyiduna 'Umar's (may Allah be pleased with him) exhortation to learn Arabic. Al-Hasan al-Basri (may Allah have mercy on him) advised to learn Arabic (*al-'Arabiyyah*) so that a person not fall into perdition through understanding a verse incorrectly. Abu Hurayra (may Allah be pleased with him) also said not only to recite the Quran clearly (*i'rab*), but to inquire into the rare lexical terms. This takes for granted that one would learn its common lexical terms (this being the cause for LIFE including Quranic vocabulary in its recommended Arabic programme). This is not to say that learning Arabic is individually obligatory and leaving it a sin. It is only an obligation to learn what one needs to make the testification of faith and perform one's prayer and a few other matters scholars of fiqh have enumerated. But the highest priority for a Muslim after knowing their individual obligations is to understand the Quran and a few religious matters laid out in the section titled Religious Instruction.

2.2.3 EMBODYING

Learning the adab of the Quran and embodying it comes through two means: a) The teacher of the Quran conveying etiquette to the child and b) focusing on embodying the Quran while it is being memorised. In fact, the second meaning opens up the matter of how *hifz* should be translated; not only as memorisation, as will become clear below.

Scholars who came through the *kuttab* state that the Quran teacher conveys character through living with the students (*muʿayashah*) in the manner of a nursery (*hadanah*) or kindergarten (*rawdah*). Elementary education (the *kuttab*) is built on the character of the teacher. The character of the teacher and their treatment of the students should make them love lessons and Islam. The method, whether or not this is the right term, is that the character of the teacher imprints on the mirror of the child's mind.

The most important writing to begin learning the etiquette of the Quran is Imam al-Nawawi's *al-Tibyan*. He conveys the method in a unique passage from our heritage thus: '[The Quran] teacher should refine (*yuʾaddibu*, or inculcate adab) the student gradually through sublime etiquette, praiseworthy character traits, and disciplining the soul through hidden fine points. He should accustom the student to protect their soul and reputation from any inward or outward indecency. The teacher should exhort the student through his words and actions towards sincerity, earnestness, a goodly intention, being mindful of God Most High in every moment. He should teach them that through this the lights of knowledge will open up, their heart will expand, the springs of wisdom and subtle matters will pour forth from their heart, there will be *barakah* in their works and states, and they will have success Divinely bestowed in their actions and words'. This presumes that the teacher themselves as a person of the Quran has the character of the Quran, which leads us to the second question of how one embodies the Quran in the first place and what it means.

Scholars have contested whether *hifz* should be interpreted merely as memorisation. The word in Arabic means 'to protect', and also comes in the hadith found in Imam al-Nawawi's *Forty Hadith* collection in which the Prophet ﷺ instructed Ibn ʿAbbas (may Allah be pleased with them) who, as a child, rode behind him on their mount, saying, 'Protect Allah; He will protect you'. Here, 'protecting Allah' is interpreted to mean to know His laws and observe them, but also relates to giving Allah what is due to Him of veneration and remembrance. The great Moroccan scholar Farid al-Ansari, Allah have mercy on him, stated:

> "Verily, protection is that which was practiced by the Companions of the emissary of God ﷺ, who would receive transmission of five to ten verses. Then, they would embark on bravely wrestling with their credal meanings as much as Allah wills. Verily, he who does not endure the rank of *Surat al-Ikhlas* and does not discipline his soul according to its impenetrable fortress and does not imitate and take on his character the declaration of the sole unity of Allah in everything—out of hope and fear—cannot be considered as one who has memorised *Surat al-Ikhlas*. Furthermore, verily, the one whose inner feelings are not ablaze with longing for the night prayer (*tahajjud*) cannot be of the people of *Surat al-Muzzammil*."

Thus, the LIFE approach is to teach memorisation in an age-appropriate manner, applying Arabic grammar (or what these early Muslims called *i'rab*) to the parts of the Quran being memorised and practicing translation into one's native language, which is also necessary for most Arabs today due to the distance between colloquial and classical Arabic. The teacher should be chosen with the utmost care. If one is the teacher and has shortcomings in practice, one should make the intention to repair what is between them and Allah, which is more precious than whatever else they are concerned with and to recite, 'They said: "Our Lord! We have wronged ourselves. If Thou forgive us not and have not mercy on us, surely we are of the lost"' (Quran 7:23).[37] Thus it is hoped they do not fall under the verse, 'Great is Allah's wrath for those who command others to that which you do not do yourself' (Quran 61:3).

2.3 THE SPECULATIVE SCIENCES

2.3.1 MATHEMATICS

The science of discrete quantity is termed arithmetic; the science of continuous quantity is geometry. The reality is that like other subjects, maths has three levels: sacred, symbolic (or liberal), and secular (or profane). While it is possible to 'just get on with it', but with what, and learn maths, assuming modern maths is a default, we can at least appreciate what a BBC presenter alluded to was a Faustian exchange occurring early in modern times in which the timeless natures and truths of Being studied in Greek

---

37 We add the transliteration for those not fluent in reading Arabic: '*Rabbana zalamna anfusana wa-in lam taghfir lana wa-tarhamna la-nakunanna min al-khasirin*'.

(and Islamic) mathematics were sold to gain power and domination of the constant flux of the world of decay and becoming.

The other end of the spectrum, in which one is aware of the philosophical changes which occurred to mathematics over the last two centuries, but which starts already with Galileo and Descartes tells us that modern mathematicians moved from the timeless geometry and geocentric roots of the Greeks to constant change, a Faustian deal. Thus, while Muslims advanced Greek mathematics such as the science of trigonometry, modern Europeans developed the calculus of change.

So, we must return to principles: the practical truth is that *kuttab* aimed to teach all Muslims basic reckoning, or at least the four basic arithmetical operations (termed *kara cümle* in Ottoman records). In some pre-modern Islamic circles, traditional mathematics was important as a means of sharpening the mind in youth so that after learning it they could approach other subjects like theology and natural science. It is for this reason that it is called 'the pedagogical science' (*al-'ilm al-ta'limi*). Much has been written in European languages on the Islamic contribution to maths, such as the introduction of Indian numerals which fueled development of mathematics making development in natural science possible. Relatively little has been written on the role of mathematics in Islamic education and its place in the curriculum. Clearly, the central Sunni Indian and Ottoman (and Shi'i Safavid) curricula involved the study of a nearly identical set of works discussed below. One finds important indications in the educational work of Saçaklızade *Tartib al-'ulum* and in the classificatory and bibliographical work of Taşköprüzada. The lack of presence of mathematics on many madrasa curricula should not deceive one: maths was often learned at home or outside formal education because it was considered associated with the teaching of children and therefore easy and not requiring instruction within the madrasa.

Taşköprüzada addresses the four topics of the quadrivium systematically, though somewhat briefly. His terse comments are valuable as they go beyond a transmission of philosophers' statements, include a Sharia viewpoint, but also show understanding of the topic. Thus, they avoid the extremes of pure reason and pure transmission, representing a synthesis. In brief, it may be said that the quadrivium sharpens the mind, trains one to overcome vain imagining (*wahm*) via true demonstrations, and opens up the wonders of cosmology. The only impermissible aspect (which is not coincidentally also the weakest aspect) is the branch of astronomy called 'the rulings of the stars', which we would call astrology. This still does not amount to advice for a primary curriculum, though it is clear from Taşköprüzada and Saçaklızade and the Indian curricula that in each of the four areas of the quadrivium, core madrasa texts were part and parcel of the curriculum:

- Geometry (*handasah*): *Tahrir Uqlidis* (Euclid) of Nasir al-Din al-Tusi. Geometry is the key to astronomy according to Taşköprüzada.)

- Astronomy (*hay'ah*): *al-Mulakhkhas (fi al-hay'ah)* of Mahmud al-Jaghmini. Taşköprüzada also mentions *Sharh al-Majisti*, i.e., Ptolemy's *Almagest*, which canonised the geocentric model of the universe up to modern times. The Dars-i Nizami included *Tashrih al-aflak* by Baha' al-Din al-'Amili.

- Arithmetic (*'ilm al-'adad* or *al-arithmatiqi*): *al-Kitab al-muhammadi* by 'Ali Qushji (which perhaps should be pronounced Qushju). This includes algebra (*al-jabr*). Reckoning (*al-hisab*) is an important branch represented in the Dars-i Nizami curriculum by Baha' al-Din al-'Amili's *Khulasat al-hisab*.

- Music (*al-musiqa*): Not represented on the curriculum, but Taşköprüzada lists standard works by al-Farabi, Ibn Sina, and a work on rhythm (*iqa'at*) by a later scholar.

2.3.2 THE NATURAL SCIENCES

The importance of understanding what we term 'science' and putting it back into an integrated whole with 'natural science' and theology is addressed within the primary level subject of natural science under the sub-title 'Why?' Here, we present the much-needed solution based on the insight that modern science filters reality through instruments, collecting and analysing primarily mathematical data.

What is lost is what the intellect 'sees', which is intelligible form, intrinsic value, and meaning, and even the aspect of form which, relating to a part of mathematics, is relatively neglected in modern science: proportion. Natural science was once a branch of philosophy, whereas it is now part of a dichotomy against philosophy and other humanities subjects. Thus, it fits into a cultural war, and we mention in passing that this plays out in the Muslim world in deep social divisions put in place by colonialism into a crude secular and religious culture which struggle to speak to each other. So, the solution proposed has potential for healing not only the individual, but society. This also highlights the crucial importance of teaching a proper classification of the sciences. Our solution is not a pure antagonism to science, but to understand its place and temper its effects on the developing student. Those who would not relinquish modern advancements and technology that reshape hospitals and nearly every other field of life should grasp the sobering fact that nearly all the vaccines and other discoveries which powered the scientific revolution were simply the result of having the right instruments (and perhaps the infrastructure); they were not directly the result of the 'worldview' or philosophy of modern science. They are not the conclusions arrived at through its premises. For example, Galileo was able to look at Jupiter through a telescope. What he found—that the planets are corporeal—was not unknown centuries earlier to John Philoponus nor al-Ghazali for that matter. We advocate that a child learn both and be able to navigate them intellectually. This is necessary for the individual soul and collectively for a sound and healthy culture. The modern world will likely not go away in the coming decades unless there is some natural or manmade cataclysm. Thus, we need to be able to navigate it. A principle of pedagogy is that what should not be there must be removed before adding virtue, truth, and what should be there. In this case, as soon as one wakes up—let alone goes out the door to the street and local mall—there is a built environment which implicitly speaks the assumptions of modern science. So, it pervades our own thought and must be addressed for proper tarbiyah to occur. the forms of the natural world are windows and archetypes that point to the Divine names, and thus can be studied as signs (*ayat*). Here we note a pattern that has emerged: modern approaches treat the outward purport of things, while the traditional approach treats their essential, intelligible, and permanent reality. This is very clear in science, and it gives one key to treating the subject as a whole. We offer how to repair and complete the treatment of natural science which has been split into two in Western history.

In terms suitable to the primary curriculum:

Humpty Dumpty sat on the wall (whole: one natural science). Humpty Dumpty had a great fall (starting in the 16th century – the emergence of mathematisation and revival of Greek atomism leading to a culmination in positivism and the split into two views on one subject). All the king's horses and all the king's men (post-positivists and critics such as Husserl and Heidegger) couldn't put Humpty back together again (except for a minority of Neo-Aristotelian, Thomist, and Muslim thinkers.)

What is called 'science' is now limited to appearances, while our approach teaches how to integrate this limited view with a holistic view in such a way that the sensible and intelligible aspects of the natural world mutually illuminate each other inside the student and their community. Crucially, psychology is a branch of natural science; so, handing it over to those limited to studying through a so-called empirical method is highly dangerous. As we teach students, the problem with an empirical method is not that one uses the senses; it is that modern empiricists stop with the senses. They only occasionally use the senses to arrive at rational truths, so they basically stop with studying the appearances and their correlations, rather than their causation and nature.

2.3.3 THE PRODUCTIVE SCIENCES

The context of education could not be more important, yet more overlooked. Education must be relevant to the lifestyle which the student is likely to actually adopt, lest it become absurd or actually harmful, leading them away from their immediate concerns and, what's worse, teaching them to under-appreciate what they have. This could not be worse in our own times of those in villages across the world encouraged to sell their ancestral land for peanuts and pour into the city, often into slums. They see no value in the village and the land. This is often because the nation-state directs whatever funds exist into growth projects, usually around tourist locations or a capital associated with their legacy. This is not entirely a historical anomaly, but it is harmful and makes living in the village seem impractical: one must earn a living and there is no living with rising prices of electricity and even water needed to water plants. But we should think twice before permanently settling in the city. When Gandhi was asked about how to educate children in the city, he said his efforts were made to rightly educate villagers and he had nothing to say to those in the city. This is partly because city life is so artificial and disconnected. Modern office jobs are just an extension of what used to be a clerk or scribe, rushing and addressing one's attention to whatever those with accumulated money deem in the interest of their company. The only possibility for seeing nature-in-nature study in a city is often to search for a few odd trees in a park (or weeds if not in a Western city) or insects and birds which manage to thrive in the city.

In the village, Charles Ashbee observed that there are also limitations. Timidity amongst teachers, poverty in the students. But they should learn to preserve their beautiful and often sacred local culture, often in the crafts and songs or hymns (and what Muslims would refer to as qasida, na'at, ilahi or nashid). If the area has access to the sea or is a farming community, this will be reflected in an integral way of life which locals should be encouraged to preserve in an intelligent manner (not of course in a crippling manner). But their access to nature and land and lack of rush in their life are great boons which others long for who do not have them. To this list should be added the strong bonds between local families and friendliness and helpfulness between neighbours. Rather than encouraging rural folk to leave the land, they should be encouraged to preserve sustainable means of production, perhaps introducing more efficient irrigation systems and knowledge of organic farming, and simultaneously thereby saving money and making a more valuable product. In the city, there are resources, but they are difficult to capitalise on due to loss of fitrah, community, and religious identity. Many resources are spent to merely preserve social status by those of some sort of class, but this status is not served by true education anymore. Aside from a few pockets in the Muslim world, and a few European families (in England, France, Belgium, and Italy), and a few pockets in the US such as Boston, Vermont, and Maine, a city or two in California, there is no notion of class outside quantity of possessions (and knowing the right places to vacation). Class is not what is sought, but rather education; but education suffers as a result of priorities. To its credit, the US hosts a few great books colleges, but even these institutions do not hold up to the standards of wisdom and true class.

2.4 THE AUXILIARY SCIENCES

2.4.1 GRAMMAR

Teach Arabic language and literature in a manner similar to the English liberal arts: the trivium, true great books, and literature. The Arabic or wider Islamicate culture is the best culture on earth. It combines revelation with literature, true philosophy, and spirituality. It lacks the pagan baggage Christians agree is so difficult to remove from Western culture. What does the right approach to grammar, language, and literature look like? A language is just that: a language. But a language is a gift fitting Adam as Caliphate of Allah on earth. This is not modern standard or communicate Arabic. Classical Arabic goes beyond this into a language which embodies a) the trivium and b) Islamic and Quranic culture. So, the first step to a real education is to abandon using communicative schemes to do anything other than act like oil when a joint is stuck. You can master *al-Kitab* but not know the first steps of how to understand Allah's book. You also will not know how to sparse a sentence, which even a beginner *tafsir* will require to understand the Arabic which is the basis for understanding Quranic verses. There are countless stories of people completing the Arabic courses available in the US and UK (and abroad), but when they open up even a contemporary and beginner *tafsir* like *Safwat al-tafasir*, they struggle and must look up every word. Or they can construct spoken sentences such as: '*Uridu an adhhaba* (not *adhhabu*) *ila al-hammam*' (I want to go the bathroom), but they cannot explain a single classical grammatical rule, let alone perform parsing (*i'rab*) of even a two-word sentence. The answer is: teach classical Arabic and teach it interactively. There is no intrinsic contradiction between the two methods (classical and interactive); rather, they complement each other in practice. But so many people struggle to learn Arabic. Many try on their own, and others go to Arabs for help. But one should as if anyone ever recommended that one learn the way non-native Muslims learned Arabic for the last six-hundred years, in their own language? This is the method explained here: the manner that foreigners (*a'ajim*) learned Arabic in Persian, the Eastern languages (like Xiaojing),

THE AUXILIARY SCIENCES   *Grammar*

then Ottoman, then Urdu, and now English. There are key texts written by scholars of the Arabic language in various other mother tongues. The way a scholar explains language is clear and powerful and invigorates the mind. It opens the door to understanding higher sciences, especially but not limited to *tafsir*. It uses the same apparatus as not only jurisprudence, but some of the apparati of sciences like classical logic, maths, and natural science, and of course Islamic theology.

Arabic, like other languages, deals firstly with terms. The LIFE curriculum advises that your child learns Arabic calligraphy when age-appropriate, at least after seven to learn basic *naskh* style. We will remember from the introduction that all human knowledge is arranged in four levels: the shell of the shell, the shell, the kernel, and the kernel of the kernel. Script and pronunciation (including the important science of tajwid) deal with the shell of the shell. These sciences should not be neglected as mastery of them leads to them becoming second nature and roots our thinking in the earth of the body, in sound and sensation, and physical movements to form letters on paper (and only then on a screen). Thereafter, Arabic and all languages encounter the shell: speech. Speech is first divided into two in Arabic: what relates to the singular (words) and the compound (*murakkab*). The singular is divided into vocabulary and morphology (*sarf*). Arabic morphology teaches one how Arabic words are constructed of roots and forms. In English, the construction of words is often based on Latin and performed by adding prefixes or suffixes. In Arabic, more flexibility exists, and a plethora of meanings can be generated from root letters: the active and passive participle, adjectives, etc. Verb conjugation is also more powerful and flexible. By learning morphology and a few roots, thousands of words can be generated or learned and much of the Quran understood. Alongside vocabulary, morphology and grammar are the two basic sciences needed to understand the Quran.

The second part of speech concerns the connections between words: so, we move from building blocks to the forms holding words together. Students could think of roots as the material, morphology as the shape of the blocks, and grammar as the structure for building walls of a castle or grand mosque.

Rhetoric is a second order science of choosing vocabulary and structures which are eloquent, add meaning to the basic meaning, or suit the situation. One cannot learn rhetoric before grammar. One can, and should, learn at least basic rhetoric before logic. In our curriculum which follows in the next sub-section, we advise that students move quickly from grammar to basic reading and from basic reading to literature, which exemplifies the language arts skills of grammar and rhetoric. There is a longstanding Azhari tradition of using *al-Burdah* and *al-Shifa'* to learn Arabic vocabulary and literature. So, the greatest praise and description of the Prophet Muhammad ﷺ is what your child will spend the next years of their childhood with, absorbing the love for Allah's beloved one.

This is thus the best of a classic culture which has no comparison in Western culture. The Bible has some inspired speech in its original languages. Western culture never resolved the tension with pagan culture, so there is no pure and robust well-spring to drink from in English, not free of contradictions. High scholastic culture has gems including some poetry and mystical texts, but this is different from what is available in Arabic, as explained in the secondary stage.

2.4.2 The Liberal Arts

Several issues are summarised in bullet points inside the primary curriculum in the subject of 'Liberal Arts' under the sub-title 'Why?' One may ask, 'Why learn English?' or, 'Why learn another language than Arabic?' Some of us will want all our true education to happen in Arabic, for others the obvious language of education will be English which worldwide is the lingua franca of industry, communication, and technology (i.e., the world of work which education should prepare for). LIFE's approach is to note first that Muslims in English-speaking countries have struggled so far to be 'fully lingual' in Arabic such that it is a language of learning. Second, even for those of the Arabic persuasion, one needs to be able to conduct religious discussions in English. Previous madrasas taught Persian or Urdu as scholarly languages, and the process is already well under way for English. Third, if one is in a given land, and becomes a citizen, one should be educated in that language, whatever it is. In the case of English and many other languages such as French and Persian, there is already a tradition of the liberal arts in that language which is very rich (French and English drawing most of their roots from Latin and Greek, Persian drawing greatly on Arabic). Learning concepts and learning language are distinct even though they are related. The most economic manner of teaching concepts and language is in a manner whereby they reinforce each other. In a curriculum where two languages are important—Arabic and English—learning in Arabic and English should reinforce each other. So, one will see when we turn to Arabic that a similar list is presented. Some students may struggle to learn in a second language. The fact that they have studied sentence diagramming and the types of sentences (declarative and non-declarative), word roots, logic, etc. in English at around the same time they study it in Arabic will reinforce their learning. And learning these matters in Arabic will ensure they know what their tradition has to say on the matter.

Modern students are not taught how to write essays, nor how to think, but are only given the general guidelines regarding how to be critical regarding sources and other nonformal guidelines. The classical tools outlined in the LIFE curriculum not only make one into a superior writer, but possessing this timeless cultural capital would transform the image of Muslims.[38]

What about literature, imagination and matters of acculturation?

Imagination is a multifaceted reality. Different schools also see it differently, and we attempt to strike a middle path. Those using the intellect see the imagination as a faculty of the soul, and as below the intellect, needing control so that it does not cause vain imaginings. Those using the method of illumination see imagination as having two levels, the higher being a cosmic reality without which physical things are not even possible. A scholar sympathetic to both views is al-Ghazali, who sees the imagination as an isthmus to higher worlds, so long as one's soul is strong and the imagination does not distort what the soul sees. This is needed for true visions and revelation. Our approach is to train students in the instrumental sciences, including logic, that help to rule out false imaginings. We also expose them to nature and poetry. We choose some poetry by those whose imagination is illumined such that things become windows unto meanings—and the Divine attributes—for them. We are sympathetic with those who wished to populate the imagination with symbols of virtue and sacred realities, such as the Inklings. One of their members, J. R. R. Tolkien, not only composed some of the greatest literature embodying this but wrote essays on the theory of imagination that should be read by teachers and students alike—when children are more mature. Even for those whose eye of insight is not entirely open, the fitrah allows images that resonate with reality to impact on the soul. In this sense, literature can be edifying and inspiring. This is not utterly distinct from reading the biographies of the prophets, saints, and righteous scholars, but also literature on the wisdom in Allah's creation (*al-hikma fi makhluqat Allah*).

Penmanship, typesetting, and design

With more people giving over to computers to teach their children or believing learning should start on computers, it is important to temper this approach by noting that penmanship is still necessary in the modern world. The LIFE approach to penmanship recommends the work of Rosemary Sassoon. Her policies are flexible and practical, while simultaneously being connected to a living tradition of calligraphy. Her years of practical experience setting policies for primary and secondary schools result in

---

38 One only has to think of Augustine's advice to learn the trivium which transformed the socio-economic position of Christians in Europe.

policies our own experience shows to be true. If children are not taught letter forms in a practical and flexible manner, handwriting becomes frustrating, and the beauty of letters is the last thing which might occur to the child. Children need clear instruction and guidance about when to move to joined up writing so that they do not abandon proper form when the pressure comes to speed up. The ideal which should also be a practical aim is that children are taught to take pride in their own writing and to appreciate the beauty and proportion in letters. They should be introduced to the language of letters and their styles (such as serif and sans serif). They should be given choice, so long as it falls within a valid range.

My own experience of not being taught in this manner is the most important experience I have. Children need to be supported in avoiding certain mistakes. They need to embody correct letter forms before or separate to being expected to compose. So, the ideal time to embody letter forms is in dictation or copy work, not in composition exercises where ideas and creativity are the focus. If we as parents and teachers skip over this step, we deprive students from basics like posture and sensation which should be the basis for them to then transcend into the world of thought and expression. Unlearning mistakes is difficult, something many of us experience in tajwid and Quran memorisation, but the same applies to handwriting. Handwriting and calligraphy can open up to the world of art and print design (including website design). This is an art completely amenable to Islamic practice, and the beauty of print is not something that Muslims can afford to skip over in a race to hothouse children at the expense of true, solid development. Typesetting and design are good forms of work, and if based on sound principles, they are a rare way to spread beauty in the world and influence people towards truth, while so many use print and design to call people to the false.[39]

2.5 THE PRACTICAL BRANCHES

The principles of tarbiyah were addressed above. It was pointed out that there is a fundamental distinction between ethics as a science of right and wrong—and how to find happiness and felicity and tarbiyah in the sense of perfecting character through repeating those right acts until they become a habit in the soul. Here, we address the subject of ethics and tarbiyah.[40]

---

39 More will be said on typesetting in the secondary level, but it all starts by getting foundations right in primary education.

40 Note that there is also a distinction between what the science of ethics and scriptural and other religious statements of right and wrong. The latter may be called 'moral theology'. It is not developed as a science, but merely indicates what the truth is and often motivates one to act according to truth.

What follows are preliminary notes on the subject of ethics as it is addressed in the primary curriculum. In reality, it is woven into the liberal arts, Islamic instruction, and it is found in certain prophetic traditions and matters such as the prophetic biography and poetry such as *al-Burdah*. There are also sections or whole books devoted to tazkiyah which borderlines on not only tarbiyah but *taraqqi*: spiritual discipline and upbringing. These include even rudimentary texts such as *al-Risalah al-jami'ah* taught as early as Year 1, but more clearly in texts such as the *Book of Assistance*. In later years, options include teaching key chapters of Books XXII (and to a degree also XXI) of the *Ihya' 'ulum al-din*, which address the nature of the soul and how to purify it, and *Mizan al-'amal*.

In terms of the liberal arts, stories are chosen in Years 1 & 2 which are crucial for tarbiyah, but also in particular towards the specific goals set out in the resource *Finding True Happiness*, described in the 'Tarbiyah' above. These are found for instance in the *McGuffy Reader*, but their moral value should be seized on. In general, the manuals written by the Haddad scholars such as *The Book of Assistance* convey tarbiyah with the important ingredient of adab. This carries on in secondary education where the proper science of ethics (*akhlaq*) is studied, including *Mizan al-'amal* if not drawn on in a simplified fashion in elementary education.

2.6 ANSWERS TO OBJECTIONS

2.6.1 HOW CAN ONE TEACH CLASSICAL TEXTS TO YOUNG PEOPLE?

Teachers may ask how 2nd to 4th graders are expected to learn grammar, logic, and rhetoric, and to apply it to the Quran, for instance. We may know 7-9-year-olds that learn very simple materials. Or it may be that we may simply do not know and have not heard of 6th or 7th graders learning classical texts in logic.

Is this just a matter of Arabic? Maybe they could understand books in these sciences if they are fluent in Arabic by the time they start them. But the very concepts that are advanced in books such as *Tahdhib al-mantiq* before the 10th grade or *Sharh Mulla Jami* (in grammar) and *al-Shamsiyyah* (in logic) seem inaccessible unless the children have been on a very good track and reach the 11th or 12th grade. Right? Or is the LIFE curriculum only designed for students who are exceptionally gifted and precocious? Have we thought of the average student? How intelligent or talented do we expect students to be? Are there not adults that struggle with these books?

And how can a child learn fiqh which deals with marriage and financial transactions. What, for instance, is an 11-year-old going to understand of these matters. They may not yet have desires, and they may have zero financial responsibility or awareness. Is it not feared that they will simply be memorising (if they are clever), but not really understanding? What if—presupposing they are intelligent enough to memorise—it merely appears that they understand, while in fact they do not understand what they have memorised? Should we consider the context, in which children remain children till eighteen or even twenty-five sometimes.

In reply, we must admit that we know very few children who have started on a good classical education from the beginning of their education. True, there are some homeschooled children that are far behind those in public schools. But there are also examples of students multiple grades ahead of their level, and gaining a full, classical education.

Teaching a traditional syllabus requires the following principles to be understood and adhered to. We have all had the experience of going back to a book we read previously and feeling like we never read it before. This is natural but is especially so if our teacher had not absorbed it themselves. It does not mean there is no benefit. While children are young, there will be a partial absorption. The more they engage with the ideas in classical texts, the more they will unfold in their experience. All education is like this. We learn mathematics, but if we study the humanities, we largely forget it. If we become a physicist, we understand it in ways that make us feel like we had never studied it before.

Another traditional principle that aids in this absorption is to use the gradual method set out by al-Ghazali and tweaked by Ibn Khaldun. This principle explained in the theoretical writings and courses explaining LIFE pedagogy is that, in each science, one should go through three levels of text minimum in each science: summary, intermediate, and comprehensive. This allows much of the said unfolding in one's experience to happen naturally in a structured pedagogical experience. This generally does not happen in textbooks, though some authors attempt to deploy something vaguely similar: a spiral curriculum in which topics are circled back to at progressively higher levels.

Another principle is that, if we are to invest our energy, it should be in the best books. These best books should also relate to the timeless sciences that guide the unfolding of our practical, theoretical, and productive faculties, in a way aiming for human perfection in a social context. This is what classics do, and this is what the madrasa sciences do, so long as education is not dumbed down.

Another principle is that one should learn the ten principles of the sciences. The ten principles of the sciences are the introductory points and principles by which one identifies and knows each science, as well as identifying its relation to other sciences. Young students may suffice with the first three, most fundamental principles: the subject, definition, and benefit. But as soon as they are capable, students should be taught the logical scope of each science and from what principles it is obtained. Aristotle noted that if one does not search for knowledge from its principles, one may dissect 10,000 frogs and learn nothing of biology. One may spend one's entire life looking up at the night sky without establishing one topic in the science of astronomy.[41] Learning to seek knowledge through its principles is termed 'paideia'. So many forms of contemporary reductionism can be avoided if one knows the full classification of the sciences and its value. One comes to learn that lower sciences—such as natural sciences or the social sciences—cannot establish universal rules for higher sciences such as metaphysics. Without knowing these principles, one is sure to be confused by figures such as Richard Dawkins who professes that he is not a philosopher, yet unknowingly makes philosophical claims into metaphysics and theology that extend beyond his discipline.

Children should learn fiqh with all subjects covered, attempting to memorise important rulings, including the conditions and pillars of acts of worship and of common contracts. Again, this makes a foundation present when they reach the age when they are able to understand but find it hard to memorise. Emphasise worship, including ritual purity, but do not neglect books like *Matn Abi Shuja'*, which are brief classics covering all the sections of fiqh.

If children become strong readers and strong in the instrumental sciences such as grammar and logic, they will be able to read complicated books of fiqh after they graduate. The combination of memorising a short text or two covering all sections, then reading a larger book or two on worship, then graduating and being able to read complicated works such as the daunting *Tuhfat al-muhtaj* of the Shafi'i scholar Ibn Hajar al-Haytami is a known, successful formula. Another model is to work up inside the madrasa to *al-Hidayah*, a top madrasa book in Hanafi fiqh, but is this not more suitable for someone already committed to a full-time *'alim* course? On that course, one will plow through books, bigger and bigger, reviewing and memorising rulings. One would hopefully see how *fatwa* is given in and outside the madrasa. But there are many madrasa students who graduate and genuinely do not understand what they have memorised.

As a principle, LIFE never advises curriculum without knowing that it has worked for a child who is not highly exceptional. We also insist on

---

41 See James G. Lennox, *Aristotle on Inquiry Erotetic Frameworks and Domain-Specific Norms* (Cambridge: Cambridge University Press, 2021).

not developing a curriculum for the student who struggles most. We design our curriculum for the average or slightly above average student whose parents have protected their fitrah since birth as much as they were able. This allows LIFE and the wider community to develop a tried and tested, common path, termed in Arabic *al-muwatta'*. You can only make versions if there is something to make versions of. You can only individualise for a given learner or learning style if something already exists to individualise. You can only bespeak a curriculum if that curriculum exists. So, this is our first priority. We attempt to cater for all the schools of fiqh.

If your child has gaps and struggles, in a homeschool you are at liberty to take the time to fill their gaps and repair their confidence and interest.

A secret of pedagogical success is to break things down, especially if pushing the boundaries of what is age-appropriate.

2.6.2 Should we Teach Grammar to Young Students?

Should we teach grammar at all or use the tried and tested methods of communicative language teaching?

The ancient Roman rhetorician Quintilian was confronted with the all-too familiar question, 'If it takes longer when younger, why do we not wait until children are older and can learn these concepts and skills faster? Why teach them at an age in which they do not truly understand what they are learning'. This question is often posed now by those trained in modern education. However, the same sentiment is increasingly reflected in common statements passed around Muslim educational circles. One may see this as progress: Muslim educators benefitting from modern educational research and increasing their professional qualifications. Or this might relate to patterns by which religion survives in the modern world through adopting a formation fitting modern culture.[42] Perhaps the greatest ancient educator, Quintilian, replies virtually to this question (in paraphrase), 'True, they may learn faster and understand better later, but anything they acquire younger is more firmly fixed than if they acquire it later. And, if you start early, no matter how slow you are going you will be ahead in development over others that are not acquainted with new materials yet'.[43] Those children will be ahead. Similar arguments say, you cannot study mathematics early because it is so abstract. However, one encounters a great deal of centers in the US where there are large Chinese and Indian populations where children are

---

42 For instance, it either conforms to science and liberal ethics, or it becomes New Agey, or renders itself an (individualistic) cult, when not outright secularising. (See Graham Ward, *True Religion*, Oxford: Blackwell Publishing, 2003).

43 See Smail (tr.), "Method of Primary Instruction," in *Quintilian on Education.*

entered into preschool or after-school maths programmes, finishing high-school programmes by the 6th or 7th grade. This is not to agree with or even be intimidated by such arguable hothousing. It is just to strike a parallel: they use different techniques; they do not truly understand every detail until some point in their life when they do a deep dive into the topic. But they understand enough such that if the topic is encountered later in life, they do get the benefit of it. What better to ground oneself in than the sciences of Arabic, which Allah says His Book (and final revelation) is written in, and liberal arts in general designed to lay the foundations of human development (before state economic development).

We advocate the approach of scaffolding. In scaffolding, one uses knowledge of English and Arabic grammar to mirror and support each other and to lead to repetition and reinforcement. One may ask, 'How can these two languages mirror each other, considering they are so different from each other?' The answer is that many languages have a deeper agreement with each other than might be supposed. We bring this out, and thus when we teach the parts of speech in Arabic, we show that English can also be conceived as having three basic word types: verb, noun, and particle or preposition.[44] We show how sentences universally involve predication: saying 'X is Y', as in, 'Zayd is standing'. Most of what is added is restrictions to this predication: 'Zayd was standing yesterday in his room'. Here we introduce non-essential parts of the sentence, such as adverbs, and we teach parent and student alike how to diagramme the most common ten additional parts of the sentence. Then, they can analyse 90% of both English and Arabic sentences.

One may object, 'How do you expect students to speak about nouns and pronouns and other elements in Arabic if they cannot speak or understand Arabic?' To this end, we devote daily lessons for a few months to speaking the basic Arabic sentences in context. After they can use the basic sentences, we ask them first to identify words that perform certain roles as they themselves use them in their speech. If they have learned to speak Arabic, then it is just as easy as learning English grammar. They already have the language, and you are merely picking out and identifying. They already have the implicit information to know grammar in a natural way; one is merely clarifying. We may ask them, 'Do you say it this way or that?' Then ask, 'Can I say it this way?' to which they will respond, 'No, that is wrong'. Then one may ask them why it is wrong. They do not know. 'Why don't I say, "Me is happy"?' They will say, 'It sounds weird'. 'Why does it sound weird?', and then one says in the case of Arabic, 'The verb conjugates', or, 'The pronoun is not inflected (i.e., the *damir* is *mabni*)'.

---

44 See the masterful guide of Bryan Garner, *The Chicago Guide to Grammar, Usage, and Punctuation*, 'I. The Traditional Parts of Speech', University of Chicago Press: Chicago, 2016.

2.6.3 SHOULD WE NOT USE SIMPLE, MODERN TEXTS THAT TEACH THE SKILLS WE WANT TO TEACH?

'Doesn't teaching classical texts put additional and unnecessary burden on the teacher and child? Isn't the point the skills, and should we not adopt the path of least resistance in obtaining those skills?'

Put simply and clearly, true knowledge requires proof. Learning without proof produces memorisers, not scholars.[45] Proofs require at the very least logic, as it is the universal tool for learning. Even the practical and productive sciences have principles gained through experience and stated as a 'practical science' or 'productive science'.[46] So, one must know logic for every science, and to know logic one must be able to access the primary meanings primarily through grammar. But one cannot learn logic from the beginning of education, so what is the proper order of any education aiming at knowledge?

Education (setting aside tarbiyah for the moment) should begin with the acquisition of high language skills, including grammar, and experience of the world through the senses and careful watching—and sometimes engaging with nature and the world. Without experience, one's definitions are limited to what books convey abstracted from nature and condense into words. Without strong language and grammar, one's capacity to think, convey thought, and receive other's thought is not firm. So, the curriculum should focus on experience, language, and grammar in the first formal years. Language should ideally be literary, including the flares of rhetoric, metaphor, and turns of phrase. The basics of rhetoric can be learned earlier than formal logic. Verbal thinking skills can be learned from the beginning of education. Logical and deductive puzzles can begin in Grade 2. Logical fallacies can be learned in 4th or 5th grade, and formal logic can be started in 6th grade. As a prerequisite to starting logic, the basic grammatical structures of the language of learning should be mastered.

---

45 The difference between different types of learners was referred to in a well-known prophetic tradition which likens knowledge to water. Some people are like rock pools: they store water for others, but do not themselves benefit.

46 This is lost in contemporary medicine and even in engineering, which is a technocratic application of industry standards, rather than an art requiring the virtue of craft (techne). See Ivan Illich, *Limits to Medicine: Medical Nemesis: The Expropriation of Health* (London: Marion Boyars, 1976) and Hans Gadamer (tr. Jason Gaiger and Nicholas Walker), *The Enigma of Medicine: The Art of Healing in a Scientific Age*, Stanford University Press: Redwood City, California, 1996. See also Jacques Ellul, *The Technological Society*, which speaks more directly to civil engineering and architecture, but also applies to medicine. For a summary of and argument that Illich's book remains an accurate and insightful analysis of contemporary medicine, see https://medhum.med.nyu.edu/view/16963.

Following Ibn Khaldun, LIFE emphasises that the best pedagogy is one that deploys disputation and research methodology on the given text. *This is* the classical method for engaging with the text that is used between the teacher and student, full stop. All classical teachers speak of *fakk al-'ibarah* as a method of teaching: unpacking the sentence in terms of its linguistic and logic contents. Note that this method requires that the text *deploy* the sciences of grammar and logic and even rhetoric. Classical texts do this; contemporary schemes and textbooks generally do not. Based on this, primary education centres around grammar. It is studied in itself and used to unpack the classical text. As such, parents need at least a crash course in grammar, discussed in the following objections and answers (no. 9).

In sum:

Primary

Years 1-6: Grammar focus

Years 3-6: Introduce more and more rhetoric, starting with use of metaphor and simile

Secondary

Years 7-12: Logic focus

Years 8-9: Learn and begin to apply disputation and scientific method (*adab al-bahth wa-l-munazarah*)

One may think we use the instrument to achieve knowledge, but there is no need to transmit that knowledge in a particular, classical format. This is not true. We may summarise the truth about the proper method by saying, 'Classical sciences are sought through certain instrumental sciences, then they are taught through certain instrumental sciences'. This prevents wisdom from calcifying.

Thus, LIFE's training course discussed immediately below focuses on grammar for primary education, and logic for secondary. They also offer rhetoric for primary, and disputation for secondary, and explain how they are used to teach classical texts.

2.6.4 If Schooling is Bad, Should we Adopt Unschooling?

To increase motivation, should all children choose what they wish to study? Should we avoid technical sciences which are 'heavy' on the children?

We are attempting to embark on a real education, which is the classical form of education. Classical Islamic education used to be visible in every

Muslim city. That classical education was a continuous but developing tradition carrying wisdom and centuries of collective experience. In our time, these living chains have broken in most cities, largely due to the deluge of mass education in the last century, plus the destruction wrought by colonization in preceding centuries. LIFE have worked hard to connect to living traditions. However, there is a trend amongst those looking for classical or traditional education to make the following arguments:

P1   All that is modern is bad.

P2   Schooling is modern.

C1   Therefore, all schooling is bad.

P3(C1)   All schooling is bad.

P4   Everything with organisation or some rigour is schooling.

C2   Therefore, all organisation and rigour are bad, and we must therefore adopt unschooling.

This argument it clearly fallacious in several points. I also argue that it fits a widespread mentality: New Agism.

One sign that something is New Agey, rather than truly traditional, is that it contradicts tradition. Can you imagine trying to realise your bodily potential and become an athlete without organisation and rigour? If one looks carefully at the educational norms of Ibn Khaldun, Ibn Sahnun, and Ibn al-'Arabi al-Maliki, one sees that one must learn specific sciences in a specific order to develop and to do things right. For instance, one must learn Arabic poetry early to appreciate the Quran, ideally before memorising it. Then one must memorise, and finally one must learn debate skills (*munazarah*) to gain the noetic disposition needed for knowledge, which is contrasted with mere memorisation. This cannot happen through an unorganized and unplanned curriculum. That is not what tradition did. But, then again, neither does the tradition adopt modern hothousing. 'And seek between this and that a (moderate) path'. It did not adopt toxic parenting.

There is a great onus on the teacher to keep lessons interesting and to break things down to facilitate learning. The child will ask some days, 'Can we do something besides (memorisation or grammar, etc.)?' This sound like a perfectly valid question, so one has to be prepared. It will occasionally be the right thing to do to go outside and build snow forts instead of study.

2.6.5 How can Parents & Teachers Teach Classical Texts if They are not Trained?

How are parents not trained in the trivium able to teach classical texts properly? This is a legitimate question. To avoid the impression that parents or teachers must learn every subject taught to students before they may begin, LIFE focusses on grammar in primary education and logic in secondary education. We simplify these sciences to crash courses, and train parents on applying them to classical texts. Then, with these basics, one may learn on the job.[47] Certain LIFE or LIFE-recommended resources are scripted to ease learning on the job. By teaching your children and working things out in front of them on whiteboards, etc., you will absorb it and join them on the learning journey. In the future, we hope a community will upload videos to help get past sticking points.

A teaching strategy adopted by LIFE is teaching English and Arabic grammar in parallel. If one is stronger in English, then one grasps the grammatical concepts, and English is a firm crutch to rely on. Either way, learning the two reinforce each other. We offer sentence-diagramming/parsing in Arabic which mirrors that of English. So, by seeing how the two languages express the same meanings, one sees each in the mirror of the other.

---

47 We have noted this is not ideal, but not everyone can send their child to a boarding school, nor afford private tutors, nor set up a satisfactory school or co-op.

3

THE PRACTICAL PRE-ELEMENTARY CURRICULUM

3.1 From Now to Conception

The mother and father of the child are the basis for the child: you will imprint on their imagination and they will naturally copy the way you move, speak, and the activities you engage in. Whatever relationship they develop with a teacher in the future—as spiritual mother or father—will build on this basis. They may reject messages from a future teacher because they sense that those ideals are not a reality in their home. So, educate yourself with the following priority:

3.1.1 Rectify your State with Allah

This requires sound belief and practice and some daily litany of remembrance. We recommend that teachers and parents read *The Beginning of Guidance* (*Bidayat al-hidayah*) of Imam al-Ghazali, translated into English more than once. This book teaches beliefs, practice, and remembrance. Moreover, it gives something of the right attitude and etiquette of these practices. Without this adab, our efforts only weigh us down. With it, they lift us up. And after they become a habit, it will be harder to leave them than to do them. And we will have a new source of meaning and motivation in our life that we never expected. This book will also give you the capacity to explain to children the significance and etiquette of fiqh, 'aqidah, and purification of the heart when you come to the early years of the student's curriculum.

How do we expect our hearts to be right with Allah if they are busy with the world all the time. Do we really believe that we are busier than Allah's chosen messenger, the Prophet ﷺ? Find friends that practice and remember Allah, and keep their company.

Learn your basic beliefs, as these are the foundations without which practice is invalid. Then learn the basics of practice so these are valid with their preconditions, including ritual purity.

Thereafter, set up a litany (*wird*) for yourself. This should include as many Sunnah prayers as possible, starting with the twelve which the Prophet ﷺ never left. We should from the Quran daily, even if one verse. We do not need to understand it perfectly, but we can look at a translation and read it to remember Allah. The most important litany is exalting Allah after the five prayers: 33-33-33. Then, some of the daily and nightly remembrances of Allah from the Sunnah, including at occasions of waking, sleeping, eating, etc. These occur as we go through our day, not by setting aside time for them. Then, set aside time to implement copious advice from the Quran and Sunnah: try to ask forgiveness, send blessings on the Prophet ﷺ, and say, '*lā ilāha illa Allāh*', one-hundred times in the morning and one-hundred times between '*asr* prayer and when you sleep. If you wish, ask a scholar for the proofs behind this practice of the righteous.

From a scientific viewpoint, our stress and anxiety imprint on the child at all levels of development. So, start now to manage such states and set good habits. The point is not to force oneself to be perfect; the point is that wherever one is on a scale, turn the dial towards the middle. If you are stressed often, try to fake not being stressed. Or handle the same matters that stress one with a certain degree less of stress than normal. Keep doing this until it comes without effort and has become a firm habit.

3.1.2 Learn your Obligatory Religious Matters

After reading al-Ghazali's *The Beginning of Guidance* and putting as much as possible into practice, learn your basics of fiqh, 'aqidah, and purification of the heart. One way to do this and prepare to teach is to learn the books listed for these Islamic sciences from Year 1 & 2, and perhaps 3, from the LIFE curriculum. This will also enable you to teach the early years of the primary curriculum based on your own learning and allow you to review and expand.

If you cannot find a teacher, contact us directly. Even after you learn with a teacher, keep in contact with them and other scholars so that you can ask questions when you teach your child or when you help your child review their lessons.

3.1.3 Begin Learning Arabic

Enrol in an Arabic programme, but also consider encouraging your local mosque to teach Arabic. For instance, ask them to have a class for young mothers, including offering childcare.

3.1.4 CHOOSING A SPOUSE

Choose a spouse for their character and religion. Think of how happy your future child will be in the afterlife that their parent made it easy for them to be close to Allah and have a high station in the afterlife. Think on the other hand of how you will explain to Allah why you chose a spouse who did not raise them well or who was not practicing and therefore made it very difficult for them to take practice seriously.

To this end, set expectations with your family before they raise the topic. Be firm and polite. Be responsible about allowing your heart to get attached to someone. Learn the prophetic guidance on choosing a spouse, and this will help guide the heart to someone that you will love not only in this world, but in the next. Many people are attracted to the wrong people, so learn something about compatibility and personality types. Finally, challenge dichotomies of secular and religious: many 'good' families cannot imagine marrying their child to a person who looks religious. This is in part because they cannot imagine a religious looking person being successful in a world where business is secularised. Learn to navigate this space in a mature and perspicacious manner, and be a leader, not a follower. Future generations will thank you.

3.2 BETWEEN CONCEPTION & BIRTH

Make a good intention for having children in the first place. This should include, but not be limited to, a) obeying the command to proliferate (*takatharu*) and b) hoping for the benefits of a child that focuses on the afterlife, such as their praying for you after you die. Remember the two supplications surrounding marital relations when trying to conceive. After conception, be extra careful to eat only what is pure and permissible. Remembrance Allah as noted above, and spend extra time reciting Quran aloud, and know that your remembrance will affect the baby. Visit places that benefit your state, including trying to go for *'umra*, or visit Muslim countries where scholars and righteous people from Islamic history are buried. Research shows that children in the womb are able to hear sounds from 16 weeks and form memories from 22-3 weeks.[48] Thus, hearing the Quran and nashids can benefit them. Have the husband draw close to the womb and recite Quran and sing a song; pick a particular song to repeat, such as *Tala'a al-badr, Inna fi al-jannah*, or other nashids known across the Islamic

---

48 Heidi Murkoff and Sharon Mazel, *What to Expect When You're Expecting*, 5th ed., Workman Publishing Company, 2016 and Hugo Lagercrantz and Jean-Pierre Changeux, *The Emergence of Human Consciousness: From Fetal to Neonatal Life*, Pediatric Research 65, no. 3 (2009).

world.[49] When your child is born, perform the Sunnah practices: reciting the adhan (call to prayer) and iqamah in their ears, and repeat the same nashid to them. They will connect between your presence they felt before birth and you. Later, when they are crying or distraught, sing the same nashid of your choice to them. Improve your state along the lines mentioned above, or keep the company of righteous scholars, especially trustworthy spiritual guides. Take counsel from the righteous about how to improve your state.

This is all a foundation for educating your child properly. It removes conflicts between the so-called ideals and realities of Islam and between our inward and outward state. Such conflicts cause cognitive dissonance when children mature, and we can avoid it now and strive to have our own inward and outward in accordance with each other. Doing so after the children are old enough to understand can lead us to feel hypocrisy.

3.3 AGES 0 TO 3

Arrange with your doctor or midwife for the child to spend time with you after birth, not to immediately be taken away to be weighed, cleaned, and left in an incubator to cry often in room of crying babies. If the baby opens its eyes, make contact and speak in a soft voice. Either way, place them on the skin of the mother and father and connect with you. Breastfeeding is now known to impact not only the immune system, but to form a connection needed for a stable and balanced personality.

Though children are too young for formal learning, they are born in an angelic state and placed in our custodianship. There are many activities for keeping the fitrah alive; in addition to those listed below, one might add: art activities and gymnastics or martial arts. Even a two-year-old can be impacted forever just by meeting a master of martial arts, especially if the person inculcates the virtues of self-discipline. Four aims are essential if they are to succeed in a real education later in life:

Their fitrah should be preserved through staying off screens,

seeing as much of nature and animals as possible,

having a good grounding in language, and

seeing their parents practice and hearing forms of Islamic practice such as the recitation of Quran and nashids.

Let us take these points in turn.

---

49 Two collections of such nashids are *Breezes from Paradise*, Vol. I & II, edited by Mustafa Styer. These are available for sale on Amazon and through other sellers.

3.3.1 Screens

Put simply, as one scholar interviewed told us, 'These devices ruin (*tufsidu* or spoil) the child'. If given the choice, they will choose screens over activities. I almost said, 'other activities', but realised this is a mistake, as looking at a screen is not an activity. Perhaps we should call it a passivity. Why do they prefer it? It represents the path of least resistance, just like eating sweets and junk food. It requires less effort, is easier, and more instantly stimulating. But it does not produce deep satisfaction. Perhaps that is why each may be termed, 'morish'. Each experience on the screen leads to them wanting it, and not wanting or enjoying other things. Conversely, every set of hours they do not see the screen and instead get on with other things, with or without you, the less they miss the screen and start to find other things stimulating and fulfilling.

This leads back to you in two ways. One is that they really want your attention, which helps replace the screen. Second is that you will have to sacrifice your own screen-time and hide the moments you look at a phone and laptop. There will come a time when you can and should make them realise that you have things they cannot. In this vein, treat the screen like a cooking knife. Adults can use it when they need; children cannot. But if they see you looking at it all the time, then it is hard to argue that it is needed to take care of adult matters such as shopping and navigation.

There was a period where it was difficult to convince people of the harms of screens, but the time is ripe to separate from screens. In decades past, one could say that toys produced by corporate toy companies were part of a product umbrella and pathway that might be innocent, momentarily, but lead on to certain products whose value includes a false vision of happiness. Consumerism consumed human identity, as it were, and even matters such as idiosyncratic self-expression were encompassed by corporations into their product umbrella. Now, phones profile us and work not only to identify and type us, but to gradually alter our behaviour, including the amount of time we spend on the screen. Demand to have a real life like people had before 1994. Demand actual company and return to activities involving real people and real things, especially those that have a local significance, not merely being part of an international chain that homogenises our environment till every part of the globe looks like every other part.

To recap, there is both old and new[50] research on the impact of screens

---

50 For a review of Jane Healy's work on the impact of screens, see https://www.amblesideonline.org/ReviewHealy.html. Also see Happé and Frith, "The Weak Coherence Account: Detail-focused Cognitive Style in Autism Spectrum Disorders", *Journal of Autism and Developmental Disorders 3, no. 1* (2006): 5–25, doi:10.1007/s10803-005-0039-0; Booth and Happé, "Evidence

on the brain and social skills: the skills needed to connect with others, such as making eye contact and avoiding overt signs of boredom. Research aside, it is clear that children who spend time on screens run the risk also of finding reality less interesting than the online world. Even if they cannot put words to it, it is like any other addiction. One craves it because it stimulates the pleasure parts of the brain, but is not beneficial, generally.

Or you may make a truce and allow them to watch certain programmes for thirty minutes a day, or when they or you are unwell, etc. In other words, limited and exceptional times. If you opt for the latter, be aware that each ten years media experts increase the speed of movement of items on screen, and in fact increase the rate at which there is movement from one angle or object to another. These movements stimulate the reptilian parts of the brain, and the trick wears off.[51] So, like other addictions, more and more extreme stimulation is required to grasp one's interest. What can one do about this? One suggestion is to try to find old recordings and those that involve nature. Beatrix Potter, Wind in the Willows, Noddy, and if you are a die-hard American, Little Bear or Curious George and other programmes from twenty or more years back will be found to be much more civil. The recordings of Peter Rabbit and the stop-motion version of Wind in the Willows are literally beautiful and have musical scores that seem from another universe than today's children's staple diets. Much of the new cartoon industry is designed with AI and shows the signs of someone who never made it outside their

---

of Reduced Global Processing in Autism Spectrum Disorder", *Journal of Autism and Developmental Disorders* (2016), doi:10.1007/s10803-016-2724-6. It is worth noting that the superior colliculus not only receives but also shapes attention direction; malformation of neurons in the superior colliculus may not only result, that is, in an inattentiveness, but exacerbate it. See Heffler, et al., "Association of Early-Life Social and Digital Media Experiences With Development of Autism Spectrum Disorder-Like Symptoms," *JAMA Pediatrics*, 174.7 (2020): 690– 696 [DOI: 10.1001/jamapediatrics.2020.0230], Zhao et al. 2022: "Association Between Screen Time Trajectory and Early Childhood Development in Children in China" in *JAMA Pediatrics*, 176.8: 768-775 [DOI: 10.1001/jamapediatrics.2022.1630], Kushima et al. 2022: "Association Between Screen Time Exposure in Children at 1 Year of Age and Autism Spectrum Disorder at 3 Years of Age: The Japan Environment and Children's Study" in *JAMA Pediatrics*, 176.4: 384-391 [DOI: 10.1001/jamapediatrics.2021.5778], and Sarfraz et al. 2023: "Early Screen-Time Exposure and Its Association With Risk of Developing Autism Spectrum Disorder: A Systematic Review" in *Cureus* [DOI: 10.7759/cureus.42292]

For the underlying neurology of the superior colliculus as mechanism for attention of any kind, see Krauzlis, "Attentional Functions of the Superior Colliculus," in Nobre and Kastner (eds.), *The Oxford Handbook of Attention*, 2014, doi: 10.1093/oxfordhb/9780199675111.013.014. (Kind appreciation to Dr. Brian Kemple for sharing his research ahead of publishing a paper on the subject.)

51 The reptilian parts of the brain, mostly the brainstem, are those parts that control basal functions, such as breathing, coordination, eating, etc. These parts and functions of the part share a similarity to the classical concept of the vegetative and animal souls and their functions. See Alfred Ivy, "Arabic and Islamic Psychology and Philosophy of Mind," *Stanford Encyclopedia of Philosophy* (May 2012), https://plato.stanford.edu/entries/arabic-islamic-mind/.

house, let alone had a profound relationship with nature. {*Travel through the land and see how Allah originated creation*}, Quran 29:20.

3.3.2 SEEING NATURE

Part of the screen solution is a green solution. Get out into nature. Couples should arrange their schedules and even choose where to live based on nature and, if necessary, parks. Try to get children from birth to three into nature or a park every day. That way, if you fail, they will still see a lot of green. Nature imprints on the soul. There is a vast, vast difference between what Allah creates, and what humans generate, between nature and culture. Humans can potentially perfect nature, but only if they know it inside out. Otherwise, their imagination is weak, their minds empty, and they produce the kind of drivel that is found in modern cartoons and architecture.

Even before children can speak, take them out of the house to get fresh air and see nature. Frustration leads to bad habits. Avoid the temptation to let the screen replace this outside time, though family time can replace a certain portion of it without harm, especially if the wider family has children for your little one to play with. Still, some educators say you should be out of the house six hours a day.

3.3.3 LANGUAGE LEARNING

If in the home you speak more than one language that you want the child to learn, make a plan for each person to primarily speak in one language. This helps the child represent the language in a person and keep the languages distinct. If they want to speak to that person, they have to speak that language. After birth, connect with them through using speech they can understand. Rather than excitedly saying, 'Stay away from the light socket. You could be electrocuted!' Say, 'Dangerous!' Or even, 'Ouch!' Some of the frustration of children nearing the 'terrible twos' is not understanding and not being understood. Decrease this by being as clear as you can, and they will learn better as well and hold on to words, rather than merely thinking that if you want something, you merely blurt out a long string of syllables. Prioritise words such as 'food', 'water', 'no', 'dangerous', 'momma', and 'baba'.

3.3.4 SEEING PARENTS & FAMILY PRACTICE

Let the child see and hear you saying the basmalah and other adhkar and practices, most important being the prayer. If not in a Muslim country, let them hear the adhan in the home.

3.3.5 Books & Toys that Work: Birth to Three

Ages 0-1

Let them hear lots of Quran, nashids, and nursery rhymes.

In general, expose them to beauty. This works in the background of their minds and souls to love beauty and prepares them for higher realities of religion.

For Quran, try to listen to Egyptian reciters such as 'Abd al-Samad 'Abd al-Basit and those before him such as Mustafa Isma'il and Muhammad Rif'at. There is a big difference between their recitation and modern reciters, even if you prefer the modern. Modern recitation and music makes use of a more and more limited range of modes (*maqams*), aiming toward the deprived Western music in which most music is in one mode, and often in just a few keys in the mode. Also, the spirituality of these reciters is better than the sentimentality of modern reciters that create an atmosphere through the same techniques as modern music.

As for English nursery rhymes and lullabies, we may list a few.[52]

Row, row, row your boat (include silly verse, 'If you see a crocodile, don't forget to scream'.)

Where is Thumbkin?

The incey wincey spider

Twinkle, twinkle, little star[53]

Ba, ba black sheep

Hey diddle, diddle

Hickory, dickory, dock

Here's Tom Thumb

Ages 1-2

Continue repeating nursery rhymes, encouraging them to join along. Buy them an anvil and hammer where they hammer shapes into the anvil. Give them balls and balloons. Read picture books to them that have 1-2 sentences

---

[52] For a list of around 75 well-chosen English nursery rhymes, see Clifton Fadiman, *The World Treasury of Children's Literature*, Quality Paperback Book Club, New York, 1984, pp. 4-31.

[53] This and the previous two with gestures. Open and close your hands for twinkling, make a diamond by touching the thumbs and forefingers of each hand, and make your hands step up one over the other further and further towards the ceiling for 'up above the world so high'.

per page.[54] Show them how to play with figurines, or even pretend various scraps of wood or fabric or wool are figurines. Spend quality time with them, and you will find in the years to come that they play confidently and independently, as your attention to them makes them have a lasting feeling of security. Play *Peek-a-boo*, *Hide-and-seek*, and *Thumbkin* with them. Take them in a push chair into nature, gardens, parks, botanic gardens, and zoos.

Introduce some activities from *Slow and Steady, Get Me Ready*,[55] which teach object permanence. Hide objects in socks or under cushions or between parts of furniture and take them back out or let them find them. If you find it fruitful, progress through the said book.

Ages 2-3

Carry on with previous activities, but all puzzles starting with two pieces, then progressively moving up to 8, 16, etc. Buy a sand and water table. Introduce them to playdough, making it at home. Buy them magnetic blocks, which are quite incredible in terms of what they can do with them. Let them play on swings and slides, and visit parks to feed the ducks or throw pinecones into the water. Give them paper or notepads and egg-shaped crayons. Later, they can hold proper pens and pencils and markers, but watch that their grip is not crumpled up. If so, give them fist crayons and then come back to other materials months later.

Set up their room with floor-level cubby holes. Dolls and toys can not only be stored there, but it becomes a natural play space and backdrop for action, or a cozy home for characters.

Buy toys that are either lacking detail—leaving matters to the imagination of the child—or toys which, if they have details, are realistic. Avoid toys and cartoons where children are purple or look like they have never been in the sunlight, like vampires or children with bags under their eyes that stay up all night on screens. Avoid the wave of toys in which everything lacks its natural form and is shaped like a blob whose features are painted over it. This seems to have begun around the time of recent, popular Nickelodeon cartoons, then the introduction of aliens. The point is that it is unnatural. The cartoonists of today could not draw a realistic plant or animal if their job or life depended on it. So, cartoons are often now made through pulling an image off the net and manipulating it through software.[56]

---

54 We list a set of board book below.

55 June Oberlander, *Slow and Steady, Get me Ready: A parents' handbook for children from birth to age 5*, Bio-Alpha, Burke, Va, 2002.

56 See the discussion of the history of design in the works of Rosemary Sassoon in this manual. (Cf., https://tedium.co/2021/10/27/anthropomorphism-early-animation-history/.)

Encourage them to start to develop independence, for instance getting their own water or choosing their own book.

3.3.6 READ-ALOUD BOOKS FOR THE VERY YOUNG

Many of these books can be read again and again over many years. Some will appear in our preschool and Reception/Kindergarten curriculum. Some ideas to get you started are:

- Interactive baby-books introducing colours, shapes, and animals[57]
- *Montmorency's Book of Rhymes* by T. J. Winter (Shaykh Abdal Hakim Murad), Kinza Press, 2013
- A. A. Milne, *When We Were Very Young*[58]
- Janet and Allan Ahlberg, *Peepo*, Penguin, New York
- *The Very Hungry Caterpillar* (and around ten other books) by Eric Carle
- Michael Rosen, *We're Going on a Bear Hunt*
- Beatrix Potter: simple board-books drawn from her stories
- *Winnie-the-Pooh Story Treasury*, Egmont, London, 2018
(The illustrations and rendering of this particular edition have nothing to do with Disney.)
- *A First Discovery Book* series by Scholastic. These will hold their interest at anywhere from 1-5 and are genuinely informative

Find engaging books in Arabic, such as *Sirat al-Rasul Muhammad* (Biography of the Prophet Muhammad ﷺ) by Kidsotic. The same publisher, Kidsotic, has a number of other books containing books with one to two sentences per page, including their multi-volume series on the prophets.[59]

It is very difficult to find books friendly to small children that are not

---

[57] A lot of what is out there is terrible. The older it is, the better, in general. So, find towns that still have used bookstores, or look online and find good sources.

[58] Though Milne wrote these poems for his three-year-old son two years before he wrote Winnie-the-Pooh, only a few of these poems can be read to those who are indeed very young. Many others should wait until children are school- aged. One may select the poems oneself or purchase the board-book by Rosemary Wells, *Poems from When We Were Very Young*, which is approximately 80 pages and published by Norton Young Readers, 2021. Milne's poems can be found read on BBC in 1941 with the BBC orchestra. A selection was also set to music by Disney in 1968 and is more innocent of a progressive agenda than later Disney productions.

[59] http://www.kidsotic.com/shop/view-book/9789948193067/syrt-alrswl-mhmd-sly-allh-lyh-wslm.

merely translated from European languages or known Disneyfied stories. Also, nearly everything is in colloquial dialects. Even the modern standard Arabic shows that authors cannot speak classical Arabic, and often write through translating English phrases into Arabic.

Perhaps the best alternative is a temporary solution: find the books of Julia Donaldson or even Dr. Seuss translated into Arabic. There is a good amount of dual-language literature for children that appears in the counsels throughout England and perhaps other parts of Europe. *The Very Hungry Caterpillar* and *The Snail and Whale* exist in dual-language, and one is likely to find many, many more titles.

3.4 Ages 3 to Kindergarten/Preschool

Children who attend a well-run play-based preschool seem to have an enormous advantage throughout elementary school, and perhaps beyond. They will often be put into accelerated or gifted programmes. At three, children are generally confident enough in speaking to begin to learn and retain simple ideas and words. Children have a certain receptivity at this age and are learning, whether we teach or not. Those who spend the ages of 3 to 6 or 7 learning through play will have spiralled through the topics of the world several times at further levels of depth by the time they begin formal learning in grade 1 or 2. If not, the sensitivity to acquire words and concepts that they possess at that stage may be lost, or worse, spent watching YouTube cartoons and playing video games.

Children in the UK and US start Reception/Kindergarten (Rec/KG) at different ages. The consequence is that those starting in the US will make it through one additional year of the present preschool curriculum. One in the UK may accept having one less year of preschool. Or they may choose to start Rec at the same age as the US starts KG: five going on six. They may even start the preschool curriculum earlier if their child of two-and-a-half is speaking confidently and able to begin memorising through play. Some children are, while other require reaching the age of three-and-a-half. If you are unconcerned about what others are doing at school, you may enter your child into the Rec/KG curriculum early if they are ready, or alternatively delay till the age of six going on seven.

3.4.1 The Preschool Curriculum at a Glance

Between the age of 3 and the beginning of Rec/KG, children learn topics orally through play, start phonics when ready, and scaffold Arabic learning on English. This is explained below through the following:

- Advice for learning through playful exploration of topics
- An outline of the preschool subjects
- Approaches for timetabling these subjects
- The subjects (one-by-one)

3.4.2 LEARNING THROUGH PLAY

Topic-based language learning

Our topic-based learning is broadly based on the Reggio Emilia approach, though with elements from our traditional scholars and insights from Pestalozzi.[60] The principles by which students in preschool learn language and concepts around certain topics is as follows:

- Students select topics based on interest and seasons
- Speak to children and take note of their interests. This allows topics to come from them.

Note briefly that in practice, very young students tend to be interested in the same topics. The Scottish early learning curriculum topics can be cross-checked, but one will notice that children will usually ask about insects, seasons, cars and transportation, buildings, family (and topics such as, 'my father is traveling'), so it happens naturally and does not need to be forced.

Even if one prepares set topics knowing they are likely to emerge, one may make this emergence more natural through being flexible in the order they emerge. They may arise to the awareness of different children at different times.

We advise scaffolding a second language (Arabic) off of this conceptual learning in the main language (English). To facilitate this, you will find below in 'The Subjects' under 'Arabic' a list of Arabic vocabulary which covers the major topics and the major words that appear under them. This is to ease for educators, who are not confident in Arabic, learning a limited number of words to be able to lead the Arabic learning if needed.

Further, if in a school setting, students may follow an individual curriculum

---

60 Learning through exploration and experience for us does not entail constructivism: that we construct our concepts subjectively. Rather, LIFE considers that there is a pre-scientific reflective mode of concept-acquisition. This comes from the tradition of great Sunni scholars such as al-Sayyid al-Sharif al-Jurjani, but it is also found in the educational philosophy of Pestalozzi: students must have intimate and deep experience with matters before they either try to define it or, worse, are merely given a definition to memorise. Students who have little experience outside the school or madrasa risk a brittle dogmatism or formalism.

through primary and secondary topics as follows: as individual students become aware of a topic they wish to investigate, make this their primary topic. Secondary topics are those raised by other students. They are welcome to sit in the topics of other students as other teachers guide those activities.

Topics reflect local culture

The Reggio Emilia approach emphasises that children and education are rooted in their local culture. The curriculum you produce should use materials from their local culture and environment. If your local area has no coal or coal mines, do not make activities involving coal central. If you are in a desert, you cannot have a forest school. Similarly, you cannot have a desert school in England or the Netherlands which emphasises how to reclaim land from deserts and give it natural and agricultural life.[61]

LEARNING THROUGH EXPERIENCE AND EXPLORATION: LEARNING TO LEARN

Learning through experience and exploration leads to learning certain general knowledge and habits, rather than facts that may be easily forgotten or are trivial in themselves compared to deeper learning. For example, it is not so important to learn to distinguish a car from a truck as it is to learn how to learn about cars, including how to deduce this distinction from one's own experience and learning how to pursue topics further that are not merely cut and dried facts.

One flaw with learning through memorisation or superficial discussions is that children do not learn to retain specifics unless accompanied with much repetition. The 'prepare for school' nursery often gives this repetition in circle time and other activities, where the content likely to come up in school interviews is reinforced. What is more important for the child's development is general knowledge and habits: to gain the confidence and knack for deducing this knowledge and similar kinds of knowledge themselves. They may deduce it directly from their own experience, consult an expert, or learn to find answers in books and other resources. As a practitioner of the Reggio Emilia approach stated it: 'The teacher's purpose then is not to answer the child's questions promptly, but rather guide them in a journey of discovery and investigation'.

It is widely accepted now to say that if you teach children to learn, this is the greatest service you could do them in their education. This is true, but only if combined with several notions from traditional wisdom that are not

---

[61] In fact, some well-known philosophies of childhood education are commercialised and promote a set agenda with a set culture.

normally taught by those who promote learning to learn.[62] The core part of the truth is captured in the following points:

- Answering questions immediately sometimes kills curiosity.
- Better is to encourage a learning journey, but this requires identifying sources.
- Sources include the environment and experts.
- Learning from the environment requires developing a rich learning environment that leads to experience or taking children out to places where they can obtain such learning.

So, when you are the teacher, remember that teachers are in fact three: parent, teacher, and environment. Some things need to be learned from experience, so set up a rich environment. Try to bring certain fruitful items and play centres into the learning environment. What you cannot obtain, go out and visit. Make experiential educational trips frequent. Teach children to contact experts, including religious scholars and muftis. To avoid answering everything through the internet, attempt to acquire certain child-friendly resources in hard copy.

Note that such methods are often described as co-constructive, a term often interpreted to imply that knowledge is purely a subjective production of the human mind. However, traditional learning often teaches definitions of things without giving experience or even alerting learners that experience might be a necessarily ingredient to knowing a thing or defending a definition. In our context, many traditional definitions are being challenged, sometimes on good grounds, sometimes not. So, experience is crucial. Further, it is not experientially satisfying to come to something so complex as a tree and simply offer a two-to-three-word definition, as though the details of the roots and moss or vines growing on it were not important and a cause of wonder. Finally, traditional learning indicates that there is a natural process in which concepts are formed through non-scientific reflection that goes on often unconsciously in the back of the mind. To build this on the right direct experiences roots students in their bodies and senses. The senses should not be seen as at odds with their minds, but as a sound basis. If they are rooted on earth, as humans, they may reach the sky without their feet coming off

---

62 Other elements include true thinking skills, the need to purify the soul through learning ethics and gaining the virtues, and the more sophisticated reality that the sciences are related to each such that they cannot be learned without knowing this relationality. To simplify this latter point made throughout our curriculum, the very evidence needed to advance in some sciences necessarily comes from other sciences. If students are not taught this or do not stumble on it themselves, they may not advance in a science one iota. This point was taken up in the theoretical introduction, objections and answers, 'How can one teach classical texts to young people?'

the ground as happens in so many students that are sparky and disconnected from their bodies, and often unconnected from others socially.

BUILDING 'ISLANDS OF EXPERTISE'

Encourage children to develop deep and rich knowledge of a topic, rather than sketchy, superficial knowledge of many topics. This may be done with children as young as two through family and teachers encouraging the building of islands of expertise. Island of expertise may be defined as 'a topic in which children happen to become interested and in which they develop relatively deep and rich knowledge'.[63] Modern education often subtly encourages students who flit from topic to topic or who make fast, sparky thinking to link topics in their minds, but fails to develop a disposition of thinking skills in those same students who lack rick experience and knowledge.

The notion 'islands of expertise' derives from research which shows that it is far, far more beneficial to return several times to the same museum than to move from one 'experience' to another. In addition, you should follow up by taking children to related museums, investigating related topics, and purchasing related items, even as their toys. An example mentioned in this research is trains. Children may read books about *Thomas the Tank Engine*. They may learn about steam engines and visit them in local museums or when they travel. They may learn about steam itself, or coal, and coal mining. Through purchasing toys related to the topic, conversations unfold and may be followed, taking up new related topics that emerge.

While new 'experiences' are entertaining, they do not lead to real, valuable experience of the topic. Think of it this way: if children dig for three minutes here and three minutes there, they will never dig deep enough to hit water. If they do hit water, they may slake their own thirst, reach real satisfaction, and be able to offer others water to drink.

Interest may be raised based on the season: it is summer, so we think about heat. Heat may lead to the discussion of cooking, or how heat transfers through certain materials such as metal pans and their wooden or rubber handles.

3.4.3 LANGUAGE LEARNING: ARABIC & ENGLISH

As noted elsewhere, language-learning is crucial, so ensure that your

---

[63] See Kevin Crowley and Melanie Jacobs, "Building Islands of Expertise in Everyday Family Activity", in Gaea Leinhardt, Kevin Crowley, Karen Knutson (eds), *Learning Conversations in Museums*, Taylor & Francis, London, 2011.

child is not semi-lingual: speaking one or more languages in a broken manner. While we may be tempted to follow a classical method of teaching the nursery/preschool as Arabic immersion, this requires hiring someone, unless a parent is fluent. It also risks that students struggle to understand such a teacher, and it risks students being semi-lingual in English, especially if parents are not themselves confident English-speakers. If you do offer immersion, ensure that the teacher is educationally trained and ideally speaks enough English to help if children are entirely confused.[64]

What we recommend for most circumstances is a dual-language programme. As we note below, there are three ways this can happen. Our preferred model is that topics are taught or explored in English, and after a break students learn the related Arabic vocabulary, discussing how to use the terms and beginning to speak or listen to Arabic itself when and if they are ready.

In both cases, the items in the home/school should be labelled in Arabic. Even if children cannot read, this will remind them to use the Arabic name sometimes. In all cases, label items in the learning environment in Arabic and teach the Arabic vocabulary (including in mathematics) as outlined presently in the levels of our preschool curriculum. Ensure that students in the subjects taught are understood cognitively in English through the topics and method outlined below, and then introduce and discuss the Arabic terms for topics.

Native Arabic-speaking parents wishing to expose children to their 'home' dialect of Arabic should either do so outside of instruction time or further split the languages of the preschool. Like it or not, if you wish to transmit this dialect, children will thus need three languages to be educated Muslims, even if not aiming to be scholars.

---

64 While some disagree, we believe that immersion is best offered through a fluent speaker, not necessarily native, and someone who ideally speaks the child's first language in case they struggle to build their concepts through scaffolding. Obviously, most native speakers will not speak the child's language, but hopefully Arabic speakers in an English- speaking country will acquire English in many cases.

Note that French immersion courses in Canada require that at least one parent of the child in question speaks French. This is precisely to avoid the child being lost and failing to benefit from the instruction. In our case, we encourage parents to learn with their children, and Arabic is around us in the Quran, the Friday sermon, and especially in Ramadan. Also, we reinforce their Arabic learning year after year in the Arabic curriculum and apply it in the Islamic instruction and Quran curriculum. Parents should even attempt to teach Arabic by attending LIFE courses to stay just ahead of students as they develop and learn. For the first several years, parents only need to learn comely pronunciation (tajwid) and around one-hundred words. If they apply this to the Quran, they will soon be understanding the basic meanings of the Quran themselves.

3.4.4 Transforming the Self & Home

Education occurs in a context, and this context imposes upon us that we compensate for certain missing experiences. The world around us presumes we consume and—if we wish to join the middle-class—manage or form part of technological society. Either way, we do not produce, and we lose the knack of producing in and around the home. And when we serve, we do so through a set of institutions and abstract standards that intervene (or mediate in an artificial way) between us and our community. This often involves a product or software or social media platform that monetises the relationship and is really only in it for money. So, we need to have our own clear idea of family, community, and service and seek to raise children who do not end up trapped in entertainment and studies. Having children focus on their studies is good, but not when they expect parents to serve them all the time as they sit in their room with the door closed. As such, we list a set of activities that transform this:

- Pick up toys
- Put dirty clothes in the hamper
- Help sort, fold, and put away clean laundry, especially small towels
- Set the table before meals
- Put their own dishes by the sink after meals
- Help put away groceries
- Help feed/water the family pet
- Be responsible for keeping a nature display or vase of wildflowers fresh
- Unload utensils from the dishwasher
- Straighten bedding/help make the bed
- Clean up spills
- Collect small trash cans from rooms
- Pick up sticks, pinecones, and outside other yard debris

These are activities that grow their natural intelligence before school such that school does not weaken their relationship to the home and family but may strengthen it and it leads to embodied intelligence.

In this line, you may draw benefit from Charlotte Mason's preschool activities found in the following link: https://amblesideonline.org/ao-y0-activities.

3.4.5 Laying the Foundations (*Mabadi'*) of Their Islamic Personality

A fourth principle is to teach through play in a manner that is simple but looks at the great potential in learning about the world and religion. These matters may be explained through introducing concepts and terms and indicating whatever of their significance the child is able to understand. Many of them will understand that smiling in the face of one's brother or sister is charity and that this is a good thing for various reasons. They may understand they are purifying their character, pleasing Allah, or improving social bonds. Memorising and applying etiquette and prayers and invocations unfold in them over the years. Those who lack these often have religious sentiments but lack these seeds which should naturally grow and unfold in oneself and in one's years, like a good tree. Many of us have learned to survive without this basic knowledge; others hunger for it when they are too busy to easily learn, and they regret, and then pass on their lack to future generations. These aspects of religion are made to integrate with a busy life; they are not the special remit of a religious class, which, after all, Islam does not recognise as a formal entity. Every soul should worship Allah as much as it can, and every soul has capacity in the form of the fitrah.

3.4.6 An Outline of the Preschool Subjects

Required

- Quran: Oral memorisation
- Local language: Engage children's interest in child-friendly topics
- Arabic: Use conceptual knowledge in local language as scaffolding, linking it to the Arabic language
- Introduction to the Arabic alphabet through play
- Maths: Use Oxford Owl or another scheme designed for 3-year-olds
- Religious instruction
- Etiquettes and invocations (*al-adab wa-l-ad'iyah*) memorised
- Tawhid (including the 99 Names)
- Fiqh: learn prayer and ablution through acting them out.
- Stories of the Prophets (read-aloud in local language)
- Natural science/nature study
- Arts and crafts

Optional or informal learning

Physical education/*futuwwah* disciplines (including swimming)

Music: Recitation and singing

ADVICE FOR TIMETABLING THESE SUBJECTS

LIFE offers three recommendations for timetabling: minimalist, mean, and maximalist. The minimalist may suit a home-schooler with little support. The maximalist is based on what suits a child in terms of an organised day of playful learning. The mean position recognises that even in schools and co-ops, organising a full day of rhythmically dispersed playful activities throughout the day is not possible due to limited resources, such as the inability to consistently find supporting teachers who might guide activities such as woodwork or even Quran teaching.

3.4.7 MINIMALIST APPROACH

Offer three daily sessions as follows: a) topic-based language learning, b) religious instruction, c) a rotation of other subjects, one each day of the week. Similarly, one finds the primary curriculum divided into daily and weekly subjects. At this age, draw from the subjects we have listed, including arts and crafts, nashid, and nature study.

To keep the number of 'planned activities' from exceeding three daily, consider the following activities as habits rather than sessions. Many 'habits' can lead to learning while you are engaged in household activities or taking care of your own routine. Here are ways to incorporate other parts of the curriculum into your day.

MAKE QURAN DAILY

The least amount that should be learned are those *suras* that are part of one's daily routine: a) *al-Fatihah*, b) *Surats al-Ikhlas, al-Falaq,* and *al-Nas* (i.e., 'the three *Quls*) and ideally c) *Ayat al-Kursi*. They should hear *Ayat al-Kursi* and others verses such as *'amana al-rasul...'* Quran 2:285-6, before bedtime or after prayers. If you do not have your own Sunnah adhkar, use the *Talqin al-sabah* found in the 'Prayers and Invocations' section of the preschool religious studies curriculum, and add the Three *Quls* to it and read it after *'asr* prayer or after maghrib prayer as well.

Play certain parts of the Quran on a loop in the background while engaged. Focus on *al-Fatihah* and the last three chapter, especially al-Ikhlas and al-Nass. Read the three *Quls* twice daily with your children. This is a Sunnah of the Prophet Muhammad ﷺ, and you could take this opportunity to ensure it is part of your daily routine. Encourage the children to repeat to you what they can when it begins to become natural to them. You do not have to put pressure on them, but simply ask if they are able to either say it themselves or repeat it verse by verse after you say it. It will come naturally. As described in the subject description for Quran in this preschool curriculum, you may also take one verse as recited by al-Husari and repeat it in the background. When they show some capacity to remember and repeat back, play a verse several times on loop, letting them repeat what they can (even if with mistakes and omissions) and then do the same with the next verse.

Try to find a consistent tutor for Quran. This would serve as a break from the children. It also structures your activities on the day the tutor is unavailable, as you will help children structure any homework.

ARABIC

LIFE highly recommends that all educators learn at least very basic Arabic via the various courses that are available. You may take the vocabulary from the present preschool curriculum as a basis, making flash cards or finding a tutor. If you are unable to do this, you may find a tutor. Even if the tutor is only available once a week, try to get more than an hour, and break this meeting up with playing games, etc. This now becomes the equivalent of 2-3 lessons per week, and may suffice, especially if they set homework you supervise.

If you do manage to learn or already know very basic Arabic, you may integrate Arabic into the minimalist schedule in several ways. First, you may alternate days. After teaching the subjects in English, think of the key concepts you have learned and see if they are in the preschool vocabulary. If there are other concepts not listed there, you may learn to use dictionaries—online or a hardcopy—or access a native speaker. Also try to be aware of the high frequency Quranic vocabulary words and draw from these when possible.

A second but more demanding possibility is to follow English sessions with at least ten minutes of explaining how to speak about topics in Arabic.

Third, you may hire a tutor. Explain to them the topics learned the previous day. This requires a fair amount of time to think through the topics and key vocabulary you taught and to communicate it regularly to a tutor. Preschools or co-ops that have an Arabic speaker are in a great position to do this regularly within the school. The Arabic speaker (not necessarily a native speaker) may sit in the English language lesson (whether it be a language topic, mathematics, or other lesson) and explain to the children how to say the same things in Arabic, taking turns with the teacher or taking over the lesson when they finish, being sure not to exceed the children's attention span.

MATHEMATICS

While involved in household tasks or playing or in nature, introduce and discuss basic mathematical vocabulary and skills. There are vocabulary words for each major topic. At the preschool age, only seven to eight topics need consideration, such as numbers, counting, adding, subtracting, shapes, time, and money. A basic skill such as counting or adding and subtracting has for instance the one-to-one principle: that numbers have cardinal values and ordinal values. Know that there are certain errors the child will make without these principles. For instance, if children do not understand that numbers have a cardinal value and they count objects to ten, when they pass five, they may count the next object as three again or start over and count from one to five. They do not understand that three or five finished. With a few principles and topics, an average educated person can lead mathematics activities in the playground, nature, or while engaged in household tasks. They just need to identify the basic topics and skills. For instance, children need to learn to count up and to count down. Now, you can encourage mathematics learning without planning a specific session. There are also books which are full of activities, linking them to other daily activities and topics suitable for early years learning.[65] Without buying resources, you may bring maths in when you play by counting aloud, when eating by sharing (dividing), and teach children to count and encourage their early ability to subitize: the ability to look at a small set of objects and know instantly without counting how many there are. Taking them shopping can be a way to teach a large portion of maths, including how scales work when buying fruits. 'How many apples makes a kilo? How many bananas? It is different. How many watermelons?' Sequences and multiples may be taught by practicing counting two at a time or five at a time: 2, 4, 6, 8, and so on. This teaches them the basic idea of patterns. For preschoolers, you can integrate these skills without putting pressure on the educator or teacher. The basic vocabulary suitable for 3-5 year-olds can then easily be translated into Arabic, a task partially completed in the present preschool curriculum.

NATURAL SCIENCE/NATURE STUDY

Take the children into nature or at least a park as much as possible, ideally every day, based on what is available to you. If the nearest park or nature area is 30 mins or more away, start with going weekly, but try to increase this, or even look into moving house. While there, talk about what you see and draw on the activities listed in the nature study curriculum. If you can, during the day or at night, look at the Arabic vocabulary list for

---

65 See, for instance, Alice Hansen, Games, *Ideas and Activities for Early Years Mathematics*, Longman: London, 2011.

nature study and teach the children the words through repeating them and discussing them with them.

Nature study can be taught while you are involved in your normal daily habit of cooking. For example, teach science through teaching about heat, fire, water, diffusion, mixing or crushing substances, and bonding, as in dough.

PHYSICAL EDUCATION

Exercise in front of your child, not in a gym or outside. They will learn from you, and you can teach them to do movements that they can do while you work out.

Or take your child to swimming lessons or tumbling and gymnastics. The latter will not only make them healthier and stronger and more coordinated, but it will give them a basis if they wish to start to learn grappling or jiu-jitsu from a young age as we recommend in the LIFE curriculum.

Nashid: Buy quality, traditional nashids and play them while you drive or while in the house. Purchase a *daff* (frame drum) and play even the simplest of rhythms while the nashid is playing.

3.4.8 A Maximalist Approach

While not necessarily recommended, a maximalist approach is based on the child having eight productive hours, provided a) sessions are limited to 20 minutes, b) meals are included, and c) rest and breaks are rhythmically woven into the day. If one is scheduling their time more formally as is needed in a nursery with multiple teachers, we recommend at least 15 mins at the beginning of the day for a) a light workout to remove stress of travel and ensure students are awake and b) a reading of morning litany (such as *Talqin al-sabah* mentioned in the subject, 'Prayers and Invocations'.)

A child may arrive at a nursery at 8 am and be collected at 4 pm. If a nursery is well-resourced, they may have supplementary teachers taking children for Quran and woodwork while teachers plan. In that case, the schedule may be built around the child rather than the limits of the educator. Educators will need at least an hour and a half to prepare for lessons and up to an hour to keep records, in addition to their contact time with children. Consider that a 20-minute session actually takes 30 minutes, as children will need to be gathered, settle, and listen before starting an activity. They will need time to rest between. There should be a minimum of 15 minutes, though we recommend having long play sessions if in a nursery. With the said rhythm, an 8-4 schedule would be thus:

8-12:30	6 sessions[66]
12:30-1:15	lunch
1:15-3:30	3 sessions
3:30-4	1 30-min session of read-aloud, nashid, or play

Nine sessions would enable having Arabic following each of the four core subjects daily: language topics, religious instruction, maths, and nature study. If you alternate English and Arabic, you open up a huge amount of free, extended playtime. The final session or the last 30 minutes allow the weekly subjects such as arts and crafts, nashid, and read-aloud to be offered daily, alternating between them. Afterwards, the subjects become like the weekly subjects in the rest of the LIFE K-12 curriculum. Then, you would have four core daily subjects and one non-core session daily. It is of course not necessary as we have said to have a planned daily maths and nature study session.

3.4.9 MEAN APPROACH:

SEVEN SESSIONS & EXTENDED PLAY

- Local language topic
- Arabic
- Religious instruction
- Arabic
- Alternate or integrate Nature Study and Maths[67]
- Arabic
- Weekly topic: Arts and Crafts, Nashid
- Extended play: an extra hour and a half, including a read-aloud session, or individualised reading between teachers and particular students or groups of students based on interest and level

ADVICE FOR HOME SCHOOLERS

Home schooling is very particular, based on your child and your circumstances. Your first task is to sit and ideally write down the answer

---

66 Note that this schedule produces a 15-minute break leading into lunch, which is unneeded. This may be borrowed to have a morning routine to start the day as mentioned.

67 By merely getting into nature daily and integrating this trip or another part of the day with maths.

to four questions. 1) What subjects will you child learn from you? Some children firmly resist learning certain subjects from their parents. 2) What subjects are you capable of teaching, perhaps after taking a course or two? 3) What subjects can be taught through a tutor or a co-op in your area? 4) How organised are you and your family? Write your answers down in a notepad.

If your answer to question 4 is that your organisation is average or below average, and you your question to answer 3 is that you have little or no support from a local co-op, three learning sessions per day is a good number. This is what we have termed the 'minimalist approach' above.[68]

To make three sessions per day work, think of subjects such as Quran, nature study, and physical education as a 'habit', rather than as a 'session'. We spoke above about how to incorporate them into the minimalist approach.

If your level of organisation is average or above, the mean approach may suit you. If you are able to combine Arabic with the lesson, alternate days, or arrange a tutor or co-op to teach the Arabic, you greatly reduce this schedule. For the mean approach, we encourage you to try to find a Quran tutor to ensure that every day the child has a lesson, or at least homework. So, if a teacher gives significant homework every day, you could meet with them only once every other day.

Whichever approach you adopt, write down which you are committed to in a notepad. Home-schoolers do not have to adhere to this structure, but it is still very much needed to write down what you are committed to. Some parents are very good at receiving guests without letting the schedule go out the window. When it is time for a session, parents excuse themselves for as long as necessary. Older children can simply be told briefly what to do and at what time, and their parents can then get on with tending to the guests. There are many other commitments, such as work, which we do not discard when a guest comes. Many home-schoolers even encourage their children to benefit from guests, learning from them or showcasing their own learning.

RHYTHM VERSUS STRUCTURE

The difference between rhythm and structure is that, when using a structure, it is a *problem* to finish early, just as it is a problem to finish late.[69]

---

68 Mind that this is not an absolute minimum: some parents will find it hard in some circumstances to offer even one learning session per day, especially at those inevitable times where there are health issues in the family, including tiredness and other issues related to pregnancy.

69 See, Rudolf Steiner, Roberto Trostli, *Rhythms of Learning*: What Waldorf Education Offers Children, Parents & Teachers, Steiner Books, 2017 and A. N. Whitehead, *The Rhythm of Education*: *An Address* delivered to the training college association, Christophers, London, 1922.

With a rhythm, you may have a practical time allotted to activities, but you may go over or end early when appropriate based on the topic of the interest of the children. Also, a rhythm allows for wider rhythms in which we live by no choice of our own: holidays come, and in winter days are shorter, and the prayers which punctuate the day fall closer together. We recommend 20-minutes learning sessions in preschool. You may wish to start with 10-15 minutes for a few das, and you may find it appropriate to increase to 30 later or based on the topic. For instance, if your location forces you to travel to find your closest park or natural setting, it does not make sense to end your activity there after 20 minutes. After a 20-minute session, a parent may tend to house chores. A teacher in a nursery may divide responsibilities with other teachers. Some may supervise children at play, while others take a break or prepare activities.

A second basic principle of timetabling alongside rhythm and an age-appropriate duration is that certain subjects should be taught each day. Language based on topics is most central as a daily subject. But there is an argument that the following are daily subjects:

- Religious instruction (teaching basic fiqh, adab, and prayers, but also 'aqidah and sirah)
- Nature study (in part to get children outdoors and into nature daily, and engage with God's creation—as opposed to human productions and the concrete jungle—and engage with outdoor learning)
- Maths
- Quran

We have noted though that maths and even Quran can be more of a habit integrated into your routine and that of the children, rather than a planned session. Maths, as noted, may be incorporated into other activities, even free play time. Rather than always incorporating maths into other subjects, you may do so sometimes, yet offer a maths session 2-3 times per week. You may wish to dip into resources such as Oxford Owl listed above.

A third principle which effects timetabling is the mode of Arabic teaching. At this tender age, children are receptive. Undoubtedly, learning basic vocabulary and meanings will benefit them as a basis through which their later learning can go further on a sound foundation. They should use their local language to learn concepts through topic-based play. We recommend a list of topics which are known by experience to emerge naturally, but feel free to change the order based on children's interest

---

The latter is available in the public domain. In it, the author introduces his own conception of the stages of development: romance (exploration), mastery (precision), generalisation.

or even the topics if you are capable of producing the Arabic equivalents to new concepts. After the concepts are learned through discussions and activities, introduce the Arabic equivalent orally.[70]

This method of scaffolding language learning on local-language acquired concepts is theoretically sound. It may be enacted in three ways. One may guide the activity in the local language and then spend the remainder of the time introducing Arabic terms and explaining their use. Or you may do this in a separate lesson after break. Or, finally, you may use a lag technique: around a month after you introduce the topic in the local language, re-offer it in Arabic. We think that immediately teaching Arabic terms in the same session will lead to exceeding the natural attention-span of young learners. We believe the third method is harmed by the need for teachers or parents to review materials after a month, which multiplies work. Also, students may feel they have moved on and do not wish to arbitrarily return to the same topics as a matter of policy after one month.

Summary of notes useful for timetabling:

- Most topics repeat, taught first in the local language, then in Arabic.
- Quran, read-aloud and nashid do not repeat (they are taught once in one language).
- Nature study is refreshing, almost a form of a break in terms of rhythm, and one need not plan a session. Ideally, if one learns about a plant or animal, etc., they will look for the word in Arabic.
- If one struggles to timetable, many 'subjects', such as physical education, maths, nature study, and even Quran, may be integrated into one's routine or other subjects.

A list of subjects to consider when timetabling:

- Local-language topic (20 min)
- Arabic topic (20 min)
- Local-language religious learning (20 min)
- Arabic religious learning (20 min)
- Local-language nature study (40 min, including travel)
- Arabic nature study (20 min, done on site unless one lacks Arabic for matters that emerge)

---

[70] While we recommend introducing the children to the whole alphabet one letter per day at the beginning of preschool, children are still not expected to read nor write, nor even to identify written words.

- Local-language maths (20 min)
- Arabic maths (20 min)
- Quran (20 min)
- Read-aloud in stories of the prophets (20 min)
- Nashid (20 min)
- Physical education and *Futuwwah* disciplines (including swimming; variable)
- Arts and Crafts (variable)

ARRANGING A TUTOR OR *MU'ADDIB*

Parents have to balance being teacher and mother or father. So, if they arrange a tutor or *mu'addib*, the parent helps retains their primary role of being a parent. Traditionally, educational institutions and educators such as the *mu'addib* were always crucial. Taking sole responsibility for teaching in the homeschool thus poses a problem: you have to be curriculum developer, headteacher to ensure the curriculum is being followed and on time, and school counsel to make big decisions or resolve problems.

Even merely having a shaykh or experienced educator that directs learning is a great help. A community or educational co-op may play this role, but parents will generally struggle with the same questions and thus be unable to help each other unless they collectively reach out to others or research the matter. Or each person will have their own opinion or conflicting schedules and cannot meet to discuss matters properly. With an organisation, you have the benefit of an imam/leader to determine a solution and a course of action. Note that everyone acts like an expert or shaykh when it comes to education and other social sciences because they feel that they have the experience of going through life and handling the problems that arise. But they would not act like an expert when it comes to other areas in which they have no experience. For instance, they would not pretend to have the knowledge and capacity to make decisions of a doctor.

3.5 THE PRESCHOOL SUBJECTS

1 QURAN: ORAL MEMORISATION

The following addresses schools or home educators. Some of it overlaps with the Quran elementary curriculum. But a 3-year-old is in a special transition. Some speak confidently but may struggle with Quranic letters.

Some speak only odd words. Others may speak a few words in more than one language, if parents speak two languages or if the home language differs from the language of the country or school. This impacts how children will be able to memorise. Also, the guidance for Quranic memorisation will be greatly impacted if parents speak Arabic in the home, as children will immediately understand some of what they hear and memorise, and learning meanings requires less work to attach those meanings to the Quranic words themselves.

QURAN PREREQUISITES

a. Teaching to encourage love of the Quran

Teachers need to balance the respect due to the Quran with the gentle age of the child: yes, children should treat the Quran as special, but perhaps the highest etiquette with the Quran is to love it. If they love the teacher and the lesson itself is fun, this means the world. In the past, teachers of Quran, just as teachers of the classics in both ancient and modern times, taught with a scowling face and a stick in hand. These days are finished. Preschool children should be given choices: ask if they want to sit or want to walk under the trees while they recite. If they show natural affection for the teacher, excessive formality should be avoided. I have seen Quran teachers that were warm with children in a public space and ended lessons by playing games with the children to ensure they enjoyed the lessons.

b. Basic tajwid

The teacher needs basic tajwid, whether they are the parent or a tutor/teacher. Even if parents find a tutor, unless the tutor reads with the child daily, they need some tajwid to ensure the child is not making major mistakes. To a certain degree, if the tutor comes once or twice weekly, they may oversee the playing of a recording, such as the learner-friendly recitation of al-Husari. [71]The same goes for schools if they do not have a daily Quran teacher who has the time to ensure that every child is learning 20 minutes per day.

So, if the parent or school does not have acceptable tajwid, one person there should seek it, starting with having a person with permission to teach (*ijazah*) in tajwid give them permission to teach in their *al-Fatihah*.

---

71 Listen to his recording called *al-Mus-haf al-Mu'allim al-atfal* (Pedagogical Recitation) in which he reads slowly and clearly (referred to as tartil in tajwid.) Often, these recordings include the repetition of a child. The most common recitation is Hafs. (See, https://archive.org/details/Hafs_Al-Hussary.) In certain countries Warsh, for instance, is more appropriate. (See, https://archive.org/details/16kb---mp3---Quran--------alhosary----by--warsh---by--teacher---repeat--- kids-)

Additionally, Quran teachers in non-native Arabic countries have a practice of teaching tajwid of a single verse that has all the Arabic letters: a) the last verse of *al-Fath* (verse 29) and b) verse 154 of *Al 'Imran*.[72]

c. Quranic vocabulary

Know very basic Quranic vocabulary and some of the lessons to be taken from Juz' *'Amma*. This point is elaborated below.

GETTING STARTED WITH QURAN

a. Test for readiness for oral transmission (*talqin*)

When the child turns three—though you could just as well start at the age of two—recite a few words of Quran to them. If they are able to repeat them back to you without too much difficulty, then they are ready to memorise directly through oral transmission to those unable to read from the Quran (*talqin*).

If children are not able to repeat back correctly, even after several repetitions, then they are only ready for indirect memorisation. This is still very important. If no effort is made, children may unnecessarily take years to begin *talqin*. *Al-Fatihah* may be too long, so start with *al-Nas* or *al-Ikhlas*.

b. Play on a loop in the background or repeat from a small number of verses

Play *al-Nas* or *al-Ikhlas* (or *al-Fatihah*) on a loop in the background for half an hour at some point in the day. Recite it joyfully for the child as one would recite *Twinkle, twinkle little star* or *Ba, ba black sheep* or a nashid such as *Tala'a al-badr*—though not singing it of course. Have other children recite it in front of them when the chance arises.

Recite (if you have tajwid) or play repeatedly one of a few verses *al-Nas* or *al-Ikhlas* (or *al-Fatihah*).

c. Repeat a few verses repeatedly to the child

When the child is able to partially repeat, not fully but with regular mistakes, sit with the child for a 20-minute slot, or till they tire. The aim is not direct memorisation, but to accustom their ear to the sound of the words. One may move through a whole chapter of the Quran even if there

---

72 If they were to read a *khatam* of Juz' *'Amma*, this would allow them to oversee the whole of the preschool education, but this may take months if weak in tajwid. Imagine how inspiring for children and even students in a school to see their teachers learning alongside them and valuing the Quran.

are mistakes, partial repetition, and no ability to recall previous verses. The aim is that they attempt to recite back what they hear.

If the child says part of what they hear or says parts incorrectly, praise them sincerely for their efforts and correct them subtly, encouraging them to say it as corrected. Make this fun. Change verses if it becomes tiresome to the child and integrate games and walking and other means to avoid boredom. Take note of the increase in capacity, even if nothing is visible over a span of weeks in some cases. When the child begins to repeat accurately, they are ready for *talqīn*.

d. Oral transmission (*talqin*)

When the child's ability to speak and repeat increases to where mistakes are not regular or can be corrected rather quickly in most cases, begin oral transmission for memorisation. In the beginning, they may only be able to memorise one, two, or three verses. This is fine, and one may begin discussing as much as possible the meanings, to which we turn now.

TEACHING BASIC QURANIC MEANINGS

When the child is able to converse and also memorise through oral transmission, begin explaining some of the meanings, lessons, and words in the verses being learned, even in the form of activities. An instance that relates to our time is that children have learning or play equipment—like pencils or a swing. They may each have their own pencils and erasers, but they must share swings. We discuss with them how to share. They may not linguistically be able to understand the Arabic words, '*Wa-yamna'una al-ma'un*', Quran 107:7, but they can understand the lesson of the verse through examples and an activity pointing out how to share properly and take turns. Then one can return to the discussion of orphans (*yatama*). How does one interact with an orphan? What if their parents were killed in Gaza and they are not dressed like others and do not behave like the others? How do I treat them? How should I treat them? Should I also do the same with my little brother or sister?

Then focus on oral memorisation of the Quran with the Arabic vocabulary listed in 2b. Point out when words from this list are found in the verses they are memorising, and select certain verses that are accessible and convey the meaning to them. Further, skim the Quranic high frequency words list referred to in the Year 1 Arabic curriculum (see, 'Elementary' section), and choose common words to explain to students.[73] Keep these words on a visible list in the learning space, and review them from time to time.

---

73 See the Leeds website, Quranic Corpus at the following link: https://corpus.Quran.com/.

THE PRESCHOOL SUBJECTS

Level	No. of Surahs	Name of Surah
1	4	al-Fatihah to al-Ikhlas
2	8	" " " al-Kawthar
3	13	" " " al-'Asr
4	18	" " " al-Bayyinah
5	28	" " " al-Fajr and Ayat al-Kursi

List of Surahs

1	al-Fatihah	8	al-Kawthar	15	al-Qari'ah	22	al-Sharh
2	al-Nas	9	al-Ma'un	16	al-'Adiyat	23	al-Duha
3	al-Falaq	10	Quraysh	17	al-Zilzilah	24	al-Layl
4	al-Ikhlas	11	al-Fil	18	al-Bayyinah	25	al-Shams
5	al-Masad	12	al-Humazah	19	al-Qadr	26	al-Balad
6	al-Nasr	13	al-'Asr	20	al-'Alaq	27	al-Fajr
7	al-Kafirun	14	al-Takathur	21	al-Tin	28	Ayat al-Kursi

2 ENGLISH (LOCAL LANGUAGE OR L1)

Build conceptual knowledge through developing units around children's interest.

- Just as in Arabic, expose the children to one letter per day for the first month or so, not expecting mastery. Devote whatever time this requires and delay topical teaching as needed.

- Use the topic/unit-based teaching described towards the beginning of the preschool curriculum. As noted, use this conceptual basis upon which to scaffold the introduction to the Arabic vocabulary.

- Engage playfully in pre-writing skills started to prepare students for Rec/KG. Suitable activities include a) using hands and later crayons to connect dot-to-dot drawings, b) making patterns that involve counter-clockwise circles (such as the steam emerging from a locomotive), and c) making letters from clay, forming them with the body, and writing letters in sand.

Optional

Pre-phonics by working through the Modern Curriculum Press' *Phonics* (or *Plaid Phonics*), Level K. If your child is ready and willing, introduce them to this book. If they find it difficult, put it away for a couple months, and then try again.

3 ARABIC (L2)

Integrate tawhid into Arabic teaching.[74] This is how it is done. Point out that there is one Creator, and everything else is created, and creation usually comes in pairs, and these pairs are often opposites. Additionally, created things may be divided into two: substances that exist independently, and what are called accidents, which are the attributes that exist *in* things, and may come and go. So, some created things like trees and humans are substances. Other created things like hot, cold, sickness, and health are accidents that must exist in substances to exist at all. These accidents always have opposites, which is not true of substances. This alternation of opposite—like hot and cold, night and day—shows us that these created things change. Change is a sign that they are not eternal and unchanging, while Allah is eternal (*qadim*) and unchanging. Even in us, opposites of happiness and sadness, pleasure and pain come and go.

a. Introduction to the Arabic alphabet through play

Expose the children to the whole alphabet in the first month. Do not expect mastery. If you teach the second year of preschool, repeat this at the beginning of the coming year.

Introduce letters one at a time and one per day through art activities, such as playdough, or through forming them in sand through tracing them with a finger. You may wish to focus on this at the beginning of the year so that students encounter Arabic vocabulary already familiar with the alphabet.

There are approaches to teaching the letters: a) *alif, ba', ta'*—group letters that look alike (such as *ba', ta',* and *tha'*), or b) based on points of pronunciation (*makharij*), or c) link to the child's name: the name's letters to start with. Collectively, the names in the room will cover most/all of alphabet. Include father's name or family name.

b. Learn basic vocabulary orally[75] and label any objects found in the home/classroom[76]

Vocabulary for preschool involves more than one level, as there is

---

74 This is done again in Year 1 but may be begun here.

75 We are not limited by letters known, because we are learning orally.

76 One could modify the vocabulary to include that found in the UK Reception topics.

potential of circling back through topics in a more sophisticated manner.[77] Initially, Arabic vocabulary must be introduced orally. Learn words ordered to tawhid, but also linked to concepts they are learning in English. These include greetings, family, animals and insects, colours and numbers, body parts and feelings and actions, environment, such as school/nursery, not only classroom equipment, but food and regime and whatever is in the given facility and outdoors, such as forests and animals in some schools, including the city or country (animals).

VOCABULARY FOR LANGUAGE TOPICS

Greetings (13)

Making acquaintance (7):

al-salāmu ʿalaykum (Peace by upon you)
..... *wa-raḥmatu Allāhi* (and Allah's compassion)
.... *wa-barakātuhu* (and His blessings be upon you)

maʿa salāmah (with peace)
..... *ilā al-liqāʾ* (until next time)
.... *fī amāni Allāh* (in Allah's security)

mā+ism+pronoun (*ka, ki,* and *kum* for instructor for politeness),

salām (peace)   *shukran* (thank you)

ma-smu-ka (what is your name?)   *wa-anta* (and you?)

kayfa hālukum (how are you?)   *ana bi-khayrin* (I am well)

Interacting (6):

ʿafwan (you're welcome)   *ayna* (where is....?)

in shāʾa Allāh (If Allah wills)   .... *al-ḥamām* (the restroom)

min faḍlik (please)   .... *al-masjid* (mosque)

---

77 One may include basic Islamic concepts (*niʿmah, barakah, shukr*), including the most common words of Quran and concepts related to tawhid. Think how learning other parts of the Islamic curriculum will need to have vocabulary taught, introducing them first in English, then Arabic. But note that the most appropriate time to teach abstract (*iʾtibari*) concepts is after the age of distinction (*tamyiz*).

ana bi-khayrin (I am well) .... *al-ḥadīqah* (garden)

tafaḍḍal (welcome) .... *al-maṭʿam* (cafeteria)
(*tafaḍḍalī, tafaḍḍalū*)

Family and community (16)

Community (5):

jār (neighbour) *ṣadīq* (friend)

ṭālib (student) *zamīl* (classmate/companion)

muʿallim/ustādh (teacher)

Family (11):

umm (mother) *ab* (father)

jaddah (grandmother) *jadd* (grandfather)

akh (brother) *ukht* (sister)

ʿammah/khālah (aunt, paternal and maternal) *ʿamm/khāl* (uncle, paternal and maternal)

abnat al-ʿamm(ah)/abnat al-khāl(ah) (female cousin) *ibn al-ʿamm(ah)/ibn al-khāl(ah)* (male cousin)

murḍiʿ(ah) (foster mother)

My self (56):

Body parts (12):

5 senses 4 limbs

baṣar (sight) *raʾs* (head)

samʿ (hearing) *dhirāʿ* (forearm)

lams (touch) *rijl* (legs)

dhawq (taste) *yad* (hands)

shamm (smell; olfactory)

THE PRESCHOOL SUBJECTS

Others (3)

iṣbaʿ (finger; pl: *aṣābiʿ*)   *ẓuhr* (back)
ṣadr (chest)

Colours (12):

7 Rainbow (*qaws qazaḥ*)   3 Tones
aḥmar/ḥamrāʾ (red)   *aswad/sawdāʾ/sawād* (black)
burtuqālī/burtuqāliyyah (orange)   *abyaḍ/bayḍāʾ/bayāḍ* (white)
aṣfar/ṣafrāʾ (yellow)   *ramādī/ramādiyyah* (grey)
akhḍar/khaḍrāʾ (green)
azraq/zarqāʾ (blue)
nīlī/nīliyyah (indigo)
banfasjī/banfasjiyyah (violet)

Sounds (3):

muwāʾ (meow)   *nabaḥ* (bark)
zaʾīr (roar)

Feelings (9):

saʿīd (happy)   *taʿbān* (tired)
ḥazīn (sad)   *nashīṭ* (energetic)
khāʾif (fearful)   *muftakhir* (proud)
qaliq (worried)   *khajlān/maksūf* (embarrassed)
muḍṭarib/mutaḥayyir (confused)

Daily actions (20 listed in Tarim's *Ḥaḍānah* curriculum):

yaqūmu (stand)   *yatakallimu* (speak)

yajlisu (sit)

yabkī (cry)

yaḍḥaku (smile)

ya'kulu (eat)

yashrabu (drink)

yanāmu (sleep)

yurattibu (tidy or put in order)

yaghsilu (wash)

yuṣallī (pray)

yaskutu (be silent)

yamsuku (grasp)

yaktubu (write)

yamshī (walk)

yasmaʿu (hear)

yanẓuru (look)

yasquṭu (fall)

yalbisu (wear)

yalʿabu (play)

Environment (22)

Parts of building (5)

jidār (wall)

saqf (ceiling)

arḍiyyah (floor)

nāfidhah/shabbākah (window)

mirḥāḍ (toilet)

Equipment (5)

qalam (pen)

kitāb (book)

qirṭās (notepad)

sabūrah (board)

waraqah (paper)

Food (8)

khubz (bread)

arz (rice)

fākihah (fruit)

laḥm (meat)

bayḍah (egg)

khaḍār (vegetable)

ḥalīb/laban (milk)

zabādī/laban (yoghurt)

Home (4):

luʿbah (toy)

kurrah (ball)

thallājah (refrigerator)

sayyārah (car)

THE PRESCHOOL SUBJECTS

Characteristics (16):

qaṣīr (short)	*mubtall* (wet)
ṭawīl (tall)	*jāff* (dry)
ṣaghīr (small)	*ḍaʿīf* (weak)
kabīr (large)	*qawī* (strong)
laṭīf (nice)	*salis* (smooth)
laʾīm (mean)	*khashin* (rough)
ḥārr (hot)	*ʿālī* (loud)
bārid (cold)	*hādiʾ* (quiet)

VOCABULARY TAUGHT IN OTHER SUBJECTS

Nature (35):

Animals (and their sounds and actions), insects, and sky/earth/sea

Animals including insects (must be individualised for one's own location; 22): Bird, mammal, insect; cat, dog, horse, cow, sheep, goat, camel, bear, bee, fly, mosquito, beetle, chicken, sparrow, pigeon, robin, crow, stork, owl

Plants (9): tree (*shajarah*), flower (*zahrah*), herbage (grass (*hashāʾish*), herb (*ʿushb*), pasturage (*marʿah*)), shrub (*najm*), garden (*bustān, hadīqah, jannah*)

- *Jamādāt* (4):
- *arḍ* (earth)
- *baḥr* (sea)
- *nahar* (river)
- *ḥajar* (rock, stone)

Seasons (explore topic in English and identify vocabulary, translating into Arabic): including changes to weather and plants and animals (visiting them in nature study to see observe their changing of leaves, flowers, and fruits)

- *rabīʿ* (spring)
- *ṣayf* (summer)
- *kharif* (fall, autumn)
- *shitāʾ* (winter)

Maths (27):

Numbers (12): 0-10, 20

Shapes (15): listed in maths below

VOCABULARY FOR RELIGIOUS TOPICS

This vocabulary occurs in the religious topics below. For instance, each prayer should be memorised and practiced in Arabic. The words which are common should be taught and eventually incorporated into an English-Arabic vocabulary poem.

Teaching is through following teaching of the concept in English, then linking to English the word/concept, plus any necessary and basic explanation of the Arabic word in English, e.g., what *barakah* means. When capable also explain in Arabic.

Reinforce words through games and songs, such as pointing to body parts and saying Arabic term. You can make songs and games where you say the Arabic and the English term if this helps, which may help learning.

Teach them to sing the Arabic letters and numbers through songs recorded on the following links:

Letters of the alphabet: https://www.youtube.com/watch?v=IOOgJe0ajQE

Numbers: https://www.youtube.com/watch?v=Aa3afnmQps0

Label items in the classroom, and when referring to them, read the labels. Some of the children will begin to sight read some of the words even before they learn the full alphabet.

4 MATHS

The LIFE approach to preschool maths is to integrate mathematical learning into real-life situations and to follow the learning experience with a subsequent focus on Arabic. Below, you will find a set of tables that set out the age-appropriate topics to be learned, followed by a table on Arabic vocabulary.[78]

To integrate maths, one has to look for or generate suitable events for teaching maths. So, while educators do not need to plan and deliver separate maths lessons, planning is still required. At least monthly, educators should identify the topics that follow in sequence and ensure they are prepared to teach them when the opportunity presents itself, or to generate such an activity. This planning should be based on an awareness of how much of

---

78 In 'Arabic', above, you will find more mathematical vocabulary.

THE PRESCHOOL SUBJECTS

the previous topic the child understood. If needed, educators should take the time to repeat and reinforce, rather than marching ahead and confusing the child.

Examples of opportunities for teaching maths include:

- Count objects in a real set, such as toys.
- Divide food amongst family or friends.[79]
- Divide an apple.
- Count how many grams are in an apple.
- Count how many bananas are in a package.
- Count while waiting for turns ('How many people are ahead of us?' 'How many turns till our turn comes?')
- Reflect on how the fin of a fish is a type of triangle.
- Look for shapes at the supermarket.

Rather than put pressure on the child, know what they should learn in this age-range, and wait for or generate the appropriate activity. The key is to keep it simple and understand that maths at this stage is not difficult. The number of topics is not great. Nonetheless, learning by play at this stage will lay a foundation of basics that make later learning easier. The concepts here are abstract, but the way they are learned is highly concrete and integrated with real life. It expands their vocabulary.[80]

One very introductory video on the concepts behind counting at the age of 3-4 is found here: Early maths skills: counting by Oxford Owl, https://www.youtube.com/watch?v=soQMufAUUfY. Based on interest, LIFE is prepared to offer a training course to empower parents to understand the concepts below and how to turn them into activities, plans, and assessments. A full, research-based resource for early years is Mathematics in Early Years Education.[81] This book includes tables and summaries at the end of its chapters. These summaries are replete with activities and ideas known to be effective, integrated, and fun for 3–4- year-olds and the early years in general. While the book is written for teachers, all educators may find useful explanations of math teaching and advice on teaching in the early years.

---

79 You may intentionally give food to the child in order to practice this 'division'.

80 And note that a great source of frustration in the terrible twos is inability to express oneself.

81 Ann Montague-Smith, Tony Cotton, Alice Hansen, Alison J. Price, *Mathematics in Early Years Education*, 4th edition, Routledge, London, 2018.

MATH TEACHING PRINCIPLES

a. Know what maths is

Mathematics in a generic sense is a science studying quantity, and quantity divides into discrete (separate) quantities, such as ordinal numbers, by which we count discrete objects (arithmetic), and continuous, which studies quantities that are connected, such as the surface area of a football (geometry).

b. Identify its topics, vocabulary, and activities

We have attempted to condense the topics, vocabulary, and activities needed to integrate maths teaching into daily activities. Take some time to familiarise yourself with this, as this will lead the teaching of natural topics flowing at the natural time.

c. Accustom oneself to mathematical vocabulary and concepts

Educators should accustom themselves to mathematical vocabulary, how to model that vocabulary, get children to absorb it and use it, and how to and correct them. Maths in early years is to a high degree about language. Teaching is not through structured activities, but through understanding the map and setting aims and then finding the age and context appropriate ways to achieve those aims. So, educators need to plan mathematics monthly, even if they have no abstract or specific planned activities focussing on maths. We do not mean that you should not plan the activity by which you teach maths, but you want the activity by which you teach to be intrinsically important or interesting to the child and to have a practical outcome ideally. So, you can cook, or go outside to count trees or planes fly overhead. This teaches to count distant objects, which is more difficult than counting objects one can manipulate.

Numbers represent quantity and order, something simple and profound that many educators themselves are unaware of. So, what numbers are and represent needs to be grasped by educators, and on that basis, children should be taught all mathematical topics, but initially educators should focus on laying a strong foundation in counting and 'numbers'. 'Such that you come to know the number of years and calculation *(hisab)*' (Quran 17:12). So, we lay out the three main things educators need:

a) topics,

b) vocabulary, and

c) some examples of general activities applied in real contexts.

You will need to add to these three by attending a crash course on teaching maths or extract these yourself.

As for linking subjects, take some time to show that subjects such as mathematics and religion are not 'separate'. This can be through showing the maths needed to pray properly, calculating rewards in blessed times such as Ramadan, or calculating inheritance. In reality, every corporeal being has quantity in terms of not only weight, but surface area and shape, etc. And there is a unity in the multiplicity we see around us, and multiplicity is a type of quantity. An important instance of quantity is the rhythm in music, as it is a type of pattern that moves in time. Teaching traditional rhythms, such as dum, dum, tak, as are in the LIFE music curriculum, are a fantastic introduction to patterns and lay the groundwork for strong, natural apprehension.[82]

Numerical skills (i.e., counting, ordering, and identifying) are the foundation of mathematics education, especially in the early years. Sufficient numerical skills are acquired by accumulating relevant numerical vocabulary and understanding underlying numerical concepts and principles for counting.

Primary numerical skills we are looking for include:

- Counting on and counting backwards.
- Counting objects from afar.
- Subitizing of a few objects. (Subitizing is taking a number in quickly, at a glance.)
- Number conservation.
- Counting through sorting items.
- Addition and subtraction.

Underlying number concepts include:

- Nominal value: numbers may represent a name, as in the example of a jersey number of a sportsman or a bus number.
- Ordinal value: numbers may represent order, such as the first in a class or second turn.
- Cardinal value: numbers may represent quantity.
- Zero: nothing, emptiness.
- Fractions: part of a whole, as in half of a sandwich.

Underlying counting principles include:

- Stable order principle: the order of numbers does not change.

---

82 In Greek and pre-modern Islamic maths, music is one of the four branches of mathematics.

- Order irrelevance principle: the order or organization of items in a set does not affect the number of items in the set.
- One-to-one correspondence: assigning one number to one object in a set.

The following list organises these topics into their subtopics. In each case, skills and key vocabulary suitable for the child is included, as well as activities by which to learn the related skills.

NUMBER CONCEPTS

- Nominal value: numbers may represent name, as in the example of a jersey number of a sportsman or a bus number.
- Ordinal value: numbers may represent order such as the first in a class or second turn.
- Cardinal value: numbers may represent quantity.
- Zero: nothing, emptiness.
- Fractions: part of a whole, as in half of a sandwich.

Vocabulary: number words, what order, first, second, last, how many, 'number', zero, nothing, empty, whole, part, share, portion

Skills: reading and identifying numbers (numerical symbols), differentiating number symbols from other symbols and alphabet, identifying zero, nominal numbers (identify the number of a bus, car, house, or phone number, and postcode), using proper vocabulary to describe order (I am first, he is second), identifying and using appropriate vocab to describe a part of a whole and part of a set (I finished half of my plate).

Activities: talking through using the skills, modelling the appropriate numerical vocabulary, discussing with child and gently correcting; organising play situations with numbers where the child can use different concepts of numbers, playing games with rules: he is first, she is second; reading aloud and pointing to page numbers when reading a book (We are now on page two) or verse number when reading the Quran, house numbers, car numbers, prices in the supermarket, weight on a scale; pointing to other numbers you find in the environment, such as shirt and shoe sizes, and explaining the different meanings of numbers in these situations.

- Stable order principle: the order of numbers does not change.
- Order irrelevance principle: the order or organization of items in a set does not affect the number of items in the set.
- One-to-one correspondence: assigning one number to one object in a set.

Vocabulary

Number words: count, how many, a lot, few, many, take away, give, add, more, less

Skills

Counting on hand, counting onwards and backwards, counting solid objects by grouping and sorting, counting items visually, using simple addition and subtraction of few numbers

Activities

Counting items in any surrounding environment, counting for waiting turns, singing counting rhymes, grouping and categorizing activities while counting items in groups and sets.

FURTHER SUBJECTS

The following list provide concepts, vocabulary, and activities for further subjects important for early learners. Note: Shape and space/place will both become geometry in later years. The heart of both, which shows their unity, is that they both involve classification and transformation of shapes and their positions.

UNIFORM SHAPES AND PATTERN

Concepts

- Explore and describe shapes, construct and deconstruct them.
- Explore lines and the simple properties of 2D and 3D shapes.
- Understand that a square of any size is still a square (shape conservation).
- Distinguish between a square and cuboid (such as a box), circle and sphere.
- Symmetry and similarity.

Vocabulary

Straight, curved, triangle, square, rectangle, corner, circle, round

Skills

Describe shapes and modelling adequate vocabulary to move them beyond inadequate expressions: 'it looks nice', 'not nice'. Explore texture, colour, feature, differences, and size. Fit shapes together, take them apart, rearrange, and reshape. Explore the shape, thickness, outlines, and direction of lines. Combine 2D shapes, sort them, and understand them as faces of 3D objects. Understand face shapes of 3D objects, and their movement, arrangement, and their properties of solidity and hollowness.

POSITION AND PLACE

Concepts

- Reflection and symmetry
- Position and movement
- Interpret pictorial representations of spatial relationships

Vocabulary

Above, below, right, left, in front of, behind, in, and on.

Practice

Turn, move, or flip objects. Make symmetrical patterns. Observe and describe objects from different viewpoints. Explore relative positions, directions, and distances. Describe the pictures of 3D objects. Model things in pictures and describe their own pictures of objects. Approach these matters through building things like animals with blocks.

TIME

Concepts

- Naming segments of time

Vocabulary

Today, yesterday, tomorrow, the day after tomorrow, months, weeks, hours

Practice

Introduce words and encourage them to use them in their own speaking. Relate future times to events: when school is finished, time for lunch, waking up (tomorrow), time to go to the park, after brushing teeth, time to read a story, etc.

MEASUREMENT AND COMPARISON

Concepts

THE PRESCHOOL SUBJECTS

- using many different measuring units,
- weight, length, height, distance, time, etc.

Vocabulary

Length, height, heavy, light, big, small, near, far, fast, slow, dark/dim, light/bright, nearly, just over, almost, about.

Practice

Use many different units, even using students/humans or parts such as their feet. Measuring is really about comparison with a standard, which is typically an abstract unit or concrete object of known size. Compare the height of a dinosaur to other lengths. Show application of units or comparison with objects to new things measured. Practice estimation and use of approximative language.

MONEY

Concepts

- Know the function of money and how to use it

Vocabulary

Value: 'How much is the bill or coin worth?' (i.e., how much can you buy with it.) [Money vocabulary depends on local currency and whether it has coins, bills, and multiple levels of value such as dollars and cents, pounds and pence, gineas and filses, etc.]

Practice

You cannot merely take things from the market; you have to pay. The value is not the number of notes or coins; rather, each note or coin has a number on it signifying its value. Now you will need addition and subtraction, etc., to purchase properly. Cross-curricular question: how old does one have to be to buy and sell to make a valid transaction in the Sharia, and why?

ARABIC VOCABULARY

(taught after concepts are taught in English)

square	مُرَبَّع	rhombus	مُعَيَّن
triangle	مُثَلَّث	cube	مُكَعَّب
circle	دَائِرَة	pyramid	هَرَم

THE PRESCHOOL SUBJECTS

rectangle	مُسْتَطِيل	sphere	كُرَّة
oval	بَيْضَوِي	cylinder	أُسْطُوَانَة
star	نَجْمَة	bow	قَوْس
crescent	هِلَال	trapezium	مُنْحَرِف
heart	قَلْب		

addition and subtraction   الْجَمْع وَالطَّرْح

Note: a parallelogram whose sides are the same length is a rhombus.

d. An alternative scheme

A more structured alternative than the one found above is Oxford Owl, designed for the age of 3-4. Their website includes:

- Recommended activities for home which cut across the spectrum of maths skills: https://home.oxfordowl.co.uk/maths/maths-at-home/. Some of these activities are appropriate for 3–4-year-olds, while others are too advanced.

- Recommended activities specific for 3–4-year-olds: https://home.oxfordowl.co.uk/maths/primary-maths-age-3-4-early-years/. This link includes games and videos and the manner in which one talks about numbers found in the real world.

- *Numicon: 1st Steps with Numicon at Home Kit*: A resource pack offering step-by-step guidance, including an activity book and numicon manipulatives (physical resources for teaching maths concepts. The link is https://home.oxfordowl.co.uk/product/numicon-at- home-first-steps-kit-9781382020831/.

- Manipulatives: Of course, you may purchase the Oxford Owl manipulatives which are sold separately and could use them to support a more integrated, less structured approach to teaching the same skills. On the Oxford Owl website, you will find a guide for parents explaining the numicon system including videos and worksheets (starting for 4-year-olds) here: https://owlhomestage.wpengine.com/maths/numicon-guide-for-parents/.

5 ETIQUETTES AND INVOCATIONS (*AL-ADAB WA-L-AD'IYAH*)

Integrate teaching these adhkar with studies of the Arabic language, pointing out words that are on the vocabulary list listed in the Arabic part of this preschool curriculum. Optionally, draw on the Quran high frequency words referred to in the Year 1 curriculum for the Arabic language. To teach the adhkar listed here well, it is recommended that teachers (including parents)

THE PRESCHOOL SUBJECTS

Level 1 (6 items)

Action	Transliteration	Translation	Arabic
starting to eat, drink, study, or do anything important.	Bi-smi Llāh	in Allah's name	بِسْمِ اللهِ
finishing eating, drinking, or receiving a blessing of any kind.	al-ḥamdu li-Llāh	All praise belongs to Allah.	الحَمْدُ لله
waking	al-ḥamdu li-Llāhi l-ladhī aḥyānā baʿda mā amātanā wa-ilayhi n- nushūr	All praise belongs to Allah Who gave us life after He make us pass away, and to Him is the resurrection.	الحَمْدُ لله الَّذِي أَحْيَانَا بَعْدَمَا أَمَاتَنَا وَإِلَيْهِ النُّشُورُ
sleeping	aṣbaḥnā wa-aṣbaḥa al- mulku li-Llāh	We have entered the morning, and the dominion has entered the morning, for Allah.	أَصْبَحْنَا وَأَصْبَحَ المُلْكُ لله
To start the day [if and when unable to recite the full morning recitation listed in the next level.]	Bi-smika Llāhumma amūtu wa-aḥyā	In Your name, dear Lord, I die and live (again).	بِسْمِكَ اللَّهُمَّ أَمُوتُ وَأَحْيَى

THE PRESCHOOL SUBJECTS

Level 2 (9 items)

Action	Transliteration	Translation	Arabic
finishing reading Quran	ṣadaqa Allāhu al-ʿaẓīm	Allah the Mighty said the truth.	صدق الله العظيم
morning recitation (to be done every morning before starting to study)	aṣbaḥnā wa-aṣbaḥa al-mulku li-Llāh	We have entered the morning, and the dominion has entered the morning, for Allah.	أصبحنا وأصبح الملك لله
	aʿūdhu bi-kalimāti Llāhi t-tāmmāti min sharri mā khalaqa (x3)	I seek refuge with Allah's perfect words from the evil of what he created. (x3)	أعوذ بكلمات الله التامات من شرّ ما خلق (٣)
	Bi-smi Llāhi l-ladhī lā yaḍurru maʿa smihi shayʾun fī al-arḍi wa-lā fī s-samāʾi wa-huwa s-samīʿu al-ʿalīm (x3)	...in the name of Allah with whose name, nothing in the earth or heaven can harm, and He is the Hearing, the Knowing. (x3)	بسم الله الذي لا يضرّ مع اسمه شيء في الأرض ولا في السماء وهو السميع العليم (٣)
	ṣallā Llāhu ʿalā sayyidinā muḥammadin wa-ʿalā ālihi wa-ṣaḥbihi wa-sallim	May Allah bless Muhammad and his family and Companions and send [them] peace.	اللهم صلّ على سيّدنا محمد وعلى آله وصحبه وسلّم
	(Ayat al-Kursi)		(آية الكرسي)

THE PRESCHOOL SUBJECTS

Level 2 (contd.)			
	ashhadu an lā ilāha illā Llāhu wa-ashhadu anna muḥammadan rasūlu Llāh	I testify that there is no god but Allah, and I testify that Muhammad is Allah's messenger.	أَشْهَدُ أَنْ لَا إِلَهَ إِلَّا اللهُ وَأَشْهَدُ أَنَّ مُحَمَّدًا رَسُولُ اللهِ
	raḍitu bi-Llāhi rabban wa-bi-l-islāmi dīnan wa-bi-sayyidinā muḥammadin ṣallā Llāhu ʿalayhi wa-sallama nabiyyan wa-rasūlan	I am pleased with Allah as my Lord, with Islam as my religion, and with our master Muhammad as a prophet and messenger.	رَضِيتُ بِاللهِ رَبًّا وَبِالْإِسْلَامِ دِينًا وَبِسَيِّدِنَا مُحَمَّدٍ صَلَّى اللهُ عَلَيْهِ وَسَلَّمَ نَبِيًّا وَرَسُولًا
	Allāhu rabbī, muḥammadun nabiyyī, al-qurʾānu kitābī, al-islāmu dīnī, al-kaʿbatu qiblatī, al-muslimūna ikhwānī	Allah is my Lord, Muhammad is my prophet, the Quran is my book, Islam is my religion, the Kaʿba is my prayer direction, the Muslims are my brethren.	
	Āmīn	Amen	آمين
	(Surahs: al-Fatihah, al-Ikhlas, al-Falaq, al-Nas)		قِرَاءَةُ سُورِ الْفَاتِحَةِ وَالْإِخْلَاصِ وَالْفَلَقِ وَالنَّاسِ

Level 3 (12 items)

- Add the invocation for entering the lavatory, exiting it, and wearing one's clothes.

Action	Transliteration	Translation	Arabic
entering lavatory	Allāhumma, innī aʿūdhu bika mina l-khubuthi wa-l-khabāʾith	Dear Allah, indeed I seek refuge in You from evil and the evil ones (or from evil male and female jinn).	اللَّهُمَّ إِنِّي أَعُوذُ بِكَ مِنَ الخُبُثِ وَالخَبَائِثِ
exiting lavatory	Ghufrānak	Your forgiveness (O Allah)!	غُفْرَانَك
wearing clothes (whether or not they are new)	Al-ḥamdu li-Llāhi l-ladhī kasānī hādhā th-thawba wa-razaqanīhi min ghayri ḥawlin minnī wa- lā quwwa	All praise belongs to Allah Who has clothed me with this garment and provided it to me, without any power or might on my part.	الحَمْدُ لِلَّهِ الَّذِي كَسَانِي هَذَا الثَّوْبَ وَرَزَقَنِيهِ مِنْ غَيْرِ حَوْلٍ مِنِّي وَلَا قُوَّةٍ

THE PRESCHOOL SUBJECTS

Level 4 (15 items)

- Add the invocation for riding one's riding mount or other mode of transportation (such as a car), and for entering the home, and exiting it.

Action	Transliteration	Translation	Arabic
Riding one's riding mount or other mode of transportation (such as a car)	{Subḥāna l-ladhī sakhkhara lanā hādhā wa-mā kunnā lahu muqrinīn wa-innā ilā Rabbinā la-munqalibūn}, Surah al-Zukhruf: 13	Glorified be He Who has subdued these unto us while we were not capable (of subduing them ourselves), and to our Lord, indeed, we shall return.	‹سُبْحَانَ الَّذِي سَخَّرَ لَنَا هَٰذَا وَمَا كُنَّا لَهُ مُقْرِنِينَ وَإِنَّا إِلَىٰ رَبِّنَا لَمُنقَلِبُونَ›
Entering the house [Make a prayer involving the basmalah. Then great the people of the house.*	Allāhumma innī asʾaluka khayra al-mawlaj wa-khayr al-makhraj. Bi-smi Llāhi walajnā wa-bi-smi Llāhi kharajnā, wa ʿalā Llāhi Rabbinā tawakkalnā. As-salāmu ʿalaykum	O Allah, I ask You for the best entrance and the best exit. In the Name of Allah we enter, in the Name of Allah we leave, and in Allah our Lord do we trust. Peace be upon you.	اللَّهُمَّ إِنِّي أَسْأَلُكَ خَيْرَ الْمَوْلَجِ وَخَيْرَ الْمَخْرَجِ، بِسْمِ اللَّهِ وَلَجْنَا وَبِسْمِ اللَّهِ خَرَجْنَا، وَعَلَى اللَّهِ رَبِّنَا تَوَكَّلْنَا. السَّلَامُ عَلَيْكُمْ
Exiting the house	Bi-smi-Llāh, tawakkaltu ʿalā Llāh, wa-lā ḥawla wa-lā quwwata illā bi-Llāh	In the name of Allah, I rely on Allah, and there is no power or change except by Allah.	بِسْمِ اللَّهِ، تَوَكَّلْتُ عَلَى اللَّهِ، وَلَا حَوْلَ وَلَا قُوَّةَ إِلَّا بِاللَّهِ

* For beginners, say the basmalah and send greetings on the people of the home.

THE PRESCHOOL SUBJECTS

Level 5 (18 items)

- Add the invocation for walking to the mosque, entering it, and exiting it.

Action	Transliteration	Translation	Arabic
Walking to the mosque	Allāhumma jʿal fī qalbī nūran, wa-fī lisānī nūran, wa-fī samʿī nūran, wa-fī baṣarī nūran, wa-min fawqī nūran, wa-min taḥtī nūran, wa-ʿan yamīnī nūran, wa-ʿan shimālī nūran, wa-min amāmī nūran, wa-min khalfī nūran, wa jʿal fī nafsī nūran, wa aʿẓim lī nūran, wa ʿaẓẓim lī nūran, wa jʿal lī nūran, wa jʿalnī nūran	O Allah, place light in my heart, light in my sight and light in my hearing. Place light on my right and place light on my left. Place light above me and place light beneath me. Place light in front of me, place light behind me and grant me light, and make me light.	اللَّهُمَّ اجْعَلْ فِي قَلْبِي نُورًا، وَفِي لِسَانِي نُورًا، وَفِي سَمْعِي نُورًا، وَفِي بَصَرِي نُورًا، وَمِن فَوْقِي نُورًا، وَمِن تَحْتِي نُورًا، وَعَن يَمِينِي نُورًا، وَعَن شِمَالِي نُورًا، وَمِن أَمَامِي نُورًا، وَمِن خَلْفِي نُورًا، وَاجْعَل فِي نَفْسِي نُورًا، وَأَعْظِمْ لِي نُورًا، وَعَظِّمْ لِي نُورًا، وَاجْعَل لِي نُورًا، وَاجْعَلْنِي نُورًا.
Entering the mosque	Bi-smi-Llāh, Allāhumma ftaḥ lī abwāba raḥmatik	In the name of Allah, and may blessings and peace descend upon the Messenger of Allah. O dear Allah, open for me the doors of Your mercy.	بِسْمِ اللَّهِ وَالصَّلَاةُ وَالسَّلَامُ عَلَى رَسُولِ اللَّهِ، اللَّهُمَّ افْتَحْ لِي أَبْوَابَ رَحْمَتِكَ.
Exiting the mosque	Bi-smi-Llāh, wa-s-ṣalātu wa-s-salāmu ʿalā rasūli Llāh, Allāhumma innī asʾaluka min faḍlik	In the name of Allah, and may blessings and peace descend upon the Messenger of Allah. O dear Allah, indeed I ask You Your favour.	بِسْمِ اللَّهِ وَالصَّلَاةُ وَالسَّلَامُ عَلَى رَسُولِ اللَّهِ، اللَّهُمَّ إِنِّي أَسْأَلُكَ مِن فَضْلِكَ.

THE PRESCHOOL SUBJECTS

learn Imam al-Ghazali's The Beginning of Guidance (*Bidayat al-hidayah*) and draw from their understanding of it for students when appropriate. To get educators started, we provide an example of one way of teaching a three-year-old the *dhikr*, 'al-ḥamdu li-Llāh', after eating or drinking. For parents not fluent in Arabic, we provide translations so parents can discuss the basic religious meanings involved. Notice that basic meanings such as thanks, provender, creation, and resurrection appear. While children may struggle to understand, there our aim is to start planting seeds early. For instance, compare thanks (shukr, given to people) to praise (hamd, deserved by Allah). At first, they know they are obliged to give thanks, so they have a vague understanding of thanks. This vague meaning transfers to praise of Allah. Now, in conversations, you can start to differentiate the two. You cannot make distinctions if you do not start planting basic conceptual seeds, so start with slowly, but start now, and build. Speak to them about thanks and praise outside the 'lesson', both in the home and outside.

Etiquettes and invocations is broken into levels. Teach the etiquettes of a) eating, b) drinking, c) sleep, d) entering and exiting the lavatory, e) putting one's clothes on, f) entering and leaving the home, and g) seeking knowledge. For example, the etiquettes of eating are to say the basmalah, say the supplication for eating, eat with one's right hand, to eat from what is closest to one, to eat small mouthfuls, to chew well, and thank Allah for this blessing. And the etiquettes of seeking knowledge are to sit with adab, still in one's place, not to play or be silly, bring forth one's intention, not speak to others sitting next to you during the lesson, listen to the lesson, have adab with the teachers and one's brothers and sisters in Islam, and know that Allah makes the lives of those who have adab longer.

An example of how to teach 2 above to a three-year-old would be the following. With a whiteboard and marker, after giving the child something to eat or drink which they enjoy, draw a table on the board, the child sitting at it eating or drinking, and their mother or father on the other side of the table providing the food. Tell them that the mother or father gave them the food or drink, but it really came from Allah. Write the name of Allah, most high, at the top of the board. On the right edge of the board, write *al-ḥamdu li-Llāh* (in Arabic or English or both). On the left, write shukran, particularly after they learned to say shukran or thank you. Tell them, when a parent gives us, we say shukran or thank you. When Allah provides for us, we say, *al-ḥamdu li-Llāh*. Show them on the board that the food or drink really comes from Allah. Just as we say shukran to our parent, so we say *al-ḥamdu li-Llāh* to Allah.

Older children may understand providence (*rizq*), creation, or the difference between *shukr* and *ḥamd*. For now, repeat after the lesson that everything comes from Allah and that one should say *al-ḥamdu li-Llāh* often.

6 BELIEF ('AQIDAH), INCLUDING THE 99 NAMES OF ALLAH

Here, you will find tables and ideas for teaching the following:

a. The two testifications

b. The Divine Names (memorised and discussed at the most basic level)

c. The three pillars of religion: Islam, iman, and ihsan

d. Selected lines from the poem: Beliefs for non-scholars (*'aqidat al-'awwam*)

How to teach

In addition to encouraging memorising, teach the concepts through stories. Starting with a 3-year- old, you cannot tell stories about Allah, angels, and the Prophet Muhammad ﷺ without laying groundwork. But whatever words you use, the children will begin to pick them up as a habit. So, start with what is most basic, and do not give too many words or concepts at a time.

A simple idea for organising beliefs for children is to visualise a chain:

Allah sent to the

- angels

- books which the angels gave to the

- Prophets

{ *'The Messenger believes in what has been revealed to him from his Lord, and so do the believers. All believe in Allah, His angels, His Books, and His messengers...'* }

- Quran 2:285, as created by Allah -

Have a whiteboard and marker handy and start with 'Allah'. You may have already taught the supplication for eating and drinking, saying *al-ḥamdu li-Llāh*. If so, remind them of how you taught them to ask politely for something and to say, shukran and 'thank you', and how gifts are really from Allah so, one says, al-ḥamdu li-Llāh. Now, state (or repeat) that Allah created everything. Accustom them to saying 'create', which is only for Allah, because only He is strong enough to make the sun, the moon, and the seas. Mention that only Allah can make something from nothing. If the child is fascinated with dinosaurs, dolls, or cars, make sure to add this to the list. Tell the child clearly that mother and father get food, toys, etc. from the store, but the store gets it from the sea, and the sea is created (or made) by

Allah. Now draw a chain on the board:

From Allah at the top,
...... to the sea (and sun and moon),
.... to the store,
.... to mother and father,
.... to the child's plate.

Separate the levels with a line, draw something for each level, and draw arrows between the levels. Talk the child through the levels and ask if they have any questions.

For the rest of the names and poem memorised in this part of the preschool curriculum (six pillars of belief – 'aqidah), strike a balance suiting your child between memorisation and discussion/activities. (We offer another example activity below which lays a basis for further discussions you produce.)

Level 1:

- The two testifications and the principles of declaring unity

Transliteration	Translation	Arabic
ashhadu an lā ilāha illā Llāhu wa-ashhadu anna muḥammadan rasūlu Llāh	I testify that there is no god but Allah, and I testify that Muhammad is Allah's messenger.	أشهد أن لا إله إلا الله وأشهد أن محمدا رسول الله
raḍītu bi-Llāhi rabban wa-bi-l- islāmi dīnan wa-bi-sayyidinā muḥammadin ṣallā Llāhu 'alayhi wa-sallama nabiyyan wa-rasūlan	I am pleased with Allah as my Lord, with Islam as my religion, and with our master Muhammad ﷺ as a prophet and messenger.	رضيت بالله ربا وبالإسلام دينا وبسيدنا محمد صلى الله عليه وسلم نبيا ورسولا
Allāhu rabbī, muḥammadun nabiyyī, al-qur'ānu kitābī, al-islāmu dīnī, al-ka'batu qiblatī, al-muslimūna ikhwānī*	Allah is my Lord, Muhammad is my prophet, the Quran is my book, Islam is my religion, the Ka'bah is my prayer direction, the Muslims are my brethren.	الله ربي * محمد نبيي * القرآن الكريم كتابي * الإسلام ديني * الكعبة قبلتي * المسلمون إخواني

* Note that the latter part is reinforced daily as part of the 'Morning Recitation'.

Level 2:

- Review the two testifications and their meanings, and memorise and discuss the first ten Divine Names.

Transliteration	Translation	Arabic
Allāh	Allah (the proper and chosen name for God)	اَللّٰه
Al-Raḥmān	The Benevolent	الرَّحْمٰن
Al-Raḥīm	The All Merciful	الرَّحِيم
Al-Malik	The King	الْمَلِك
Al-Quddūs	The Holy	الْقُدُّوس
As-Salām	Peace (some people say, 'Source of Peace')	السَّلَام
Al-Muʾmin	The Protector	الْمُؤْمِن
Al-Muhaymin	The Guardian / Governor	الْمُهَيْمِن
Al-ʿAzīz	The Mighty	الْعَزِيز
Al-Jabbār	The Overwhelming	الْجَبَّار

Sing the Divine Names song daily. Play in the background if not possible to devote time to this. Find a link to an authentic recitation in the footnote.[83] Take the names one at a time and mention the translation and discuss what the word means.

Discussion/Activity

Your discussion may not be fully understood, but that is ok. Get children to use certain words and to pick up ideas which will enter into their thought and imagination. The earlier you begin, the more progress you will make. Just keep it child-friendly.

Remind children that Allah created everything. He is the only one who can create something from nothing. We make things from materials we get at stores (like flour for bread and wood for the carpenter) or from the earth, or by planting seeds. Allah made the seeds and created the oceans

---

83 https://www.youtube.com/watch?v=3FNnVM0bKGA

from which we get fish. Not only do things come from Allah, but His names connect to them. He keeps them in being. An optional activity is to turn on a screen plugged into a laptop. Put up a picture showing the vastness of nature, ideally including the sky and forests or ocean or other habitats. Say, 'Allah's power is like the electricity in the screen. What happens if we put the cord out of the socket?' Let the child do this. Say, 'The world is like this. If Allah and His Names do not protect it and keep it, it will vanish.'

We may put this another way that helps us teach the adhkar from above: It is related[84] that the Prophet Muhammad asked his companion 'Uthman what would happen if he recited, 'In the Name of Allah with whose Name nothing is harmed on earth or in the heavens, and He is the All-Hearing, the All-Knowing,' three times every day and every night. He told him that nothing would harm him. (If you wish to expand, there is an interesting story in the previous link related to Hazrat 'Uthman's son.[85]) Tell the children that all power and barakah comes from Allah and His names. When we remember this and mention Allah and His names, we are with Allah, His protection and His light. We are in a state of remembrance (*dhikr*). The one who remembers Allah and the one who does not are like the living and the dead. When we do anything with the basmalah (saying *bi-smi Llah*) and remember Him and His names, we are away from harm and darkness through mentioning Him and His names. Allah gave to His beloved prophet, Muhammad, upon him be peace and blessings, these ways to protect ourselves. They protect our body and our heart. They protect our body from sickness, and our heart from darkness and Shaytan. (You may wish to repeat this lesson, first leaving out certain concepts which may be new such as Shaytan, and later adding them if the child is attentive.)

[We teachers may see how 'aqidah, adhkar, and other topics are all linked in a certain way. If we lay foundations, children will worship from their hearts, rather by wrote and habit.]

Level 3:

- Memorise the next ten names, discussing meaning and translation.
- Memorise the following, discussing according to the child's understanding, and make activities like those that preceded.

---

84 Ibn Majah 3869. For the Arabic and full translation, see https://sunnah.com/ibnmajah:3869.

85 He was struck by paralysis on one side of his body. He had related this tradition to a man, and the man stared at him when he was partially paralysed. Hadhrat 'Uthman's son, Abana, said, 'Why do you stare at me? One morning I was angry and forgot to recite the words, and then I was struck (with this paralysis.).

Transliteration	Translation	Arabic
Al-Mutakabbir	The Supreme	المُتَكَبِّر
Al-Khāliq	The Creator	الخَالِق
Al-Bāri'	The Maker	البَارِئ
Al-Muṣawwir	The Form Giver	المُصَوِّر
Al-Ghaffār	The Forgiving	الغَفَّار
Al-Qahhār	The Overmastering	القَهَّار
Al-Wahhāb	The Bestower	الوَهَّاب
Al-Razzāq	The Provider	الرَّزَّاق
Al-Fattāḥ	The Opener	الفَتَّاح
Al-'Alīm	The All Knowing	العَلِيم

The pillars of religion are three:

4. al-Islam (practice: actions),
5. al-iman (belief), and
6. al-ihsan (spiritual excellence).

The pillars of Islam are five:

1. The testification that there is no god but Allah, and that Muhammad is the messenger of Allah,
2. upholding the prayer,
3. giving the poor-due (zakat),
4. fasting Ramadan, and
5. making the pilgrimage to the sacred mosque for those able to travel to it.

The pillars of belief are six:

1. to believe in Allah,
2. His angels,
3. His books,

4. His messengers,

5. the Last Day, and

6. the good and evil of destiny being from Allah, most high.

Spiritual excellence is to worship Allah as though you see Him, for though you do not see Him, He sees you.

Level 4:

Discuss and memorise ten more Divine Names.

Study and memorise the first ten lines of *'aqidat al-'awwam*.[86] (These lines are a complete set on the topic of theology.)

Level 5:

Complete memorising the Divine Names. Discuss ten more.

Study and memorise lines eleven to twenty of *'aqidat al-'awwam* (on the topic of prophecy).

[Optional: memorise the next eight lines on the angels and revealed scriptures (lines twenty-one to -eight.)]

7 FIQH

Learn prayer and ablution through acting them out.

Matters such as pillars and conditions of prayer and ablution do not have to be taught, but children can correct each other: 'He did it right.' 'He did it wrong.' 'Why?' 'Because....'

You can also enact circling the Ka'ba, especially in the sacred month of Dhu al-Hijja.

8 STORIES OF THE PROPHETS

Informal read-aloud: English stories of the prophets (on them be peace).

9 NATURAL SCIENCE AND NATURE STUDY

Winter activities

- Help bake cookies

---

[86] For a free, downloadable copy, see https://archive.org/details/aqidat-awam-dual-trans-1.

- Look for bird nests, squirrel nests,[87] and mistletoe[88] in bare trees
- Make paper snowflakes[89]
- Make snowmen or animals, such as sheep
- Pour hot maple syrup on cups of clean snow to make snow candy[90]
- Grow seeds in a cup to be transplanted in spring and watch them grow

Spring and summer activities

- Observe a worm crawling
- Look at stars and pick out the Big Dipper
- Play in a puddle or stream
- Throw pinecones into a pond and feed ducks
- Pull plants out of the ground (either vegetables or weeds)
- Catch some tadpoles/polliwogs (if it's legal in your area; they may be endangered) and watch them turn into frogs[91]
- Pick (but do not pull apart) flowers and put them in a vase of water
- Watch an ant's nest
- Make juice popsicles (or ice cubes to crush and eat with a spoon)
- Be aware of dew in the morning that dissipates
- Collect flowers for your teacher to press between wax paper with a warm iron[92]
- Keep a pet insect in a jar
- Blow dandelion seeds

---

87 https://www.woodlandtrust.org.uk/blog/2020/06/squirrel-nests/
88 https://www.discoverwildlife.com/plant-facts/facts-about-mistletoe
89 https://www.hgtv.com/design/make-and-celebrate/handmade/how-to-make-paper-snowflakes 92 https://happyhooligans.ca/make-maple-syrup-snow-candy-3-simple-steps/
90 https://happyhooligans.ca/make-maple-syrup-snow-candy-3-simple-steps/
91 93 https://www.wikihow.com/Catch-Tadpoles
92 https://www.ehow.com/how_6246603_press-flowers-wax-paper.html

- Watch a spider trap, wrap, and eat prey in its web
- Paint the sidewalk with a cup of water and a paintbrush
- Taste honeysuckle nectar[93]
- Press prints of leaves, seeds, flowers, rocks into playdough or clay
- Watch a snail leave a slime trail
- Dig the biggest hole in the world (reference: 'The Real Hole' by Beverly Cleary)
- Find colours in nature that match your child's shirt, shoes, etc.
- Count rings on a cut tree
- Make a fairy (or toy dinosaur) garden[94]
- Look for a bird's nest with eggs and keep track of the hatchlings (from a distance)
- Squirt a fence or plants with water from a spray bottle
- Excavate for buttons, beads, or small toys hidden in sand or mud
- Grow sunflowers[95]
- If legal in your area, keep a pet turtle, lizard, frog, or toad for a few days
- Find the red spot in Queen Anne's Lace
- Collect elder flower and make a cordial
- Look for a four-leaf clover
- Make sun prints by leaving items on construction paper outside
- Identify shapes in clouds
- Transfer a cocoon or chrysalis to a jar indoors to watch the moth or butterfly emerge[96]

---

93 https://www.instructables.com/Honeysuckle:-Harvesting-the-Sweet-Nectar-of-Life/
94 https://rhythmsofplay.com/start-your-own-fairy-garden/
95 https://www.gardenhealth.com/advice/plants-flowers/how-to-grow-sunflowers
96 https://www.wikihow.pet/Hang-a-Monarch-Chrysalis and https://homeguides.sfgate.com/rehang-cocoon80989.html

THE PRESCHOOL SUBJECTS

- Identify bands of colour from a real rainbow after a rain
- If in North America, catch fireflies in a jar
- Explore what lives and grows on and around a tree

Fall activities

- Make leaf rubbings with crayons
- Look for plant galls[97]
- Try catching leaves as they fall
- Collect acorns and look for squirrels gathering nuts
- Cut up leaves with child-safe scissors to make confetti
- Collect leaf pairs and play at mixing and matching them up
- Make tent-style forts from sticks for tiny toy people/animals
- Collect leaves for your teacher; press between wax paper with a warm iron[98]
- Buy nuts (even peanuts) in the shell and crack them open
- Activities for all seasons
- Pour water from containers of various sizes
- Notice their own shadow and how it moves with them
- Set a bird feeder near a window and watch the birds[99]
- Sort a box of buttons or beads by colour or by size
- Watch coloured light made from an object that acts like a prism[100]
- Notice how puddles decrease in the sun
- Run rice or sand through the fingers
- Recognize the garbage man or mailman or other regular service person

97 https://www.discoverwildlife.com/how-to/identify-wildlife/how-to-identify-plant-galls/
98 100 https://www.wikihow.com/Preserve-Leaves-in-Wax-Paper
99 101 https://www.discoverwildlife.com/reviews/window-bird-feeders/
100 102 https://www.hunker.com/13411944/the-best-ways-to-hang-crystal-prisms/

and say 'hello' to them

- Watch squirrels, rabbits, birds and/or other backyard wildlife
- Build a blanket fort
- Notice where the sun comes up and sets; locate East/West
- Help bake a loaf of bread
- Play with magnets (but not near computers)
- Stop and listen to what do they hear (dogs, birds, cats, crickets, frogs)
- In a tub of water, explore what sinks and what floats
- Look for circles and straight lines in nature
- If you have a large appliance delivered, save the box to make a castle or car

10 MUSIC: RECITATION AND SINGING

- Recite your favourite chapters of the Quran: practice with your teacher (or alone if shy) and then recite for your family and friends (listen to reciters such as Mustafa Isma'il and Muhammad Rif'at for inspiration)
- Learn *Tala'a al-badr* and other songs from *Breezes from Paradise vols. 1 & 2*
- Learn some folksongs; this is Wendi Capehart's YouTube playlist of folksongs for Year 01[101]
- Learn four folksongs by heart

11 ARTS AND CRAFTS

Everything in Islam requires an intention (*niyyah*); it is not just play. Similarly, physical education is about a discipline, not sport. Topics may include cooking and woodwork. It is facility dependent: all can do cooking, but reviving handy skills is important and requires effort.

Concluding note

If you wish to follow the British timing or start Rec/KG at 4 going on 5 for any other reason, there are opportunities to make up for elements of the Preschool curriculum not covered in Rec/KG, or even in the beginning of Year 1. For instance, the hours of Religious Instruction in Year 1 are handed

---

[101] https://www.youtube.com/playlist?list=PL2IR3x_bkyR6hUrO5A1IE4qtltKKIRPSt

over to reading *Qasas al-nabiyyin* to consolidate Arabic before beginning to read in Arabic. You may instead study one or more level of the Preschool/Rec/KG fiqh curriculum.

3.6 Reception/Kindergarten Subjects - Outline

RECEPTION (AGE 4-5)/KINDERGARTEN (AGE 5-6)

1. Quran
- Oral memorisation

2. Arabic
- Tajwid (here meaning approximately phonics): Competence in decoding written Arabic
- Learn basic vocabulary (and label any objects found in the home/classroom)

3. English (local language)
- Phonics and reading, as in UK Reception (tempered by Steiner practices)

4. Maths
- As in UK Reception (tempered by Steiner teaching practices and including Arabic terms for numbers and shapes)

5. Etiquettes and invocations
- (*al-adab wa-l-adʿiyah*) memorised

6. Tawhid
- The 99 Names

7. Fiqh
- Begin level three of Preschool and Rec/KG curriculum

8. Stories of the prophets

- Informal read-aloud of English stories of the prophets (on them be peace)

9. Natural Science

- Nature through narrative, activities and nature specimens.

10. Art and Design

- Integrated learning of drawing and script, option activities

11. Physical Education

- Start swimming and wrestling: general development activities.

SUBJECT BY SUBJECT IN DETAIL

1 QURAN: ORAL MEMORISATION[102]

Carry on with the Preschool curriculum.

2 ARABIC

a. Tajwid (here meaning approximately phonics)

- Competence in decoding written Arabic[103]

Move from 'alphabet through play' to what is effectively phonics. Before the children reach First Grade/Year 1, they should have not only learned a good amount of Arabic spoken vocabulary, but also gone through *al-Qaʿidah al-nuraniyyah*. Here, our recommendations overlap with Level 2 (Primary). We recommend *al-Qaʿidah al-nuraniyyah* be broken down into individual slides and taught by a qualified tajwid teacher, or at least an adult whose Fatiha, and ideally whole Quran, has been tested by one qualified in tawjid. The book needs to be supplemented as already happens by many experienced teachers in the US, UK, and abroad. The Malaysian resource Iqra has more extensive teaching of each letter. It alone has sufficient material and exercises such that students having finished a topic are likely to have mastered it sufficiently to move on. This tajwid is required for those wishing to move

---

[102] Teach with joy, voices raised, remembering this is an invocation, and tapping one's hand to the rhythm of the short and long vowels, as performed in al-Azhar Mosque to this date (in al-Madrasah al-Taybarsiyyah). Tajwid (comely recitation, equivalent of phonics) is taught in the Arabic lesson.

[103] Learn via traditional phonics book. These include *al-Qaʿidah al-nuraniyyah*, the Malaysian equivalent, or *Muʿallim al-qiraʾah*. Also, learn the alphabet song which exists on same tune as English alphabet.

into our curriculum for First Grade/Year 1.

b. Learn basic vocabulary

- Label any objects found in the home/classroom

Carry on with the Preschool curriculum, but now children should start being able to read the notes on things in the learning environment or to use flash cards and identify words in sentences (whether these sentences are in the Quran or other subjects such as tawhid and *adab wa-l-ad'iyah*).

By the age of three or four, children who can speak may be asked about parts of speech. Ask the questions of nouns. Children who can speak know what a person, place, and thing are. Ask them about adjectives. They can answer questions about adjectives (whose, how many, what kind?) and adverbs (how, where, when, why?). Start orally, linking it to any reading, asking them questions as they read, or as you read to them if easier. Adopt activities from Waldorf to ensure gross motor skills are in place, and when children are writing one may sentence diagramme, even if earlier than recommended in the rest of our curriculum. It will take longer than in later years; there is no reason not to start if children are able. Children enjoy sentence diagramming: it is effectively drawing with sentences. This introduction to syntax allows one to avoid front-loading the curriculum with the properties of nouns and verbs (such as tenses and moods). Then one can safely go into the characteristics of words.

3 ENGLISH (LOCAL LANGUAGE)

Phonics and reading

As in UK Reception, tempered by Steiner practices.

Read-aloud should begin well before this stage but carry on reading aloud to children. Some children will exhibit pre-reading skills or even begin to read without being taught phonics. Phonics is a means to an end, so if reading occurs, one should limit oneself to complex elements of phonics which overlap with spelling.

If your child turned four (in UK) or 5 (in US) by September 1, start teaching them phonics and other subjects 10 minutes a day, incorporating playdough or clay to make learning letters tactile. Children may also act out letters, shaping themselves into them and singing the alphabet song until it is naturally memorised. As their maturity and attention span will allow, increase this gently and gradually to 30 minutes.

If students finish phonics well before the year ends, begin spelling (using *Spelling Workout* also by Modern Curriculum Press) and reading.

RECEPTION/KINDERGARTEN SUBJECTS

- Spelling: Note that Spelling Workout A devotes much time to reviewing and applying phonics to spelling.
- Reading: Working through a graded reading scheme or begin McGuffy's First Reader. The first thirty lessons are quite simple.
- Writing (script and penmanship): Introduce the letters of a print scheme using the advice of Rosemary Sassoon (*Handwriting: The Way to Teach It*).

Devote some time, even if not a 10-30 min slot, to memorising poems, including 'Grammar in Rhyme' in the 'General Resources' at the end of this chapter.

Organise the above through gently introducing the following tracks (a.-d.), starting with 10-minute slots dispersed throughout the day.

a. Read-aloud with discussion for comprehension: 30 mins

As most students are not reading at this stage, read-aloud to them.

Board books

(Other board books may be or become available from the picture books below)

- Janet and Allan Ahlberg, *Peepo*
- Eric Carle, *The Very Hungry Caterpillar* (and around ten other books)
- Michael Rosen, *We're Going on a Bear Hunt*
- The entire Beatrix Potter (Peter Rabbit) series (available in selections in a board book under the title: *Meet... including Peter Rabbit, Hunca Munca, Squirrel Nutkin, and Mrs. Tiggy-Winkle*)
- Large-shaped Peter Rabbit books (books are cut, often to shape, of lead character; there are always 1-2 sentences per picture)[104]
- A. A. Milne (and selection by Rosemary Wells), *Poems from When We Were Very Young*, Norton Young Readers, 2021.
- *A First Discovery Book* series by Scholastic (these will hold their interest at anywhere from 1-5 and are genuinely informative)

Picture books

- *Winnie-the-Pooh Story Treasury: A Collection of illustrated stories* (based on the stories of A. A. Milne with illustrations by Andrew Grey, having something of the classical feel of E. H. Shepard's) DEAN Egmont, London, 2018.[105]

---

104 https://www.abebooks.com/9780241304716/Large-Shaped-Peter-Rabbit-Board-0241304717/plp

105 This abridgement has many of the original phrases and songs yet makes it closer to a

- A. A. Milne, *Winnie-the-Pooh*
- A. A. Milne, *The House at Pooh Corner*
- A. A. Milne reading from writings in 1929[106]
- Beatrix Potter, *The Tale of Peter Rabbit and the tales of the Flopsy Bunnies, Tom Kitten, Mrs. Tiggy-Winkle, Mr. Jeremy Fisher, Jemima Paddle-Duck, Mrs. Tiddlemouse and Two Bad Mice*, or obtain *The Complete Tales of Peter Rabbit*[107]
- Shulamith Oppenheim, *The Hundredth Name*, Astra Young Readers, 2020.
- Kelly Cunnane and Hoda Hadadi (illustrator), *Deep in the Sahara*.
- Hena Khan, *Golden Domes and Silver Lanterns: A Muslim Book of Colors*
- Hena Khan, *Crescent Moons and Pointed Minarets: A Muslim Book of Shapes*
- Watty Piper, *The Little Engine that Could*[108]
- Robert McCloskey, *Blueberries for Sal*[109]
- Kate Greenaway, *The Language of Flowers*
- Edward Lear, *Complete Nonsense Poems*
- *Treasury of Mother Goose* (Linda Yeatman (ed.) and Hilda Offen (illustrator) or edition of your choice)[110]
- Robert Louis Stevenson, *A Child's Garden of Verses*

For additional read-aloud resources, see Ambleside.[111] Also, see the Burgess nature books listed in below in '9. Natural science'.

Valuable collections

- Clifton Fadiman (selected by), *The World Treasury of Children's Literature* (especially vols. 1&2)

b. Script

Determine whether children are able to hold a short pencil and begin to learn an English script. If not, return to pre-writing activities listed in 'Preschool' above. When ready, transition from fist crayons and making

board book with copious illustrations and sturdy paper.

106 https://www.openculture.com/2013/05/hear_the_classic_iwinnie-the-poohi_read_by_author_aa_milne_in_1929.html, also https://www.youtube.com/watch?v=3Sr3-541IIw

107 https://shop.peterrabbit.com/collections/books

108 https://www.christianbook.com/little-engine-could-original-classic-edition/watty-piper/9780448405209/pd/405202?event=AFF&p=1231043&

109 https://www.christianbook.com/Christian/Books/product?event=AFF&p=1231043&item_no=0169X

110 Here is an essay on the benefit of Mother Goose's nursery rhymes with specific reference to many, many of them and their significance and how to teach them: https://amblesideonline.org/art-mother-goose.

111 https://amblesideonline.org/ao-y0-bks

letters in clay and sand to introducing a script with a short pencil (as opposed to fat preschool pencils): 10-5 min

c. Phonics

(McGuffy's *Eclectic Primer*): 10-5 min

If students started Modern Curriculum Press in Preschool, you may continue with it or switch to McGuffy's *Eclectic Primer* or *Jolly Phonics*. If you carry on with Modern Curriculum Press, pick up where they left off in Preschool and complete Level A this year.

If students did not start with Modern Curriculum Press's *Spelling Workout*, but wish to pursue it here, start with Level K, and advance to Level A when they finish.

Some children will begin reading this year, rather than in Year 1. For these students, use the following board books:

- Harriette Taylor Treadwell, *The Primer*[112] and *First Reader*[113] (available online for free)
- Else Holmelund Minarek, *Little Bear readers*[114]

The second volume in the series of Reading-Literature readers, whose purpose is to train children in reading and appreciating literature through the reading of literature, contains thirteen of the best folk tales, of gradually increasing difficulty, and 33 of the best rhymes and jingles suitable for young children. Includes 'The Three Little Pigs', 'The Cat and the Mouse', 'The Bremen Band', 'The Straw Ox', 'The Town Mouse and the Country Mouse', 'Little Two Eyes', 'Little Half Chick', 'The Fisherman and His Wife', 'The Sheep and the Pig', and others. Attractive black and white illustrations are appealing to children. These are suitable for ages 6-8.

- Russell Hoban, Frances books (including the Frances Collection)[115]

d. Oral poem memorisation (including nursery rhymes): 10-20 min (or every other day)

Include copious time for review of previous poems. Memorise from books listed above (Stevenson, Lear, and Milne's When We Were Very

---

112 http://www.gatewaytotheclassics.com/browse/display.php?author=treadwell&book=primer&story=_contents

113 http://www.gatewaytotheclassics.com/browse/display.php?author=treadwell&book=first&story=_contents

114 https://www.amazon.com/Little-Bear-Can-Read-Book/dp/0064440044

115 https://www.amazon.com/Frances-Collection-Russell-Hoban/dp/B003F31AJ4 119 LIFE is refining its own list for publication.

Young) and other poems.[116]

4 MATHS

As in UK Reception, tempered by Steiner teaching practices and including Arabic terms for numbers and shapes.

One may use the following for resources and an overview of skills appropriate to Rec/KG: https://home.oxfordowl.co.uk/maths/primary-maths-age-4-5-reception/. One may use the skills and manipulatives recommended here to teach the topics listed in Arabic as one continues to work through the Arabic mathematics curriculum listed in the Preschool section above.

Informal activities

- Read numbers off the back of a can or box at the grocery store
- Count how many different kinds of bolts or washers are sold at the hardware store
- Play dominoes[117] or make a line of them to topple
- Count the number of petals on different kinds of flowers

5 ETIQUETTES AND INVOCATIONS

(AL-ADAB WA-L-AD'IYAH) MEMORISED

Continue where one left off in the Preschool curriculum.

6 TAWHID (INCLUDING THE 99 NAMES)

Continue where one left off in the Preschool curriculum.

7 FIQH

Begin level three of the Preschool and Rec/KG curriculum.

8 STORIES OF THE PROPHETS

Informal read-aloud of English stories of the prophets (on them be peace).

9 NATURAL SCIENCE

---

116 LIFE is refining its own list for publication.
117 https://www.dominorules.com/the-basics

RECEPTION/KINDERGARTEN SUBJECTS

Read *The Adventures of...* and *Bedtime Stories* by Thornton Burgess

If these books are not read-aloud to children (or independently by confident readers), they may be used in Y1. There are 20 full books in total, each around 100 pages, starting with *The Adventures of Reddy Fox and Mother West Wind's Children*. Burgess's stories are found read-aloud in the public domain.[118]

Activities for 5-year-olds[119]

- Adopt a tree in your yard and track its changes over a year; mark off a square foot in the grass and watch it for insects, crawling and otherwise
- Visit a local children's science/activity centre
- Identify the birds, plants, and bugs in your backyard
- Make a daisy or clover chain[120]
- Create a nature scavenger hunt, finding three different kinds of leaves, flowers, bugs, etc.
- Gather nature items in a box, look for two minutes and then cover; ask how many can be remembered
- See what lives in a cup of pond water; if you're lucky, you'll find a dragonfly larva
- See if flowers, leaves, etc. have symmetry using a mirror image[121]
- Make a sundial with a stick and mark the hours around it on the ground with rocks[122]
- Look at bugs and plants with a magnifying glass (younger children may not be able to use a magnifying glass)

Nature Specimens

- Mobile: Herbs (child chooses and plants)
- Permanent: Frog (ideally multiple frogs in an aquarium, part dry and part water, encouraging them to mate and lay tadpoles)

---

118 https://librivox.org/reader/1121?primary_key=1121&search_category=reader&search_page=1&search_form=get_results

119 Five-year-olds might venture outside the home more, and their activities might involve counting, or be slightly more advanced.

120 https://www.wikihow.com/Make-a-Daisy-Chain

121 https://www.youtube.com/watch?v=O7zV-7IoiWk 125 https://www.wikihow.com/Make-a-Sundial

122 https://www.wikihow.com/Make-a-Sundial

10 ART AND DESIGN

Use the text *Draw Write Now, Book 1* (over three half-terms).

Activities

- Kneading and shaping bread roles
- Teasing wool into thread and dying it
- Knitting using plain and edge stitches

Optional

- Make a wooden, drop spindle.

Inter-curricular

- Children will be learning letters in both Arabic and local language. In natural science, they will begin gardening.

11 PHYSICAL EDUCATION

- Swimming may be started at 4, as children have enough coordination for most basic strokes.
- Jujitsu may be started at 5.

General Developmental Activities

- Visit the library
- Make a sandwich
- Sketch a map of your town's few main roads large enough to play with toy cars; let your child draw houses and buildings
- Use a hammer to pound nails into a board
- Play rhyming games and how many words rhyme with 'game'
- Try balancing a stack of rocks
- Make salad for the family dinner

GENERAL RESOURCES

Parts of Speech Poem

1. All names of persons, places, things,
Are NOUNS, like Caesar, Rome, and kings.

2. PRONOUNS are used in place of nouns:
My thought, her work, his book, your frowns.
When the kind you wish to state,
3. Use an ADJECTIVE, like great.
4. But if of manner you would tell,
Use ADVERBS, such as: slowly, well.
To find an ADVERB this test try,
Ask how? Or when? Or where? Or why?
5. PREPOSITIONS show relation,
Like with respect, or in our nation.
6. CONJUNCTIONS as their name implies,
Are joining words; they are the ties
That bind together day and night,
Calm but cold, dull or bright.
7. Next, we have the VERBS, which tell
Of action, being, and state as well.
To work, succeed, achieve, and curb—
Each one of these is called a VERB.
8. The INTERJECTIONS show surprise,
Like Oh! Alas! Ah me! How wise!
Thus briefly does this jingle state
The PARTS OF SPEECH, which total eight.

4

THE PRACTICAL ELEMENTARY CURRICULUM (YEARS 1-6)

The LIFE practical curriculum divides into daily subjects and weekly subjects. The former consists of obligatory knowledge, Quran, the Trivium and English literature, Arabic liberal arts, and mathematics. The latter consists of the study of nature; arts, crafts, and design; music; physical education; and history and cultural studies. Under each subject, you will find a 'What', 'Why', and 'How', each of which explain the LIFE approach to the subjects and offer advice for instruction.

4.1 DAILY SUBJECTS

The daily subjects are the foundation and roots of the entire curriculum. For this reason, children will have a unit on each of these subjects daily.

4.1.1 RELIGIOUS INSTRUCTION

a. What?

What is religious instruction? In reality, there is no subject called religious instruction, nor is there a subject termed 'Islamic studies'. There is something called religion (*din*), and it is four subjects listed in the Jibril tradition: iman (belief), Islam (Islam), ihsan (spiritual excellence), *amarat al-sa'ah* (signs of the end times). Here is an eternal root to a holistic education, for these sciences relate to the mind, body, and heart or spirit, respectively. The hadith refers a fourth science: the science of the end times (or eschatology, *amarat al-sa'ah*). This last science is important not because we may accurately predict when the Mahdi will come, but rather because the end times come with corruption which may affect (and has affected) our religion. For this reason, scholars have written sound books already translated into English which enumerate in a rooted manner the broad categories of corruption, including social and financial. The very starting point of religion is now affected by our time, and it is this change of our social environment which makes Islamic instruction a challenge in our time. Thus, we have for starters, four subjects. We may see immediately that 'Islam' or 'Islamic studies', is not properly speaking a subject. Rather, we have so far:

- 'aqidah (and at a more advanced level, tawhid and *kalam*),
- Fiqh, written down within a madhhab or school,
- Tazkiyah and *tasawwuf* or (roughly, purification of the heart), and
- Knowledge of the signs of the end-times.

The first three, along with tajwid (comely recitation of the Quran), are generally considered the core individually obligatory subjects which every Muslim must know (to please Allah and avoid sin and leaving duties and dues unperformed).

As noted in this manual's introduction, we draw from the wider syllabus when the madrasa taught all subjects in an integrated manner. Many sciences we would not think based on our being shaped by modern culture and its notions of hyper-specialisation are considered Sharia sciences. For instance, great scholars such as al-Taftazani and Shaykh Zakariyya al-Ansari considered logic a Sharia science: you can give zakat to fund its teaching. The wider subjects that appear on the primary curriculum are divided according to al-Azhar into two:

a) Sciences that are instrumental (*'ulum al-alah*, many of which are linguistic sciences) and

b) Sciences that are sought for themselves (*maqasid*).

INSTRUMENTAL SCIENCES DIVIDED INTO LINGUISTIC SCIENCES AND THOSE THAT ARE NOT.

Linguistic sciences include:

- Recitation of the Quran (and pronunciation of Arabic, tajwid)
- Grammar (*nahw*)
- Morphology (*sarf*)
- Literature (*adab*)

Other instrumental sciences include:

- Logic (*mantiq*)
- Rhetoric (*balaghah*)

Here we see the full, classical trivium represented – grammar (including morphology and literature), logic and rhetoric. Importantly, note that many of these sciences are taught in the subject 'Arabic'.

Sciences taught for their own sake include:

- 'aqidah and *kalam* (representing iman and the theoretical sciences)
- Fiqh (sacred law, representing Islam and the practical sciences)
- Tazkiyah and *tasawwuf* (purification of the heart and character, ihsan)
- Biography of the Prophet ﷺ (sirah)

This is ten sciences in sum. We teach the instrumental sciences in Arabic (and local language) and liberal arts, centring on the trivium. So, of the religious sciences in the stricter sense, there are four.

b. Why?

Why classical texts rather than contemporary schemes? LIFE has opted for the learning of classical texts for both its learning pathways: learning Arabic and learning *in* Arabic. There are now classical texts translated into English by scholars sufficing for the first several years.[123]

In 'General Resources' below, we list many of the numerous Islamic instruction schemes that have been painstakingly produced over the last twenty years. A universal feature of the said schemes is that they are generally based on traditional texts, but these schemes do not read like scholarly texts. Scholarly texts, even extremely simple texts for beginners, are written by scholars to be the highest degree of eloquence and exactness. They are simple and accessible from one viewpoint; from another viewpoint, they can be examined and explained endlessly to show how the knowledge of the scholar is reflected in them. They capture the subject they study just as a thumbnail sketch captures the map of a whole country. If we are to produce thinkers, we need to use texts which deploy the tools of learning in English so that the teacher may explain how they do so.[124]

Were someone to respond that English is not a scholarly language and that only Arabic can have these features, we would remind them that there have existed many scholarly texts in Persian, Urdu, Ottoman, and Kurdish. What is required is a communal effort to translate technical terms into English in a way conveying the same concept and referent as the classical

---

123 LIFE has a number of classical texts in the production pipeline.

124 This being one of the most important roles of a teacher and qualities rendering a text 'pedagogical'.

text, or redefining terms when necessary. The LIFE team has been engaged with this process in its courses produced over the last ten years—such as the translation of *al-Sullam al-munawraq* (*The Comely Ladder*, our course being titled, 'The Ladder of Light to the True Sciences'), and also in its upcoming publications of *Mughni al-tullab* (*Seekers' Sufficiency*) of Mahmud al-Maghnisi and *al-'Awamil* (*Grammatical Agents*) of al-Birgili. ASIPT has produced a large glossary of terms across the sciences. It is only a matter of time until a scholarly language exists in English across the traditional sciences.

Towards the attributes of the perfect person, the following must be considered:

- Growing the seed through 'aqidah and watering it with goodly acts
- The role of 'aqidah, fiqh, and sirah in perfecting character
- Spirituality in the primary years
- '*Finding True Happiness*: *Is Ethics possible in modernity?*', a LIFE text
- Forming stable dispositions

The attributes of the perfect person include perfections that are productive, practical and theoretical. See the daily subject, many of which treat the productive attributes.

We should raise children in tawhid and sincere piety; they should both see and engage in worship. We should help them from a young age to work on their practical soul, ensuring that it is directed to the true causes of happiness. Towards this end, LIFE offers a dual-language pack of the strongest sayings on true happiness and its opposites, drawn from short hadith, poetry, and other genres. The sayings are commented on to argue cogently that consumer and celebrity culture do not lead to true happiness. The pack also has enough materials to directly empower youth not to fall under peer pressure. In normal circumstances, the traditional curriculum we offer of 'aqidah, fiqh, spirituality, and sirah would suffice, but we clearly live in the end times in which the cultural, social, and economic corruptions—alluded to in hadith—exist in our everyday lives, and now even chase us into our homes, laptops, and phones.

Character perfection requires knowing what to do and repeating the correct action enough for it to become a habit. 'aqidah plays a significant role here, for one who believes Allah is watching and in control of everything behaves differently and gives up the pseudo-benefits of the material world for higher goals much easier. Also, this awareness infuses the action with a meaning and intention. Intention is fundamental to the type of act we are doing: the same outward act, such as giving to the mosque, may be almsgiving (*zakat*) or it may be ostentation (*riya'*). Fiqh should be taught with the proper adab and applied such that one knows God's ruling for every action one does.

Sirah unifies these matters and infuses in them the utter love for Allah's beloved ﷺ. Everything becomes easy when one's heart inclines to the beloved.

Spirituality should inspire from within to draw close to God and purify the heart from sins, which prevent the other aims of the curriculum. Imam 'Ali (Allah be well-pleased with him) said to his son al-Hasan (Allah be well-pleased with him): 'I start you with adab'. Imam Zarruq, the sixteen-century Moroccan jurist and mystic said in his *Principles of Spirituality*:

> "Whatever is incorporated in one's nature is an aid to obtaining what it seeks, depending on one's capacity. This is why it has been said: 'If a child learns that which his soul is inclined to [what he or she likes], he or she will become a leader in it; if a seeker embraces the invocations and prayers that his true self prefers, this will aid him to reach his goal by his continuing to do so'. [This is because] what you start in a state of spiritual expansion (*inbisat*) is more likely to last."[125]

Between the ages of 5 and 12, the fitrah must be protected and pre-virtues (good habits) must be inculcated. The irrational parts of the soul (anger and desire) must be guided. This requires reducing contact with advertisements and street/gang culture to a minimum and empowering children with the four subjects of religious instruction and the said packet. Moral education must convey clearly what the soul should love, aim for, and respect, in order to bring true happiness and felicity. If one's desires, respect, and notions of entertainment—as opposed to true recreation—are not aimed at the target of true happiness, how can one sharpen the will to hit that target; and, importantly, learning theoretical ethics will lead to a great deal of cognitive dissonance within oneself.[126] A key LIFE approach is to make the best attempt to avoid the soul being corrupted in the first place. However, if this corruption happens, tarbiyah then aims to purify the soul and direct it to true happiness, but also to ameliorate some of the said dissonance a person will feel within themselves.

The theoretical perfections take as a prerequisite that the practical soul has been purified. Without the purification of the practical soul, the practical intellect lacks control of anger and desire, and they undermine the purity required for contemplation. There is a habitual element here as well: theoretical perfections are not mere flashes of sparky understanding, but an enduring cognitive capacity and *habitus* (*malakah*). To achieve *habitus* in the theoretical sciences, one must begin with language, including morphology and grammar. If a person cannot speak the local language, they cannot express the goodness of their religion nor participate in making the locality a better place. If a person

---

125 Ibn Zarruq, *Qawa'id al-tasawwuf*, principle 98.

126 The dissonance between ideals and realities is part of what is called a hidden curriculum: one teaches one thing, but what the student receives may be quite another.

cannot speak the scholarly language of Islam and its revelation, Arabic, then they must at least read translations of the meanings of the revelation and read the tradition produced on its roots: the largely Arabic scholarly tradition.[127]

c. How?

Reception/Kindergarten

Teachers and parents should study *The Beginning of Guidance (Bidayat al-hidayah)* of Imam al-Ghazali or an equivalent text which instructs on the very basics of pious Muslim practice.[128] This includes the importance of intention and sincerity (*niyyah* and *ikhlas*), ritual purification (*taharah*), and the importance and role of the litanies of day and night (adhkar *al-sabah wa-l-masa'*).

Basic beliefs should be taught in the local language through resources designed for extra-curricular teaching.

Shaykh Faraz Rabbani, *The Absolute Essentials of Islam*, (pp. 3–6). This is perhaps the clearest and shortest yet thorough summary of Islamic beliefs in English)

Islam for Young Boys, Pt. 2, English and Urdu, 'Beliefs' (approx. 15 pages)

Islam: Beliefs and Teachings, 'Introduction and Basic Beliefs' (approx. 25 pages)

Reliance of the Traveller, 'True Faith' (pp. 809–14, omitting certain paragraphs). This exposition of the integrals (*arkan*) of iman is drawn from commentary on the Jibril Tradition.

We provide a list of more companies offering such materials below in 'General Resources'.

The meanings of adhkar and the ritual prayer should be distributed between Arabic instruction and religious instruction time. Wudu' and salat should be taught by exemplifying the steps for those who do not know them.

Years 1-6

The LIFE curriculum uses whole, traditional books from Year 1 on.[129] The supplemental school schemes listed in 'General Resources' below are designed

---

127 Do not forget the great traditions in Persian, Ottoman, and—more recently—Urdu languages, in which scholars wrote serious works in the local language. This is just beginning to happen in English.

128 There are several translations of this text, as discussed below.

129 Think of the 'whole books' movement here which sought to avoid the splintering of real books that occurs when they are excerpted, and even worse when turned into textbooks.

for students who are already attending school, which is already more hours of instruction than is healthy. Some educators argue that this important element of context explains why these schemes generally differ from traditional texts. Some may also argue they cater for another contextual element: disadvantaged students or those for whom English is not the first language spoken in their home. Our approach rather is to avoid disadvantage through gaining cultural capital: use the very best English, which does not mean to be archaic. Mind that our minds and bodies can adjust to almost anything, but they are like electricity: they will take the path of least resistance. Second, note that in many parts of England, eloquent speech is valued or even demanded. Elsewhere, this may be perceived as inappropriate, but our speech adorns us in a manner more important than even our clothing. There is a middle way between ostentation and chauvinism, and cowardice in front of chauvinism means one cannot perfect oneself on the model of the Prophet Muhammad ﷺ. Before nationalism, all Arabs were eloquent and many could compose poetry, and the Prophet ﷺ was the most eloquent of them.

THREE LIFE APPROACHES IN SUMMARY

Learn classical texts in Arabic

Here, the student learns through Arabic texts, but unless they comfortably understand spoken Arabic, the text should be explained in English. While this method is often forgotten, we explain that it was the norm in what were classically termed foreign (*a'jami*) contexts (see 'Introduction'). In the West, one still sees this in Urdu or Gujarati Darul Ulums where teachers explain Arabic texts in those languages, and others, including Bangla. The teacher should reinforce the grammar and thinking skills taught in other subjects.

Learn classical texts in translation

Many of the texts we recommend are now available in English. So, if you do not have the time or capacity to teach Arabic texts, to tutor, form a co-op, or attend our courses ahead of time or with your student/child, you do not have to jump all the way from a classical text to modern textbooks. Classical texts make traditional people, modern texts make modern people. Many of these texts are translated in a manner such that they bring across the value of the original in terms of grammar, forms of reasoning (i.e., providing essential definitions and logical arguments, and in terms of the very structure of a classical text (containing a classical introduction and being logically structured to bring about knowledge of a science built around a logical subject).

Learn through units composed of lesson plans

LIFE designed a scheme to cater for the dominant classroom practice, but we are moving away from this form. As the Junior Great Books amply demonstrate, it is possible to use classical and even whole texts for those who are in a classroom. Such schemes in general contain units whose length fits the school year (and its terms or semesters) and whose format is designed to engage thirty students in a classroom. The lessons of these units progress through introducing a learning objective and a starter activity and move through a main topic, activity, and plenary.

For those willing to consider it, we advocate the classical model. The benefits of a lesson-unit model are not exclusive to this model and may be obtained even to a higher degree by use of classical texts and methods. In the classical method, if one is constrained to teach a large number in a classroom, one merely breaks up the text and organises the active interaction both between student and teacher and between the students themselves. One might prepare worksheets to a higher degree than necessary in the classical method. One could also deploy modes of teaching texts derived from the Montessori, Junior Great Books, or Classical Writing series, going through the *progymnasmata* (Gr.: fore-exercises applied to narrative, maxim, and poem) and authored by Weitz, Jaqua, and Vance.

HOW TO TEACH CLASSICAL TEXTS

Whether in English or Arabic, most of the same principles apply. The only difference is that in Arabic, you will need to spend more time in reading, vocabulary acquisition, and sentence diagramming. Children should have experience reading and memorising Quran before this. While children can learn many sciences in English, to properly be a religious scholar (*'alim*) there is no way around being able to understand the Arabic revelation directly.

But being a scholar does not mean one cannot also pursue another career. We have many examples of scholars who are practicing physicians. The trick is to pursue a curriculum from a young age that avoids missed opportunities. Mind that before WWII, many or even most famous scientists such as Michael Faraday completed a classics education before becoming a scientist. This makes all the difference, as technology without wisdom is like a monkey, or Dr. Faustus, opening Pandora's Box. In a word, obtain a general education, then specialise. This can be done naturally with a good curriculum. Do not throw away the one chance for an education.

Not everyone has to become a scholar as an aim, though, and reading classical texts translated by scholars into English gives your child the opportunity to still get a classical education. You may also want to start with English and try after a term, a year, or two years to start to return to the Arabic texts. As noted, we try as far as possible for the English texts in Islamic instruction to parallel the Arabic. However, after a certain number of years, one finds that the needed texts have not yet been translated.

THE SHARED PRINCIPLES ARE
THE ADAB & PEDAGOGY OF READING A TEXT:

ADAB

We already mentioned our recommendation that parents read the Beginning of Guidance *(Bidayat al-hidayah)*, a book that will give you the ability to provide the adab of sacred learning and give you the stories and background needed to explain many of points we make presently. In addition, we make the following recommendations:

- Make the intention to please Allah. Before beginning in Year 1, tell the students the story of the angel that worshipped Allah for 500 years then insisted on entering Heaven through his works of worship. Do not make your intention to enter with your works, but to please Allah through striving to obey and submit to His will and to draw close to Him through worship. This is far superior to the bank model.

- Make one's intention to be a seeker of knowledge and to fulfil the obligation of seeking the individually obligatory *(fard al-ʿayn)* knowledge in particular. Again, read students the hadith and discuss what individually obligatory knowledge means.

- Make the intention to practice what one learns. Parents and teachers should be good examples, practicing what is learnt. The Prophet ﷺ was sent for this reason: to provide a goodly example in front of our eyes of how to embody practice with wisdom, sincerity, and humility.

- During each lesson of Islamic instruction, try to be on ablution. This makes these lessons and the Quran special. Make the intention of being in remembrance *(dhikr)* throughout the whole lesson, even if certain topics are dry or mere memorisation.

- Learn about the author and build a bond with him or her. At the beginning and end of each book, read *al-Fatihah* for the author and intend that the author be in the company of the Prophet Muhammad ﷺ in the hereafter, and intend the same for everyone who conveyed knowledge from the Prophet ﷺ to you in a chain.[130]

- Start every lesson with the basmalah and saying *al-ḥamdu li-Llāh* (the hamdala) and sending benedictions *(tasliyah;* the prayer of peace and blessings

---

[130] This includes from the author to the Prophet ﷺ, but also from the author to the student, including the teacher, even if they be you.

upon the Messenger ﷺ).¹³¹ End every lesson with at least the benediction (*tasliyah*). For the basmalah and saying *al-ḥamdu li-Llāh* (*hamdala*), make the intention of practicing the hadith which commands this.

PEDAGOGY

Classical texts open up classical learning because of their organisation and content. Before stating the steps of classical pedagogy, we enumerate the parts of a classical text that must be referred to throughout learning.

The Parts of a Classical Text

Have it clear in your own mind that classical texts include certain features. Referring to these parts are part and parcel of classical teaching, but also helps to consolidate learning with the student.

A proper introduction must offer a definition of the science at hand, and it must state the benefit of the science. Some beginner texts do not, so you should offer it. For instance, fiqh is a science that studies the actions of religiously responsible Muslims.¹³² The benefit of fiqh is ultimately to please Allah and enter Heaven. However, other benefits are to know Allah's ruling regarding all our actions, to know the adab of drawing close to Allah and entering His presence through purifying the body and its acts, to fulfil the obligation of knowing what is individually obligatory (*fard al-'ayn*), to know how to make our acts of worship valid, and to be able to submit to Allah's will which requires knowing the rulings He has willed for us. Following Allah's rulings allows us to fight our ego in our actions, to follow Allah, and also to be with the Sunnah of His Beloved, the Prophet ﷺ in all our actions and states. We can replace our actions with his Sunnah and our awareness of ourselves with our awareness of and love for him ﷺ.

The science of fiqh consists of propositions stating the ruling of those actions. For instance, the action of eating pork is haram.¹³³ Actions are studied by putting them into propositions that tell us their Sharia ruling. So, action x = ruling y (haram, halal, etc). In many cases, you will also need to define the action or the ruling. For instance, you need to ask, 'What exactly is prayer or usury (*riba*), and what exactly does haram or disliked (*makruh*)

---

131 There are, respectively: *bismi-Llah, al-hamdu li-Llah, allahumma salli 'ala sayyidna muhammad wa-sallim* (and similar phrasings).

132 The importance of this definition will become clear when we turn to the body of the fiqh text below.

133 Notice that pigs are not haram. Why? Because they do not have a ruling. Why? Because they are not an action. It is only actions that are studied in fiqh, and it is only actions that have a Sharia ruling.

or recommended (*mustahabb*) mean?'

The propositions will fall under main topics, and then sub-topics. For instance, the first Shafiʻi text in the curriculum, *al-Risalah al-jamiʻah* (*The Encompassing Epistle*), is divided roughly into an introduction, iman, Islam (fiqh), and purification of the heart and limbs from sins (ihsan/tazkiyah/ tasawwuf). The beginning of the book is divided into a) the basmalah, saying al-ḥamdu li-Llāh (the *hamdala*), and *tasliyah* (defined above in this section), b) the address (*khutba*; or what has been called problematically the 'religious introduction'), and c) the introduction proper.[134] Once you define the science, especially if you name its subject, then you already begin to have a sense of the structure of that science.

Although *al-Risalah al-jamiʻah* (*The Encompassing Epistle*) is divided in the manner noted above, the author begins the work with the pillars of Islam. After this brief section, he picks up with what is titled 'the basis of belief'. One may detect that he goes through the six pillars of belief. One should point this out to students and help them consolidate what the author says around each of the six. Then, one can be sure that one has achieved the lofty task of having learned the basic iman required to enter Heaven. In terms of mentioning the benefit, reflect with students on the amazing impact possible for each of these pillars. They are not merely keys to get a reward out of a treasure chest. They open up a world of meanings for us. For instance, if Allah exists, has power and knowledge, and creates everything, then the world is like a book in which His signs are written. The things in the world become windows in which His names and attributes appear. If prophets exist and something of their miracles also appear on the righteous of their community who follow them closely, then humans are not just upright animals, but are capable of reaching amazing heights and drawing close to Allah and knowing amazing things.

Primary Lesson Format for Classical Texts

1. Preview (*mutalaʻah*)
2. Core lesson (*tadris*)
   a. Topical lesson
   b. Textual lesson
3. Review (*mudhakarah*)

---

[134] We noted that the introduction must include the definition and benefit of the science being taught, and that if a beginner text does not do so, one should add it for the student. Some authors merely allude to these, and the teacher needs to clarify these allusions.

PREVIEW (*MUTALA'AH*)

For mature seekers of knowledge, preview is done independently. In the early years, it is teacher-led at the beginning of each lesson. Here is how you do it. Estimate how much you will read in one lesson. Try to cover full topic or sub-topic.

Write this topic and key vocabulary on the board. If teaching in Arabic, put up the Arabic and its English translation, if you are able.

Ask the students what they know about the topic. If they have background knowledge, bring this out through a brief discussion. Then, briefly state the main idea covered in your own words. Explain the importance of the topic. Engage students with the importance of the act both in terms of its pleasing Allah and in terms of its benefit and wisdom.[135] Consider mentioning differences of opinion on the subject, if this will not confuse students. Ask students to say or write a question they may have about the topic.

Define the terms on the board.

CORE LESSON (*TADRIS*)

Topical Lesson

Draw from these activities:

- Reflection: How is the ruling a sign of one of Allah's attributes, such as wisdom? How would it improve me or my society if it were practiced? What is the best way to implement it?

- Dramatization: This could simply be enacting the act of worship mentioned. It could be to discuss how it could be applied in spite of challenges, or how best to implement it and what impact it could have.

- Interpretive art activity

- Creative writing: If it is difficult to get started with the creative activity, reverse the order and start with textual analysis.[136]

Textual lesson

- Read the text selected for the day's lesson. Point out the vocabulary mentioned in Part 1 of the lesson, as well as any definitions that come in the text itself.

---

[135] When possible, mention hadiths stating the virtue of an action, or mention how it allows us to follow the Prophet's Sunna, on him peace and blessings, or how it improves one's soul or the society around one.

[136] Either way, start with the preview.

DAILY SUBJECTS　　　　　　　　　　　　　　　　　　　　*Religious Instruction*

- Have students practice saying key terms and using them in sentences (especially if teaching in Arabic).

- Analyse sentences (*fakk al-'ibarah*): Traditional sentence analysis consists of bringing to bear the mastery of grammar and morphology on the sentence to bring out their meaning, including clarifying what pronouns refer back to. One surely does not parse every sentence, but when there is a possible obscure meaning, one parses certain words to clarify. For those getting started, it is helpful to take some sentences and parse completely, writing the sentences out on a board or a worksheet.

- What to expect is contextual. For the first text, e.g., *al-Risalah al-jami'ah* for Shafi'is, simply start with identifying the subject and predicate and add elements as they are learned in grammar. One may either use LIFE's parsing method (drawing lines under sentence parts, applied both to Arabic and English) or colour coding, each described below. Also ask the question: 'What exactly does this pronoun refer back to?' Either way, from time to time, write a set of sentences on a board or worksheet and parse the subject and predicate and whatever is possible beyond that. While this may seem challenging in Arabic, sometimes parsing a set of sentences—the teacher modelling this—is the key to the door of confidence and grasping sentences in a foreign language. One may take parts of the introduction. Taking sentences from the beginning of the body would ensure the text is begun with understanding and may facilitate memorising the text. One may also return to parsing when one senses that understanding is slipping. So, check from time to time.

Definition work

Start by giving students definitions which are correct, but as concrete and simple as possible. Show students how this definition includes what one is defining but rules out other things one is not defining. When students are ready, show the role of each part of the definition. Each part makes the definition more and more qualified or restricted. For instance, if I define 'human' as 'rational animal', start with 'animal'. It excludes plants and minerals, but it includes millions of things that are not humans. Then, when I add 'rational', there is only one animal that is rational: human beings, and that is the goal of a definition.

Here is what to expect for the rest of Year 1 and into Year 2 and 3. In Year 1 and 2, students begin to parse through diagrammes, adding more and more complicated sentences. By the end of Year 1, they should be able to parse common English and Arabic sentences using the following tactile or simplified method: LIFE introduces parsing of English and Arabic through scaffolding the two languages on each other and starting with the most simple form and going through the most common ten or so additions. This method of parsing is set out in other subjects (Arabic and English) but suffice to say that one draws a line under and then between the subject and predicate—and object when present—and then adds modifiers slanting down from each of these. Another method known in Montessori education and not requiring rewriting the sentences is to colour-code where red indicates the subject (being *marfu'*) and the indicative mood for verbs (also *marfu'*), green the predicate (also *marfu'*), purple the object and subjective mood (being *mansub*), blue for prepositional and possessive phrases (*majrur*, including *idafah*), and orange for the jussive mood (*majzum*). In fact, the parsing with lines can be combined with colour-coding: the lines themselves may be coloured instead of black.

By the end of Year 2, they should know the rules for parsing a wider variety of sentences. By the end of Year 3, they should have memorised the classical parsing of al-Jurjani's *'Awamil*, and thus be competent in parsing all but rare Arabic sentences.

Once proficient in parsing, it is enough to ensure the grammar does not cloud the understanding of what is being said. It is enough to point out the basic parts of a sentence and to work out precisely what pronouns refer back to.

REVIEW (*MUDHAKARAH*)

Review for mature students is performed with other students.[137] For now, the teacher will need to facilitate this. Also, it should happen after the lesson, but for young students being led by you, review immediately after teaching. Model for them how to go back through the main topics and reproduce the main statements, divisions, and definitions. Work out the divisions on a board in front of the student: what a Muslim is obligated to know is divided into iman, Islam (fiqh), and ihsan (tazkiyah). The pillars of Islam are x, y, and z. The pillars of belief are x, y, and z. Make a flow diagramme (*tashjir*) of these divisions. State the main definitions and the main rulings. Feel free to go back through the text, until the time when the student is confident, and this is unnecessary.

Make time in teaching for this, and by the end, one will develop the mind and know the science of fiqh, for instance. This is a great accomplishment.

---

[137] If there are no other students, the student may repeat the lesson, 'even to the wall', as is sometimes said. In a homeschool, the student may repeat the lesson back to the parent or to a tutor. In a traditional madrasa, students may repeat the lesson to students that are several years younger or older, within reason.

Finding True Happiness: Making Ethics possible in modernity

This text starts in Year 1 with basic habits of orderliness, introduces ethical teachings in Year 2, and then receives a fair degree of concentration of the Islamic instruction curriculum in Years 3 & 4. While this work is absolutely necessary in the modern world to avoid cognitive dissonance and a hidden curriculum, it remains a work in progress. A schematic overview of its contents for Years 1 to 4 is provided at the end of this section. (Note that under all circumstances, the stories from the Eclectic Reader listed in Year 1 of this curriculum should be taught in Year 1 to lay the basis for good and pious habits.)

Here is the set of texts designed both to cover the basics and to be transformative in our context:

YEAR 1

Term 1

Stories of the Prophets (*Qasas al-nabiyyin*) by Abu al-Hasan 'Ali al-Nadwi (as an extension and consolidation of 'Arabic arts'). This text allows gentle development of first steps in Arabic language. Teach this text as we have outlined below in 'Arabic'.

Terms 2 & 3

Comprehensive manuals teaching iman, Islam (fiqh), and ihsan

- Hanafis: *Maraqi al-sa'adat* (tr. as *Ascent to Felicity*, Faraz Khan)[138]
- Shafi'is: *al-Risalah al-jami'ah* (tr. as *The Encompassing Epistle*, Musa Furber) then *al-Maqasid* (tr. as *Al-Maqasid: Imam Nawawi's Manual of Islam*, Nuh Keller)[139]

  Manuals teaching purification, prayer, and some of the other acts of worship

- Malikis: *al-'Ashmawiyyah*[140] (tr. as *Matn al-'Ashmawiyyah*, Abu Zahrah Nkosi)[141]
- Hanbalis: *Akhsar al-mukhtsarat*, Ibn Balban (tr. as Hanbali *Acts of Worship: From Ibn Balban's The Supreme Synopsis*, Shaykh Musa Furber)[142]

---

138 Covers beliefs and the acts of worship.

139 Covers beliefs and the acts of worship.

140 Covers purification, prayer, and fasting. Confident students attempt to learn and memorise the text.

141 https://www.muwatta.com/ebooks/english/matn_al_ashmawiyyah_en.pdf

142 Covers purification and the acts of worship.

YEAR 2

Hadith

- *al-Arbaʿin al-Nawawiyyah*, draw from commentaries, but focus on explaining vocabulary. A benefit of hadith is the holistic way matters of religion are addressed. Use this opportunity to reinforce the three pillars of religion (iman, Islam, and ihsan) through the hadiths.

Fiqh

- Shafiʿis: *Matn al-Ghayah wa-l-taqrib* (tr. as *The Ultimate Conspectus*, Musa Furber)
- Hanafīs: *Maraqi al-saʿadat* (continued from Year 1) or consider *Nur al-idah* (tr. as *Nur al-Idah: The Light of Clarification*, Wesam Charkawi)
- Malikis: *al-Murshid al-muʿin*, Ibn ʿAshir[143]
- Hanbalis: *Bidayat al-ʿabid*[144]

ʿAqīdah

- Select one of the longer texts cited from the resources provided above for ʿaqidah in Reception/KG. Accessible ʿaqidahs are also summarised at the beginning of *al-Maqasid*, *Maraqi al-saʿadat* (*Ascent to Felicity*), and three and one-half pages in the Maliki fiqh text, *al-Risala* of Ibn Zayd.
- Stories from the Quran
- Stories of the righteous and *awliya'*

YEAR 3

Hadith

Choose from:

- *al-Silsilah al-dhahabiyyah* (200 hadiths drawn from *al-Mudawwanah* of Imam Malik)[145]

---

[143] Covers beliefs and worship. As this is a poem, work towards memorisation of the lines that are learned. A number of translations are available, some in part and some in full. See Shaykh Abdullah Hamid Ali's commentary and translation of the creedal section, found at: https://lamppostedu.org/wp- content/uploads/2018/06/Creed_Ibn_Ashir.pdf. An English translation of the complete poem by Asadullah Yate is available from online retailers.

[144] Covers purification and the acts of worship. A number of translations are available online, such as John Starling's (Bidayat al-ʿAbid: Commencement of the Worshipper) and Mohammad Zahid's series (https://www.inkoffaith.com/post/bidayat-al-abid-water).

[145] The first selection does not require further summary. One will find a translation of these

- *Mukhtasar Riyad al-salihin* of al-Nabahani (tr. as *Riyad as-Salihin: The Meadows of the Righteous*, Turath Publications, selections)

Fiqh

- Hanafis: *Nur al-idah* (first half, tr. as *Nur al-Idah: The Light of Clarification*, Wesam Charkawi)
- Shafi'is: *Sharh al-Ghayah wa-l-taqrib* (first half, tr. as *The Accessible Conspectus: A Commentary on Abū Shuja' al-Asfahani's Matn al-Ghayah wa-l-Taqrib*) or read *Safinat al-najah* (tr. as *Ark of Salvation*, Musa Furber)
- Malikis: *al-Murshid al-mu'in*, Ibn 'Ashir (continue with worship from Year 2)

YEAR 4

'Aqīdah

- *al-Jawahir al-kalamiyyah*, (tr. as *The Jewel of the Theologians in Light of the Islamic Creed*, by Hafizurrahman Fatehmahomed, answerstofatawa.com)

Fiqh

- Read the second half of the book started in Year 3. Malikis may attempt to complete the fiqh of the poem *al-Murshid al-mu'in*, with memorisation.

  Overlap with 'Arabic liberal arts'

Sirah (Prophetic Biography)

- *Burdat al-madih*: Recite, memorise, and learn vocabulary (and very basic commentary if one sees fit)[146]

  Overlap with Arabic instruction

Grammar

- *Tasheel al-Nahw*, tr. Aamir Bashir (based on *Hidayat al-nahw* which itself is a summary of *Kafiyat Ibn al-Hajib* and its commentary referred to simply as *Mulla Jami*)[147]

---

hadith in 200 Golden Hadiths from the Messenger of Allah ﷺ by Abdul Malik Mujahid from Darussalam publishers.

146 A commentary and translation is Commentary of the Qaseedah Burdah by Ebrahim Desai, which can be found online.

147 The proper title being *al-Fawa'id al-ḍiya'iyyah*.

Rhetoric

- *First Steps to Understanding Balaghah* by Hashim Muhammad (around 120 pages and taught in English with Arabic examples, particularly from the Quran)

  Overlap with 'English liberal arts'

  Pre-logic is taught in Year 4

YEAR 5

'Aqīdah/*Kalam*

- *Qawa'id al-'aqa'id* by al-Ghazali (tr. as *Al-Ghazali: The Principles of the Creed*, Khalid Willams)

- Imam al-Laqqani, *Jawharat al-tawhid* (with brief commentary)[148] or *Bad' al-amali* (study and memorise)[149]

  Overlap with local-language liberal arts

- *The Fallacy Detective: Thirty-Eight Lessons on How to Recognize Bad Reasoning* by Nathaniel Bluedorn and Hans Bluedorn

- Introduction to logic: Introduce students to the basic terminology of logic (centring around definitions, propositions, and arguments.) Draw examples from the Quran using al-Ghazali's work *al-Qistas al-Mustaqim* which exemplifies the forms of logic deployed in the Quran.

YEAR 6

Sirah

al-Shifa', Qadi 'Iyad (tr. as *Muhammad: Messenger of Allah* ﷺ *Ash-Shifa of Qadi 'Iyad*, Aisha Bewley)[150]

Alternative: *Fiqh al-sirah al-nabawiyyah*, Ramadan al-Buti (tr. as *The Jurisprudence of the Prophetic Biography & Brief History of the Rightly Guided Caliphs*, Nancy Roberts)

Overlap with Arabic Instruction

---

148 Translations of the Jawhara can be found online, including Haroon Hanif's (https://lote.org.uk/wp-content/uploads/2021/11/Jawharat-Al-Tawhid.pdf) and Faraz Rabbani's (https://muslimanswersfiles.wordpress.com/wp-content/uploads/2014/02/jawharatal-tawhid.pdf).

149 Translations of the Bad' can be found online, including that of Abu Hasan (https://ridawipress.org/wp-content/uploads/amali.pdf).

150 Including its literary value; study as much as time permits.

Tazkiyah (options)

- *al-Arbaʿin fi usul al-din*, al-Ghazali (tr. as *The Forty Principles of the Religion*, Nasir Abdussalam), or
- *Kitab al-maʿunah*, ʿAbdallah b. ʿAlawi al-Haddad (tr. as *The Book of Assistance*, Mostafa al-Badawi)

Overlap with local-language liberal arts

- al-Abhari, *Isaghuji*, (tr. by Feryal Salem, tr. by Faraz Khan, and tr. with commentary *Mughni al-tullab* by LIFE)[151]

Cross-Curricular Notes

Note that some sciences such as logic are Islamic sciences in the wider sense of the term.[152] For those learning Arabic, pre-logic (critical thinking skills) and logic are taught in the English liberal arts. For those learning in Arabic, they are taught in the Arabic liberal arts.[153]

d. How for those lacking resources?

For all or most of primary, most parents will be able to teach most subjects from traditional texts. For the special case of tajwid, see the subject: 'Quran'. LIFE agrees with Elizabeth Y. Hanson that even topics like grammar can be taught by parents who are not masters and who do not even know the basics. How? They are adults with fully formed minds and language; so long as they read through the lesson ahead of time and think through it, they should be able to read the lesson and conduct activities (especially where materials are scripted).[154] Parents learn along the way. To aid them, we are producing courses targeting the key skills of each age, both for teaching and tarbiyah. For instance, all primary teaching centres around memorisation and grammar. Secondary teaching centres around logic and disputation.

Ideals of knowledge transmission

It is ideal to have an illuminated and pious scholar teach your children. If you have the means, you should have them sit at the feet of a scholar to produce a well-rounded education and prepare them to succeed in the

---

151 Forthcoming from Zaytuna College, insha'allah.

152 See the second, theoretical part of the 'Introduction'.

153 We and others are in the process of carefully translating the classical sciences, ideally in dual-language editions. That way a) students can apply skills in their local language and b) if they struggle with Arabic, they use the English. If they learn the English, they can see immediately how it relates to the scholarly terms in Arabic.

154 Some of the early LIFE resources in the pipeline such as Arabic are scripted. As such, parents only have to be able to read Arabic fluently to get going.

world. Scholars and the elite have always tutored their children. So, neither schooling nor even homeschooling are ideals. But your means determine what is obligatory on you. This is a principle of fiqh. And parents should undergo the learning journey with their children: if you do not, you are telling them implicitly that this is not important enough to get you off the sofa or phone. Finally, people say that teacher training should proceed curriculum development. One of the founding fathers of modern curriculum development, Lawrence Stenhouse, effectively agreed with Elizabeth Hanson: teachers may learn by training and preparing for and teaching curriculum. The more beneficial that curriculum is, the bigger change is affected in education through this process.

LIFE also offers a consultation process, available through our website. We offer limited support for putting parents in contact with scholars and encourage communities to share such contacts organically.

If unable through these avenues to teach classical texts or to progress in Arabic, then look at the schemes listed below under 'General Resources'. Still try to purchase and peruse the classical texts and compare them with how materials are presented in the part-time schemes. Draw from the classical texts where possible. Attend our courses where possible. Consider encouraging those in your community to start a co-op to share the responsibility of teaching and organising. This will also raise awareness of true education. There is a high number of Darul Ulum graduates in the North of England and Azhari graduates around the world who are qualified to teach. When you make an intention and an effort, Allah will provide the avenues.

General Resources

A unit-based curriculum is available from LIFE but remains a schematic curriculum requiring a confident teacher to work out the units which are described in brief terms of lesson objectives and activities. This scheme attempts to teach children to integrate the teaching of essentials with their origins in the words of the Prophet Muhammad ﷺ, including how and under what circumstances he himself taught or instructed. The scheme recommends use of eloquent translations of the Quran and hadith to inspire and deploys language similar to that found in texts written by scholars (or recommends translating this text itself as it is). The aim of this scheme is to inspire practice and the beginnings of true scholarly knowledge. It is sounder to inspire Islamic knowledge and practice than to cater directly to building Islamic identity. Were this scheme to be piloted and edited, subsequent teachers would not necessarily need to be fluent in Arabic to instruct, but only to give the texts and learning skills contained their due of attention.

Schemes designed for part-time education include

See the following resources: Safar Academy, Tasheel (a carefully graded system written by Darul Ulum graduates based on traditional texts), Muhammad Imdad Hussain Pirzada and al-Karam Publications, Iqra (Chicago), MET (Muslim Educational Trust), An Nasihah (for 6–14 year olds, including a tajwid book that improves on *al-Qaʻidah al-nuraniyyah*), Islamia College (from Cape Town, directed by Ali Adam Nadwi), and the beautifully designed series of Osman Nuri Topbas (Erkam Publications). Safar Academy and Islamia have both made efforts to include inspiring stories and a form of spirituality such as coming to know Allah through His Most Beautiful Names. Muhammad Imdad Hussain Pirzada of Nottingham has been publishing resources with al-Karam Publications for decades and has books teaching basic beliefs (such as *Islam for Young Boys, Part Two, English and Urdu*).

General Resources and schemes on Islam

Shaykh Faraz Rabbani, *The Absolute Essentials of Islam*, White Thread Press, Santa Barbara, California, 2005.

Muhammad Imdad Hussain Pirzada, *Islam for Young Boys, Pt. 2, English and Urdu*, Al-Karam Publications, Retford, 2004.

Ghulam Sarwar, *Islam: Beliefs and Teachings*, Muslim Educational Trust, London, 1989.

Shaykh Nuh Keller, *Reliance of the Traveler*, Amana Publications, Beltsville, Maryland, 1997. (*The Reliance* includes ʻaqidah and other aspects of religion in its appendices.)

Abu Hamid al-Ghazali, *Bidayat al-hidayah*. (tr. Montgomery Watt)

Abu Hamid al-Ghazali, *Imam al-Ghazali's Deliverance from error and the beginning of guidance*, Islamic Book Trust, Kuala Lumpur [Malaysia], 2005. (tr. Mashhad al-ʻAllāf)

Abu Hamid al-Ghazali, *The Beginning of Guidance,* 2nd revised edition, White Thread Press, London, 2010. (tr. Mashhad al-ʻAllaf)

Abu Hamid al-Ghazali, *Book of Piety and Islamic Manners: The Beginning of Guidance*, Light Publishing, 2020. (no translator listed)

Safar Academy (https://safarpublications.org/all-safar-publications/)

Tasheel (https://www.albalaghbooks.com/education-schools/tasheel-series/ and https://kitaabun.com)

Iqra (https://www.iqra.org/School-Curriculum_c_221.html)

MET (Muslim Educational Trust, https://www.metpdx.org/)

An Nasihah (for 6-14 year olds, https://an-nasihah.com/)

Islamia College (Ali Adam Nadwi, Cape Town, South Africa)

Shaykh Osman Nuri Topbas (Erkam Publications, Istanbul)

Stories of the Prophets

Abu al-Hasan 'Ali al-Nadwi, *Stories of the Prophets*, Academy of Islamic Research and Publications, Lucknow, India, 2012. (*Qasas al-nabiyyin*)

Sirah and characteristics of the Prophet Muhammad

Al-Imam al-Busiri (with commentary of Shaykh al-Azhar Ibrahim al-Bajuri), *Burdat al-madih*, Maktabat al-Safa, Cairo, [no date.]

This summary commentary focusses on vocabulary. (Available for free download at: https://archive.org/details/KwakebDorriaBosiry)

'Iyad ibn Musa (tr Aisha Abdurrahman Bewley), *Muhammad messenger of Allah : Ash-Shifa of Qadi 'Iyad*, Madinah Press, Granada, Spain, 2011.

Muhammad Ramadan al-Buti (tr Nancy Roberts), The jurisprudence of the Prophetic biography & a brief history of rightly guided caliphs (Fiqh *al-sirah al-nabawiyyah*), Dar al-Fikr, Damascus, 2008.

Hadith

Yahya al-Nawawi, *al-Arba'in al-nawawiyyah*

Imam Malik (tr Abdul Malik Mujahid), 200 hadiths drawn from *al-Mudawwanah* of Imam Malik.

Riyad as-Salihin: The Meadows of The Righteous - Abridged And Annotated (by Shaykh Yusuf al-Nabahani), Turath Publishing, 2018.

'Aqidah and *Kalam*

Tahir al-Jaza'iri (tr. Hafizurrahman Fatehmahomed), *al-Jawahir al-kalamiyyah*, (tr. as The Jewel of the Theologians in Light of the Islamic Creed), Answers to Fatawa, London, 2016. (Available for free download at: https://archive.org/details/AlJawahirAlKalamiyyahFiIdahAlAqidahhAlIslamiyyah.)

Abu Hamid al-Ghazali (tr. Khalid Williams), *Kitab qawa'id al-'aqa'id, The principles of the creed: Book 2 of the Ihya' 'ulum al-din, the revival of the religious sciences*, Fons Vitae, Louisville, Kentucky, 2016.

Ibrahim al-Laqqani, *Jawharat al-tawhid*. Translations available include:

https://muslimanswersfiles.wordpress.com/wp-content/uploads/2014/02/jawharatal-tawhid.pdf and based on the lessons of Shaykh Faraz Rabbani, and https://lote.org.uk/wp-content/uploads/2021/11/Jawharat-Al-Tawhid.pdf

Imam 'Ali al-Ushi (Abu Hasan), *Bad' al-amali*, Ridawi Press, [no place of publication mentioned], 2017. (Available for free download from: https://ridawipress.org/wp-content/uploads/amali.pdf.)

FIQH

For the Shafi'i school:

Ahmad ibn Zayn al-Habashi (tr. Shaykh Musa Furber), *al-Risalah al-jami'ah: The Encompassing Epistle*, Islamosaic, [Place of publication not identified], 2015.

Imam al-Nawawi (tr. Shaykh Nuh Keller), *Al-Maqasid: Imam Nawawi's Manual of Islam*, Islamic Texts Society, Cambridge, 1996.

Ahmad ibn Shuja' al-Isfahani (tr. by Shaykh Musa Furber), *The Ultimate Conspectus: Matn al-Ghayah wa-l-taqrib*, Islamosaic, [Place of publication not identified], 2012.

For the Hanafi school:

Maraqi al-sa'adat (tr. as *Ascent to Felicity*, Faraz Khan)

Hasan ibn 'Ammar Shurunbulali (tr. and commentary by Wesam Charkawi), *Nur al-idah* (tr. as *Nur al-Idah: The Light of Clarification*,) al-Rashad Books, [Place of publication not identified], 2010.

For the Maliki school:

Translations of several Maliki texts are available here for free download: https://www.muwatta.com/category/publications/

Shaykh 'Abd al-Bari al-'Ashmawiy, *al-'Ashmawiyyah* (tr. as *Matn al-'Ashmawiyyah* by Abu Zahrah Nkosi), (published for free distribution at the following link: https://www.muwatta.com/new-translation-matn-al-ashmawiyyah/), 2014.

Ibn 'Ashir (tr. Asadullah Yate), *Al-Murshid al-Mu'een: the Concise guide to the basics of the deen*, Diwan Press Ltd., Bradford, UK, 2018.

Ibn 'Ashir, *al-Murshid al-Mu'in: A supplemental Text For Users of the Guiding Helper*, The Guiding Helper Foundation, 2005. (Available for free download at: https://archive.org/details/al-murshid-al-muin-arabic-english-2005.)

Ibn 'Ashir (translation of the creedal part, with commentary by Shaykh

Abdullah Hamid Ali), *al-Murshid al-mu'in*: https://lamppostedu.org/wp-content/uploads/2018/06/Creed_Ibn_Ashir.pdf.

For the Hanbali school:

Muhammad Ibn Balban (tr. Shaykh Musa Furber), *Akhsar al-mukhtsarat*, (tr. as Hanbali *Acts of Worship: From Ibn Balban's The Supreme Synopsis*), Islamosaic, [place of publication not identified], 2016.

Abd Al-Rahman Abd Allah Al-Bali (tr. John Newton Starling III), *Bidayat al-'Abid: Commencement of the Worshiper*, Two Palms Press, [place of publication not identified], 2017. (Available for free download at: https://archive.org/details/bidayat-al-abid-commencement-of-the-worshiper-1/mode/2up.)

Tazkiyah

Abu Hamid al-Ghazali (Nasir Abdussalam), *The Forty Principles of the Religion: An Adapted summary of Ihya' 'Ulum ad-Din*, Turath Publishing, London, 2016. (*al-Arba'in fi usul al-din*)

'Abdallah b. 'Alawi al-Haddad (tr. Mostafa al-Badawi), *The Book of Assistance*, Fons Vitae, Louisville, Kentucky, 2003. (*Kitab al-Ma'unah*.)

Finding True Happiness: Taught across Years 2-4 with selected stories beginning in Year 1

This LIFE resource referred to above is an essential ingredient for reasons mentioned above, herein, and in the introduction of this book.

YEAR 1

Teach:

- how to use a space properly (taking off coat and putting in proper place)
- how to wait in line properly
- how to share (including intentionally bringing more than you need for yourself; the food of two suffices for three)

McGuffy's Second Eclectic Reader recommended in English liberal arts has many stories that are perfect for teaching basic habits. These stories include:

- Lesson 54: 'Grandfather's Story' (two fighting over a fish both lose it)
- Lesson 55: 'God is Great and Good' (God rains blessings on us so we should be thankful)

- Lesson 56: 'A Good Old Man' (happiness in serving: old man served children while father was away travelling, and they served him after their father returned)[155]
- 'Lesson 57: 'The Greedy Girl'
- Lesson 58: 'A Place for Everything' (teachers' orderliness and self-dependency, not selfishness)[156]
- Lesson 59: 'My Mother' (the pains and joys of motherhood which incline one to gratefulness)
- Lesson 60–1: 'The Broken Window' (conscience to repair what one has damaged rather than running away out of fear)
- Lesson 62: 'Frank and the Hourglass' (like the hourglass which always works, we can accomplish much learning if we are consistent)

Finding True Happiness: Taught across years 2-4

Finding True Happiness is a resource which straddles what may be termed ethics, tazkiyah (purification of the soul), and hadith (prophetic traditions). Tazkiyah is arguably the ultimate aim of Islam, but for it to work, the context and the particular challenges it raises must be met. This is the task of this invaluable resource. It marshals hadiths and other materials to ensure tazkiyah will 'work' today, particularly addressing the end times culture which offers a very strong and clear alternative view of happiness and what is deserving of respect. Another way of saying this is the traditional notion of matters known to remove belief (*sawalib al-iman*) and perhaps preventatives (*mawaniʿ*) which might undermine the intended effect of scripture, tazkiyah literature, and the methods of tazkiyah. In the modern context, we identify these as false notions of respect and happiness which direct the soul in the wrong direction. It works to perform the removal (or divestment, *takhliyah*) of wrong ideas that are part and parcel of modernity so that youth born in our time have as much hope as possible for tazkiyah being effective and for being able to transform their souls. Some of what we may consider present corruption is alluded to in descriptions of the end times, and as such, we investigate this topic in that light for teachers but also inform students of the basics of this so that they can protect themselves.

The following background needed for educators is presented here before the materials for students:

---

[155] Many modern children spend all their time entertaining themselves on screens or being served while they study, but not serving others or being part of the home and community.

[156] Prophetic injunction to take care of one's own matters, even if you drop something from your camel to go down and get it yourself.

- Tazkiyah is the goal of religion, but requires certain habits being in place from youth.

- Taqwa may be defined as 'obeying commands to do actions and to leave what is prohibited'.

In pre-modern times when more people practiced, many people fasted and prayed, but only those with taqwa left off sins which could be done in private, etc. Further, to leave vices and sins of the heart, one must acquire character virtues and closeness to Allah, so tazkiyah entails not just two matters, but at least three: obeying commands, leaving sins and vices, and obtaining character virtues that are the higher branches of belief (as obedience and leaving sin are also branches of belief). Having a basis in these habits leads to an accord between them and obligations of the Sharia. This itself leads to their insight becoming strong and their resolve being embodied in these habitual practices (not being at odds). This being at odds we may term in modern parlance 'cognitive dissonance', which may or may not be removable through efforts in late youth and adulthood.

Good education and tarbiyah in a 'virtuous polis' (*madina*, or state) involves habituation of youth into good practices that organise the non-rational parts of the soul. This enables them when their intellect dawns on them (at age of discernment and the maturity) to respond well to what reason comes to understand.

The Jibril hadith refers to financial and social (i.e., cultural) corruption which are signs of the end times that bring specific challenges, religious and otherwise. 'Competing in tall buildings', may indicate taking material development as an end, undermining ethics and religion, but also having economic consequences.

'The slave-mother giving birth to her mistress', may indicate a youth culture in which children from as early as 3rd or 4th grade detach from parents and become comfortable only with their age group. This undermines inter-generational transfer and bonds. It contravenes the basic prophetic injunction: 'Whoever does not show mercy to the young and honour the old is not of us'. When in a society where youth of various ages play together, there is more wisdom, less cruelty, and a healthier framework and ethos exist such that habits are more or less guided towards what is healthy. Purely horizontal social networks are often shallow and even boring, as they have nothing to offer each other, and cruel: they look to each other for so much, have so little, and are fickle and immature.

This culture equates to a 'bad polis': one inducting us into false images inevitably misshaping our soul to some extent through false notions of:

   a. *satisfaction* through a happy life purchasing objects in advertisements

b. *freedom* lies in 'choosing' these objects

c. *honour* is due to the very wealthy or those owning fashionable material goods (car, house, clothes, designer goods, etc.)

d. *learning* is a means to a pay package and consists in following celebrity politicians.

> "I do not fear polytheism for you,
> but love of the dunya (i.e., this world)."
>
> - The Prophet ﷺ -

The Prophet upon him peace said, 'Be in the dunya as though you are passing by on a path.' This is the proper attitude to the dunya: do not act like you are staying here. Do not act like this world is the only world on your travel plans. Do not act as though this world is better than the afterlife. Regarding the latter, the Quran tells us otherwise, and Sunnah tells us otherwise in *great* detail. When you love the dunya, your heart connects to it; you want more of it and take it as an end, not a means to purify yourself.

YEAR 2

Being between 6 and 8, Year 2 students achieve or draw close to discernment (*tamyiz*, around seven years of age) and the time they should be taught to pray. The dawning of intellect is an appropriate time to discuss who they are.

> { *And when I proportioned him and breathed into him of My spirit...* }
>
> - Quran 15:29, as created by Allah -

The soul is what is ordered and prohibited by Allah and is what receives reward or requital in the afterlife. The body and soul affect each other. The body affects the soul through repeating acts that lead to immaterial habits in the soul. The hand is thus an instrument to perfect or corrupt the heart.

The body inclines to physical pleasures so must be aligned with good goals and form habits to find felicity/happiness. True satisfaction occurs through doing what is right and accustoming the body to align itself with this. Then, the body does not trouble one, and a more real satisfaction arises. This allows one to think of the soul as a sculpture one is perfecting and polishing in order to give it back to Allah after perfecting it.[157]

Activity

Think of acts that one or others do in the wider culture that do not bring true satisfaction: eating, purchasing things online (which releases endorphins but fades and is often not matched by what is felt with the item itself), social-media relationships as opposed to meeting with real friends and family. Mention that there is a whole industry trying to devise ways of pulling us the online world and out of the real world and real relationships.

YEAR 3

Peer pressure: friends drag us into doing things and being a certain way (*al-sahib sahib*).[158] How to avoid peer pressure through noticing it, and negotiating it and knowing what we are about, and what we want from this world.

Video games: attempt to convey how they affect us (They present a world more perfect than our world and they move quickly, so they activate our attention more than people and the world, and capture your imagination till it does not want to be free to imagine greater things yet. So, they effectively addict us through being more effective at activating our attention and motivation than the real world. The effect: we leave off the purpose of this life.

{ *The one who perfects (the soul) has truly succeeded.* }

- Quran 91:9, as created by Allah -

The children we know are on the conveyer belt to get there through corporate culture: toys not made from their locale and culture but made to be purchased and replace local culture. How to counter this? Pointed reminders from Sunnah, pious scholars, and wisdom tradition. For instance:

d. Ask ourselves, what do we really need? Allowing someone to convince us of other needs makes us a slave to more than one god. Why sell yourself into slavery simply because you were tricked by attractive packaging and marketing appeal?

e. Remember the advice of the wise regarding knowledge versus wealth, how one brings true happiness, gathering the other brings distress

---

157 The teacher can explain this as a metaphor of polishing a mirror as well.

158 Pronounced '*al-Sahib sahib*'.

and one ends up serving it (and therefore serving more than one master, which is impossible).[159]

YEAR 4

Topics above are symptoms, but what are they symptoms of?

What kind of society do we live in? Capitalist, which is not a neutral space, but rather constructs us as consumers and manufactures our assent to politics. It takes a Christian and theological notion of happiness in the afterlife, removes the notion of the need for purification and salvation (through removing vice and obtaining virtue and contemplating, etc.) and replaces it with economic salvation and progress and the populist idea of egalitarianism: righting previous financial wrongs and bringing more financial equality. Basically, modern life centres around wealth and technological development. These are important religiously, but only as a means, not an end. And there must be room for human development,

---

159 There are many good sources in such writers as al-Raghib al-Isfahani and Ibn Abi al-Dunya and Imam al-Ghazali. Two sayings may be referred to here:

a. Imam 'Ali ibn Abi Talib's wise counsel to Kumayl ibn Ziyad, of which the following is only an interpretive selection: (for original Arabic, see: https://www.alukah.net/sharia/0/74676)

   Knowledge is better than wealth:
   1. Knowledge protects you, whereas you have to protect wealth.
   2. Wealth decreases with spending, whereas knowledge increases with it.
   3. Knowledge is a faith to be followed. It helps you practice obedience to your lord in your lifetime, and leaves a beautiful legacy of remembrance after your death; whereas the benefits of wealth cease with its ceasing.
   4. And knowledge rules, while wealth is ruled over.
   5. Those who hoard wealth are dead even as they live, whereas the learned remain as long as the world remains – their persons may be lost, but their teachings live on in people's hearts.

b. Proverbs 24: "1 Be not envious of evil men, nor desire to be with them; 2 For their minds plot oppression and devise violence, and their lips talk of causing trouble and vexation. 3 Through skilful and godly Wisdom is a house (a life, a home, a family) built, and by understanding it is established [on a sound and good foundation], 4 And by knowledge shall its chambers [of every area] be filled with all precious and pleasant riches. 5 A wise man is strong and [a]is better than a strong man, and a man of knowledge increases and strengthens his power; 6 For by wise counsel you can wage your war, and in an abundance of counsellors there is victory and safety. 7 Wisdom is too high for a [b]fool; he opens not his mouth in the gate [where the city's rulers sit in judgment]. 12 If you [profess ignorance and] say, Behold, we did not know this, does not He Who weighs and ponders the heart perceive and consider it? And He Who guards your life, does not He know it? And shall not He render to [you and] every man according to his works? 13 My son, eat honey, because it is good, and the drippings of the honeycomb are sweet to your taste. 14 So shall you know skilful and godly Wisdom to be thus to your life; if you find it, then shall there be a future and a reward, and your hope and expectation shall not be cut off."

not merely economic development. The people we know are consumed in consuming and developing a CV pointing to a certain pay package.

No notion of enough: wider culture says you should always seek increase.

4.1.2 QURAN

a. What?

To teach Quran, do the following:

- Strike a compromise between traditional scholars who recommend starting with memorisation, and those who recommend waiting until enough grammar and poetry are learned to appreciate the beauty of the Quranic language. (See, 'Proper Learning and Memorising of the Quran' in the second half of the 'Introduction'.)
- Start before 1st Grade (Reception/Kindergarten) by learning 'phonics' and correct recitation of the Quran (tajwid).
- From 1st Grade till 12th Grade, devote approximately one hour per day to the Quran.

Other subjects taught outside the Quran hour will complement it and help bring about natural understanding. These include Arabic grammar and poetry and the Islamic sciences that are themselves drawn from the Noble Quran. LIFE's teaching of Arabic includes a careful scheme (Arabic 101) which explains how to teach Quranic high-frequency vocabulary.

- In 1st Grade, memorize through oral transmission. Also, during the 1st Grade, complete a *khatam/nazirah* of Juz'/Separa 30.
- In 2nd Grade, students may begin to memorise from written text of the Quran, but one's tajwid must be checked regularly and carefully.

In the daily Quran hour, educators should spend a fair percentage of time devoted to the meanings of the Noble Quran. When the students learn more and more vocabulary and grammar starting in Years 1 & 2, this should include translating the meanings and parsing the verses they are memorising. (While translation seems intimidating, this has been a traditional practice for beginners even in places outside the Arab world for centuries. The Quran is full of simple phrases that can be translated without deep exegesis and many resources exist which translate the Quran into English and other languages one word at a time.) Use this time to reflect on the message. If you do address a passage which is complicated or unclear, use this as an opportunity to contact scholars to ensure how to interpret or apply certain verses.

- Each student should memorise as much as possible for their individual capacity, though we do recommend certain juz's/separas for each year.

We also describe an optional focus in the early years, which decreases, but does not remove, all other learning. While ideally one may become an 'alim and a hafiz, it is more likely that one must choose between the two. And it is a reality that some who set out to be a hafiz will 'drop out'. It may be better to devote time to memorisation each day and be content with what *rizq* is given by Allah.

b. Why?

If you read English academic writings in education departments, you will hear a stated purpose of Quranic study that is almost entirely wrong. Commonly there, it is said that teaching the Quran while children are young is a means to seal their Islamic faith or identity to ensure they do not leave Islam when they mature. I only mention this type of well-intended ignorance because it is so common. The Quran is revelation: God revealing Himself. To increase our capacity to receive the realities of God and live with a profound presence of God in our life, that revelation teaches mankind the practical and theoretical truths needed to embody and maintain those truths. This procedure is one with the path towards reaching felicity, as an individual, and as a society—the latter needing a law and a social vision. To be of benefit, these realities must be conveyed in an appealing way, and the Quran is the most beautiful of speech and is inimitable. (To appreciate this inimitability requires some knowledge of Arabic but also pre-Islamic Arabic poetry to see how it is superiour to the best human speech.) To remain Divine, human hands and desires must be kept from these realities, so they must be transmitted with conclusive certainty to us today. Thank God, the Quran has been mass transmitted both orally and in writing, it being the only untainted revelation left to mankind.[160]

We should not begrudge any efforts to learn the language of Allah's

---

160 These realities must also be understood and explained; one principle of Quranic sciences is that the Quran is often explained by the Quran itself, but in other chapters that treat the same topic. A second principle stated in the Quran itself is that the Prophet Muhammad, on him peace, was sent to explain the Quran to mankind. In the recorded prophetic tradition, there are two examples of this. In many traditions, the Prophet Muhammad, upon him peace, speaks of the meaning of a certain verse. Secondly, while not necessarily referring to a give Quranic verse, the Prophet upon him peace often describes or performs actions that give crucial details needed to understand the revelation or how to practice it. For instance, the traditions that relate to the obligatory prayer could fill a full volume even without commentary. The Islamic sciences described in the previous subject listed in the present curriculum take these meanings and turn them into truths and actions to harness their potential for contributing immediately towards producing the perfect human. For they lay out the truths and acts that perfect the theoretical and practical intellects if one embodies them. (See, 'Introduction II.6. Traditional Guidance on How to Memorize, Learn, and Embody the Quran.')

Book, *din*, and Islam's culture. Past generations could afford for only madrasa students and other scholars (in fields like astronomy and medicine) to learn Arabic because there was so much Islamic culture in their language. In Persian, for instance, Saʻdi's *Gulistan* is an Islamic education in one book and was used for centuries to teach native speakers of Persian. *The Mathnawi* of Rumi is referred to (respectfully of course) as the Persian Quran. It contains a commentary on a large share of Quranic verses, woven into stories that relate it to the life and community of pre-modern Muslims. Those who do not learn Arabic and are limited to English—or even native speakers of Arabic who cannot read classical Arabic—are in a very different situation. The Islamic writings in English are increasing, but there is a qualitative difference. Works in Persian (and also Urdu, Turkish, Kurdish, Malay, etc.) were often written by scholars and masters of Arabic and local-language literature. This means the text they wrote contains a quality which makes it suitable for pedagogical purposes. When most contemporary people think of a pedagogical text, what comes to mind is making things simple for the uninitiated. But this (and texts with word counts and silly topics like aliens) are all part of a dumbing down process which claims to aim at literacy but actually destroys it. The only solution is to maintain and uphold that it is possible for a text to be both accessible and of value in terms of literary style and content. A few such books exist in English, and they have been listed in the local language section. Note also, in Persian the same tools of learning taught in Arabic were alive and taught. So, one could learn Arab (or more technically Arabic) logic in Persian. This is a possibility in English, but one cannot educate a child on the hopes of a possibility. (LIFE is working to translate Arabic texts in such a way that they maintain their original quality in English and can be used as a living science once translated. The key to this is glossaries with very carefully translated terms.)

One cannot be a sharia scholar without being able to understand the Quran in Arabic and having access to various texts that help one understand and interpret it. Without Arabic, none of us can go further than the translations available in the languages we speak. These translations and the other sources helping one to understand the Quran are increasing in languages such as English, but they are still very far from what one has access to in Arabic. Without Arabic, you rely on someone else: what they explain (when it is correct!) you may grasp and what they remain silent on becomes your limitation. In such a state, one cannot go back to the revelation itself.

Memorisation should not be neglected. As a rule of thumb, a scholar should aim to memorize at least five juz's/separas. One way to do this is to memorise Juz' 'Amma (30), and the suras *al-Baqara* and *Al 'Imran*.

For the pious, the Quran opens up to the closeness to Allah in a way that human descriptions and kalam proofs do not. For knowers of Allah, there is an infinite and eternal beauty that opens up to God's word, and there are subtle indications that offer guidance regarding matters in which there is difference of opinion, and there are subtle etiquettes conveyed. The Quran in Arabic is irreplaceable not simply because it is sacred. Rather, it is sacred because for those who are not ignorant of what the Quran is, it truly is irreplaceable. As in all matters, we should not worship for good deeds, treating the *din* like a cash register or bank. Some Companions only had one sura by memory. It is better to love the Quran and memorise a little than to resent it and memorise it all. The way of the Companions was to learn how to implement what was memorised, and only then proceed to memorise more.

c. How?

You will need the Quran (i.e., a mushaf) with the script you and your child find easiest to read, one of the books of tajwid described below, and some access, at least, to a teacher qualified in tajwid unless you are one yourself. Ensure that the Arabic and Quran lessons connect with each other by alerting students to what they have learnt in the Arabic lesson: vocabulary, parts of speech (noun, verb, and particle), and parts of the sentence (subject, predicate, adverb, etc.). Arabic lessons give you these basic tools and should be applied in the Quran lesson. Islamic Studies lessons often involve Quranic verses, and again the educator needs to make the links clear in the children's minds.

YEARLY GOALS FOR QURAN

Preschool curriculum

See 'Preschool Curriculum' for advice on memorising short suras orally, and starting to become acquainted with the letters, and learning to speak very simple vocabular from the Quran (as found in classical Arabic).

Reception/Kindergarten

Complete *al-Qa'idah al-nuraniyyah* (or *al-Qa'idah al-baghdadiyyah* or the Malaysian equivalent) to recite fluently. Continue oral memorisation of the shortest suras (which can begin as soon as children start to speak). Engage with physical activities to learn the letters such as writing in sand and making letters from clay. See 'Reception/Kindergarten Curriculum' which also takes forward the oral learning of Arabic vocabulary.

Year 1

Memorisation: Memorise through the teacher repeating the verse, bit by bit, until memorised. Once students begin reading from the Quran, they may consolidate what they have heard through looking in their own mushaf.

Tajwid: Complete a *khatam* (reading) of the final juz'/*separa*, i.e., Juz' 'Amma (30), with correct tajwid.

Understanding and translation: Begin to take parts of the Quran and apply to *al-Fatihah* or suras from Juz'/*Separa 'Amma*. For instance, from morphology, identify active and passive participles in *al-Fatihah* (e.g., *mālik* and *maghḍūb*). In grammar, identify subject, predicate, past and present tense verbs. Learn Quranic vocabulary and begin to translate two- to three-word sentences which relate directly to Arabic lessons.

Year 2

Memorisation: Learn to memorize independently from the Holy Quran.

Tajwid: While learning from the Quran, frequently check for proper tajwid with a teacher.

Understanding and translation: Carry on learning Arabic vocabulary and performing parsing (*i'rab*) and translation of more complex sentences and eventually whole *ayat*.

Optional: Some students may opt out of all but basic English, maths, and natural science and aim to memorise the Quran by the age of 10 or even earlier if they are motivated to do so.

Years 3-6

Carry on with daily memorisation, vocabulary for what is memorised, and parsing and translation for understanding.

Year 4

Apply their learning of rhetoric to the Quran. Even the outward aspect of the Quran is not understood by grammar and vocabulary alone. Rather, Allah tells us that the Quran was revealed in Arabic. In line with this, it deploys the richest of rhetoric, some of which is absolutely necessary to understand even the basic meaning of a given verse. Al-Ghazali lists these aspect of the outward meaning as omitting words, using words with multiple meanings (homonyms), revealing information on a given topic gradually in different suras, and altering word order for rhetorical effect.

Year 5-6

Those who complete the memorisation of the Quran begin *Alfiyyat Ibn Malik* in grammar and continue working towards understanding of the Quran as above.

Year 6

Tajwid: Aim to complete a reading (with correct tajwid, *qira'ah*) of the Quran before graduation from elementary school.

Memorise key suras (for those not completing memorisation of the Quran, these being spread out over the elementary years). All should memorize Juz' *'Amma* as it is needed for prayer. Thereafter, one may either move on to Juz' 29 and 28 or memorize *al-Baqarah*. Juz' 29 and 28 are relatively easy as the verses and chapters are short. Memorisation of *al-Baqarah* is facilitated by the fact that it contains many stories. There are numerous hadiths about the *barakah* and benefits of learning *al-Baqarah*, and it contains the source text for many practical rulings.

Our Recommendation for Yearly Memorisation

Year	Memorisation	Phonics/ Recitation (tajwid)	Interaction with meanings
Preschool: Age 3+[1]	**Test for readiness to memorise orally, then work flexibly, memorising from *al-Fatihah* towards *al-Fajr* orally.**	Simply ensure that children hear correct pronunciation. Correct clear mistakes when they recite by repeating the correct pronunciation to them (or playing a recording of a trusted authority such as al-Husari).	1. Introduce children orally to very basic Quranic vocabulary, especially from *Juz' 'Amma*. 2. Teach basic Quranic meanings, applying them in the home and or learning space.
Reception (4-5)/KG (5-6)	Complete preschool curriculum (to *al-Fajr*), then carry on in *Juz' 'Amma*.	1. Phonics (tajwid): Complete 1 introductory book (*al-Qaʿidah al-nuraniyyah* or *al-baghdadiyyah*, or Malaysian book: Iqra). 2. Learn letters through physical interaction (involving clay, sand, fingerpaints, etc.).	—
Year 1 (5-7)	1. Continue to memorise orally (*talqin*) until confident in reading from Quran. 2. Memorize at own pace (complete *Juz' 'Amma* and some students may memorize *Juz' Tabarak*).	Complete *khatam/nazira* of *Juz' 'Amma*.	Apply Arabic lesson to simple verses (grammar and morphology). Learn Quranic vocabulary and begin to translate.

Table 3.1

DAILY SUBJECTS   Quran

Year	Memorisation	Phonics/Recitation (tajwid)	Interaction with meanings
Year 2 (6–8)	Memorize at own pace (complete Juz' *Tabarak* and some students may work towards Juz' *Qad Sami'a*).	Ensure students have successfully transitioned to memorising correctly from the Quran.	Apply Arabic lesson to simple verses (grammar and morphology). Learn Quranic vocabulary and begin to translate from Quran. 3. Begin simple grammatical analysis (*i'rab*, parsing.)
Year 3 (7–9)	Memorize at own pace (complete Juz' *Qad Sami'a* and some students may begin Juz' 1 & 2).	Beginning at *al-Baqarah*, begin working at own pace towards completing a *khatam/nazirah* of full Quran by end of primary.	1. Learn Quranic vocabulary and translate from Quran. 2. Grammatical analysis (*i'rab*, parsing.)
Year 4 (8–10)	Memorize at own pace (recommended: complete Juz' 1 & 2 and some students may begin Juz' 3 & 4).	Beginning at *al-Baqarah*, continue working at own pace towards completing a *khatam/nazirah* of full Quran by end of primary.	1. Learn Quranic vocabulary and translate from the Quran. 2. Grammatical analysis (*i'rab*, parsing.)
Year 5 (9–11)	Memorize at own pace (recommended: complete Juz' 3 & 4 and some students may begin Juz' 5 & 6).		1. Learn Quranic vocabulary and translate from the Quran. 2. Grammatical analysis (*i'rab*, parsing.)
Year 6 (10–12)	Memorize at own pace (recommended: complete Juz' 5 & 6 and some students may begin Juz' 7 & 8).	Complete a *khatam/nazirha* of Quran before year's end (and completing primary.)	1. Learn Quranic vocabulary and translate from the Quran. 2. Grammatical analysis (*i'rab*, parsing.)

Table 3.1 (*contd.*)

More detail on the teaching of reading/phonics/tajwid are found at the end of the Arabic curriculum under: 'Detailed Advice for Learning Arabic to Read & Write in Arabic script'. There we explain which resources to use, how to use them, and how much to progress through them each day.

The teaching of Arabic reading and writing necessarily overlap between Arabic language-learning and Quran. We also mention how to capitalise on the natural overlap between art and Arabic calligraphy.

4.1.3 THE TRIVIUM & ENGLISH LITERATURE

a. What?

The liberal arts are in fact a *set* of subjects; the closest single name for this set is 'English', though many countries still refer to them as 'the language arts' or simply 'language arts'. There is much confusion over what the term liberal arts means. The best way to understand it is as a part of a liberal education: an education designed to free the human being through perfecting the faculties that make us human. These faculties are the practical intellect—which is perfected and purified through character virtue—and the theoretical intellect. The practical intellect is perfected through the practical sciences—and applying them in one's own character. The theoretical faculty is perfected through the theoretical sciences, though it is a precondition to first perfect one's character to purify the soul. But the two sets of sciences, practical and theoretical, cannot be approached directly, but rather require a set of tools or instruments. The sciences teaching these tools are the liberal arts, though one may also term them the instrumental sciences.

The liberal arts are termed arts because they each enable us to perform an act, either an act of speech or thought. (As speech and thought are what distinguish humans from animals, what could be more important.) Traditionally, the liberal arts are the trivium, which consists of grammar (in a wide sense including poetry and other matters), logic, and rhetoric, and the quadrivium. The quadrivium comprises the four branches of mathematics, and in a full liberal arts education, mathematics is one of the theoretical sciences. So, we are concerned primarily with the *trivium* when we say liberal arts (as maths is taught elsewhere in a full classification of the sciences).

It is important to recognise that the liberal arts are only part of a 'liberal education'. The trivium is what Dorothy Sayers termed the 'lost tools of learning' (more on this below). But what is the value of tools if one never learns to use them or does not learn the right material on which to use them. Tools (or instrumental sciences) are a *means* allowing one to move on to the ends which are the theoretical and practical sciences. But, as we noted, they are very important in themselves.

There are different models of classical education, and we have searched extensively for the best model. Classical curricula often focus on literature, but we aim to perfect the human and prepare them for life and society, and we think literature is important, but the focus should be on perfecting character and learning the true sciences. While a Roman (and to a degree Greek) curricula aimed to produce orators who could lead society, we think that a person with perfected character is able to lead others as they have learned to lead themselves. And if they know the truth about the theoretical and practical sciences, then they will be natural leaders and be able to produce a better world than the pragmatist and utilitarian world we have, whose pragmatism slides more easily into corruption and greed than it does into virtue and justice.

So, what is at stake is a matter of models. The most unfortunate model is what is simply termed 'English'. Mere modern communicative language does not give one the tools to write and think. It is well-known that once modern education removed classical learning, it struggled to teach writing. At best, students read examples of good writing and learn things like how to structure an essay as an argument or in a persuasive form. Most of the details added to this or the exercises used to develop students are either truisms or have no known impact on their ability to write. On the other hand, using classical techniques, such as the progymnasmata, produced the likes of Shakespeare and John Milton, two authors who literally shaped what it means when we say excellent English. Further, 'English' does not set one up to seek knowledge—even if it might help your business in the short-term.

The madrasa once encompassed the full gamut of sciences, the sharia and rational sciences, and a few madrasas on this model still exist. This model includes these liberal arts under the term 'instrumental sciences'. A full list of these liberal arts and instrumental sciences must include not only grammar, but before it the science of script and what are termed 'vocabulary', but which was termed 'lexicon' in the past, and included the study of word etymology. To be thorough, one should include how to decode script, and this is what is now termed phonics and resembles the basic and practical part of what is termed 'tajwid' (Quranic recitation without the science of rules).

The compound aspect of language is the links between the building blocks. The basic rules of the compounds (called syntax) are taught in grammar. Rhetoric studies the secondary meanings which take off where grammar leaves off, and which often include rules for achieving eloquence. Logic is not taught till students are ready, which usually occurs around the age of 11. However, the top year of the elementary stage will include pre-logic.

So, to summarise, a sound, holistic education in the instrumental sciences is the best way to start education and LIFE sets this down in the following sciences:

Script

- Penmanship/calligraphy: the basics in English being to properly learn a script for separate and joined up (cursive) writing,

Speech (singular elements)

- Vocabulary
- Etymology/word roots

Speech (compound elements)

- Grammar (including the parts of speech and sentence diagramming)
- Rhetoric (pre-rhetoric termed 'classical composition' at this stage)

Speech (successful examples in a specific genres)

- Literature

Thought

- Logic (mostly pre-logic and thinking skills, though in Year 5 informal logic begins, and in Year 6 logic proper begins)

b. Why?

Taking our aim as human perfection on the prophetic model, we said that perfection is through the practical and theoretical sciences, and that there is no approaching them except through the liberal arts. Also as noted, certain of the liberal arts are developmentally prior to others, or have a specific time at which abstract abilities appear, for instance. Thus, for the liberal arts, we are dealt a clear hand:

From birth to three we preserve the fitrah and speak and read to children copiously. [Key to preserving fitrah is get into nature and get off screens and feed them halal and let them see religion practiced in a wise and spiritual fashion.]

In preschool (from three to the start of Rec/KG), introduce them to letters and pre-phonics.

In Rec/KG, start phonics, and, if ready, start them reading in board books or a classical reading scheme (see Rec/KG).

YEAR 1-3

Progress with them in reading/literature, increase vocabulary and spelling, but focus on grammatical knowledge of the unit of meaning: the sentence. Additionally, emphasise the learning of a script not only to know how to write, but as a matter of grounding oneself in the body and leading on the good drawing (and literally being a form of drawing).

YEAR 4-6

Continue to progress in reading, vocabulary, and spelling (and indeed grammar), but shift the focus to pre-rhetoric via the progymnasmata. Introduce pre-logic, then in Year 5 study informal logic (fallacies), and in Year 6 introduce the first short text in logic. (If students struggle, continue pre-logic in Year 6, and start one's first logic text in Year 7 at the outset of secondary school.)

This liberal arts curriculum is designed to encourage focused growth of the human soul. It works with the other strands such that synergy occurs. While studying these liberal arts, one studies their like in Arabic. And, while these liberal arts are accompanied with a focus in practical sciences suitable to this age (orderly habits, pre-virtues, and then virtues), one is fully aware that one is being raised in less than a virtuous polis *(madinah)*.

Accidental but crucial considerations for application

While we have just outlined how to perfect the soul with little consideration of our cultural context, there are a number of challenges that we may term cultural, linguistic, and practical. Several of these topics were addressed in the (theoretical) second half of the introduction, so here we will adhere to statement of principles in bullet-point form:

- Classical and liberal learning simultaneously may accomplish the language-learning achieved by communicative local language programmes, but the opposite is not true.
- Liberal arts learning gives cultural capital, which is still valued from what is left by the true elite of the contemporary world.
- Liberal learning prepares children to enter a workforce that is strikingly dynamic, such that it is often said that a. university does not prepare students for the world of work and b. in the United States the average person changes career, not job, a startling seven times. The only way to prepare for this is general learning.
- At the same time, general learning is the only way to counter hyper-specialisation. Specialisation has reached the point where one learns

more and more about less and less, until finally one knows absolutely everything about absolutely nothing!

- The LIFE model is universal, and thus we refer to the liberal arts as 'local language', but this first edition of LIFE's practical curriculum manual simply takes English as its local language.

- In many countries, the local language is not a classical language, let alone a classical Islamic language. While English is not a classical language, it is yet relatively gifted in that many Greek, Latin, and French—and now Arabic and Persian—classics have been translated into English. Until the last few decades, it was considered important to learn classical Latin (and sometimes Greek) even though to an extent classics existed in English, and the liberal arts were to a certain degree *applied* in English.

The status of contemporary English is an extensive topic, and we must direct the reader to the more extensive discussion in the introduction and limit ourselves here to outlining certain crucial points:

- Very few English classics such as Chaucer demonstrate use of the trivium. Most writings, even those considered classics, do not.

- There are groups of thinkers such as the Inklings (notably Tolkien, Owen Barfield, and C. S. Lewis) that attempted to revitalise English, but English remains a language resistant to synthesis. As such, we must accept it to a degree as it is.

- Its vocabulary is depleted from the meanings of its classical roots. Attempts to alleviate this must be done with utmost care to avoid awkwardness.[161]

- Application of many of the trivium arts results inevitably in awkward deviations of what is considered 'normal' English.

- It is secular and exact but in a limited, empirical sense befitting positive sciences.

- It shows a very depleted range of etiquette (compared to Arabic or Japanese) and, for instance, romantic expressions (compared to languages such as French).

Our challenge then is the need to learn classical thought and expression and have access to the rich Islamic culture's etiquette and symbolic universe of discourse incorporating elements from Islamic religion, piety, and mysticism. Then we must be able to convey some element of this into

---

[161] John Ruskin has written a most insightful essay on this topic, terming the study of classical roots and meanings as the most central requirement for true reading of texts. The question remains whether this would apply to modern texts written without such sensitivity.

English, or else hope that English-speaking communities develop a culture of reading and writing in the best Arabic or other classical Islamic language. As the latter seems unlikely, or at least is out of our control, instead we propose to learn two languages well: English and Arabic.

In these circumstances, several strategies or aims impose themselves. In English, one may find materials—written by Muslims or otherwise—which convey truth and virtue. One may find a small amount of material written by Muslims or accurate translations of their works which have at least an acceptable literary quality, and some of these convey truth and virtue. Another section of English materials offers valuable critique of modernity such as is not found in either classical or contemporary Muslim writings. This is highly valuable to divest oneself of falsities, an example being the literary classic *1984* of George Orwell. A final consideration is that there are genres of literature which deserve to be mastered even by those not specialising in literature, which in some cases cannot be exemplified through materials alerting to truth, falsity, or virtue. They nonetheless must in some cases be studied. (Even the nursery rhyme is such an example, there being very few nursery rhymes that are beneficial aside from their undeniable linguistic benefit.)

To aid the learning of a classical language, Arabic and English reinforce and scaffold off of each other.

In some cases, it will prove redundant to learn a science such as logic in both languages, but then the vocabulary and practice surely cannot be expected to transfer from one to the other. In such cases, we recommend that one learn the science in both languages. However, if it comes to be that facing page translations of these classical sciences are translated successfully into English and a given student struggles to learn both, then they may learn merely in the local language/English, though at the price of never being a 'scholar' so long as not learning the language of revelation (Arabic).

Avoid over-canonizing literature and merely lock-stepping through 'classics', especially merely literary classics (as opposed to classics in a given science or for impact on character).

Ensure that, in addition to being literary and edifying, literature is inspiring and age-appropriate, but still fulfils the goals of education.

Note importantly that it is possible to produce a liberal arts curriculum with no 'children's literature'. One easy way to overcome any challenges in this is to include in Years 1-6 a fair number of classics simplified for children. This way, the ideas are still 'great': we do not need to reify childhood—speaking to children as we imagine children should be spoken to. Even *Aesop's Fables* which may be taught in Year 1, 2, or 3 include some child-like characters and were used at certain points of history to entertain children, but they were not solely for children, but were a means of conveying right and wrong, and sometimes political messages.

It is theoretically possible to produce a curriculum entirely written by Muslims. It is also entirely possible to produce a reading list of works it seems every adult should read, whether these be books on health, political corruption, or where these meet such as big pharma. Be careful not to err in Islamic pietistic reasoning by trying to pour too much of an Islamic worldview into the literature selected. There is a balance to be obtained between good literature and teaching (or preaching). So, Muslim scholars in the past have been correct to note that certain secularised literature dominated certain Arab countries (notably Egypt), especially for children. But their response was to draw from materials exemplifying the Islamic spirit, but in a way that differs from how the Dars-i Nizami curriculum encouraged the mastery of Persian. It did so with five of the best works in the language, period. Now, were one to argue that the works of Mulla Jami were both superlative in terms of literature and piety, then including them would not be 'pietistic'. Otherwise, it may very well be.

c. How?

RESOURCES AND PEDAGOGY

Rec/KG

See the separate section, 'Reception/Kindergarten', where all subjects are explained in one location for ease and integration. (We advocate certain pre-phonics matters such as read-aloud from 3, and Modern Curriculum Press Phonics, Level K which is actually suitable for 3–4-year-olds. In Rec/KG, we advise four strands: read-aloud and comprehension, script, phonics, and oral memorisation of poetry.)

Years 1-6

Four major tracks should be followed:

- Script: Penmanship (handwriting)/Copying/Dictation/Writing
- Singular elements (words): Phonics/Spelling, word roots and vocab
- Compound elements: Grammar
- Literature: Guided Reading of Literature

These elements need to be woven to come together and come alive for the student. So, the skills themselves need to be known, but they should be integrated. (Though the two elements are distinct, their concurrence is not impossible: it is possible that a child can memorise a grammar rule and simultaneously be able to get over a hurdle of understanding by applying that rule to ensure the text is properly understood.)

'Literature and reading lists' are presented in full immediately after Year 6 so that it may be seen at a glance and used as seen fit. You will find McGuffy's Reader listed in literature, Years 1-6, but this is just one option. You may also draw on a literature list you find and teach it using classical methods. McGuffy's Reader is effectively a guided reading scheme, so while other readers such as Junior Great Books also increase in difficulty through the months and years, McGuffy's is more carefully designed to achieve this. The price you pay for this is that McGuffy's Books Primer, 1, 2, and 3, are written by the author rather than being drawn from known authors. Books 4 and 5 draw from a mix of authors, but only a few are what would clearly be termed classics. There is a great jump in difficulty to Book 6.

Other classical reading schemes include that of Harriette Taylor Treadwell which also begins with a primer. One may use Junior Great Books which begins from Kindergarten with a read-aloud resource.

Other integrated classical schemes exist such as *Classical Writing* of Kathy Weitz, but this is designed to begin from 3rd or 4th grade. This is very similar to James Selby's *Classical Composition* series from Memoria Press which we recommend for pre-rhetoric in Years 4-6, except that Weitz provides her own texts, so the scheme is relatively complete, rather than teaching only one strand (i.e., rhetoric).

YEAR 1   65-80 MINS

Script to writing: 15-20 mins

Select a script (involving child if you wish) and learn individual letters (or carry on from where they reached in Reception). Then do copy work from famous sayings (considering using *The Content of Character Copybook* (Kinza Press), a collection of prophetic hadiths published as a copy book for this purpose). Ensure that correct letter formation is established before moving from copy work to composition, as composition requires focus on content. Begin writing letters to family and friends, then introduce other simple genres such as stories. Once moving from script to writing, make the time longer, but less frequent, e.g., three times per week.

Words: 10 mins

Spelling Workout A (which moves from phonics towards spelling and vocabulary). Confident students may complete this in the first half of year, and move on to *Spelling Workout B*.

Grammar: 10-5 mins

Learn the canonical parts of speech (using relevant parts of *Simply Grammar* (clearly labelled as such in the 'Contents') or *First Language Lessons*) and apply to real sentences. The importance of this aspect of grammar is exaggerated, so do not linger on it. Merely teach their definitions with examples, exercise till student is competent with a given part of a sentence in isolation, and after you have gone through more than one, test whether they are competent to identify parts of the sentence when mixed in real sentences.

When this is accomplished, learn the parts of the sentence. The sentence is the unit of meaning, and hence grammar actually makes more sense when working on sentences and their parts than on the attributes of individual words (such as whether they are singular, feminine, etc.). So, work quickly through the lessons from *Simply Grammar* that relate to the parts of the sentence. Then, move on to sentence diagramming using *Rex Barks*. [This should parallel as much as possible the elements of grammar learned in Arabic.]

Literature: 30 min

Eclectic Reader, Book 2 (read, discuss, and apply language skills). The exercises listed here are performed orally until the children are able to write. They may be divided into three broad types:

a. Analysis

While teaching parts of speech, take sentences from readings and label them with a single letter or colour code them.

When teaching the parts of the sentence, do the same, using the colour-coding laid out elsewhere in this manual, and the mode of simplified sentence diagramming.

Later on, one may add the identification of:

- sentence types
- capital letters (as well as explaining them)
- end punctuation (' ')
- direct and indirect quotes
- nouns and identifying whether they are persons, places, things, or ideas, and common or proper
- pronouns
- antecedents
- verbs and identifying the action they refer to

- verb phrases
- subjects, and
- predicates.

b. Imitation

- Change sentence or quotation types.
- Reposition quoted and explanatory words.
- Vary utterances.
- Make up new quotes for characters.
- Produce synonyms for nouns, modifiers, and verbs.

c. Summarise

Invert the order (tell the story backwards).

Retell it in past, present, or future tense, or first, second, or third person.

Poem memorisation [fit into timetable]

YEAR 2   65-80 MINS

Writing:

Writing should introduce new, age-appropriate, classical genres, from progymnasmata, beginning with *Aesop's Fables* (see 'General Resources' below). Introduce copy-work (leading on to dictation when ready) of classical writings, including from *Aesop's Fables*.

Words:

Spelling Workout B, and carry on to *C* when ready.

Grammar:

Begin *Harvey's Grammar* and applying grammar to more complex sentences from literature (Charles Dickens)

Literature:

Eclectic Reader, Book 3 (read, discuss, and apply language skills)

Poem memorisation [fit into timetable]

(Optional)

Primary Logic: Grades 2-4, by Judy Leimback, Dandy Lion Publications, 1986

Bond Starter Papers in Verbal Reasoning: 6-7 Years

YEAR 3 — 75-80 MINS

The same as above, but advancing to:

Dictation in classical writings

Spelling Workout C

Eclectic Reader, Book 4

Gwynne's English Grammar

Advanced English Grammar, Kitridge and Farley

Optional:

Primary Logic: Grades 2-4 (cont.)

Bond 11+: Verbal Reasoning Assessment Papers: 7-8 Years

Problem Solving: Logic-Based Activities (Grade 3; Mead)

YEAR 4 — 75-80 MINS

The same as above, but advancing to:

Spelling Workout D

Eclectic Reader, Book 5

Rhetoric: *Classical Composition I: Fable*, James Selby [From Year 4 on, writing skills now addressed via exercises in the literature and rhetoric strands.]

Primary Logic: Grades 2-4 (cont.)

YEAR 5 — 75-80 MINS

The same as above, but advancing to:

Spelling Workout E

Eclectic Reader, Book 6

Rhetoric: *Classical Composition II: Narrative Stage*, James Selby

Fallacy Detective: Thirty-Eight Lessons on How to Recognize Bad Reasoning, Hans and Nathaniel Bluedorn

Introduction to logic (introducing terms from *al-Isaghuji* and examples through the Quran). [To identify logical concepts, Imam Abu Hamid al-Ghazali.]

Logic, Rhetoric, and Legal Reasoning in the Quran: God's arguments, Rosalind Ward Gwynne. [To identify and discuss logical terms, use one of the translations of the *al-Isaghuji* listed in 'General Resources'.]

YEAR 6   75-80 MINS

The same as above, but advancing to:

Spelling Workout F

Junior Great Books Series 6

Rhetoric:

Classical Composition III: Chreia/Maxim Stage, James Selby

Al-Isaghuji, al-Abhari (use the tr. by Dr. Feryal Salim or Sh. Faraz Khan, and tr. with commentary *Mughni al-Tullab* by LIFE, to be published with Zaytuna College)

COMPUTERS & LEARNING LAYOUT/PROTO-TYPESETTING

Rather than say yes or no to computers, LIFE's approach is to strive for good use of technology. If your student is champing at the bit to use a computer, insist that they learn the basics of textual design and paper layout first. Before children begin typing on a computer, they should know some basic design principles about the core elements before they begin. These include (in order of part to whole):

- fonts
- word kerning
- line layout
- paper layout (especially paper proportion, margins and how to design where elements should lay on a page)

Typing uses a font, and fonts came from typefaces. They were originally drawn by letterers. Students should know at least a few basics about fonts, typefaces, and scripts. Before beginning to use a word processor which opens up with a set of layout defaults, children should know the basics of layout and practice designing first single sheets (or folios). (Within living memory, teachers would tell students to leave 1/2-inch border on their paper, requiring them in some cases to have a ruler or straightedge to hand and to put it in themselves.) Then they should learn a few basic conventions of booklets and books. They should learn some of the basics of book conventions which are rich and as old as the woods and a veritable gold mine of human thought and rich beauty. Thereafter, children are free to do whatever they want on a word processor.

Timetabling to Learn Layout Before Using Computers

YEAR 1 & 2 (WHEN STUDENTS BEGIN WRITING)

Teach line spacing, margins, and the other basics of layout. Make good decisions about these matters and whether to skip lines for a given piece of writing. Teach proportions without mathematics. The way to do this is to introduce them to geometric shapes in nature and the idea of proportion through Wooden Books such as *Sacred Geometry*. Extract some of the shapes in Bringhurst's *The Elements of Typographic Style* which he shows to be behind certain paper sizes and shapes. Let the student themselves experiment with folding and cutting paper into squares, hexagons, and, most importantly, rectangles formed based on various proportions and taken from within various other shapes. For instance, a rectangle taken from the centre of a hexagon will have a particular ratio between the height and width. Learn the various qualities of these ratios. For instance, the pentagon is never found in inanimate beings such as minerals, but always in the living such as roses, forget-me-nots, sea urchins and starfish. This will give them a softer quality. Bringhurst summarises the four ratios used in art and nature and how to apply them to shaping the page (his apt term for page layout).

Practice using these principles to present written work, but also in natural science to present, label, and comment on one's nature drawings.

YEAR 3 & 4

Apply these matters, especially when studying sacred texts such as *al-Burdah* and the character and characteristics (*shama'il*) of the Prophet Muhammad ﷺ, or even to make art from excerpts of the Quran or certain of Allah's Divine Names.

Of course, they also need to know the conventions of paper size and how the harmonic ratios developed over the last few hundred years. The standard A0 paper conventions we have originated in Germany, and they have timeless principles of beauty woven into them. However, the ratio presented there is only one ratio, and students need to know the other typical ones and what the quality is so they may match them with their purpose. If the students learn what is taught in other parts of the LIFE curriculum, they should grow in familiarity with the language of proportion and beauty in years 3-5. If a student hungers for the computer, they could be taught the basics of proportion and layout through a pictorial introduction to the ratios and their qualities. This can be done without any mathematics and can be an eye-opening entrance into the world of sacred beauty for the student. Seeing how artists and typesetters have used these proportions for centuries to make beautiful things can make them fall in love with proper design. If that happens, the rest of their education will flow and become natural and full of gusto and pleasure, as it should be.

LITERATURE & READING LISTS

Principles guiding the selection of literature are as follows:

- Language is a means for thought and communication, and while one may ignore the dictates of good communication in limited circumstances, in the long-term a person or community must grasp or master the literary forms of communication or genres.

- Genres have become less important in the age of science and social media, but every healthy culture must have them. Genres are only exemplified in literature, though some works of philosophy and science are also works of literature. This was truer in the past.

- As our aim is perfection of the human being, we aim for a balance of linguistic skills (some only being exemplified in genres), theoretical perfection through knowledge of the 'sciences', practical moral perfection, knowledge of Islamic culture, and knowledge of modernity and one's local culture. While sciences, reasoned and revealed, are taught in separate curriculum areas, one must be able to express them well in the local language, and there are aspects of Islamic cultural literacy best taught through wider reading (even in matters such as pre-Islamic prophets and their history, or the travels of Ibn Battuta as such literature also reveals realities that no longer exist in so-called Muslim countries).

The following lists include books that may be used as an alternative to the core literature resource listed for literature. In that case, it may whichever reading scheme one is using.

Alternative literature schemes (to McGuffy):

Harriette Taylor Treadwell, like McGuffy's Eclectic Readers, is formed of a primer and six progressively difficult readers. More so than McGuffy, it draws on existing literature and merely orders it in graded steps. McGuffy generally writes his own stories and poems (though often reworking existing material) up to Book 3. Book 4 is mostly drawn from other writers, but not what would be considered classical literature until one reaches Books 5 & 6.

Note that were one to use the Classical Writing series of Weitz, et al., this series includes its own literature texts. The same goes for the Junior Great Books (which some may consider expensive, if purchasing the teacher's manual). One may explore the literary schemes of CAP (Classical Academic Press), which have received must use in the last few years.

We recommend that the moral stories from McGuffy's Eclectic Reader Book 2 be used in all circumstances as a foundation for our resource *Finding Felicity* which extends to the end of Year 4. Eclectic Reader 2 has numerous stories that begin with good habits and advance gradually to pre-virtues and even piety through practical and convincing narratives without which students would have gaps and holes not filled by fables and only filled many years later by a scholar specialising in tazkiyah or hadith.

YEAR 1

(In addition to Eclectic Reader 2 or at least the effective morals therein)

~ Gatty, *Parables from Nature*, part one of three. If one struggles with the Victorian English, the parables have been somewhat simplified by Leslie Laurio.
~ Leila Azzam, *Lives of the Prophets*, Hud Hud Books, Cambridge, 1995.
~ James Rumford, *Traveling Man: The Journey of Ibn Battuta*, Houghton Mifflin, Boston, 2001.
~ Julia Donaldson, *The Snail and the Whale*, Macmillan Children's Books, London, 2019. (narrated in poetry and available in good Arabic translation as *al-Hut wa al-Halazun*)
~ Noura Durkee, *The Animals of Paradise*, Hood Hood Books, London, 1996.
~ Mobin-Uddin, *The Best Eid Ever*, Boyds Mills Press, Honesdale, Pa., 2007.
~ Noura Durkee, *Yunus and the Whale*, Tahrike Tarsile Quran Inc., Elmhurst, New York, 1999.
~ Elma Ruth Harder *Yusuf and His Brothers*
~ Idris Shah, *The Farmer's Wife*, Hoopoe Books, a division of The Institute for the Study of Human Knowledge, San Jose, CA, 2022.
~ Idris Shah, *The Lion Who Saw Himself in the Water*, Hoopoe Books, a division of The Institute for the Study of Human Knowledge, San Jose, CA, 2022.
~ Dr. Suess, *The Lorax*
~ Marcus Pfister, *The Rainbow Fish*
~ *Thomas the Tank Engine* (by original author)

YEAR 2

- Mrs Alfred Gatty, *Parables from Nature*, Dancing Unicorn Books, S.I., 2023, part two of three.
- *The Aesop for Children*, with pictures by Milo Winter [teach using the progymnasmata methods for teaching fable]
- James Baldwin, *Fifty Famous Stories Retold* (This collection includes stories from the lives of numerous historical figures from the ancient Greeks to late-modern history.)
- John Ruskin, *King of the Golden River*
- Marguerite De Angeli, *The Door in the Wall*, Yearling, New York, 1990.
- Arthur Scott Bailey, *The Tale of Jolly Robin*, Forgotten Books, [S.l.], 2022.
- Arthur Scott Bailey, *The Tale of Solomon Owl*, Forgotten Books, [S.l.], 2022.
- Arthur Scott Bailey, *The Tale of Reddy Woodpecker*, Forgotten Books, [S.l.], 2022.
- Timothy Winter, *Montmorency's Book of Rhymes*, Kinza Press, San Ramon, California, 2013.
- Denys Johnson-Davies, *Aladdin and the Lamp*, Hoopoe Books, Cairo, 1999.
- Denys Johnson-Davies, *Maaroof the Cobbler*,
- *Tales from Syria*, Denys Johnson-Davies, Dar el-Shorouk, Cairo, 2003 (also: Sunflower Books).
- *The Alleyways of Cairo*, Johnson-Davies, Dar el-Shorouk, Cairo, 2005 (also: Sunflower Books).
- Optional:
- Laura Ingalls Wilder books, including *Little House on the Prairie*
- Dick King Smith, *The Stray*
- Frances Hodgson Burnett, *Sara Crewe*

YEAR 3

- Rumi (tr. A. J. Arberry), *Tales from the Masnavi* (This collection of 100 stories may be spread over years 3-6.)
- *Tales of Juha: Classic Arab Folk Humor*, ed. Salma Khadra Jayyusi (Interlink Books)
- Geraldine McCaughrean (retold by), John Bunyan's *A Pilgrim's Progress*
- Joanna Spyri, *Heidi*
- Kenneth Graham, *The Wind in the Willows*
- George MacDonald, *The Princess and the Goblin*
- -Diane Stanley, *Saladin: Noble Prince of Islam*, HarperCollins Publishers, New York, 2002.
- *Hood Hood Heroes of the East Series*:
- *Rumi: Poet and Sage*

~ *Saladin*
~ *Razia: Warrior Queen of India*
~ *Mehmet: The Conqueror*
~ *Ibn Sina: (Avicenna) Prince of Physicians*
~ *Cheng Ho: (Mao Sambao) Admiral of the East*
~ The poetry of Christina Rossetti and Walter De La Mare
~ (Optional)
~ Michelle Szobody, *Beowulf: Grendel the Ghastly*
~ Gwen Gross, *Knights of the Round Table*, Stepping Stone series, Random House, New York, 1985.
~ Howard Pyle, *The Merry Adventures of Robin Hood*
~ *Boxcar Children*
~ *Stuart Little*

YEAR 4

~ Charles and Mary Lamb, *Tales from Shakespeare*, Kibworth Books, Leicester, England, 1999.
~ Edith Nesbit, *Beautiful Stories from Shakespeare*
~ Sterling Publisher's Classic Starts:
~ Chris Sasaki (adapted by), *The Adventures of Sherlock Holmes*, Sterling Children's Books, New York, 2005.
~ T. H. White, *The Sword in the Stone*
~ Denys Johnson-Davies, *Stories of the Caliphs: The Early rulers of Islam*, Bloomsbury Qatar Foundation Publishing, 2010.
~ *Folk Tales from the Northern Sudan*, Abdulla El-Tayib (New Life Printing Press)
~ *The Man Who Never Laughed*
~ *Abu Kir and Abu Sir*
~ Abdul Wahid Hamid, *Companions of the Prophet: 1, 2 & 3*, MELS, London, 1985. (This series could be spread over 2 or even 3 years.)
~ Mehded Maryam Sinclair, *When Wings Expand*

YEAR 5

~ J. R. R. Tolkien, *The Hobbit*, Ballantine Books, New York, 2012.
~ Denys Johnson-Davies (tr.), *The Island of Animals*, Quartet, London, 1994 (and University of Texas Press, Austin.)
~ Ibn Tufayl (tr. Lenn Goodman), *Hayy ibn Yaqzan: A Philosophical Tale*, The University of Chicago Press, Chicago, 2009.
~ *Robinson Crusoe*, Daniel DeFoe, Bucknell University Press, Lewisburg, 2020. (Compare to Hayy Ibn Yaqzan which it borrowed from. You may read various sizes of abridgements, reflecting on why modern publishers generally remove religious discussions from the book.)

- C. S. Lewis, *The Screwtape Letters*, Collins, London, 2012. (Note: There are several study packs visible on the internet which have been prepared for this book.)
- *Hoodhood Treasures of the East: Shah Jehan and the Story of the Taj Mahal*
- Rosanne Parry, *Heart of a Shepherd*, Random House Children's Books, New York, 2009. (A boy adopts early manhood with sense of godfearingness, interesting family discussions as family includes Catholic, Quaker, and a father serving in the Iraq war.)
- *Joha and the Three Merchants*
- *The Magical Gourd*
- *Khalid and Aida*
- *The Bearded Man*
- George MacDonald, *The Princess and Curdie*, Oxford University Press, Oxford, 1990. (For a study of MacDonald's mode of writing, see, C. N. Manlove, *George Macdonald's Children's Fantasies and the Divine Imagination*, The Lutterworth Press, Cambridge, United Kingdom, 2020.)
- Madeleine L'Engle, *A Wrinkle in Time*

YEAR 6

- George Orwell, *Animal Farm*, Macmillan, London, 1985.
- Ibn Kathir (tr. Gemeiah, ed. Mischler), *Stories of the Prophets*, Islamic Book Service, New Delhi, 2004. (These stories carry a great deal of clearly conveyed information. The English is relatively classical.)
- Abdulla El-Tayib, *Changing Customs of the Sudan*, The Trust for Printing and Distributing the Works of Abdulla ElTayib, New Life Printing Press, 2nd edn, 2017. (Part of the *Finding Felicity* resource packet.)
- Biographies: Enoch (Idris, from *Stories of the Prophets*, Ibn Kathir), Pythagoras, Homer, Plato, Aristotle
- Harold Lamb, *Cyrus the Great*, Doubleday, Garden City, New York, 1960.
- Reza Nazari, *Cyrus the Great: The Inspiring Story of a Genius*, Effortless Math Education, 2024. (Cyrus the Great is said to be '2nd Messiah' in Old Testament and some Muslim scholars claim he is the real figure behind the title 'Dhul-Qarnayn'.)
- Harold Lamb, *Tamerlane: The Earth Shaker*, Garden City Publishing Company, Garden City, New York, 1928. Lamb is surprisingly respectful in an age it was common to speak of the 'white man's burden', venerating his characters. He speaks of saints and sayyids, and sends salutations on the Prophet Muhammad when mentioning him, saying, '...(upon whom and on his posterity be the peace)'.

General Resources

https://dandylionbooks.com/

Classics retold by storyteller Jim Weiss: for a long list of titles, see www.greathall.com (and https://www.jimweiss.com/.)

American Home-School Publishing catalogue (see the literature and history sections)

Greenleaf Press catalogue (see the literature and history sections)

Mughni al-Tullab, tr. Mustafa Styer, Zaytuna College Publications (forthcoming)

4.1.4 ARABIC LIBERAL ARTS & LITERATURE

a. What?

LIFE offers two options for its Arabic curriculum: the High Road and the Low Road. We recommend the 'high road', but we are also happy to guide you through the 'low' road. The main difference between the high road and the low road is whether you continue to learn core subjects *in* Arabic. The high road empowers students to learn Arabic and learn *in* Arabic, while the low road focuses on bringing the students' proficiency of the Arabic language so that they may understand Arabic texts later, as their minds mature. Students on the high road, like the low road, start by learning the basics of Arabic, then learn several of your lessons *in* Arabic. This includes learning classical grammar and morphology, and even rhetoric *in* Arabic. By *in* Arabic, we do not necessarily mean that discussion and explaining are 'in' Arabic. Though it is largely forgotten, Islamic learning outside Arabic-speaking countries has *always* used the local language to explain the Arabic text. (Think of Persian, Ottoman, Kurdish, Swahili, and now Urdu centres of learning where for centuries scholars were trained. Those scholars knew Arabic texts inside-out but could not necessarily speak fluently in Arabic. To this day, many such scholars cannot 'teach' the text in spoken Arabic.)[162]

To assist young learners, we have structured English to mirror Arabic, so that Arabic may scaffold off of grammar learning in the mother tongue. It is much easier to grasp new concepts in one's mother tongue, and *then* confidently make the connection to a second language. We also compromise between a text-based approach and a spoken-language approach, through beginning with a spoken-language intensive. We deem that when language flows in the students minds and on their tongues. We offer many traditional tricks for

---

162 For instance, if you are fluent in Arabic and wish to study in Pakistan, most scholars are uncomfortable teaching in Arabic, and one must also learn Urdu. The same matter occurs in Turkish, Kurdish, Indian, and other lands with their own local languages.

learning vocabulary that are not offered by other schemes and approaches.

If one is unable to complete the 'high road', continue to achieve milestones on the 'low road', but never entirely give up on teaching Arabic—or any language for that matter—as a liberal art. Do not accept MSA (Modern Standard Arabic) nor 'English' for a subject with elements of grammar, morphology, logic, rhetoric, and literature. Yes, it would be possible to completely forget these elements and communicate with each other as though they did not exist or were archaic and out of step with the times. Mortimer Adler stated that the worst thing that ever happened to *the curriculum*, was for the liberal arts to be named English. That is what he meant: for English to merely be taught as listening, speaking, reading, and writing, designed to foster communication (i.e., business transactions). So, if you must use communicative schemes, use them as a temporary and necessary means to build your students and children up in a gradual manner. When your child's mind is more developed, complete at least one intermediate text in grammar so that you can read *tafsir* as a graduate attribute (i.e., an outcome embodied by the graduate from this syllabus). In this manner, they will graduate not only with a basic understanding of Arabic but will also have laid a basis for reading in their tradition. Millions of Muslims now grow up not even knowing broadly where to access their tradition or feeling they do not have even the basic keys. The low road offers not only the basic keys, but also the ability to understand Arabic basic texts.

b. Why?

Some scholars of Islam have argued that learning basic Arabic is obligatory for anyone who reads the Quran and Sunnah, which would seem to be all Muslims. We all wish for ourselves and for our children during the month of Ramadan to not only stand and hear the Quran, but also to understand the Quran. We have a great opportunity if we start young to make this entirely possible.

By learning Arabic as a liberal art, not only do you understand God's final revelation to humankind, but you learn it in a way that perfects your intrinsic human faculties. All learning starts with language (and experience). The linguistic sciences are a prerequisite for logic, and they are keys to all knowledge, as we only have access to logic and the sciences it produces through language. Further, the Arabic language, even more than Latin, is a powerful inflected language. Merely learning classical Arabic grammar is half of a liberal arts programme, producing a powerful mind. (Note that only a few decades back, the leaders of European civilisation trained in Latin conjugation as a core part of their mental training.)

c. How?

For preschool and reception/kindergarten, see Section 3.5 and 3.6, respectively. You may also consider the following option: hire an Arabic teacher to run a play-based submersion programme for your children or those of a co-op you establish. Either way, attempt to teach Arabic letters to your child with clay, etc., and introduce them to child-friendly units of vocabulary and simple spoken Arabic.

RECEPTION/KINDERGARTEN

Students need to complete a tajwid book such as *al-Qaʿidah al-nuraniyyah* and *al-Qaʿidah al-baghdadiyyah* (traditional texts), or opt for a more modern version, such as *Iqra'* (Malaysia). These books teach tajwid with very little reference to rules, so they resemble phonics and teach proper pronunciation of Arabic, which greatly helps with learning classical Arabic. After completing one of these, one may study more of the rules through the accessible text *Tajweed for Beginners* by Qari Ismail Ishaq (available for free download on https://archive.org › details › TajweedForBeginners). If students learn the proper Arabic phonics before they are five or six years old, they should enjoy a flawless recitation of the Quran for the rest of their lives. Read half a page per day, then move the child on to activities and sensorial experiences such as drawing the letters in a sandbox or making them from clay. Test children regularly (every day and with every new topic). To do this properly, mix up the letters and use new examples, to encourage the child to learn and remember them clearly, rather than answering through relying on context and memorised patterns. Another useful activity is to draw a human head and show the 'enunciation point' (makhraj) of each letter and ask the children to touch that place while they are repeating the letter.

While teaching to read the 28 letters, some modern books do not mention how to read the letters in their various shapes when the letters are each joined up. Only Iqra' printed in Malaysia gives the child a chance to absorb this matter via exercises, spending around thirty pages on this. (See, 'Resources', below.)

If in a school, even a classic such as *al-Qaʿidah al-nuraniyyah* can (and has been) put into Power Point slides which allow children to focus on one word at a time and use large fonts. *Al-Qaʿidah al-nuraniyyah* ends with small excerpts from the Holy Quran. Thereafter, tajwid and Arabic are taught in separate lessons. Tajwid is taken over by the Quran teacher who works through small suras of Juz' 'Amma, completes a reading (khatam) of Juz' 'Amma, then works with the student to complete the whole Quran, according to ability and motivation.

YEAR 1

Reading & comely recitation / phonics (tajwid):

If your child did not at least read a book in tajwid before Year 1, pause the other elements of Arabic teaching until you do. Being confident readers will allow children to engage with all the strands of language in a holistic manner. During this rapid catching up with learning to read the letters and script, avoid doing what is done in some madrasas: sitting and reading for six hours a day at such a young age. This is unhealthy and probably also unproductive.

Year 1 of the 'high road' is the most complex, as learners are transitioning in Year 1 from structured play to formal learning. This is like trying to learn to ride a bike from someone speaking to one in a new language, especially if they have not undertaken the submersion experience that we recommend for preschool. You will have to pay keen attention to ensure students are learning and that they review enough such that they consolidate what they do learn, grasp what they only partially grasped in the lesson, and can confidently explain what they have learned and recite what they have memorised. As noted in the theoretical second half of the 'Introduction' to this manual, the point is not to fully understand grammar and language, but to grow into it.

For both the high road and the low road, we encourage you to start Year 1 by going through the letters of Arabic, learning to write one per day. If you have learned the letters through play before Year 1, we would still recommend now going through a book designed for teaching writing. (See the sub-section, 'Detailed Advice for Learning Arabic to Write in Arabic script' below. There, we explain many points needed to make learning Arabic writing successful and rewarding.)

Use LIFE's *Arabic 1 Textbook*, or work your way through these five stages:

Stage 1

This stage consists of 30 Lessons focussed on spoken Arabic. Speaking exercises progress gradually and cover the basic sentence structures needed to express the most basic needs and meanings. Learn to write one letter of the alphabet each day, including learning to join them up. Students learn to acquire very basic vocabulary in the spoken exercises for this stage.

The speaking focus of Stage 1 will help language 'flow' in later stages. The LIFE resource in the pipeline scripts these exercises to ease teaching and generously models all the sentence structures for young students through copious examples, to ease learning.

To learn script at this stage, one will need resources which progress through the alphabet in a practical script such as *naskh*. (See, 'General

Resources', below, which shows that such resources abound, thankfully.) Most of them devote one page to each letter. This includes showing a letter in its initial position, middle, and final positions. Many of these resources progressively include more words and sentences as the lessons progress, and most are around 30 lessons often containing dots and guiding as to the direction they should be connected.

Stages 2-4

The basics of sentence structures are now conveyed in what we term pre-grammar. We draw out from their experience of sentences accurate, even if highly simplified, descriptions of what a sentence is, what its parts are, and what they do. For instance, it suffices and is accurate for this stage to 'define' a sentence as, 'Words saying something is or did something.' This definition includes all sentences, and excludes all non-sentences, and that is a large part of what a definition is supposed to do.

At this stage, we incorporate carefully chosen, very short classical texts children can master and apply their knowledge of sentence structures to through analysing the sentences in the texts. Some texts are less than a page, others are around two pages. and can easily be read, understood, and turned into exercises. The use of Arabic dictionaries could also be utilised at this stage. New vocabulary words can be charted and reviewed, and children should be encouraged to construct new sentences with their new words.

Stage 5

If children have reviewed consistently, they should be ready for their first full, classical text, *Nahw Mir*. This truly remarkable text was written by a master Arabic linguist, al-Sayyid al-Sharif al-Jurjani to explain Arabic in his own local language. The method used in this text is that by which Arabic was taught for centuries outside of Arabic lands, and there is no good reason to abandon it. It works much better for non-Arabic speakers than the text that comes to most people's minds: *al-Ajurrumiyyah*.

How to study this and other classical texts at this tender stage

Read a section of the text, sufficing for one day's lesson to grasp the big picture. Then, return and read sentence by sentence. Make sure the grammar of the sentence is clear in whatever language one is studying, and clarify what pronouns refer back to. In each sentence, determine whether it is offering a definition or a proposition. If it is a definition, stop to understand how each word in the definition includes or excludes certain things. (Take for instance the definition of human being as 'rational animal'. 'Animal' is the genus, including birds, reptiles, etc, and of course humans, but excluding plants and minerals. 'Rational' excludes all animals, so only humans are included, which is part of what a definition aims for.) In the secondary stage, one will want to identify propositions and explore their proofs. For now, ask if there are counter examples, but focus on producing examples, and then memorising the text as if it were a tree diagramme. For example, when the text divides the word into noun, verb, and particle, take various words and determine which they are. Ask, 'Are there some which do not fit these three categories?' Then when the text begins to discuss which words are declinable and which are constructed, one has the basis to start grammar, so use it. When one comes to an Arabic word in a sentence, ask, 'Which is it?' The, 'If it is declinable, which category is it: nominal, accusative, genitive, or jussive?' Al-Jurjani offers a complete classification of declinable words in terms of how that declension shows on them. If one memorises a few pages of his book, one is well on one's way towards understanding grammar. So, do memorise. Memorise the text if possible. If not, review the logical divisions which form the structure of the book and eloquently unfold the science of grammar. Review them so many times that one memorises them and can apply them to any word. Imagine being able to parse (nearly) every sentence in Allah's holy book.

Year 1 consists of five stages which are carefully placed stepping stones. Also, teaching involves the concrete activity of sentence diagramming, modelled first in their mother tongue. A system of colour-coding is suggested, and thus one may make these meanings tactile. Time is scheduled in for review and, when needed, repetition until students are confident. The classical text they study in this year is repeated the following year with a commentary to ensure it is absorbed and unfolds slowly in their minds. (LIFE offers training for teachers, as noted below.)

The texts chosen for inclusion in LIFE's *Arabic 1 Textbook* are carefully drawn from a mixture of short hadiths, poetry for Arabic-learning, and short stories. When ready, students work through *Qasas al-nabiyyin* which is a graded book, repeating vocabulary words to facilitate learning by young language learners. (A translation of the text exists to support the teacher/parent.)

By the end of this crucial year, Year 1, ensure that children are able to: 1) read and write the Arabic alphabet, 2) use basic sentence structures in spoken Arabic, 3) parse basic sentences and (optionally) colour-code parts of the sentence, and 4) start to learn rules of proper Arabic grammar. Any area they are unable to show 50-70% competence in, review, and, if needed and possible, supplement.

YEAR 2

Grammar

Children study LIFE's commentary on *Nahw Mir* or *al-Tuhfah al-saniyyah* which is a commentary on *al-Ajurrumiyyah* that offers exercises to learn to apply the rules of grammar.

Morphology (*sarf*)

al-Bina' and application (En. resource: *Imdad-us-Sarf*)

(Optional English resource): *Arabic Grammar (Etymology) Imdad-us-Sarf, English and Urdu,* of Shaykh Muhammad Imdad Hussain Pirzada.

Children solidify their learning through numerous exercises, activities, and parents should create a space for them to use their new linguistic skills. For example:

- Vocabulary and grammatical forms should be identified and discussed in the Quran hour.
- They should be encouraged to describe things they know or love using Arabic sentence structures.
- Nature study should include teaching students the names of common birds and other animals.

YEAR 3

The focus for this year is memorising the parsing of most Arabic sentence types. This knowledge will be a treasure serving one for the rest of one's life.

Grammar

Sharh Mi'at 'amil by al-Jurjani. *Al-Jurjani,* as this text is sometimes called for short, if commonly taught with a full parsing (*i'rab*), this parsing itself being memorised. Thus, the whole text and its parsing are memorised by heart. If students struggle, insist at least that they are able to parse the full text and its examples when they encounter them. This is termed memorising the topics (*masa'il*).

Traditionally, teachers offer *i'rab* and students memorise each portion given to them. This is best done one-on-one, though in some cases a class is possible. Students review the portion they have taken immediately with their classmates (*mudhakarah*) around seven times, or, what matters, to the point that they review it before forgetting it and do enough *mudhakarah* that they will not forget it thereafter, and it settles in their memory without having to write it. In the end, they memorise the full parsing of *al-'Awamil.*

(Optional grammar text): If one needs to firm up one's foundation, one may begin with *'Awamil al-Birgivi (al-Birvigi's Grammatical Agents).* Al-Birgivi's text names all the major parts of the sentence, and gives examples, many being from the Quran or pious exhortations. This text offers an easy to memorise map of the whole of Arabic grammar. There is a benefit for all to memorise it. Later, when one encounters a word one can determine where it fits in this map. Or, when reading other grammar books that have different modes of organisation, when one comes to a topic, one may remind oneself of its place in al-Birgivi's highly intuitive map of the whole language (into grammatical agents and things operated on by those agents, and the grammatical cases that arise from this operation).

Morphology

Arabic Grammar (Etymology) Imdad-us-Sarf, English and Urdu, of Shaykh Muhammad Imdad Hussain Pirzada. Work through the chapters and complete the activities, many of which are applied to Quranic verses.

YEAR 4

After students have gained mastery of formal grammar in previous years, they now focus on increasing their Arabic vocabulary. LIFE recommends for this vocabulary the famous poem *al-Burdah* by al-Busiri. Children should be encouraged to regularly recite and memorize *al-Burdah* to master its vocabulary.

Grammar

Two options: Students either study *al-Hidayah* or *Sharh 'Abdullah al-Ardhabili* on al-*Unmudhaj*.

a) *Al-Hidayah* is short for *Hidayat al-Nahw*, a medium level text which distils and eases understanding of perhaps the most important text in grammar: *Mulla Jami*, which is a commentary on *al-Kafiyah* of Ibn al-Hajib. So, *al-Hidayah* gives one a glimpse of the highest peaks without having already traveled far into the mountain range. While the text is accessible, it is giving you the last word on the subject, though leaving many obscure topics unfit for an intermediate student. For teachers and parents that are not confident in Arabic, consider acquiring *Hidayat al- Nahu With English Q & A*, (Jamiatul Ilm wal Huda).

b) *Sharh 'Abdullah al-Ardhabili* on *al-Unmudhaj* is shorter than *al-Hidayah* but does not exist in any English edition. *Al-Unmudhaj* is a very short text written by one of the greatest scholars in any age of the Arabic language: al-Zamakhshari. Shaykh 'Abdullah al-Ardhabili's commentary is accessible, including making accessible what we may term the philosophy of grammar. If you want a simple but satisfying explanation of why certain Arabic words are inflected (i.e., have word endings that change), while others do not, and yet others are in between *(mamnu' min al-sarf)*, he will explain. Alternatively, they could study *Tasheel al-Nahw*. *Tasheel al-Nahw* is based on *'Ilm al-Nahw*, originally written in Urdu, and has been translated into an Arabic text commented on and explained in English. It was published in 2011 by Dar al-Saʿadah Publications (ilmresources.wordpress.com), revised 2014.

Morphology

Al-ʿIzzi (*Tasrif al-Zinjani*). *Al-ʿIzzi* is taught in videos on al-Qalam Institute's YouTube channel. (We recommend *Tasrifat al-Zinjani* of Pir Khadir in Year 5 of the high road, and at the beginning of secondary education for the slower version of the high road. *Tasrifat al-Zinjani* teaches the students exactly what step occurs when a word is modified in *sarf*. The rules are like mathematics: they must be applied in the right order to produce results, and thus without understanding the steps, one does not really understand how derivate words are formed from their original forms according to rules.)

Note that Islamic instruction overlaps with Arabic liberal arts in this year, as rhetoric is being taught this year: *First Steps in Understanding Balaghah*.

YEAR 5

Literature

Selections of poetry and prose (e.g., from Diwans of ʿAbbasids (al-Shafiʿi, Abu al-ʿAtahiya, and al-Mutanabbi), Ibn Zaydun (Andalusia) and Ibn al-Farid (Ayyubid) and begin *Maqamat al-Hariri*.

Begin with short, accessible, and impactful poems. Write them on a white board and have students read them aloud with proper voweling. Then explain the vocabulary and the general meaning quickly, then go back and go through the grammar and meaning. For the grammar, identify the part of sentence of each word. (Use one of our parsing techniques.) Memorise the poem when done. It is much easier to memorise while the meaning is fresh in one's mind and one has just gone through the words carefully. However, if a student struggles, it may be found that memorising before the lesson makes understanding far easier. Determine what works for you through trial and error.

One may use the literature materials for al-Azhar's *iʿdadi* level as a model and to get one started. These materials explain the meanings of poems in very simple terms and contain learning activities to structure a lesson.

[Some of these selections will be further studied in the LIFE resource *True Happiness* which comments on ethical hadiths, wise sayings, and poetry which align the soul to desire and respect what relates to true happiness, not the various false sources of happiness sought in our wider culture.]

YEAR 6

Literature

Maqamat al-Hariri (selections). Again, begin with the most accessible, memorise them, and use contemporary commentaries when possible. LIFE may offer a course on this in the future

Islamic ethics

Riyadat al-nafs (*Disciplining the Soul*, Book XXII of the *Ihya' 'ulum al-din*). This text explains the process of purification of the soul. In the process, one learns of the faculties of the soul and the cardinal virtues, and how they are obtained.

[Or devote some or even a lion's share of this hour to *al-Mawahib al-ladunniyyah* listed in Islamic instruction with aim of reading the more literary *al-Shifa'* of Qadi 'Iyad in the following years.]

Options for those who struggle with the high road

One may either take the high road at a slower pace or take the low road. As noted, the low road is complicated by the fact that communicative Arabic schemes all presume the teacher is fluent in Arabic.

The high road at a slower pace using LIFE's *Arabic 1 Textbook*

YEAR 1 & 2

LIFE's *Arabic 1 Textbook* explains the Arabic language in English, so you do not have to be fluent to start it. Also, Stage 1 devoted to spoken Arabic is fully scripted, so you only have to read Arabic. If you take our crash course and intermediate courses in Arabic, non-Arabic speakers will find themselves learning as they teach.

Teach *Arabic 1 Textbook* over two years (instead of the one year recommended above). Take more time to explain, give examples, and review heavily. It is important to generate a community of some sort where the child can review with peers when they are able to focus. If they do not have this, review their lessons with them, carving out the time to do this. If you teach Arabic 1 Textbook over two years, you will have more than enough time. Thus, you will be performing the role of a tutor for them. Or you may in fact hire a tutor, perhaps one who is fluent in Arabic. Either way, reteach and repeat certain lessons. Take more time to memorise vocabulary and the classical texts that are used. Spend more time on available texts such as Abu al-Hasan 'Ali al-Nadwi's *Qasas al-nabiyyin* (and take your own time to go through it with a dictionary). Keep reading so long as there is motivation, and until you notice an increase in understanding and confidence in Arabic.

Get more creative, and supplement with other schemes, or integrate Arabic learning with other classes, such as maths and nature study. Look up and then teach them, for example, the names of plants and animals in Arabic. (The Prophet ﷺ used to teach the Companions the names of local birds.)

YEAR 3

Merge with the high road again, though one year later. Thus, you work through LIFE's commentary on *Nahw Mir* in English or *al-Tuhfah al-saniyyah* which is in Arabic but has copious exercises. (See Year 2 above. As noted there, it would make this easier to go through our course and workbook on al-Birgili's *'Awamil (Grammatical Agents)* first.)

Milestone: Aim to complete 150 pages or as close as possible of *Qasas al-nabiyyin* by the end of Year 3, and to be able to read near fluently.

YEAR 4

If you chose to study a grammar book in Year 3, then in Year 4 go ahead and also read *Tasheel al-Nahw* from the high road. Complement this with *Imdad al-Sarf*. Also follow the high road's Islamic instruction and read *First Steps in Understanding Balaghah*. All three of these books give instructions in English, and often explain the topics in English.

If you did not study a grammar book in Year 3, complete the instructions listed there for Arabic grammar.

YEAR 5

As in Year 4, if you read a grammar book in Year 3, study *al-Burdah* as described above. If you did not start grammar in Year 3, then complete the instructions from Year 4 for grammar now in Year 5.

If you are brave and split *Hidayat al-Nahu With English Q & A* (Jamiatul Ilm wal Huda) over two years, this would be a fantastic accomplishment. If students (and their teachers) have mastered the commentary on *Nahw Mir* and Al-Qalam institute's resources.

Begin practicing sentence diagramming and translating the Arabic wisdom and poetry in LIFE's packet *True Happiness*.

YEAR 6

Read the second half of *Hidayat al-Nahu With English Q & A*.

Complete working through the Arabic of LIFE's packet *True Happiness*.

DAILY SUBJECTS — Arabic Liberal Arts & Literature

Core Studies	Supplement	Optional
Year 1: *Arabic 1 Textbook*, first half.	a. Various videos from al-Qalam Institute: i. *First Steps in Understanding Nahw*, ii. *al-Sughra fi al-nahw*, iii. *Bina' al-af'al* (in *sarf*).	After completing Stage Two of *Arabic 1 Textbook*, begin to read slowly but regularly in *Qasas al-nabiyyin* and review vocabulary
Year 2: *Arabic 1 Textbook*, second half.	Various videos from al-Qalam Institute: i. *First Steps in Understanding Nahw*, ii. *al-Sughra fi al-nahw*, iii. *Bina' al-af'al* (in *sarf*).	a. Start *Imdad al-Sarf* and b. Read regularly in *Qasas al-nabiyyin* and review vocabulary
Year 3: Grammar: LIFE's *Commentary on Nahw Mir* in English or *al-Tuhfa al-Saniyyah*, completing its exercises. Morphology: *Bina' al-af'al* or *Imdad al-sarf*	a. Start Year 3 with al-Birgili's 'Awamil (Grammatical Agents) c. Cumulatively over Years 1–3, attempt to complete reading of 100 pages of *Qasas al-nabiyyin*, keeping and reviewing a vocabulary list	Use al-Qalam Institute's recorded lessons *Bina' al-af'al* which explain the Arabic text in English (but do not translate the text)
Year 4: Grammar: *Sharh Mi'at 'amil* of al-Jurjani, learning and memorising the parsing of the text		Studied in Islamic Instruction: *First Steps in Understanding Balaghah*
Year 5: Grammar: Start with *Tasheel al-Nahw*, then read *Hidayat al-Nahu With English Q & A* in the remainder of Years 5 & 6 Morphology: *al-'Izzi*	*al-Burdah*'s vocabulary and commentary	Use the recorded lessons of *al-'Izzi* by al-Qalam Institute (Arabic text explained in English, but not translated)
Year 6: (Complete *Hidayat al-Nahu With English Q & A* and *al-'Izzi*)	''	''

THE LOW ROAD

The 'low road' simply means traversing many of the same milestones, but taking a slower, gentler, less direct road towards breaking the barrier of learning *in* Arabic. So, children learn the same prayers and vocabulary in preschool. Like the 'high road', they finish a basic book of *tawjid* (in the sense of phonics) before the start of Year 1. Also like the high road, they learn the full script of the alphabet in the first month of Year 1, one letter per day. (See the same sub-section we pointed to for the high road entitled, 'Detailed Advice for Learning Arabic to Write in Arabic script.' This advice applies to both the high and low roads.)

Then, parents are faced with an unavoidable challenge facing the low road: all the communicative Arabic recourses that I know of presume the teacher speaks Arabic.

Arabic taught through Communicative schemes

As noted above, while these schemes are more accessible for non-Arabic speaking students, they absolutely demand that the teacher reads and understands Arabic well, even to know how to teach the very first lesson. Perhaps there is a wisdom in this; it makes it easier to accept one difference between our tradition and other classical traditions in general drawn on in a classical education: we have maintained more of a focus on transmission. For instance, it is almost impossible to learn tajwid on your own. It is best to take your other religious learning from scholars, and when not possible to run matters by them and attend some of their other lessons to tap into the spirit and etiquette they embody and exude.

If you are not fluent but wish to start with communicative schemes, we advise one of the following:

For parents who cannot read Arabic script fluently

Organise a pod where at least one parent in the community speaks Arabic and ideally has children. Supply them with materials, of course.

Hire a tutor.

For parents who can read Arabic script

Parents attend our Arabic crash course and introductory course. Then they go through the curriculum themselves in slightly more detail than the children will do, keeping themselves a few lessons ahead. In some cases, LIFE (and al-Qalam Institute) has made such lessons available. We plan to make lessons for all our basic Arabic curriculum. In other cases, parents may request this as part of the expanded LCS (LIFE Consultation Service). This is not ideal, but is better than abandoning classical languages and texts, in which case classical education comes closer and closer to modern education. Some mistakes are inevitable. In the end, you will become aware of many of these mistakes and may correct them.

Encourage your local mosque to offer Arabic classes for new mothers. Attend with your children if they are old enough. Use this to empower your own teaching. It generates a beautiful spirit when parents and teachers are pursuing knowledge together.

If you are a weekend warrior and nothing is on offer locally, go through the Fawakih curriculum. (See their courses at fawakih.org. They also have well-paced materials for which you can find your own teacher.)

For some details on the individual schemes discussed presently, see, 'General Resources', for Arabic, below. Whichever scheme you choose, try to blend in Arabic grammar and translation exercises. Do this on your Tuesdays and Thursdays: practice Quranic vocabulary and Arabic grammar and script (following the instructions for Arabic script given is most detail below).

Here is a rule of thumb for how fast to progress through existing books:

- Teach Arabic daily so that skills accumulate and can be reinforced.
- Schedule time in for review. Sometimes many things click in the review that were not understood in the lesson. The aim is not to log lots of hours studying and forgetting. The aim is to focus, obtain critical mass to start reading in Arabic with as little wasted time as possible, and then learn *in* Arabic.

YEAR 1

Uhibb al-'Arabiyyah, Student Book 1 (Kitab al-Talmidh) [If your child shows readiness, start *Uhibb al-'Arabiyyah, Student Book 1* in Reception. Either way, if you finish *Uhibb al-'Arabiyyah, Student Book 1* in Y1, work from the beginning of Saudi series named *al-'Arabiyyah li-l-nashi'in* (*Nashi'in* from here on out), *Book 1*, till the end of the year.]

YEAR 2

Aim to complete *Nashi'in*, Level 2 by the end of the year.

YEAR 3

Carry on with *Nashi'in*, starting Level 3, and begin reading *Qasas al-nabiyyin* and short hadith in Arabic (explained in English) in the daily Religious Instruction.

YEAR 4-6

Continue with *Nashi'in*, reading more than one book per year if possible.

Milestones of 'low road' for this period:

- Finish *Book 6* of *Nashi'in* before end of primary school.
- On one's Tuesdays and Thursdays, by end of Year 6:
- Complete learning high frequency Quranic vocabulary words.
- Complete *al-Hidayah*, or at least one classical Arabic grammar text covering the core topics *(Nahw Mir* (English translation), *'Awamil* (English translation), *Mi'at 'amil* (English translation, though archaic), or *Tasheel al-Nahw* (English-Arabic).
- Establish the capacity to begin to understand the Quran, and ideally classical texts, including the parent who is teaching.

This road will require adjustments also to the Religious Instruction curriculum. For example, in years 1 and 2 devoted to fiqh and 'aqidah, you can use English translations of classical texts such as Imam al-Nawawi's *Maqasid* and *The Encompassing Epistle (al-Risalah al-jami'ah)*. In year 2, this becomes more challenging, but there are by now reasonable translations of al-Sanusi, etc. In year 3, it is questionable how valuable it is to study hadith purely in English. There is a reasonable translation of *Riyad al-Salihin* by Muslims at Work Publication, 2015 which draws on reliable commentaries to comment on hadiths. The Arabic is printed on facing page, so students can do their best to work through the Arabic.

DETAILED ADVICE FOR LEARNING ARABIC TO READ & WRITE IN ARABIC SCRIPT

Reading Arabic

Whether you opt to take the high road or the low road, both parties set out together and begin with decoding script. Make this the focus of your reception class (mirroring learning English phonics).

You may use the time-tested *al-Qa'idah al-nuraniyyah*, *al-Qa'idah al-baghdadiyyah*, or opt for a more modern version. Read 1/2 a page per day, then move the child on to activities and sensorial experiences such as drawing the letters in a sandbox or making them from clay. Test children regularly (every day and with every new topic). To do this properly, mix up the letters and use new examples, to encourage the child to learn and remember clearly, rather than answering through relying on context and memorised patterns.

Some modern prints skip over how to shape and join up each letter in the alphabet in one to three pages (like MLS' *Easy Steps in Quran Reading*). Only Iqra' printed in Malaysia gives the child a chance to absorb this matter via exercises, spending around thirty pages on this.

If in a school, even a classic such as *al-Qaʿidah al-nuraniyyah* can (and has been) put into presentation slides which allow children to focus on one word at a time and use large fonts. *Al-Qaʿidah al-nuraniyyah* ends with small excerpts from the Holy Quran. Thereafter, tajwid and Arabic are taught in separate lessons. Tajwid is taken over by the Quran teacher who works with students through small suras of the Juz' *'Amma*, completes a reading (*khatam*) of Juz' *'Amma*, then one may work on completing the whole Quran.

Writing Arabic

Start with the *naskh* script, the script found in the most common mushafs available today (originally produced in Saudi Arabia, not to be confused with the Mughal script found in some parts of the world). After spending reception (4-5) learning to read script (without understanding) and forming the letters in sand, out of clay, and even taking the shape of the letters with one's body, children are ready at 5-6 and 6-7 to begin very light writing. To ensure that bad habits are not acquired, begin slowly with tracing letters (connecting the dots), with very clear instruction on where to start letters and which directions strokes should take. Make sure that each stroke of each letter is known and correct, rather than rushing children through script.

Teach script either alongside Arabic lessons or set aside longer chunks of time on Tuesdays and Thursdays.

A rule of thumb of what to aim for

Y1, Term 1: Letter shapes were learned in Reception, so teach starting points and directions practiced in writing. Start by tracing letters on dotted letters, then repeating the letters on subsequent lines.

Y1, Term 2: Once each letter is taught, introduce the letter shapes for each position in the word (initial position, middle position, and final position) and how to join them up. Use a child-friendly resource like *al-Khatt al-wadih* which uses shapes of everyday objects like animals and teacups to reinforce shapes. Or use worksheets which exemplify how to join up 2-3 letters at a time, moving through the whole alphabet. Again, trace and then repeat without dots. (Dots may be needed for several repetitions at first.)

Y1, Term 3: Practice writing words, introducing the meaning of the word. (Draw a picture if you or the child wish.) Meld this into copy-work, using short hadiths (many of which are two to three words) or short Quranic verses. [Consider translating the hadith and mirroring this in

English. Remember that part of learning Arabic (and Religious Instruction) is to translate and eventually parse the Quran and adhkar that one learns.]

Y2: Work through The Content of Character Copybook, reinforcing proper letter shapes.

Y3: Introduce calligraphy (see *Arabic Calligraphy: Naskh style for beginners* below)

The learning of writing summarised in stages:

- Separate alphabet (learning proper shape, starting point and direction before writing)
- Joined up words (with the letters in all three positions)
- Sentences (from the Quran and short hadiths)

After this, one would be able to start teaching memorisation via the Maghribi method of writing on the wooden tablets (if that is one's chosen method).

If script falls behind reading, this is only a problem for exercises. In that case, rather than children writing answers to exercises, they may answer orally. If a child's motor skills and hand muscles are clearly not developed sufficiently, wait till they show signs of being ready (or try again with them after 4-6 months).

In English, *Gateway to Arabic* offers its *Handwriting Book*. Unless the child clearly shows readiness, this book is likely best started after 7, as it involves small and independent writing. *Uhibb al-'Arabiyyah, Level 1* introduces writing in Unit 3, but the teaching is not systematic. *Level 2* has exercises in which students copy sentences from the book.

Use calligraphy as a natural and often overlooked inroad to art. Calligraphy is the highest of the three strands of Islamic art design: a) calligraphy (representing the Divine Word), b) geometric design (representing the Divine Sunnah of creation through geometric proportion), and c) floral design (sometimes called *islimi*). Both the calligraphic and floral incorporate the proportion of geometry, and calligraphy introduces this to young students. Calligraphy teaches that letters should be formed through a proportion by counting out how many dots high and how many wide each part of the letter should be when it is well-formed and therefore beautiful (and thus it also introduces the basis of objective beauty in a relativist modern world). Try to find a qualified calligraphy (*khatt*) teacher. One resource which teaches how to use the reed pen and form strokes is *Arabic Calligraphy: Naskh style for beginners* produced by calligrapher Mustafa Jafar and distributed by the British Museum.

d. How, for those lacking resources?

For those who are daunted by the Arabic language, let alone teaching its grammar, we offer crash courses. These will give examples of how to go back and forth between Arabic and English sentence diagrammes, seeing in a mirror how the grammar works in the two languages. With the crash course, teachers will find it easier to read scripted lessons and pick things up as they teach.

We also offer a consultation process for individual difficulties and may be able to assist in finding qualities tutors at an affordable price. Our community is growing, and you are welcome to address questions there directly.

We are also producing a vocabulary scheme which is light and fun; students learn vocabulary and absorb it through self-directed exercises and games. It reinforces vocabulary taken in lessons and it progresses very gradually so that students learn as they go.

GENERAL RESOURCES

Phonics/tajwid resources

Shaykh Nur Muhammad Haqqani, *al-Qaʻidah al-nuraniyyah*, Markaz al-Furqan li-Taʻlim al-Quran, Jeddah, 1431 Hijri. (https://archive.org/details/islamlibrary-00030/page/n1/mode/2up)

Abu Nur ʻAbd al-Hamid, *al-Qaʻidah al-baghdadiyyah*, Maktabat al-Sahabah wa-l-Tabiʻin, al-Imarah al-Shariqah, 2005. (https://archive.org/details/216-pdf_202105/mode/2up)

Qari Ismail Ishaq, *Tajweed for Beginners* (available for free download on https://archive.org > details > TajweedForBeginners.)

Handwriting

Imran Hamza Alawiye, *Gateway to Arabic: Handwriting Book*, Anglo-Arabic Graphics, Greenford, Middlesex, 2004. (https://www.gatewaytoarabic.com/collections/arabic-teaching-books/products/gateway-to-arabic-handwriting-book?variant=41438742675626)

ʻUmar Fahl, *al-Khatt al-wadih: Qawaʻid al-ijadah fi al-kitabah al-yadawiyyah*, Dar al-Talaʼiʻ, Cairo.

Mustafa Jaʻfar (calligrapher), *Arabic Calligraphy: Naskh style for beginners*, McGraw-Hill, New York, 2002.

Shaykh Hamza Yusuf, *The Content of Character Copybook: Ethical Sayings of the Prophet Muhammad*, San Ramon, California, 2007.

Communicate, comprehensive Arabic schemes

Al-'Arabiyyah li-l-nashi'in. (Sometimes called the Saudi Series because they produced in conjunction with the Saudi Ministry of Knowledge (i.e., Education).)

Uhibb al-'Arabiyyah, Level 1, Student Book 1 *(Kitab al-tilmidh).* Printing in Riyadh (al-Riyadh, Saudi Arabia), produced in conjunction with a number of Gulf states). (https://noorart.com/collections/i-love-arabic-pre-k-6th-level-%D8%A3%D8%AD%D8%A8-%D8%A7%D9%84%D8%B9%D8%B1%D8%A8%D9%8A%D8%A9)

Anadolu Imam Hatib Lisensi Arapça (the Arabic teaching resource used by the Imam Hatib religious schools in Turkey, 'Imam Khatib' meaning here meaning the imams and khatibs of official mosques).

Imran Hamza Alawiye, *Gateway to Arabic,* Anglo-Arabic Graphics, Greenford, Middlesex, 2004. *(https://www.gatewaytoarabic.com/collections/arabic-teaching-books.)*

Mahmud Isma'il Sini, Nasif 'Abd al-'Aziz, and Mukhtar Husayn, *al-'Arabiyyah li-l-nashi'in,* Saudi Arabia, 1983. (https://archive.org/details/al-arobiyah-linnasyiin/kitab-muallim-nasyi%27in-1/)

Abu al-Hasan al-Nadawi, *Qasas al-nabiyyin,* Mu'assasat al-Risalah, 20th print, Beirut, 1996. (This work is effectively a graded entry into classic Arabic vocabulary and sentence structures. Made to introduce language to the degree that it may be retained.)

The Saudi Series gives a more well-rounded approach to Arabic, introducing literature and motivational and informative stories and in general having a more classical feel. *Uhibb al-'Arabiyyah* is highly communicative and includes writing/script lessons in which young children trace dots and work their way up to the writing expected in lessons. Both have gaps that any teacher will need to fill in, so do not think that the low road avoids all difficulty. If you are able to source them, the Imam Khatib books contain the necessary repetition for children to advance at the pace set out in the book. In both other books, teachers will have to find supplemental materials and test student learning. *Uhibb al-'Arabiyyah* in particular requires a great deal of pre-teaching to prevent the words and grammar from overwhelming students or making barriers non-native speakers cannot break through. (One will notice that in all this, some level of Arabic is required for parents/teachers. So, why not attend a course in Arabic grammar and commit time to learning the Quran's meaning?)

Etymology *(sarf)*

Al-Bina' (in *Majmu'at al-sarf*)

(https://www.salihkitaplar.com/mecmuatus-sarf-arapca-emsile-bina-maksud-izzi-mjmw-t-alsrf-1)

Hashim Muhammad, *tahdhib* and translation of *Bina' al-af'al (in sarf)*, Al-Qalam Publications.

(https://drive.google.com/file/d/1C_hzWVk0te3WnJekoiM6tnZU0NUrBW9i/view)

Shaykh Muhammad Imdad Hussain Pirzada, *Arabic Grammar (Etymology) Imdad-us-Sarf, English and Urdu*, First Edition, *Al-Karam Publications*, 2002.

al-'Izzi (Tasrif al-Zinjani)

Pir Khadir al-Shahubi and 'Abd al-Wahhab al-Zinjani, *Sharh Tasrif al-Zinjani*, Sanandij, Kurdistan, 1987. (Available at: https://takw.in/lughah/sarf/tasrif-alizzy)

al-'Izzi is taught in videos on al-Qalam Institute: https://www.alqalaminstitute.org/resources/sarf-resources/tasreef-al-izzi-resources.

Grammar (*nahw*)

Hashim Muhammad, *Al-Sughra Wal Wusta Fi An-Nahw*, Al-Qalam Publications, Leicester, UK.

Aamir Bashir, *Tasheel Al-Nahw* (English-Arabic) 'Ilm al-Nahw of Mawlana Mushtaq Ahmad Charthawali, 2nd ed., Dar al-Sa'adah Publications, 2012.

al-Sayyid al-Sharif Ali b. Muhammad al-Jurjani (tr. Asrar Rashid), *Nawh Mir: A Primer in Arabic Grammar*, 2nd edition, Dar al-Imam Yusuf an-Nabhani. (https://archive.org/details/nawh-mir-1)

Shaykh Siraj al-Din Uthman Chishti Nizami (translate and comments Muawiyah ibn Mufti Abd al-Salam), *Hidayat al-Nahu With English Q & A*, Jamiatul Ilm Wal Huda Publications, Blackburn, UK.

Shaykh Muhy al-din 'Abd al-Hamid, *al-Tuhfah al-saniyyah bi-sharh Muqaddimat al-Ajurrumiyyah*, al-Maktabah al-'Asriyyah, Beirut, 2008. (https://archive.org/details/to7fah.ss). For a dual-language translation of the prior, see: (tr. Adnan Karim), *Al-Tuhfat Al-Saniyyahh Bi Sharh Al-Muqaddimat Al-Ajrumiyyah* (Dual-language edition), Dar Al-Arqam, Birmingham, UK.

Muhammad, al-Birgivi (tr. Mustafa Styer), *al-'Awamil (al-Birvigi's Grammatical Agents)*, Turath Publishers, forthcoming.

Hashim Mohamed, *al-Hidayah (Hidayat al-Nahu)*, Al-Qalam Institute, (https://www.alqalaminstitute.org/resources/nahw-resources/hidayatun-nahw-resources.)

Hashim Mohamed, *First Steps in Understanding Balaghah,* Al-Qalam Institute (https://drive.google.com/file/d/1bfj4nWzGZqVj_t1aoAeh-oOCyi1kJUpw/view.)

'Abd Allah al-Ardhabili, *Sharh al-Unmudhaj,* Dar al-Kutub al-'Ilmiyya, Beirut, 2013.

Shaykh Siraj al-Din Uthman Chishti Nizami (tr and comments Muawiyah ibn Mufti Abd al-Salam), *Hidayat al-Nahu With English Q & A,* Jamiatul Ilm Wal Huda Publications, Blackburn, UK.

al-Busiri, *Burdat al-Madih* (see Islamic teaching curriculum where a text teaching its vocabulary is listed).

Abu Hamid al-Ghazali (tr Walter Skellie), *The Marvels of the Heart, Book 21 of the Ihya' 'Ulum al-din,* Fons Vitae, Louisville, Kentucky, USA.

—, *Ihya' 'ulum al-din,* Dar al-Minhaj, Jeddah, Saudi Arabia, 2011.

Ahmad Shihab al-din al-Qastalani, *al-Mawahib al-ladunniyyah bi-l-minah al-muhammadiyyah,* al-Maktab al-Islami, Beirut, 2004.

For all poetry (and some prose), look up the following poets:

al-Shafi'i ('Abbasid)   Ibn Zaydun (Andalusia)

Abu al-'Atahiyah ('Abbasid)   Ibn al-Farid (Ayyubid)

al-Mutanabbi ('Abbasid)

on these two websites:

https://www.aldiwan.net/   https://www.adab.com/

4.1.5 MATHEMATICS

SUMMARY OF MATHEMATICS: PRESCHOOL AND RECEPTION/KINDERGARTEN CURRICULUM

Preschool

See Section 3.5. There we present our topical coverage of age-appropriate math topics that organise the vocabulary and activities educators need to teach mathematics as integrated into play.

Reception/kindergarten

See Section 3.6. We recommend teaching mathematics as it is taught in the UK Reception curriculum (tempered by Steiner teaching practices and including Arabic terms for numbers and shapes).

One may use the following for resources and an overview of skills appropriate to Rec/KG.

https://home.oxfordowl.co.uk/maths/primary-maths-age-4-5-reception/

One may use the skills and manipulatives recommended here to teach the topics listed in Arabic as one continues to work through the Arabic mathematics curriculum listed in the Preschool section above.[163]

a. What?

What is maths? Most people assume that maths is the 'least problematic subject'. The simplest definition of maths is: the science of quantity. Here we shall only make two notes. (See, 'Theoretical Introduction,' for more a more thorough discussion.) Modern mathematics followed a similar track to modern logic, and one could argue all the sciences, natural and social: it became formal. What this means is that mathematics used to tell us about one sliver of the world: quantity. Quantity was a real quality of things. This is why negative numbers were not part of the traditional system. Modern scientists believe it is merely a fluke or mystery that mathematics sometimes describes reality. We disagree. One could even agree with *some of* the founders of modern science: the world is a book, and mathematics is its language. The second important note is that, like other subjects, maths has three levels: sacred, symbolic (or liberal), and profane (i.e., what is commonly termed secular or practical/applied). Note that in many cases, topics like arithmetic are merely practical, even in pre-modern texts.[164] While children need to learn practical maths, they should have a share of all three of the said levels.

For the practical/profane aspect of mathematics, LIFE proposes two approaches:

1. Follow one of the better modern schemes (including the option of *Ray's Arithmetic* composed in the late 1800's), complementing it with sacred geometry. [Some of the schemes listed in Section *c. How?* do not require five or even four days a week, so they leave time for other studies.]

---

163 The same integrated activities as found in the Preschool curriculum may be used to teach counting and number skills in Arabic. For instance, try these:
  - Read numbers off the back of a can or box at the grocery store.
  - Count how many different kinds of bolts or washers are sold at the hardware store.
  - Play dominoes or make a line of them to topple.
  - Count the number of petals on different kinds of flowers.

164 One should be careful though, as their very notion of what a number is was different. This is most clear when we come to zero and one, but it runs through the very notion of number.

2. Use Kumon, requiring 30 mins/day. Spend more time on the sacred geometry listed in section b., below.

For the liberal, study *Euclid's Elements* before completing elementary school. This is also one of the best preparations for logic and was formative in the education of many of the world's greatest thinkers, including Bertrand Russell.

For the sacred and qualitative aspect to mathematics, we recommend a mixture of sacred geometry and other elements listed in Section c. *How?* below.

b. Why?

Answering why we study mathematics must balance at least the following considerations:

- Some basic mathematics is absolutely required to function in society and even to worship Allah.
- Mathematics is a discipline *(riyadah)* in a specific sense of the word: it requires continual practice to learn and advance in.
- Modern mathematics is needed to progress in the sciences and is needed in case one must enter mainstream schooling.
- Mathematics sharpens the mind, for which reason it was termed 'the pedagogical science' *(al-'ilm al-ta'limi)*.
- Mathematics like many sciences has three levels: the practical, the liberal, and the mystical. Modern mathematics is not only practical, but it denies any real meaning to mathematics.
- Traditional mathematics is what is needed to perfect the person.
- Modern and traditional mathematics overlap in certain ways, avoiding duplication.

Classical thinkers not centering education on literature or rhetoric—but rather on knowing the sciences that perfect the practical and theoretical parts of the soul—ordered learning pedagogically as follows:

- logic (the trivium)
- mathematics (the quadrivium)
- natural science
- ethics, and
- metaphysics.

However, a) above tells us that students need to learn basic maths in primary school, no matter what they may specialise in in the future. And the pre-modern primary schools (*katatib*) in key places taught the four operations from very young.

Due to b), it is not practical to teach mathematics purely in stages; to some degree at least, its teaching and review need to be continual. Thus, we make it a daily subject. We must consider also the consequences were a child to be forced to enter mainstream education at short notice. It would be very difficult to catch up if they were years behind in maths. For the same reason, we at least keep an eye on modern maths at all times, addressing c). Due to d), we replace some maths learning with *Euclid* which is transformation for the mind. By keeping an eye on modern maths as a true science, we are economical and avoid spreading students thin, noting where traditional maths like *Euclid* replaces certain topics and units from the modern syllabus. Also, there is a strong developmental benefit in working with proportion and harmony: this impacts the soul in ways those who experience it can feel. After working with compass and straight-edge and building up geometric patterns, one feels clear-headed, and new forms in world appear in one's mind, as though they were highlighted.

Maths & the Perfect Person

Teaching the quadrivium sharpens the mind, but many subjects may also be said to sharpen the mind. So, it is important to point out that maths specifically trains one to overcome vain imagining (*wahm*) via true demonstrations. This opens a door, and then one can apply this capacity in other sciences which require more awareness of context such that the rules which govern them appear, e.g., in natural science, but even in matters such as ethics.

Seeing form in the world requires understanding shape in its wider significance. Everything has an essential form which is intelligible, and the senses give us some access to this. So, in a way we see this, and in a way, we really see it with the mind or heart. This requires being sensitivised to not only shape, but proportion and harmony which are keys to the meanings of things. Of course, this also helps one see the manifestation of certain Divine attributes and opens an important door of contemplation closed by modern views of maths and nature.

Studying some pre-modern cosmology opens up the wonders of cosmology. The manner in which maths shows how mathematics reveals the precise nature of the movements of the heavens and even simple matters, such as the various speeds at which objects on a sphere rotate based on their position between the pole and equator.

c. How?

The focus of primary maths education is arithmetic, a subject as old as the earth, it being the same content focus as maths in the *kuttab* (which we know at least taught 'the four operations', i.e., the four operations of arithmetic). Modern and traditional maths only part ways with advanced or higher maths such as calculus which not all children need to learn. (See the secondary entry on maths which provides more theory.) In general, maths as a subject and number has three levels: secular, symbolic, and sacred. Actually, one could place an intermediate level between the secular and symbolic. This is what we may call applied versus theoretical. The point is not to expect all students to learn theoretical maths. The point is to alert students as much as possible about a) what quantity is and b) to teach proofs. Proofs introduce students to the reasoning involved in maths. It teaches them to get their head around the concepts themselves in geometry: what is a point, line, angle, surface? What are definitions? What are principles, such as those originally used by Euclid? All this goes a long way to raising children from transmitters (*naqil*) to scholars (*'alim*). For this reason, and because there exists a successful tradition, we recommend that students learn *Euclid's Elements* in year 5 or 6 of the elementary stage.

Still, whichever scheme you select, we recommend learning something about the qualitative nature of numbers in the world. This is the real change introduced in modern mathematics (in addition to what are indeed developments): a loss of the qualitative notion of maths coming largely through proportion. Proportion is the objective root of beauty and art, so it reunites what modern culture divorced and pulled asunder. So, LIFE's first approach is:

- Use an adequate maths scheme to teach arithmetic throughout elementary education.

- Supplement the study of quantity with the study of the qualitative: sacred geometry.

- By a narrow margin, LIFE's preferred approach is Ray's Arithmetic. This scheme has the following to say for it:

- There is an emphasis on word problems which develop the mind in a broader sense than merely calculating framed problems.

- The resource is engaging and yet simple to teach. So, it is popular amongst children and parents. In fact, is recommended alongside the Robinson curriculum, designed to succeed for those who do not have the time to sit down and teach all lessons.

Though it is American, it is often recommended by home-schoolers outside the U.S.

Ray's Arithmetic is a classic. Some modern schemes attract children through cartoons and silly attempts at humour which effectively become part of the dumbing down process, getting your child used to several things they should never have to get used to in order to be 'entertained'. (What, after all, is the point of homeschooling?)

Some practical notes

The first book is entirely oral. This means it can be used if children are not writing yet, but it also means teaching is completely dependent on a teacher. (Lessons do not have to be long, so this will not necessarily be overly onerous.)

While it is rewarding to purchase a hardback such as that distributed for a reasonable price by Mott Media, the larger books are experienced by some to be stiff, constantly flipping shot. In that case, one may purchase a CD from dollarhomeschool.com and print them to your own standards (and consider finding a traditional bookbinder and keeping them in business. If leather is not within your budget, ask them for another option).

The language and examples may be quaint, but they open a door into life when people were connected to the land and had a different relationship with everything around them.

YEAR 1-6

Ray's Arithmetic (4 days a week, each day having one lesson or two short lessons)

Sacred geometry (1 day/week)

YEAR 1

Trace and colour traditional geometric designs. [There are numerous resources for this. For instance, Eric Brough has several books on Islamic design which encourage drawing and tracing, including *Islamic Design Workbook* and *Islamic Geometric Patterns*, which includes a CD to bring patterns onto one's computer. There is much free material on the internet, but ensure that patterns are authentic, as there are endless vaguely eastern designs which are not based on geometric principles.]

YEAR 2

Learn to use a protractor and straightedge.

YEAR 3-5

Work through *A Beginner's Guide to Constructing the Universe: The Mathematical Archetypes of Nature, Art and Science*, Michael Schneider and its five accompanying workbooks.

YEAR 6

Study *Euclid's Elements*. [Optional: Leave this to the beginning of secondary school, in spite of it being the best opening to logic and needing to proceed it. If you have any doubts as to the crucial importance of this text being taught early enough to inform later development, read: https://afterthoughtsblog.net/2012/11/teaching-euclid-in-homeschool-part-i-by.html/.]

Other schemes may be used, particularly Singapore Maths and Saxon Maths. While the success of the Singapore Maths is sometimes said to be due to a mathematics culture of Singapore, some of its features are of universal value. Studies have shown that each culture informs the way its teaching takes form. In the U.S., successful teaching centres around the teacher's personality, and therefore they make maths painless through clear instructions. When maths problems have an added layer of thinking required, the teacher stops class and explains. Taking too much interest in maths exposes one to criticism from chauvinist currents. In such a culture, students are not as inclined to take risks. In the Orient, maths is important, and the culture encourages diligence and hard work. Students pay attention and work through and discuss the complexities of a maths problem without being told a clear-cut method. This method of maths learning exercises a completely different thought process, at least one step closer to something like proofs. One at least has to engage with how to apply algebraic techniques involving conversion principles and to justify steps, rather than being spoon fed them. Such a method is less likely to completely leave one later in life when encountering a problem and is more likely to result in transferable skills.

An alternative option to make room for other studies

Maths is listed as a discipline rather than a science by Shaykh al-Islam Zakariyya al-Ansari, a pious Egyptian polymath who wrote important works in spirituality and nearly all the Sharia disciplines in the wider sense including logic and metaphysical theology. He deemed maths a discipline because, like archery or purification of the heart, it requires consistent effort to advance and complete. Kumon offers a perfect model: consistent worksheets which cannot be completed without mastering skills that are then a prerequisite for further skills. Worksheets require thirty minutes a day, two days of which must be completed in a Kumon centre. This suits home-schoolers wishing to focus on certain subjects without falling behind in maths.

No other subject is so hard to catch up in as maths, something many experienced when moving from one state to another or from one school district to another with a more advanced maths programme. The two visits to the centre can be a way of increasing motivation, getting fresh air, and keeping connection to the outside world. Other schemes are noted for their compatibility with self-learning and decreased parental time. This includes our preferred scheme, Ray's Arithmetic and Saxon Maths used in the Robinson Curriculum, made for those only able to mark their children's work as they proceed independently. Any of these schemes and techniques which can decrease the burden of maths may make it possible for us to achieve challenging tasks in other parts of the curriculum. Even the sacred geometry recommended in years 1-5 could be decreased or made informal, removed, or placed into the art curriculum if it is a burden at some point.

4.2 WEEKLY SUBJECTS

Most of LIFE's weekly lessons are designed to give children holistic development rooted in a sacred manner in life and the world. However, getting things right in terms of science, history (of culture), and other subjects takes children away from their immediate environment and its institutions: the home (and kitchen and hopefully a back garden/backyard), the neighbourhood, and wherever their wider family may be. Our weekly subjects blend these two areas, tapering gradually towards the initially abstract wider world, offering children the understanding required to inhabit the wider world with authenticity and to re-enchant it. One of these weekly subjects, natural science, is now a key subject for exit examinations, so it requires particular care to negotiate.

The unique principles shared by most of the weekly subjects:

- They help children be embodied—in tune with and in control of their body—rather than merely in the head, sparky, and flitting from one thought to another. As we try to do something physical every day, let us remember Quranic recitation, penmanship, and other parts of the curriculum have a strong physical element.
- They make children capable producers, not merely consumers. 'If you want or need something, learn how to make it.'
- They develop the productive virtue of *techne*, not merely the ability to use technology as and how its designer designed it.
- They encourage knowing the natural resources specific to your locality. Be able to source and use them and make things from them.

- They make the house a place of production, not merely a sleeping pod from which the family shoots off in the morning to work, school, and nursery.

- They retain or regain a connection with animals and plants, not merely as pets and decoration.

GENERAL POINTS FOR ORGANISING THE WEEKLY SUBJECTS

We have organised the weekly schedule such that one weekly subject occurs each day. However, in either a home or a school, educators are free to reorganise the weekly subjects into blocks, focussing on one subject at a time, then moving on to another subject at a time which suits the student (or availability of a tutor or resource.)

LIFE would ideally like some element of production to occur every day, or at least several times a week. To this end:

- All production requires drawing and penmanship before being deployed in various materials. Thus, these two activities are part of daily devotion to production.

- Also, art and digital design could be integrated to work towards the same end: developing a strong and confident capacity to draw.

- What you draw is important as a general capacity, and good artists must grasp the masterful forms Allah has put into nature in the early years of natural science.

- Devote one of the mathematics lessons weekly to sacred geometry, again as part of production. (Sacred geometry could also be taught daily for periods and thus put together into a block and would also contribute to overall development in the skills of art and design.)

4.2.1 THE STUDY OF NATURE

a. What?

Getting natural science right is absolutely essential to the LIFE vision; offering an integrated solution to re-unite 'science' and natural science is important for *any* curriculum which seeks truth and human development, not merely economic development. (This solution turns out to be highly related to overcoming the divorce in our culture between science and the humanities.) The importance of understanding what we term 'science' and putting it back into an integrated whole with 'natural science' and even theology is addressed below under *'Why?'*

(How to 'put them back together again' was addressed in the theoretical part of the 'Introduction'. The much-needed solution explained there stems from the understanding that modern science studies objects mostly mathematically, which produces a quantitative abstraction which acts like a lens. But most people forget that this mathematical model or data is merely a lens. When we remember, we can reunite this lens—which only helps with prediction—with our experience not filtered through instruments to produce a holistic natural science in which these two modes of knowing enlighten each other.)

LIFE's approach to natural science is to begin in the early years with nature study, then slowly introduce a literacy in modern science after a holistic sense of nature has been established. According to one manner of dividing the natural world, it is one of the major three fields of knowledge: God, nature, and man. It is called the lowest science (*al-'ilm al-adna*) because it studies material bodies, most of which are not endowed with intelligence. However, the forms of the natural world are windows and archetypes that point to the Divine names, and thus can be studied as signs (*ayat*).

As we incorporate the two said perspectives on nature, we simultaneously incorporate careful thought on child development.[165] At the primary level, children will take the time to learn about things they can see and experience—such as plants and animals—before they jump to abstract concepts they cannot see—such as friction and other forces. Because these are abstract and have to do with motion rather than substantive things, they require mathematical models, even if simple models. Gradually, their studies will fan out to cover more and more of the UK National Curriculum itself each year. (You may adjust this based on our rationale and your home country.) Students will learn to think about the seasons and habitats and to be observant regarding the forms of plants and animals and to see carefully. They will learn to see how the aspects of the forms of living things contribute to the unity and perfection of the individual and the preservation of the species. Out of this observation of the natural world, their natural interest in taxonomy, classification, and careful observation will grow. Their desire to deepen their knowledge and understanding will be gently encouraged by you as their teacher in accord with their developing minds, as described by the great educationalists' models of child development. In short, the children first learn the names and qualities of the natural world, the grammar of it, then they will learn to think logically and mathematically after they have a foundation of experience and knowledge. In using the UK National Curriculum, some

---

165 This is perhaps a weak point in traditional natural science: it does not ensure that students develop first-hand experience with their hands and senses. It merely offers the definition abstracted from this experience. Then, when students wish to engage critically with the definitions of things, they can go a little further than their experience. This is close to a critique of the great Swiss educationalist, Johann Pestolazzi, which we take into great consideration as noted below.

of the older QCA units or aspects of the New National Curriculum will be used as they were produced; others will be modified, and others will be covered by similar units with another point of view. Important aspects such as cosmology will be added, showing that the order visible in this world (which was not produced by chance) is linked to a higher principle in a way which is explanative of this world and is demonstrable.

SUMMARY OF LIFE'S STRANDS OF NATURAL SCIENCE

- Fitrah science: nature observation
- Seeing world as *ayat* and studying specific wisdoms to start to see the wisdom flowing through the whole cosmos
- Conceptual engagement
- Natural philosophy
- Cosmology

In addition, psychology is a branch of natural science. While Imam al-Ghazali indicates that natural science is not *fard 'ayn* for Muslims to know, in *Mizan al-'amal*, he indicates that one must know enough psychology to understand ethics, in order to establish that the path to felicity in the afterlife—and purification (tazkiyah) in this life—requires a particular type of *'amal* which we may translate as praxis, practical ethics, or simply purification of the soul (itself identical with tazkiyah).

b. Why?

The spiritual benefits of this method include keeping the children's natural interest alive, one commonly referred to as a 'spark' which often goes out in Year 4 and seems to 'die' in GCSE exams. Our method strengthens their *basirah* (inner vision) to enable them to notice the realities, wisdom, and power operating in the natural world which stands in front of them. At this stage in this curriculum, the iman of the children is strengthened. Through this, children are less dependent on arguments against scientific atheism of the type one often finds in faith-based education. This type of defence through arguments often has not only an apologetic tone, but a defensive tone. And the children are often not mature or motivated enough to understand such arguments. Curriculum resources for the primary level will include nature study, hands-on nature study, and National Curriculum materials with some ideas introduced at particular topics. Those ideas will come from theology (including Imam al-Ghazali) and Islamic philosophy—which transmitted and refined the Greek heritage of natural science, and cosmology. As noted above, psychology is also a part of natural science, and it is a part one needs to know to purify the soul. *If you do not know what something is, you cannot purify it.*

We noted above (Section 4.1.5 on mathematics) a certain natural order for teaching the sciences: a) logic (the trivium), b) mathematics (the quadrivium), c) natural science, d) ethics, and e) metaphysics. We also mentioned that one needs to teach maths constantly, but either way, natural science is more complicated or, we might say, messy than mathematics. One should not wait till after perfecting maths to study nature, because nature appears to the senses in a way that must be engaged with in order to have the material to form proper classifications and abstractions later on. So, nature study is required before natural science.

In the terms of the pedagogical thought of Johann Pestalozzi, if one merely learns definitions from books, they are hollow abstractions which may break down when challenged because they did not carefully observe and capture the realities of things as they appear. In a word, they are brittle, or even dogmatic.[166]

Further, careful reflection on nature gives us a sense of some basic realities that are needed to build (or rebuild) ethical arguments in our sceptical world. If we notice the different types of being and change and learn how to draw valid inferences of the intellect from the senses, then we can enter the study of theoretical ethics prepared to stand our ground against sceptics that argue that all our concepts are constructed, including ethical concepts and principles. Further, much of traditional logic is built on psychology: it includes points about what kind of information the senses bring, what is the role of imagination, what is called 'common-sense' (or the *sensus communus*), and what the intellect is and how it benefits from the senses. If one takes these elements away, classical logic is not able to be a tool to produce knowledge because it no longer addresses the human and their connection with the world through which knowledge is produced.

A critique of modern science and a solution

We argue that any curriculum aiming for true religion or wisdom and true knowledge must come to a critical evaluation of modern science. Otherwise, students will not only have to embrace a tension, but a contradiction inside themselves and their culture. We may term this 'cognitive dissonance', one most contemporary people learn to get over when they leave their idealistic youth and settle into a career and raise children.

In simplest terms, modern science denies there are truths and realities and sets up a science we may describe charitably as 'partial'. As expounded below, it is partial as it only studies the material and quantitative aspects of reality, yet it is generally assumed to be giving a thorough explanation of the world—aside

---

166 This was noted in the theoretical introduction to the present book.

from such aspects as values and beauty which are often considered subjective.

Note that some people who have thought about modern science believe scientism is a sort of detachable doctrine from modern science, like they imagine evolution or positivism to be. However, the history of science disagrees. English science in the highly influential Royal Society, for instance, as early as the 17th century rejected research built in any way on anything other than phenomena. In France, Auguste Comte encouraged generations of scientists for whom the rules of positivism were absolute: any non-empirical elements were illicit for science. Some claim that post-positivist science allowed non-empirical or non-phenomenalist notions to be considered, but by this time a developed scientific worldview had been produced without these elements, and bringing them back in is neigh impossible. (Let us ignore the taboos which still exist regarding anything which does not sound naturalistic or even materialistic. Even Newton's crowning achievements of science were rejected or questioned for decades and termed 'spooky' because gravity appeared to operate at a distance.)

Secondly, the whole framework assumed for exploring science is built on one of two possible approaches. Either things have natures human minds can grasp or they are mechanical clumps of matter and primary (i.e., quantitative) attributes whose movements are described by mathematical (i.e., quantitative) extrinsic laws. The prior is based on the pervasive traditional notion that the human faculty setting them apart from animals is the ability to perceive (or apprehend) universal natures. Logic is the science for reasoning about natures and their relations to each other, and hence it was the tool of all science before being replaced ineffectively (as attested to by history) by Bacon. Logic was thus stripped out of the whole discussion (except for a later logic which was purely relational). The only balanced way forward is to return the deductive part of logic and develop the inductive part of logic in the hands of someone who understands both traditional subjects (especially metaphysics and natural science), including logic, and also modern science.

A world of matter and quantity lacks meaning and has no purpose of its own. This leads not only to relativism and pragmatism, but nihilism, especially as it includes the human being. If the human being has no intrinsic end, then people have to make up a purpose and construct an identity around it: this is the modern personality. Because modern science assumes the universe has no meaning aside from mathematical mechanical laws, it is a blank slate on which to project our desires and is a canvas upon which to paint our project. Trees and forests and other habitats have no intrinsic value: they are simply 'natural resources' for which modern culture makes efficient modes of harvesting and leverages their financial potential; these resources are then dumped into a centralised capitalistic model which is utopian: the more capital, the more far-reaching the project. But such a model lacks a sense of intrinsic value, and it lacks quality, form, and final cause, so it tends to focus on quantity—in part because the other matters are subjective.

A human with no end has no salvation and no purification. Salvation is through this quantitative, utopian growth which has only one of two models: capitalism and communism, each with a devastating critique of the other. Aside from this critique, each are a political theology: secular forms which are modelled on and replace Christian institutions and truth claims. Economic salvation replaces salvation in the afterlife, as well as salvation through purification and development of the soul. Without natural science taking a certain form, none of this could work. 'It all goes together.'

Educationally speaking, this worldview makes one blind to form. Form and nature are synonyms from one viewpoint. Nature and form both disappear and only culture remains. This is the extreme end of a dominating theme in the social sciences: social construction. All that we call nature is our conception of nature, which is really based on our worldview and culture. So as stated, nature disappears, and we are only left with a constructed culture.

Part of the lie here is that, in fact, we always get our best ideas from nature. Only when we perfect our understanding of nature can we possibly improve on it, as is done in the very best of traditional art. One example is the British military which prides itself on studying nature to produce even things like warplanes. The theme we speak of here manifests in every aspect of our lives: mathematics, ethics, art, and the wider culture. Some Muslim educators have noted the artificial split between art, mathematics, and natural science but to my knowledge none of them have offered a full solution in the form of a well-thought out and coherent curriculum.

The tension in contemporary culture between science and the humanities is a new version of an older tension between the moderns and ancients. One irony is that natural science used to be a part of philosophy, or what we would today call a humanities subject. Most of us are unaware of how this change took place, and thus can only orientate ourselves in terms of modern maps. This is surely an aspect of the mis-education occurring through modern culture. The Renaissance began as a rebirth of ancient culture. But early modern thinkers began to think that they could surpass the ancients. Thus, they replaced traditional wisdom with their mechanistic and mathematical 'science', as noted by a few modern thinkers who are able to orient themselves in these strong crosscurrents.

The modern world functions through a set of natural and social sciences. Those sciences are not default positions but are based on a set of philosophical bases which are implicit. Most 'modern educated' persons learn how to operate the system embodied in these sciences, but they are unaware of the philosophical presuppositions. If we turn to natural science, the key presuppositions are that what is real is matter, or what we would term now sub-atomic particles, atoms, and if one is lucky, molecules. Some modern scientists claim they are realists: a person who believes that things have realities and that they are knowable, at least to a certain degree. Even these so-called realists say that anything larger than a molecule is an 'unstable category'. What is meant is that it is not real. It is not 'being'. Think about this for a minute. Are you just your atoms? Are the various biological species and all their beauty nothing but atoms? Are things just their matter? When that matter has a form, is the form just an illusion, just a passing reality like a shadow? Do the matter and form not make a reality which is more important than the matter alone? Early modern scientists revived ancient arguments for atomism and materialism through texts translated in the Renaissance. Current scientists pick them up and are unaware where they came from and likely do not think they are philosophical in origin, but that they are merely 'scientific' and 'empirical' findings which are objective. These are all dangerous biases, as they blind us to form. An ancient story told of an argument about a bridge. Is it just stones, or is it the form of the bridge which makes it a bridge, or is it both: the matter and the form?

This crucial point is illustrated brilliantly in the following story: 'Marco Polo describes a bridge, stone by stone. "But which is the stone that supports the bridge?" Kublai Khan asks. "The bridge is not supported by one stone or another," Marco answers, "but by the line of the arch that they form." Kublai Khan remains silent, reflecting. Then he adds: "Why do you speak to me of the stones? It is only the arch that matters to me." Polo answers: "Without stones there is no arch."'

c. How?

In early years, the focus should be on natural history, hands-on nature study, and nature through narrative to allow the children to absorb the world as a whole and have an emotional and rational attachment to it, to study its behaviour in its natural environment before dissection and analysis. The following resources embody this approach: *Parables from Nature, Chance or Creation: God's Design in the Universe, Hands on Nature Study*, and the overall nature study approach developed in *Pocket Full of Pinecones* and which implements the Charlotte Mason methods of keeping a nature journal.

Other activities may be adopted from the Waldorf-Steiner method (based on the Waldorf School's curriculum established under the German scientist and mystic, Rudolf Steiner), such as planting seeds in reception and KS1 (Key Stage 1).

STRANDS

The reason science is taught with many strands is that elements are being added to the National Curriculum. Also, it is worthy of note that strands 3 through 6 could easily be subsumed under one title such as 'nature study'. Finally, it should be noted that science in the curriculum went through a stage of being three strands: chemistry, biology, and physics. Some of the strands included in our approach should be on-going, such as season watch in order to monitor the changing of the seasons, and others should be on-going to maintain a qualitative and personal approach to science to ameliorate the effect of a positivistic and naturalistic science curriculum. Other units should be taught as developmentally appropriate, beginning with prerequisites and ending with what builds on that basis.

National Curriculum units are available in the well-presented Galore Parks series, though the somewhat aged QCA (Quality and Curriculum Authority) units are still available for free on the link found below. A resource such as Galore Parks is slightly more complete, and easier if one is not a trained teacher. However, the QCA units are free.

The National Curriculum units we recommend in the earlier years are far less than the NC recommends. Then, the number we recommend fans out each year such that students will be able to pass exams needed to move on to higher levels of education. It is believed that there is sufficient time at the primary level to focus on personal development and that, if a strong grounding in language and maths is established, students can learn the strands of science easily without repeating topics throughout their years of schooling to the degree as is present in the NC.

National Curriculum Units are available at:

QCA: http://webarchive.nationalarchives.gov.uk/20090608182316/ http://standards.dfes.gov.uk/schemes2/science/?view=get

[Note that at the bottom left of the page, one finds the important tab labelled, 'Print/download the unit'. There, a .doc and .pdf version of the whole unit is downloadable in a single file.]

Galore Parks: available for purchase in the UK and, for a higher price, in the US

Nature through Narrative: Y1-3: *Parables from Nature*, Y4-6: *God or Chance*, and selective use of some of Harun Yahya's books, including Ants, Bees, and Beavers.

Hands on Nature units

Nature Table and Season Watch

Nature Observation (local outdoor trips with clipboard)

Nature Observation (indoor study of seasonal and permanent nature specimen)

Resources Used in Strands

Strand 1: See QCA link above.

Strand 2: See '2. Nature Through Narrative' below for books of Thornton Burgess, Margaret Gatty, Al-Jahiz, Jean Henri Fabre and Charles Kingsley, etc.

Strand 3: *Hands on Nature*, Lingelbach, 2000.

Strand 4: Nature Observation

- *Keeping a Nature Journal*, Leslie and Roth, 2nd ed., 2003.
- *Pocketful of Pinecones*, Karen Andreola, 2002.

EXPLAINING STRANDS

QCA units:

The number of QCA units taught each year will fan out, from one in year 1 to four in year 4 and so on such that students will be sufficient prepared for SATS by Y6. In addition to those QCA units which are taught, other strands listed above will cover the same topics of other QCA units, even if it does not teach them in precisely the same way.

Nature through Narrative:

Nature through Narrative gives students the opportunity to learn about nature through the writings of natural historians and keen nature observers who weave their awareness into writings which convey their knowledge as well as sense of awe for their subject. A number of books have been selected which are appropriate for the students between the age of five and eleven.

Preparatory (preschool, reception/KG, or pre-reading):

The Adventures of..., *Bedtime Stories* by Thornton Burgess. If these books are not read-aloud to children (or independently by confident readers), they may be used in Y1. There are 20 full books in total, each around a 100 pp, starting with *Reddy Fox*.

Year 1:

Old Mother West Wind (Set), Thornton Burgess, 1997, beginning with *Old Mother West Wind*, reprint 2011. Around 200 pages each, rather than focussing on one animal at a time, the stories each involve many animals.

WEEKLY SUBJECTS — The Study of Nature

YEAR	Y1	Y2	Y3	Y4	Y5	Y6
NUMBER of Units	2	2	3	4	5	6
NAMES of units	1A Ourselves (modified)	2A Health and Growth	3A Teeth and Eating	4A Moving and Growing	5A Keeping Healthy	6C More About Dissolving
		2B Plants and Animals in the Local Environment	3B Helping Plants Grow Well	4B Habitats	5B Life Cycles	6D Reversible and Irreversible Changes
			3D Rocks and Soils	4E Friction	5D Changing State	6E Forces in Action
				3F Light and Shadows (from Y3 and link with prayer times)	5E Earth, Sun, and Moon	6G How We See Things
Units covered in other STRANDS	1B Growing Plants covered by NOi: Growing Sunflowers and eating seeds			4C Keeping Warm, covered by Season Watch	5B Life Cycles covered by tadpoles	6A Inter-dependence and Adaptation

QCA Science units taught or covered in years 1 through 6

(Optional: *Honeybees: That Build Perfect Combs*, 2005 and *The Ants: The World of Our Little Friends*, 2011 by Harun Yahya.)

Year 2:

Burgess Bird Book for Children, reprint 2004, by Thornton Burgess; *Parables from Nature* by Margaret Gatty, reprint 2006 (first half). [If students struggle with her Victorian English, they may temporarily acclimatise through relying on a simplified version by Leslie Laurio.]

Year 3:

Burgess Animal Book for Children, reprint 2003, by Thornton Burgess; *Parables from Nature* by Margaret Gatty, reprint 2006 (second half)

Year 4:

Secrets of the Woods (reprint 2007) and *Ways of Wood Folk* (reprint 2010) by William J. Long; *By Pond and River* (reprint 2008) and *Wild Life in Woods and Fields* (reprint 2008) by A. Buckley; (Optional: *The Secret of Everyday Things* (reprint 2008) by Jean Henri Fabre; *Wonderful Creatures*, Harun Yahya, ed. by Abdassamad Clarke, in Y4 while editing out statements about evolution and faith which are unnecessary.)

Year 5:

God or Chance: God's Design in the Universe, Al-Jahiz (tr. M.A. Abdel Haleem), 1996 (first half of the book); *Christian Liberty Nature Reader Book 4*, 2000, by Florence Bass; (Optional: *The Science Storybook*, reprint 2006, by Jean Henri Fabre (first half))

Year 6:

God or Chance: God's Design in the Universe, Al-Jahiz (tr. M.A. Abdel Haleem), 1996, (second half); *Christian Liberty Nature Reader*, Book 5, 2002, by Florence Bass; (Optional: *The Science Storybook*, reprint 2006, by Jean Henri Fabre (second half) and *Madam How and Lady Why: First Lessons on Earth Lore for Children*, reprint 2007, by Charles Kingsley, a defender of religion, Kingsley was nonetheless convinced of the impermanence of species. However, his belief in evolution has not stopped this work on geology from being used by traditional Christians.)

NATURE THROUGH NARRATIVE LESSONS

These will be between 45 and 50 minutes. The format will be approximately as follows:

Intro:

Teacher introduces topic of chapter by passing around objects, books, or pictures related to the topic or simply by discussion (possibly including a spider diagram).

Reading:

Teacher reads from 15-20 minutes. In younger year groups, this should be broken up more with discussion or use of pictures, books, or objects.

Snowball Discussion:

First groups of 2, then 4, then whole class discuss, summarise (including naming main points), clarify (overall or difficult points and individual misunderstandings), and predict (the implications of what they learned or discuss question that arise which they would like to answer on the topic).

Narration:

In KS1, students narrate what they learned into science notebook. They should use writing frames or work in groups with strong writers being dictated to by group members. (Product should be copied for each member and pasted into science book.) In KS2, students write as much as they remember into science books.

Hands on Nature units:

The units of these two books (*Nature for the Very Young* being used in the first year only) contain clear directions. They are roughly based on the science curricula common in the early 20th century which taught science through exploring nature and natural objects inside and outside the classroom. At the same time, the books are modern resources which offer detailed lesson plans.

Nature Table and Season Watch:

A nature table is maintained in each classroom. The colour of the tablecloth and backing paper of poems are displayed to match the season. Children bring in natural objects representing the season or, if this is difficult, natural objects in general (i.e., a rock).

In the first science lesson of each month, students use a lesson to go out with a clipboard and draw or photo the season, mark the temperature, go out as a class to bring things in from nature, or in some other way (see sheet where breakdown of observations related to earth and sky, flora and fauna are written) contribute to the **Season Watch** (see drawing and try to draw in) or be introduced to the new nature table if that month marks the beginning of the season. They learn a poem from the **Nature Table** (during lesson if time permits). At the centre of the seasons listed on the season watch, the name of the season is written at the top of a picture or drawing of that season which 'sums it up'. Near the numbers representing the months, pictures and objects of the class are placed along with a sheet recording weather (temperature, rainfall, etc.), constellations, bird and animal and insect activity, river temperatures, etc.

Nature Observation (outdoor):

As described in *Keeping a Nature Journal*, Leslie/Roth and *Pocket Full of Pinecones*, children take a clipboard out and draw something. They come back and describe it. The teacher goes through Comstock nature guide or similar to find the name of their species and basic facts about it for children to write into their journal.

Nature Observation (indoor):

This involves nature specimens (either in class or around the school) such as planting pots or a small garden outside (with seasonal plants that grow and decay) or rabbit cage (which is of more constant or permanent interest).

Seasonal

Year	Nature Specimen
R	Herbs (each child selects; watercress)
Y1	Flower (each child selects)
Y2	Sunflower
Y3	Potatoes/Tomatoes
Y4	Strawberries/Mushrooms
Y5	Tadpoles
Y6	Caterpillar/Butterfly

Permanent

Year	Nature Specimen
R	Frog
Y1	Beetles
Y2	Wood Lice
Y3	Guinea Pigs

Y4	Rabbits
Y5	Worms
Y6	Ants

LESSON ALLOCATION

78 lessons of 45 minutes per year, roughly 26 per term

YEAR 1

QCA units: 2 QCA units	26 lessons
Nature through Narrative: Parables from Nature over	15 lessons
Hands on Nature units: (2 units of 7/8 lessons each)	15 lessons
Nature Table and Season Watch	10 lessons
Nature Observation - outdoor	6 lessons
Nature Observation - indoor	6 lessons
	78 lessons

Nature Observation Topics

Autumn: Trees (their parts, common local varieties, in class observation of branches, leaf rubbing, and draw pinecones)

Spring: Mammals (squirrels drawn under large trees in a park, etc.)

Summer: Wild flowers (draw and use http://www.mywildflowers.com/ or Handbook of Nature Study (HNS) to identify wildflowers)

YEAR 2

QCA units: 2 QCA units	26 lessons
Nature through Narrative: Parables from Nature	15 lessons
Hands on Nature units	15 lessons
Nature Table and Season Watch	10 lessons
Nature Observation - outdoor	6 lessons
Nature Observation - indoor	6 lessons
	78 lessons

The Study of Nature WEEKLY SUBJECTS

Nature Observation Topics

Autumn: Insects

Spring: Birds

Summer: Garden flowers/weeds

YEAR 3

QCA: 3 units		38 lessons
Teeth and Eating	(12 lessons)	
Helping Plants Grow Well	(13 lessons)	
Rock and Soil	(13 lessons)	
Nature Through Narrative		10 lessons
Hands on Nature		8 lessons
Nature Table and Season Watch		10 lessons
Nature Observation - outdoor		6 lessons
Nature Observation - indoor		6 lessons
		78 lessons

Nature Observation Topics

Autumn: Reptiles

Winter: Flowerless plants/crops

Spring: Fish and amphibians

YEAR 4

QCA units: 4 units over		48 lessons
Moving and Growing	(12 lessons)	
Habitats	(12 lessons)	
Friction	(12 lessons)	
Light and Sound	(12 lessons)	
Nature Through Narrative (read-aloud)		11 lessons
Hands on Nature		8 lessons

WEEKLY SUBJECTS   *The Study of Nature*

Nature Table and Season Watch	10 lessons
Nature Observation - outdoor	6 lessons
Nature Observation - indoor	6 lessons
	78 lessons
Parables from Nature (read-aloud)	11 lessons
Nature Through Narrative (read-aloud)	11 lessons

Nature Observation Topics

Autumn: Mammals and wildflowers

Winter: Rocks and minerals

Spring: Fish and amphibians

YEARS 5 & 6: TWO APPROACHES

At Years 5 & 6, we offer two approaches:

a) a more reflective and text-based approach and

b) an approach which hugs closer to the British (or your local) National Curriculum.

National curriculum science represents contemporary science and its limitation but attempts to generate wonder and interest in topics and 'the world'. It tends, especially in secondary education, to be about problems and computation. While the argument goes that this makes it more relevant, hands on, and even interesting, it represents one side of two-sided argument. One side is captured in the famous quip: 'Shut up and calculate'. The other position represented by Einstein has been expressed thus: 'No, look, the job of physics is to know and understand how the world is, not just to make predictions about the results of experiments and that sort of operationalist view. Well, fine, that's useful but that doesn't give us real understanding.' While this sentiment is in the right direction, modern science has for centuries depleted itself of the bases needed to explain things rather than merely predict. It has committed itself to a model in which things are just inert matter moving passively under the influence of extrinsic laws, rather than due to their own nature and form and attributes.

Our view goes one step further than Einstein's sentiments of seeking understanding (on a model that will not really allow it). Modern science has

Year 2 Long-term Overview

Autumn 1 7 weeks	Autumn 2 6 weeks	Spring 1 7 weeks	Spring 2 6 weeks	Summer 1 7 weeks	Summer 2 6 weeks
Nature Observation outdoors 1 lesson	Nature Observation outdoors 1 lesson	Nature Observation outdoors 1 lesson	Nature Observation outdoors 1 lesson	Nature Observation outdoors 1 lesson	Nature Observation outdoors 1 lesson
Nature Table & Season Watch 2 lessons	Nature Observation Indoors 3 lessons	Nature Observation indoors 1 lesson	Nature Observation Indoors 1 lesson	Nature Table & Season Watch 2 lessons	Nature Observation Indoors 3 lessons
Hands on Nature 8 lessons	Nature Table & Season Watch 1 lesson	Nature Table & Season Watch 2 lessons	Nature Table & Season Watch 1 lesson	QCA 11 lessons	Nature Table & Season Watch 2 lessons
Nature Through Narrative 3 lessons	Nature Through Narrative 7 lessons	QCA 10 lessons	QCA 2 lessons		QCA 2 lessons
			Nature Through Narrative 1 lesson		Nature Through Narrative 4 lessons
			Hands on Nature 7 lessons		

Year 3 Long-term Overview

Autumn 1 7 weeks	Autumn 2 6 weeks	Spring 1 7 weeks	Spring 2 6 weeks	Summer 1 7 weeks	Summer 2 6 weeks
Nature Observation outdoors 1 lesson	Nature Observation outdoors 1 lesson	Nature Observation outdoors 1 lesson	Nature Observation outdoors 1 lesson	Nature Observation outdoors 1 lesson	Nature Observation outdoors 1 lesson
Nature Observation Indoors 1 lesson	Nature Observation Indoors 1 lesson	Nature Observation Indoors 1 lesson	Nature Observation Indoors 1 lesson	Nature Observation Indoors 1 lesson	Nature Observation Indoors 1 lesson
Nature Table & Season Watch 2 lessons	Nature Table & Season Watch 1 lesson	Nature Table & Season Watch 2 lessons	Nature Table & Season Watch 1 lesson	Nature Table & Season Watch 2 lessons	Nature Table & Season Watch 1 lesson
Hands on Nature 8 lessons	8 QCA lessons	8 QCA lessons	8 QCA lessons	8 QCA lessons	6 QCA lessons
Nature Through Narrative 2 lessons	Nature Through Narrative 1 lesson	Nature Through Narrative 2 lessons	Nature Through Narrative 1 lesson	Nature Through Narrative 2 lessons	Nature Through Narrative 1 lesson

Year 4 Long-term Overview

Autumn 1 7 weeks	Autumn 2 6 weeks	Spring 1 7 weeks	Spring 2 6 weeks	Summer 1 7 weeks	Summer 2 6 weeks
Nature Observation outdoors 1 lesson	Nature Observation outdoors 1 lesson	Nature Observation outdoors 1 lesson	Nature Observation outdoors 1 lesson	Nature Observation outdoors 1 lesson	Nature Observation outdoors 1 lesson
Nature Observation Indoors 1 lesson	Nature Observation Indoors 1 lesson	Nature Observation Indoors 1 lesson	Nature Observation Indoors 1 lesson	Nature Observation Indoors 1 lesson	Nature Observation Indoors 1 lesson
Nature Table & Season Watch 2 lessons	Nature Table & Season Watch 1 lesson	Nature Table & Season Watch 2 lessons	Nature Table & Season Watch 1 lesson	Nature Table & Season Watch 2 lessons	Nature Table & Season Watch 1 lesson
1 QCA Lessons	10 QCA Lessons	9 QCA Lessons	9 QCA Lessons	9 QCA Lessons	9 QCA Lessons
Hands on Nature 8 lessons					

left behind the real conceptual basis needed to understand the world as it can be known without instruments, and this needs recovery and to ideally be joined with any findings of modern science which are beyond interpretation.

So, we recommend that you favour realist and explanative science, but do not completely neglect computation and calculation. If you wish to organise your year into three terms and six half-terms, each devoted to one topic, then cherry pick one or two topics from the British (or local) National Curriculum. These units are listed below in 'Approach Three'.

APPROACH ONE

This approach is for confident teachers who can produce lessons from unit descriptions and recommended resources.

Spend six to eight weeks on the following topics each:

YEAR 5: COSMOLOGY, NATURAL SCIENCE & THE ORIGINS OF MODERN SCIENCE

- **Sacred cosmology**

Draw from scripture but also poets such as Rumi who discuss cosmogony (the origins of the universe as described in scripture, etc.), the Divine Names, and the nature of Adam, his covenant, and the names taught to him. How do the species and natural kinds reflect the Divine Names and the names taught to Adam? How can prophets and some of their followers gain this knowledge of the realities of things?

- **Realist Ontology and Epistemology**

As a simple ontology, introduce the students to a summary or summary text on the Ten Categories of Being.

Introduce the foundations of epistemology, including how we come to know each of the ten categories. Discuss knowledge itself (which is a quality of the soul, and thus one of the categories). Note how the ability to apprehend universals is what distinguishes Adam (upon him peace) from the animals. Note the medieval synthesis in which the Islamic and medieval Christian view were close to each other, though had a few significant differences. The shared view synthesises reason and revelation. Mention potential downfalls (e.g., it can give the sense that things are independent). Note that pre-modern times included scientific advancement in both Islam and Christendom (e.g., Roger Bacon, not to be confused with Francis Bacon). The difference is that this advancement was on a realist model.

- **The Renaissance**

  'The Fathers of Modern Science and the Rule of Mathematics' as a general theme, read in works such as E. F. Schumacher's *A Guide for the Perplexed*, Ch. 1, 'On Philosophical Maps,' and draw from (or even merely abridge and simplify) Philip Sherrard's *Human Image: World Image*, Ch. 4, 'Knowledge and the Predicament of Modern Science.' The shift from a sacred cosmology to a mathematical model of human sciences (which renders the quantitative mechanical and all but quantity subjective) is well set out, especially in Sherrard.

- **The Scientific Method**

  'The End of the Speculative, and the Rise of Induction and the Phenomena' as a general theme, cover from Francis Bacon to Newton's experience with the Royal Society. Note that development of induction is good, but there is no valid reason to discard deduction which is the more essential scientific method. (Maths link: Speak of the move from Greek geometry to a focus on mechanics used to give advantages of canons on sailing crafts, etc.)

- **Empiricism and Science**

  'Locke and Sir Robert Boyle'. Boyle represents the rise of Greek atomism. What are the problems with empiricism? (Can we understand the world through pure sense perception? How would that be different from animal perception? How can cause and effect be perceived with the senses? 'The Rise of David Hume'.)

- **Newton, Scientific Method and Freedom**

  Speak of how Newton's system was perceived as leaving no room for human free choice. What was the European response to this (particularly that of Kant)? (For a good writing on freedom and scientific determinism accessible to confident educators, see Yves R Simon, *Great Dialogue of Nature and Space*, Chapter X-Chance and determinism in philosophy and science.)

YEAR 6: THE MODERN WORLD & SCIENCE

Year 6 should accomplish the following:

- provide a basic narrative of the period,
- explain how the assumptions about science shaped not only science, but the rest of human disciplines, and
- offer a balanced inquiry into the harms and benefits of modern technology.

  It should empower students to engage with questions such as:

- 'Could technological development carry on if a balanced view of all the sciences was returned?'
- 'Could modern science and technology be disentangled from its metaphysical assumptions?'
- 'Are bureaucracies requiring the mass of educated citizens in a country required for technology to tick over?'
- 'Why do we work more than ever, when from the time of Bacon there was a notion of a utopia where people worked optionally or not at all?'
- 'Can one be a full and coherent person working in bureaucracies and with machines and factories?'
- 'Does a person need a connection to land and nature to be healthy and happy (and to preserve the fitrah)?'

CORE UNITS

- **Cosmology**

Teach the links between this world and the higher worlds starting from discussions of Quranic terms and key verses. The aim of the units on the philosophy of science will be simply to show that science is limited in the claims it can make because of the methods it adopts. The impact of a loss of cosmology may be studied through readings in C.S. Lewis' *The Discarded Image* which may be taught in science or in liberal arts.

- **The Basic Principles of Realism**

Realism is defined as the belief that things have realities and that they are knowable. What are basic principles that have to be in place to underpin and understand this? How are they to be argued for in our time? This unit should elaborate these in simple but clear terms. These include a) that things have an intelligible nature, b) that we have the capacity to know natures without intellects, and c) that in spite of our first contact with the world being through the senses that we can learn about intelligible natures via the senses.

- **Technology's Impact on Society and Epistemology**

Technology requires massive infrastructure to operate and expand. It has in the past relied on commodification, industrialisation of many sectors of human life (including food, medicine, and art) and bureaucratisation/technocratisation of work and society to build this basis. The aim is not to remove technology, but to learn the good usage (good *mu'amalah*) of technology, to learn its proper place and keep it there. Technology has had a huge impact on epistemology and culture. The humanities are often labelled subjective and useless, and Neo-liberal economics which drives tech and infrastructure drives our work (where we spend our most productive waking hours), our universities, and even our schools. Technology leads to mediated experiences (using tools and graphs, data, etc), including our social experiences (more and more on online media platforms). All of this leads to the commodification of the human and knowledge, showing the intimate link with economics as well.

ELECTIVE/OPTIONAL UNITS

The Steam Engine and Electricity: Study the economic and cultural impact of the industrial revolution in history and art.

The Rise of the Machine and Factory: Technology, production, and ethics.

The Rise of Departments, Specialisation, and 'Big Science', the Decline of Integrated, Human Knowledge

Modern Science and New Age Religion, Teilhard de Chardin, Rupert Sheldrake, and the Quantum Gurus, the Virtual World (and decrease in the value of the real world).

APPROACH TWO

Anthony Rizzi has a set of resources which are very important yet do not amount to a full curriculum. (Further resources are found in the secondary section of this book.) His approach though is aimed at one of the central problems we noted above: that contemporary science is a mathematical abstraction which excludes the common sense/philosophical reality that appears to our minds via our senses. His two works for children not only speak of the everyday intelligibility of worldly objects which is missing from physics, but it also performs a traditional role of physics: to study the changing natural world as the effect of what Rizzi terms the 'Unchangeable Changer'. This is a classical form of reasoning from effect to cause—or in this case Cause.

The first of two 'kid's' introductions to physics lays the foundations to study abstract science in general on the basis of common sense. After making these crucial connections, which transforms physics, the second book addresses mechanics, electricity and magnetism, and quantum mechanics from that basis, at a very simple level.

A Kid's Introduction to Physics (and Beyond), Volume I, which is 70 pages, we recommend for Year 5.

A Kid's Introduction to Physics (and Beyond), Volume II, which is 107

pages, we recommend for Year 6.

The Science Before Science: A Guide to Thinking in the 21st Century. [Also available on an audiobook of around 12 hours for busy teachers and parents.] This book speaks of how to reconcile modern science and traditional, wisdom based 'physics' and lays out something of the history of science. Teachers who are able should acquaint themselves with the wider vision of how Rizzi describes the two modes of studying science, and how the two distinct modes of study may be reunited. The manner we express this central challenge of study of the physical world is that the technical or ideoscopic (or empirio-metric) mode of studying science operates through abstractions generally expressed in modern mathematics and logic, both of which we have noted in other LIFE publications to have been formalised. As put by one of the LIFE team, imagine you look at a car tire and abstract away from it a circle and you simply study it as a disembodied, abstract circle. What is the reality of this circle? Traditional, pre-modern wisdom of all sorts would say this circle is only real when we realise that it is a certain type of abstraction that is embodied in a particular way in the physical (or metaphysical) world. The mathematisation and abstraction of modern science are agnostic as to whether the forms we study match the outside world, and as to how they do so if they do. As such, it is often not known how certain theories such as string theory or quantum theory match the world, or whether they are just models that help us predict future events, or whether they are just a best fit, etc. Especially in popular science, writers let their imagination get away from them and discuss all sorts of issues from worm holes to mysticism in ways that capture the readers' imagination—making them think the future is near. But decades later, these dreams turn out to be a mirage, and here we are in our real world. (Some would say this focus on the future leads to a decay of morals, community, family, and human development...and attention span! But that is another matter.)

APPROACH THREE

If you are obliged by inspectors or potential entrance exams to hug close to the British National Curriculum (or your own local education system), the following is laid out to assist you.

YEAR 5

National Curriculum Units: QCA Unit	(number of lessons)
Life cycles: 5B	12 lessons
Reversible changes (of state): 5D	12 lessons

Earth and space: 5E	12 lessons
Keeping Healthy: 5A (Optional)	12 lessons

[The first three units mentioned are available in Galore Parks' *Science Year 5*, by Sue Hunter. 'Keeping Healthy' is a unit from an older iteration of the British National Curriculum. These units are still available on the net, etc.]

Combined Nature Table, Season Watch & Nature Observation:	12 lessons (6 indoor + 6 outdoor)
Selected units in Cosmology and the History of Science:	30 lessons
	78 lessons (total)
Parables from Nature read-aloud at end of school day	11 lessons

YEAR 6

British National Curriculum: QCA units	(number of lessons)
Life Cycles: 5B	12 lessons
Changing State: 5D	12 lessons
Earth, Sun and Moon: 5E	12 lessons
Combined Nature Table, Season Watch & Nature Observation:	12 lessons (6 indoor + 6 outdoor)
Cosmology and the History of Science:	30 lessons
	78 lessons
Parables from Nature read-aloud at end of school day	11 lessons

(Optional) Scientific Classification and (dichotomous) Keys[167]

Contrast contemporary classification with that taught in works of disputation (*al-bahth wa-l-munazarah*)[168]

---

[167] Resources for the 6th to 8th grade include:
- https://www.nps.gov/teachers/classrooms/dichotomous-key.htm,
- https://www.bbc.co.uk/bitesize/articles/z9cbcwx, and
- https://dloft.stanford.edu/sites/g/files/sbiybj25171/files/media/file/designing_a_classification_tool_lesson_1.pdf which refers to many resources such as https://www.quia.com/pop/324544.html?AP_rand=1559298521.

[168] See the upcoming LIFE publication which translates al-Gelenbevi's *Adab* into English with topical introductions to matters raised in the text and an accompanying course.
   This topic would befit most students in secondary after or while studying classification in the science of disputation (also known as debate and scientific research methodology).

4.2.2 Art, Craft & Design

a. What?

What is taught in art, craft, and design in primary schools is especially riddled with fallacies. For instance, students often make items for years which are not useful. Outside the classroom, they could not survive. What is taught in art requires uncovering the original meaning of art and production, and very careful contextualisation. Based on these investigations, we advocate the following:[169]

---

[169] Some of this thought is beyond the scope of the curriculum, but needed to underpin it, as follows:

Art is a productive science. It tended in pre-modern times to be a specialism, not a hobby. But at the same time 'non- artists' were acquainted with many of what we might now term 'life' or 'productive skills', as these skills were needed daily in every home. Further, many 'non-artists' took up a productive science to round themselves out. (A notable tradition states that Ottoman warriors would learn calligraphy in order to soften and balance themselves.) Art in the modern condition is important for what we might term 'compensation'. In our condition, even those not specialising in art, craft, or design need to learn basic matters to do with beauty, economy (including prudence in spending one's own money to buy useful and beautiful products for the home), and how to support ethical production. This includes, for instance: a) the true nature of beauty (trans-subjective, not merely subjective, nor purely objective), b) proper household management, and c) how to produce, rather than merely consume. These three are related, especially the latter two. The house should be a place of production ('home economics'), not merely a sleeping pod from which one shoots out in the morning to go to work and school, and to nursery before school-age. Being a consumer is particularly disadvantageous now, as one does not merely consume a product, but a culture. The corporate world produces a culture, typically globalist. In late capitalism, you can of course have your lifestyle variations—which are like flavourings on the same stock/matter. If one cannot produce, one can at least distinguish beauty and sacred meaning. In that case, one may be an educated patron (not just an educated consumer), helping communities and the common good to flourish. If one can neither produce nor distinguish, then one is sure to bring home objects whose implicit message leads to a contradiction in one's values, or at least a performative contradiction. If one can distinguish beauty and meaning, one can search it out and undergo a collective effort to find it existent, serviced, and available in a manner fulfilling one's needs and circumstances.

There are of course developmental reasons for studying art. Many study it simply because it is fun, balances the curriculum, or because certain personalities incline particularly to it. These are not bad reasons; but let us pause these and return to what art is: we draw from art for the reasons stated, which are that it teaches them a) beauty, b) how to produce, and c) that which situates them in the body. This is through developmentally appropriate activities. These overlap with script/calligraphy (a type of drawing) and drawing itself is a means of being embodied in the senses in a way fundamental to developing the intellect and spirit. Without being embodied, the intellect and spirit suffer from not being grounded. Vain imagination undermines the intellect and spirit and confuses their operations and their insights. Tuning into the senses without disturbance is a necessary foundation for the higher faculties. The two main ways to do this are through nature and art, minding that calligraphy/script overlaps with the liberal arts. Islamic art (including vegetal, geometric, and calligraphic ornamentation) captures eternal principles of beauty and works like a frozen metaphysics. If a city has wealth, it should invest in this form of metaphysics in which all partake and which raises the spirits daily as one goes about one's business.

In pre-modern education, the arts and crafts were a stream of training entered at approximately nine to thirteen, by which age children would have graduated from the Quranic primary school (*maktab*)/primary school (*kuttab*). In our context, the age of minimum instruction has risen to between fifteen and eighteen. As these circumstances are imposed by necessity, it would seem, we recommend all children persist in education on the LIFE model which joins between modern instruction and traditional liberal arts and preparing those who wish to enter the trades through our art, craft, and design curriculum that involves a partial apprenticeship at the secondary level.

All students—those opting for a practical trade and those not—should aim during the current customary schooling years to compensate for the lack of capacity to produce (as opposed to consume) in our culture, and the lack of connection to land, plants, and animals.

Those students who do opt for practical trade should take advantage of the said additional years of education to gain a general education before they specialise on a vocation or other calling. Even those that are not intellectually inclined need aspects of culture and even the liberal arts to perfect their religion, character, and open their mind to meanings and symbolism found in the world, Quran, and Islamic literature.

While temporary conditions do entail certain years of education and forms of living, what remains of self-sustaining and sustainable communities and forms of life should not be allowed to disappear. In such communities, one finds work as a traditional and sustainable way of life, either as farmers, fishermen, shepherds and what suits the region and its local culture. In Islamic lands where such communities persist, one finds practices of support for madrasas through voluntary charity (*sadaqah*) and trusts (*awqaf*) and support for the guilds as imbibed with a transformational spiritual ethos of

> Thus, our curriculum weaves together these considerations. It also introduces them to a spiritual symbolism, an endangered species in our time. While symbolism may exist in any subject, it is highly important in the arts, specifically the visual and plastic arts. While we acknowledge that this was traditionally a specialisation and calling, our accidental circumstances force us to introduce students to these matters to protect their fitra, give their psyches a foundation, teach them to learn real beauty from an age before they can understand an argument, and to compensate for a consumer corporate culture that threatens to remove the very notion of a local and unified culture. Such cultures are not a luxury, nor a nostalgic romance, but were the very means by which mankind survived for eons and are reservoirs for wisdom like species of plants in a rainforest that contain remedies or are themselves remedies. Globalism cannot deny that each place has its own weather and used to have its own biocultural environment and soil and water type, etc. The global culture as it exists also contains or is a product umbrella leading on to objects that embody false visions of happiness. They thus militate against human development, while being designed to drive economic development.

chivalry. This is because there is a natural integration of the practical and theoretical, religion, and the community working together towards fulfilling the basic needs of life in a dignified and sacred manner.

Thus, as a necessary measure and a form of compensation for deficiencies in modern culture, students should be taught a combination of practical and theoretical topics such that such knowledge survive, and to complete their personalities.

PRACTICAL LEARNING

In terms of the practical, students should learn the following:

- The highest level practically possible of beautiful productive arts in order to be able to produce basic designs. The basis of all art is drawing. The ability to implement a drawing in a particular material is based on first being able to draw it, and the mastery of individual materials source to many branches coming from this root.
- Calligraphy and sacred geometry should be taught, as well as traditional floral designs which take less training. (Note though that floral designs often presuppose knowledge of the geometric to compose a piece with proper layout and proportions.)
- Introductions for the young to woodwork (and carpentry), stonework, and weaving work best where they lead to motivating fruits and where there are teachers.
- Bookbinding and typesetting are relatively easy to put into practice, and the latter may, with design, open into a career.

Students that experience the production of various items are uniquely in place to know and sense how to consume such items properly. For instance, the basics of gardening to make fruits and vegetables and preserving such as making jams, yoghurts, and drying foods and spices. This leads to valuing food, learning to care for soil, and other fundamental lessons that alter our attitude towards the world. Such learning includes the topic of home economics such as cooking (an art being attacked by the supermarket) and sewing (an antidote to the waste of the fashion industry).

At the borderline between the practical and theoretical are found developmental experiences made practical. These include encountering and seeing artists at work, and experiencing beautiful, well-designed, and meaningful architecture, best experienced accompanied by a tour with a living architect.

THEORETICAL LEARNING

Regarding the theoretical, students should be taught art and craft and key topics such as: beauty, economy, navigating the pros and cons of machines—as they effect individuals and societies, and very importantly, community—as we have been atomised in modernised parts of the world, and the very family has deteriorated, including the wider family beyond what is now termed the 'nuclear family'. These topics may be alluded to here, along with notes on their importance.

Beauty is not particular to art, but includes natural objects, human actions, and indeed anything which is well-designed and fit to purpose. Within art, it is not primarily achieved by ornamentation; rather ornamentation must be fit to the thing ornamented. Art and craft fulfil a communal role of providing basic needs for society to function and are, if seen in this light, a calling. The craftsman should do so with justice and economy, but also with beauty through form matching end well and through proper integrated ornamentation.

Some have said that the education of each person involves a general and a particular aspect. The general is the liberal, cultural, or religious. The particular is a trade one settles on. While the crafts and trades are looked down on in certain societies failing to value production's role in life, contemporary critics have realised that many of the jobs chosen for pay packages are 'pointless' even to the employer and lead to dissatisfaction due to not being fulfilled. Production on a craft model was largely sustainable as opposed to its contemporary replacement which disregards the local and the amount of waste produced in transporting materials and products (imagine two loaded lorries passing each other on the M1 Motorway, one with one brand of biscuits (e.g., McVitie's) and the other with another brand (e.g., Cadbury)). Also, traditional crafts are spiritual opportunities and means to tazkiyah. Good drawing requires suppressing excess sense data *and* excess or uncontrolled imagination. 'Only when one can draw, can one see.'

In addition to a particular trade one may settle on, a certain part of arts and crafts enter into general education. This falls under the learning set out for instance in Ibn Khaldun's thought and relates to how the arts and crafts are necessarily part of a social vision and notion of the common good. For instance, contemporary society struggles to transcend racism and 'classism' through seeing society as a spiritual whole transcending class and race barriers. While they may have such values in their minds, they fail to penetrate their hearts. Understanding the motives for forming a society and how the crafts and other valid forms of knowledge and work were traditionally conceived of as parts in a whole is transformative, especially when one practically takes part in such production or at least learns to value it. This is a higher notion of community in which all contribute a necessary role to the whole.[170]

Every individual needs to know about economy and beauty and symbolism. While people might have learned these matters naturally in a normal society, in ours they are taught these matters in a way involving obvious fallacies. No human can afford such mis-education; insisting on the beautiful is part of piety. When one cannot afford good and beautiful products, then practicing restraint until one can afford them is also a part of piety. It is better to have a minimalist furnishing than to fill the home with plastic and cheap belongings. Ugly things in one's environment effects one's state and imprint on the imagination. Implementing this requires mutual support due to the omnipresence of marketing and mass produced 'goods', and a community cannot survive without this. Beauty is decidedly not the same as luxury, so we should not assume beauty is limited to the exclusive. Beauty comes through form which is best learned through traditional geometry listed in the curriculum below. Geometry such as the golden mean and other harmonic ratios permeates creation as has been shown in nearly every living or natural thing, even in the orbits of the planets. The general impact of understanding beauty and symbolism cannot be overestimated. While in the past scholars would have known life skills such as how to saddle or break a horse and also symbolism and beauty, the ravaging of the traditional world means this is no longer to be taken for granted for those who have undergone study or even a madrasa education.

LIFE SKILLS

Life skills points to another general factor: each individual is part of a home and thus home economics affects them. The home was traditionally a place of production. Not only does being able to grow, cook, and preserve food make one's food far healthier and more spiritually beneficial (as attested to by hadith), it makes one independent and therefore confident to adhere to beliefs

---

170 A society forming a whole requires different people to take different roles. However, there is a great deal of pressure on developing societies or communities, making them willing to invest all their resources to ascend 'the social ladder'. But they are only presented with one such ladder; they know no other and cannot be picky. The social ladder dominating our society gives prestige to office jobs over labour, but this prestige is often governed by fads and passing notions of careerism in which one is unaware temporarily of how unfulfilling or literally useless many office jobs are. Even if the wider culture takes a pay package as the be-all-end-all, one should have the foresight to see the harm to others and oneself that comes from such shortsightedness. Many careers that were once prestigious such as software design are now governed by contract labour, forcing workers to stay at work until projects are completed with no compensation for their time. This type of wage labour that borders on slave labour is becoming more common, not less as we advance in time.

which do not benefit one in a big-business (only) culture. 'It all goes together.'

GENERAL PRINCIPLES

b. Why?

'Art' is a productive science (*sina'ah*), as in the third division of the sciences according to Ibn Khaldun and others. It is essentially the making of things. In a healthy society, things are made which fulfil basic human needs. Primary needs include food, clothing, and shelter, and secondary needs include legal adjudication, monitoring coinage and measures, and military protection. These 'goods' were governed by the second major division (the practical sciences) and managed with consideration of the first division (the practical sciences) to obtain human health and spend it on gaining virtue, character (including piety), and intellect. If the arts and crafts and the science governing production and trade—economics—are not subordinated to the highest ends of culture and society, i.e., the perfection of the human being, the result is irrational action in which acts are not chosen through ordering means to ends.

Challenges facing the arts and crafts

The guilds have almost completely withered since being disbanded globally around the turn of the 20th century.

Basic life-skills are being lost in homes and communities and are not generally taught in schools.

The 'fine arts' is a very specific notion related to what is termed 'The Enlightenment'. Art and craft viewed beauty as linked to the usage of objects, not standing outside usage—as in a frame on a wall or in a museum. Unfortunately, the factory model has led to handmade crafts being exclusivist and commodified them in a way undermining the spiritual unity of a healthy community.

What is termed 'education' has been extended in nearly every country so that no one dares take a trade before completing high school/secondary school, and all are embarrassed to begin work without a university degree (entailing 17 years in the UK and approximately the same in the US).

Schooling without work of the hands is frustrating to many; studies indicate this is especially so for males. The classroom forces the student's growing personalities to negotiate their identities with the dictates of a busy teacher and school. Many students are forced by the temporary circumstances of the classroom and their limited resources as a young personality to rebel to avoid feeling branded for life as a failure.

Finally, the liberal and spiritual aspects of the traditional ethos of art have survived without guilds in only the rarest instances. Thus, the arts are often blemished with elitism or being branding as exotic rather than giving a healthy understanding of them and what the individual and society need from them (as explained above).

c. How?

GENERAL NOTES ON THE BASIC STRANDS

Crafts

While we summarise the early and shared steps towards learning the crafts below to a certain degree, the crafts are necessarily determined by local realities. What arts and crafts still exist in your locality? What natural and artificial resources are (still) available? We do list one resource that can potentially be ordered to most countries: the Steiner/Waldorf crafts make available books explaining how to dye, knit, and weave, and many of the needed materials here:

https://www.myriadonline.co.uk/products/music-books/crafts-activities-books/. (We cannot guarantee the pricing will be suitable to your budget.)

Drawing & calligraphy

In addition to the crafts and production, we have noted repeatedly that drawing is the basis for all production. Educators who are not artists may make progress in developmentally friendly drawing skills with *Draw Write Now*. This resource mentioned below combines drawing and calligraphy. It is loaded with American culture. If you prefer, experiment with either altering the lessons or using: *Draw and Write Through History*, by Carylee Gressman. This resource is recommended for ages eight and up, so you may introduce it year 3 or 4—which is where the culture of the previously named resource becomes excessive.

Colour theory

Teach colour theory each year, working it into existing lessons or starting it in a suitable season such as spring. (Follow the curriculum and activities set out in Rawson and Richter, *The Steiner Waldorf Curriculum*, pp. 78-80.)

RECEPTION/KINDERGARTEN

See separate Rec/KG section for details. These include *Draw Write Now, Book 1* (over three half-terms).

YEAR 1

Draw Write Now, Book 2 (over three half-terms)

Knitting: Finger knitting, French knitting and using a knitting nancy.

Crocheting using chain stitch and doubles. Make bags, nets for balls, and round potholders to keep plants regular temperature.

Printing and stitching cloth: Print tea towels or clothes using natural dyes. They could carve shapes on an apple or cut out cardboard and glue it to the bottom of a wood block. Stitch seams with overstitch or running stitch.

(Optional): Develop bread-making, experimenting with flours (such as spelt and wholemeal) and seeds. Make yoghurt from good, local milk. Make flat dolls. Knit or felt clothes for the dolls.

Inter-curricular: Students start to learn a script in local language and carry on with gardening.

YEAR 2

Draw Write Now, Book 3 (over three half-terms)

Knit or crochet hats, jumpers or scarves. Optionally, decorate with embroidery.

Perfection and application of stitching, dying and printing.

Make structures from wattle and daub.

(Optional): Knit or crochet glove puppets. Make a clay oven or hurdles.

Intra-curricular: Begin joined up writing.

YEAR 3

Drawing

Trace Islamic patterns on tracing paper and frame to make stained-glass window.

Trace floral designs and lay over border of poems to make simple illumination.

Practice application of Arabic calligraphy in naskh script (study examples and trace or begin to design even if only using one word such as 'Allah').

Materials

Papercraft: students learn to cut frames for their work and to make models from *papier mâché*, etc. (See, Angelika Wolk-Gerche, *Papercraft*.)

Learn cross-stitch.

Make a pit forge, producing a simple poker.

Introduce symbolism (*Concentric Circles*) and explain traced traditional patterns, if known, and the materials in which they put their design and who the artists were (and introduce the notion of a guild (*ta'ifah*).

Cross-curricular: Drawing is intently pursued in nature study in this and following years.

YEAR 4

Drawing

Learn to use compass and straightedge and start making designs such as the flower of life and next steps toward underlying grid.

Learn basic elements of *Islimi* floral (or plant-based) patterns.

Carry on with Arabic calligraphy in naskh script

Materials

(including tracing designs learned in above and carving, knitting, or painting them in these materials)

Woodwork: carve cooking spoons, mallets, paper knife, small spoons, garden dibbers, etc. Discuss safe use of tools.

Knit on five needles: socks, mittens and gloves. (See, Marja de Haan, *Knit Together, Share Together*.)

Pottery: make simple bowls, pencil holders, or other useful objects.

Cross-curricular: Drawing is intently pursued in nature study in this and following years.

YEAR 5

Drawing

Carry on with compass and straightedge and apply learning of *Euclid's Elements*. Learn to perform the basic straightedge and compass constructions through repeating the five basic constructions.

Carry on with Arabic calligraphy in naskh script

Expand knowledge of *Islimi* floral (or plant-based, also referred to as vegetable Arabesque) patterns and apply to illumination *(tazhip)*. Illuminate poetry or pages from an important book studied in Year 5 or earlier.

Materials

Woodwork: Study trees and different timbres, split and chop firewood and kindling, make tent pegs with a hand axe, etc. Hollow a bird box from a large log. Encourage children to reflect on the principles of tools as an introduction to natural science: Shy is a crowbar or wrench shaped the way it is? What is the mechanical principle behind it?

Pottery: make bowls and plates, glazing them in a conventional oven.

Learn to cook a variety of soups in accord with the seasons and the vegetables found in your region and cuisine

Cross-curricular: Drawing is intently pursued in nature study in this and following years.

YEAR 6

Drawing.

Carry on or complete same straightedge and compass constructions began in Year 5. Learn the basic shapes of tessellating tile patterns. Cut them out with a hacksaw and make different designs, introducing colour in a patterned manner.

Expand knowledge of *Islimi* floral (or plant-based) patterns and apply to illumination *(tazhip)*.

If competent in the basic hand of naskh script, learn thuluth calligraphy (or Kufic script).

Materials

Woodwork: carve bowls, make toys from Reception class. Use hammer and nail to make raised growing beds, bird houses, etc.

Cook stews. Preferably, use vegetables and herbs from your garden, or at least which are seasonal.

The Art of the Book: Write out chapters of a chosen, important book, ornamenting especially the title page and chapter head. Consider illustrating core scenes.

Cross-curricular: Drawing is intently pursued in nature study in this and following years.

WEEKLY SUBJECTS   *Art, Craft & Design*

THEORETICAL & HISTORICAL TEACHING

General: Read descriptions of art and economic order in Ibn Khaldun, *Muʻid al-niʻam* of Taj al-Din al-Subki and the guilds in Lane's *The Manners and Customs of Modern Egyptians*, as well as suitable accounts of medieval European guilds written for children. Children's books include:

Reception: Golden Domes and Silver Lanterns

Year 1: *Journey Through Islamic Art*, Na'ima bint Robert & Diano Mayo (French & English)

Year 2: *A Nest for Celeste: A Story About Art, Inspiration, and the Meaning of Home*, by Henry Cole, Katherine Tegen Books, 2010

Year 3: *Shah Jehan and the Story of the Taj Mahal*, Hoopoe Books

Year 4: *Heart of a Shepherd*, Rosanne Perry.

Year 5: *The Ottoman Empire: Life During the Great Civilisations* (including construction of the great mosques)

Year 6: *The Glassblower's Children*, Maria Gripe (this story involves several crafts persons and involves the search for good work), *The Alhambra Told to Children*. For confident students: Read on ethics of production, work (including treatment of workers, and economy and including critique of political economy).

Consider drawing on simpler materials found in our secondary curriculum. This includes essays and selections from the books of Pugin, John Ruskin (*Letters to the Workmen of England*, 1870), William Cobbett, William Morris, Eric Gill, Charles Ashbee (and his education materials), Walter Shewring (particularly his collection of essays, *Making and Thinking*), C. S. Lewis (*The Abolition of Man*), and writers who directly addressed sacred art such as Titus Burckhardt and Brian Keeble.

4.2.3 DIGITAL DESIGN & INFORMATION TECHNOLOGY

a. What?

Some home schoolers and classical schoolers choose not to introduce computers until secondary age. There are many good reasons for this. Much scientific research relates to how images on a screen rewire the brain. This explains the modern child: the inability to focus and to properly socialise, starting with making eye contact and being able to consider others. The reality is that the modern model of education replaced the previously successful manner of teaching practical matters: the apprenticeship. Designers in the past had to be able to draw and write well and know the conventions of their discipline. These matters are not served well by art schools which put students into debt and guarantee a very broad portfolio rather than focus and depth. They also allow students to invoke clever hacks, rather than master the basics and develop good taste. Modern universities are modern businesses, and the more customers they can market, the more successful they are (at least on financial terms). And when it comes to when to use computers, parents must realise that Google and Microsoft are companies wishing that their products and services be adopted and used by every student, and every school. Increasingly, apps and word processors replace a person's basic abilities to organise their own thoughts and make independent decisions. Gone are the days of IBM's slogan, 'Computers work. People think.' If one does not know anything about conventions and principles of design, how can they make decisions? Even taste needs to be trained. If these matters are never discussed when using word processors, and the increasing number of national curricula worldwide do not teach these matters in ICT, then where should children learn these matters? Is not that supposed to be the role of the school or the teacher?

b. Why?

With the said context in mind, what does the perfect person need from design and what is called ICT in the UK? To begin, we need to remember that not all students, families, and communities are the same. What follows centres on computer design directed towards producing printed language materials. In some communities, it is more practical to learn the skills of drafting to produce flower beds, design a shed, or begin to think about designing machine or motor parts. A student who learns to actively design these elements is developing active mental skills and will be a different person than children used to playing with programmes and software which are designed to resemble entertainment—even when they claim they are educational. Their mind will grow, rather than shrink.

The desire for pure photography and photoshop should be resisted until students learn to control images through proper drawing and ideas through the proper art. Otherwise, they are wading into their imagination with no oars or rudder to guide them. (They will experience right-brain pleasures without possessing any left-brain guidelines. Rather than ascend into the mystical, they will descend into the mist.)

COMPUTERS

LIFE's approach to computers was set out in the section Liberal Arts above (stating that the best approach to technology is to understand good usage, rather than simply forbidding it). As noted, all design elements directed towards and needed for writing letters in the sense of penmanship are dealt with in the section Liberal Arts. Some points regarding drawing, including drawing letters (called lettering), are left to be treated here in art and design. There is inevitable overlap because all design requires layout, whether the design is directed towards the printed word or towards drawing (and design via symbols and images, etc.). In all cases, there is a need to understand proportion so that a given space (whether on paper, a screen, or a marble plaque) is designed with principles for layout.

POINTS PARTICULAR TO ART AND DESIGN

Most art and design will have some relation to text, even if merely a caption. Almost all of it will have a relation to a sheet or a designed space. In all cases, even with lettering, art and design require being capable of drawing well before a computer can properly be used even to clean up lines, fill spaces, and add colours. As explained by Rosemary Sassoon in a section quoted from extensively in the secondary part of this book, 'The effects of technology on design education', design also requires detailed knowledge of materials (not just paper and card, but also wood, etc.) and inks. Without knowledge of this, not even a hugely flexible printer or printing press can receive the right commands. Sassoon also cites the difference in time with a tutor: the point is that drawing takes time and an expert eye overlooking one. Otherwise, impatience and market forces force one quick, shoddy work and the temptation to borrow images from the internet. (Modern elementary students are likely to want to start work with images of Pokémon—or whatever corporations decide to market next—taken from the internet and to paste them into backgrounds.) Computers tend to make images look too good too soon, so one's thinking stops. Also, the computer is a tool, but drawing is a skill which must be passed from generation to generation. Disney has stopped hand-animation, but drawing is a skill, and once it's gone, it's gone. The inability to produce new drawings makes it even more tempting to plagiarise by 'drawing from' the internet rather than drawing. In some cases, one draws elements of a drawing from existing images. In the end, everything looks the same, but no one notices.

c. How?

Students should begin with learning layout of lines of calligraphy (part of penmanship), single sheets (or folios), and booklets and books in liberal arts. Calligraphy (or penmanship) and typesetting are essential to be able to complete and present work in the liberal arts devoted to text. (In the liberal arts section, we have placed a section titled 'Timetabling to learn layout before using computers'.) In art and design, students should learn the drawing and layout of letters (called lettering, and part of draftsmanship). Of course, all other drawing, symbols, and iconography, etc. should be taught in art and design too. If and when one decides to use the computer in one of these two, it is still liberal arts or art and design one is doing, and the computer is a tool. (The computer is only a tool so long as we know the principle of layout and design. Otherwise, its defaults replace our decision and thinking. In that case, it makes us dependent on it or makes us seek it for entertainment, dependency and entertainment (and addiction) being marketing hooks which guarantee a customer base.)

d. How with limited resources?

If you do not have a computer, then do not even worry about this until the secondary stage. Even if you do, you may choose not to use it at all in the primary stage, or to use it as a reward for excellence elsewhere in a student's study.

If you have a computer and wish to use it, do so whenever students are confident in at least one script and are able to consistently produce strokes correctly, etc. For inspiration, the teacher could read online material about lettering and typographical design. Teach them the origins of printing, typeface, and typesetting, including watching segments of the documentary *Linotype: The Film*. In that case, allow them to use the computer to type paragraphs or clean up and design their drawings. Again, computer design should come after learning the principles of design and becoming competent in applying them on paper or other mediums. Begin with introducing them to a word processor.

Resources:

Sacred Geometry, Wooden Books.

Rachel Yallop (and Introduction by Rosemary Sassoon), *Creative Calligraphy*. Recommended for years 8 and up.

Rosemary Sassoon, *The Practical Guide to Lettering and Applied Calligraphy*. Teacher resource, though some of the techniques could be made appropriate for the elementary age-level.

Robert Bringhurst, *The Elements of Typographic Style*. Teacher resource.

David Harris, *The Art of Calligraphy: A Practical Guide to the Skills and Techniques*.

4.2.4 Music

a. What?

Any form of melody (and rhythm) is music. As seen from the mathematics chapter above, music (*musiqa* in Arabic and very near this in Greek) is a branch of mathematics studying quantity, specifically 'sound from the perspective of its effect on the soul and the orderliness of its pitch and time (i.e., rhythm).' Whether it is nashid, qasidahs, *na'at, qawwali*, Ottoman marching band, or reciting the adhan or Quran, this is a type of individual expressions of a thing called music.

Many scholars of the four schools of fiqh today say that instruments are haram, major *fatwas* in Syria and Egypt declare them disliked (*makruh*), but Music itself is a communal obligation (*fard kifayah*). In a cultured and developed Islamic country, such as the Ottoman Caliphate, it is unimaginable that someone not be an expert on the modes in which the adhan was systematically recited. The top reciters around al-Azhar al-Sharif have always been masters of these modes called modes (*maqamat*). It is said that the Quran descended in Makkah, was recited in Egypt, and was written (beautifully) by the Ottomans (who highly developed calligraphic script). LIFE's approach to music is to introduce traditional modes and rhythms (and how to hold a hand drum) in an age-appropriate manner, gradually introducing enough through the elementary years for students to understand and partake in this form of remembrance (and to play nashids at weddings and other gatherings and recite the Quran and adhan properly). It also trains them to appreciate and even compose lyrics, but only after exposing them to quality poetry in the English and Arabic lessons, but also in the music class itself.

b. Why?

LIFE has produced a scheme in conjunction with a qualified and expert Quran reciter and munshid, constructing with his intimate participation individual lesson plans and resources introducing skills at an age very similar to their introduction in the British National Curriculum.

Teachers and parents are wise to invest in this area for the sake of the health of their child and the wider community. The WCIE findings showed great concern about the effects of modern music. It is often said that music is part of the fitrah; for each haram we enunciate, we are wise to offer four halals in its place. While there is great pressure to be politically correct in some countries, the degradation of Western (and by now Eastern) music is well-established on the basis of form and content.

Adults will naturally learn the modes and rhythms faster than small children, so if one takes training early on, one will be able to conduct the lessons if unable to find a teacher. Students would at least be able to work towards being able to lead gatherings with well-known nashids (or accompany others on the hand drum) or give the adhan in a chosen maqam.

Unless parents or a local teacher have learned and are confident, ideally, a qualified teacher would be contacted. Your child should be mature enough to learn over the internet at some point. Even if you are not confident in your learning, you may be able to convey enough to take them through LIFE's Nashid scheme until then. Music is undoubtedly a developmental discipline. Learning rhythm coordinates the whole body and nervous system. Many advanced activities such as writing or composing logical arguments have a rhythmic and repetitive element. Also, music may touch the heart of your child in a manner nearly nothing else does; this is well-known from Islamic history and from our community. Reciting Quran with presence of heart and with proper use of maqams, making sad verses sad and happy verses exultant is not only adab of the Quran, but also a beautiful way to have a deep presence with Allah and His word. If you take the time to teach music right, you will see the dividends for millions of years to come, God willing.

In terms of language and culture, some traditional songs are taught in Arabic (such as that sung by the Prophet's ﷺ Companions, *Tala'a al-Badru 'alayna*). This is because existing nashids in languages such as Arabic and Urdu may not be understood and appreciated, and Islamic history shows that local languages eventually develop a nashid tradition. Where the quality is acceptable, some English nashids are taught. Where possible, LIFE will recommend some suitable Urdu *na'ats*. (We hope that contributions from the LIFE community will support development in this direction in the future.) Some older European melodies have the rich and emotional character suitable to a sacred topic (i.e., religion), but this process needs to be guided carefully. It appears to be in continual development, and LIFE aims to incorporate whatever is produced by existing and coming generations of Muslims.

c. How?

LIFE has prepared lesson plans for the first four years for music, which include recordings needed by educators. The following is a summary of the units of the scheme for years 1-6. In the "Term" Section, 'A' refers to 'Autumn', 'Sp' refers to 'Spring', and 'S' refers to 'Summer'.

Year/ Term **Unit Title**

1/A **Sounds I Make, Sounds Around Me**

Various expressive or disguised voices and sounds of my hands and investigation of sounds heard in the city or country. An introduction to musical vocabulary through distinguishing and discussing sounds and playing games.

Duration and Pulse

Passing beanbag to pulse and speeding up songs. Investigating wood blocks, etc. for length and nature of sound, and making simple, natural rhythmic patterns taking into consideration the length of the sounds. Thinking about which sounds sound good when played at same time to make class rhythm. (Optional: Introduce meaningful theme, such as background of the nashids, *'Tala'a al-Badr'* or Dawud Wharnsby's *'Madina Tun Nabi'.*)

1/Sp **Rhythm (Rhythm: Pulse on *Daff*)**

Tap pulse to a familiar nashid (options: *'Tala'a al-Badr'* or English children's nashid) after hearing it with rhythm then without or add rhythm to Zain Bhikha song. Learning one to tap pulse for *'Tala'a al-Badr'*, tapping on floor or desk. Intro to holding *daff* and what sounds it can make.

Tap a beat on hand following teacher, teacher say dum and tak as she taps, dum with middle finger, tak with thumb. Practice getting more and more complicated. Tapping pulse to nashids.

Review tapping on hand and tapping pulse to nashid. Embellish with extra taps.

Learn to say names of dum as they tap, then add tak as they tap rhythm alone then to *'Tala'a al-Badr'* then tap on desk, etc. (saying names is easier than tapping much easier than playing *daff*).

Tap while teacher sings and sways back and forth, students tapping dum in different place. What sounds a *daff* can make. How to hold it and make dum and tak (intro).

Review dum and tak. Practicing tapping *daff* to make a good sound, then steady beat, then playing dum, tak, repeat.

Review making a good sound, then steady beat, then playing dum and tak to nashid if possible. Sing while they play.

Pitch

Sliding and jumping pitch, phrases and patterns through game. Application according to meaning of *al-Fatihah* or small surah from *Juz' 'Amma* (moved to parent's assembly).

Review singing while they play dum and tak.

1/S **Dynamics and Intro to Score (no longer pitch)**

Playing, making, and answering musical phrases vocally and through symbols if suitable. Singing familiar song with teacher assigning voices to *qarar, jawab,* and *jawab al-jawab*. Maybe boys could do *jawab,* girls *jawab al-jawab* (or according to pitch of voice).

Parent's Assembly: (Maqam: *Sika,* Rhythm: Pulse or Perform *'Tala'a al-Badr',* some as pulse, rhythm, solo, *jawab al-jawab,* etc.,

2/A **Rhythm (Rhythm: Fox):**

Add rhythms to poems or chants. Learn a recorded nashid with rhythm and to tap the rhythm (using dum, tak, and ess) with one hand. See how many sounds a *daff* can make and introduce traditional sounds for names. Introduce symbols for names and come up with rhythm for simple nashid or chant and record rhythm in symbols.

Pitch:

Review pitch from Y1. Focus on theme of one of Nadwi's *Stories of the Prophets* with suitable preparation ahead of time.

Teach of step, jump, and slide.

(Learn a nashid in a particular maqam. Consider preparing students for *bayat* in Y3 A.)

2/Sp **Sound Families, Types, and Symbols and Scoring Voiceovers**

Sounds made by instruments can be replaced

String sounds by voweled singing or *ahat* (in West by La, la, etc.), wind by unvoweled singing (humming or with open mouth), and percussion by *daff* (and voice). Symbols for high, low, increasing speed, etc. are made into games, and at end of unit students make a background music score for stages of a story of one of the prophets (*'alayhim al-salam*).

Review holding and playing *daff* and fox.

Timbre, Tempo, and Dynamic

How sounds can describe and be combined and organised to make more complex and subtle sounds.

Students write a score, discussing elements of music to make suitable performance for one of the prophets (*'alayhim al-salam*), perhaps a story in which weather is very important, i.e., Yunus (before being thrown overboard), Nuh, or one of the prophets whose people (e.g., Thamud to whom were sent Salih, on him peace) were destroyed.

Perhaps make a song (making a score for timbre [backing voices], tempo, and dynamics) or pick subject to make music not having words in foreground (such as weather or something more inspiring, even the Judgement Day)

2/S **Maqam of Hijaz**

Learn nashid and adhan in *hijaz* and improvise on simplified scale.

Parents Assembly

Sika, Pulse, Fox, *Bayat*, Score and sing *al-Fatihah* in English

3/A **Rhythmic Patterns: (Rhythm: Ayub)**

Gather lines on dreams or other topic (sleep, ocean, *Jannah*, the Prophet ﷺ, etc.) and students find suitable rhythm and tempo for subject. Practice putting rhythm and tempo to poems and review recording in symbols.

Review pulse and Fox and select a topic and provide poem. Students think of suitable tempo and rhythm. Each take a line and make suitable rhythm. All play original rhythm at start, then stop for group with first line to play their rhythm then say their line like a drum (with rhythmic expression and attention to sound). Continue through poem and at end all keep to original. Listen for suitable adornments and changes in speed as a group and jam in a way suitable to topic and feelings.

Practice saying your words with a suitable rhythm in background. Play original rhythm at start, then all jam for 20 seconds, stop for one group to say their line with rhythm, and continue to the ending with a two-minute jam.

Sing a song, or repeat chorus, with strong simple rhythm and discuss feelings and tempo. Children listen again and imagine rhythm in their heads. Next time, they tap rhythm and experiment. When ready give one or more a *daff*. Once they have a rhythm matching the words, let several play at one time.

Review with different product or use new song. Spend 20 minutes practicing Ayub.

20 Min on Ayub, then sing ('Ya Imam al-Rusli': come up with easier nashid) and see if they can play along.

Start by groups trying to keep rhythm steady for one minute. More practice singing and playing. Discuss how to record Ayub in symbols of sound and duration.

Recitation in Bayat

Memorize two groups of three ayahs each from the Quran and then soundly memorize the tune to the first two ayahs in bayat, the teacher noting ability of class in memorization and best method. Give two more lessons to another qari' also in hijaz. Model improvising the last ayah for students and encourage them to do so, discussing outcomes with class in terms of beauty, suiting meaning, or keeping to bayat or hijaz.

3/Sp **Class Orchestra**

Discuss musical phrases with simple examples (i.e., *Twinkle, twinkle, little star*). Practice answering others' phrases and making phrase accompaniments and rhythms for known songs. Make and perform rhythm and accompaniment for *'Qul ya 'Athim'* and record.

Jaharkah: **The Musical Scale of the** *Naat*

Show children that famous *Burdah* tunes from Subcontinent are in *jaharkah* as are famous *naats*. Learn suitable *na'at*(s) and practice reciting Quran in *jaharkah* and putting lyrics in praise of the Final Prophet ﷺ in *jaharkah* in style of *na'at*.

3/S **Musical Games**

Old and new, Arabic and English and Urdu according to availability and desire of class and teacher.

Parents Assembly

Perform Quran and a nashid in *bayat* or *hijaz* with a (prepared) solo connecting to *jaharkah* and demonstrate learning of year including use of accompaniments.

4/A **Sound Colour**

Respond to a picture or other stimulus including words taking into account feelings generated by background sounds. Discuss and practice rhythms and background sounds and voices. Students respond to a picture and group write lyrics or respond to lyrics provided by teacher. Suitable background sounds including humming and vocals are added.

Practice to picture and recorded spoken word of 'The Advent of Spring' or The Signs of Allah (choose easier words) to imagine appropriate tempo and mood. Listen to a couple clips of moody music backgrounds and write description of rhythm, tempo, humming, or other voices (including singing lines of poem), or other sounds recorded or made in class are appropriate.

Groups generate rhythms and play and pick best.

Groups generate voices reviewing Sound Families, Types, and Symbols.

Listen to voice harmonies and generate best.

Make other sounds (including bringing in tape recorders, etc.).

Conduct into best piece possible, each group with a role, removing or diminishing what becomes too much sound. Focus on listening, not greed.

Orchestra

(*Maqam*: *Rasd*, Rhythm: *Laff*)

Set *Tala'a al-Badr* or other known nashid to a tune containing question and answer phrases, pointing out that nashids can be set to more than one tune or rhythm.

We sing a section of a known nashid and they answer, at least changing the register (i.e., from *jawab* to *jawab al-jawab*) for those unable to improvise. Students memorize a nashid with many parts (i.e., *'Aqidat al-'awamm*) and perform. They take to nashid which they made a new tune for by question and answer and set as many parts to it as they can from high, low, repeating end of line, humming and other backing vocals, and some playing pulse or rhythm on *daff*. They could do this with a fun song (i.e., Who's Phoning?).

4/Sp **Recitation in *Rasd***

Practice recitation of the Quran in the maqam of *rasd*.

Descriptive Sounds

Pick a story with two animals that is emotive and has a moral such as *Fox and the Hound* or a story from Muslim lands such as Kalila and Dimna, etc.

4/S ***Bayat***

Learn nashids in the maqam of *bayat* and practice improvising tunes to words from teacher or other source.

Parents Assembly

Perform the *Burdah* to tunes in the maqams of *bayat*, *sikah*, and *jaharkah*.

5/A **Rhythmic Patterns: (Rhythms: *Masmudi*, *Wihdah*)**

Model writing out a rhythm unknown to the class and let them practice for a rhythm they have learned (i.e., *baladi* or *laff*). Play or sing nashids built on rhythms they have learned and ask them to determine the rhythm and try to play it to the nashid. Play nashids they have heard but whose rhythms they have not learned and see if they can write the rhythm. Then see if they can set suitable rhythms to unknown nashids after listening several times.

Learn to write out known rhythm.

Play nashids in known rhythm. They determine, play, and write.

Play known nashids in w*ihdah* and see if they can write and then play along.

Play unknown nashid in *masmudi* for same.

Let groups jam in *wihdah* and add extra dums, taks, or esses. Do the same over a nashid.

The same for *masmudi*.

Naat

Learn a variety of styles of modern performance of the *na'at*. Learn a popular *na'at* and choose an attractive style and attempt to perform *na'at* in that style.

5/Sp **Rounds**

Exploring rounds and setting harmonic phrases to known nashids.

A Gem from Sa'di or *A Muslim's Refuge* (rounds for three voices)

Recitation: (Maqam: *Sikah* or *Hijaz*)

Learn that the adhan is usually, but not necessarily, read in *hijaz*. Learn to set suitable melodies to ayahs about *Jannah* in a set maqam (*hijaz* or review *sikah* if needed).

5/S **Nashid Writer**

Learn nashids about *Jannah* and attempt to write words and melodies in group and possibly with teacher help. Attempt setting known words to other known melodies, making simple melodies in a set maqam, or writing words and a melody (according to each student's ability).

Parents Assembly

A play with Quran and nashids about a believer who lives sincerely and enters *Jannah*.

6/A Art of Performance: (*Maqam: Nahawand*)

Learn that '*Tala ma ashku*' is in *nahawand*, learning new nashids in the same maqam. Learn that in performance, one should not jump directly from maqam to maqam and that moving between maqams requires a solo which gently moves from one maqam to other. Learn a model solo between *nahawand* and another known maqam to make a short set of nashids to ready for performance.

Learn nashid in *nahawand*.

Learn short solo between *nahawand* and *bayat* (for instance).

Practice singing nashid in *nahawand*, solo, then *bayat*.

Solo between *bayat* and *rasd*.

Bridge *bayat* and *rasd*.

Put whole thing together and perform, letting one student start with Quran in *nahawand* and one end in *rasd*

The *Muwashah*

The *muwashah* is an intricate solo delivered passionately and requiring time and concentration to learn and perform correctly. Practice memorizing and performing part of a *muwashah*.

6/Sp Nashid Writer

Attempt setting known words to other known melodies, making simple melodies in a set maqam, or writing words and a melody (students trying to improve on their accomplishments in Y5).

Becoming a *Qari'*

Explore the different feelings evoked by maqams (such as joy usually associated with *sikah*) and the Quran or nashids set in them. Pick a suitable maqam for sections of Quran and improvise in it for one's section.

6/S Becoming a *Daff* Player

Learn to embellish/alter a basic rhythm by adding taks or esses to fit the words or feelings of a nashid with taste.

Parents Assembly

Preparing a *Hiflah*: Prepare for a *hiflah* by selecting strings of nashids in different maqams suitable to the occasion (i.e., a visit by an *'alim* or the coming of Ramadan).

4.2.5 Physical Education

a. What?

The Sunnah disciplines are a set of physical arts mentioned specifically by the Prophet Muhammad ﷺ: swimming, archery, horseback riding, and wrestling. They are the knowledge by which certain human actions are perfected. The fact that the Prophet, on him peace, ordered them to be taught means they take the ruling of being praiseworthy, at least. It clearly gives them a higher status than modern sports, but their status and superiority is also in their nature and transmission.

Each of these sciences has a symbolism explained by its masters. Each of these sciences is additionally known by its teachers to teach you lessons of life and character. Archery teaches failure, will, and focus. Wrestling teaches how to play—and win and lose gracefully—and submit—before you pass out! It is said that each of them was revealed to the Prophet Muhammad, on him peace, and several of them have a line of transmission to him. Archery is a clear example of an art (*sina'ah*) which was developed greatly by earlier generations, notably the Mamluks of Egypt, known as the world's best archers. Archery with a line of transmission is currently taught in Turkey, and such lines may exist in other places.

The ethos of these sacred and Sunnah disciplines is that one may experiment with or learn several but must be faithful to one discipline for the rest of one's life. While traditional teachers of disciplines such as archery agree on this, they may or may not know that this is supported by the hadith from the collection of Muslim, {Whoever learns archery (*al-ramy*), then leaves it is not one of us, or has sinned}, (Muslim: *Kitab al-Imara, Bab* 52). Wherever one lives, it is possible to find Brazilian Jujitsu, an archery pitch, a swimming pool, or a riding stable.

b. Why?

These sports are better than football which has a celebrity and egotistical culture which changes those who play it (often like Jekyll and Hyde, on and off the pitch). Football is an example of something called a team sport which becomes all about me: 'Pass the ball! Me! Me! I can score!'

Sports in general strengthen one's body which is one's earth, from one viewpoint, and one's connection to earth. Without this connection, it is all talk. {The strong believer is better and more beloved to Allah than the weak believer. In each there is good.}

It is not safe to enter adulthood unable to swim or defend oneself. Over the last 10-15 years, there has been a general rise in right-wing violence and hate crime in many parts of the world.

The greatest danger to contemporary Muslims is their food and lifestyle. So, while you may not die from knife attack, you may die from your own knife and fork. Young people need to know how to defend themselves from the much more likely sudden death of a heart attack, or the slow destruction of one's health through diabetes. Typically, Muslim cultures are honour cultures to a certain degree. So, while we now mostly have sedentary lifestyles, Muslims have been slow at taking up the habit of exercise, which often involves putting on certain clothes or jogging outdoors or exercising in the gym. Help your children develop the habit of exercise, and ensure it is done with dignity. If they go to the gym themselves, they are likely to follow the wider culture in dress and etiquette. (Let us not forget that the gymnasium played a large role in destroying Jewish religious culture, as Jews attempted to fit into Greco-Roman education systems that involved the gym and little clothing, directly contravening Mosaic Law.)

There is a plethora of research on the link between health and exercise. The two sides are primarily strength and endurance. When your child later begins work and has children and moves out of the indestructible years, they will undergo stress, lose sleep, etc. Here is where strength and endurance help. This stress will either lead to loss of bone and muscle mass over the years, and hence they need a reservoir of strength—built up in their youth—to draw from. Or it may go the other way and lead to obesity or high blood pressure which may even effect those who are thin: here they need to draw on endurance and fitness, also easiest to obtain in youth. As is often said, a strong mind depends on a strong body, and this is true for your children. If we want them to study, fast, wake up for fajr (even on summer days), the amount of health they start with will be a higher mark and they will thank their parents forever—especially when they enter *Jannah* and have more days and nights of worship because of their strong bodies.

A strong body and the discipline of working out is known to reduce errant thoughts and misgivings (*waswas*), whether this is worrying too much what other people think or verging on a mental condition. Studies show that working out gives you the ability to control your nervous system. You may start to go into fight or flight, but if you exercise regularly, you will have more of a 'break' function to keep it from accelerating into uncomfortable or harmful speeds which prevent one from achieving one's aims in life and spending precious energy.

In a general sense, the perfect human needs to be grounded in earth and the body.

c. How?

When to Begin

From preschool to five, encourage children to perform general movements to develop coordination.

Swimming may be started at four, as children have enough coordination for most basic strokes.

At four, children can start swimming and can begin grooming horses.

At five, they can begin wrestling (specifically jujitsu) and can begin horse riding.

Archery is best taught at ten and up when children have the attention span.

Timing

How you time the combination of these four is up to you. Teaching swimming at some point is necessary, best being sometime after four when children are physically mature enough to learn properly.

Whether in a homeschool, a co-op, or a school, there are break times. If you are not lucky enough to have a swimming pool or riding ground in the back garden, your breaks can be devoted to archery (with supervision), wrestling, or something else such as calligraphy. Children may pick up from youth culture the idea that a break means relax and relax means do nothing. But archery and jujitsu are actually stress relievers, especially when children are learning heady material or later on preparing for exams (even if you avoid as many as possible). As a homeschool or school, lighter subjects could run longer (in the case of a school this would be structured as an after-school club). If the child does jujitsu or swimming competitively, practicing during breaks gives them extra practice hours on the mat or on the range. The group element encourages motivation and children getting involved.

There are many notes on timing within the particular Sunnah arts listed below individually.

Swimming

As noted, swimming lessons can start at four. At four, their arm and leg coordination are good enough to start learning strokes.

Swimming is individually obligatory (*fard 'ayn*). This is not surprising, considering what is very surprising: that between the age of one and nineteen, the second leading cause of death in the U.S. is drowning. But while it is obligatory and extremely good for the health, we favour jujitsu over it. So, swimming could be your focus for two years. Some schools set aside Year 2 and Year 3 to complete a course in swimming. You can take this a rule of thumb for a homeschool.

You could go out twice a week on the same days as Kumon, if using

Kumon in maths. The ease of finding a centre will depend on your location.

Wrestling

While swimming is obligatory, the two years mentioned above could be devoted to it, but jujitsu or wrestling is a core of health and self-defence. Practice it every year unless you are making room for another sport that year. During that year, practice twice a week.

Jujitsu is a fantastic, whole-body sport with a strategic element. Strength helps, but if seeking self-defence, one hopes strength is not everything. (Otherwise, the outcome of an altercation is determined by strength, not skill in self-defence.) The techniques of jujitsu can bring someone much larger than oneself into submission, making it suitable for self-defence for females. Also, an attacker can be brought into submission without harming them. This makes it extremely practical. It is just as important to avoid hurting someone else—and the potential legal problems—as it is to avoid being hurt oneself.

Archery

Many archery clubs shoot arrows on Saturday or Sunday. Increasingly, you can find archery teachers in a line of transmission to Muslim archers. If you have a school or a co-op, arrange with an archery teacher to come to you or meet in a park which meets the necessary safety conditions.

Horseback riding

Interacting with horses can fundamentally change a child, even just through grooming and handling and being with them. Search for places to ride near you, and if travel is required, this could be done on a weekend. Otherwise, you may be able to have lessons on an afternoon.

Practical points for schools

Inter-school competitions are quite an incentive for children to get involved and motivated to excel. Schools do this for tennis and other mainstream sports such as rugby, football and netball, but not so much for the disciplines we have advocated.

Because there is less of an emphasis in most schools on the four disciplines we advocate, one needs a good model. A good model is the Arab Emirates where they are installing jujitsu mats because youth culture there was leading overweight children to spend their time in malls and going out to eat. Now the culture has become a matter of everyone, including the upper class, becoming competitive in jujitsu. The leader brought in 100 black belts to train teachers, and Dubai has now become one of the largest world jujitsu competitions. This brings to mind the command of Sayyidina 'Umar to the Arabs not to settle into cities. City dwellers tend to lose their chivalry. The impact of this move could very much change the mindset and character of coming generations. Whether one is the son of an amir with servants or a servant, on the mat they are equal. Who will they call on when on the mat?

If one is in a school, it would be good to have a PE staff with a blackbelt in jujitsu. If schools lack a specialist coach for a sport, they are required to outsource that coach, putting pressure on finances. Schools should look out to have an in-house jujitsu teacher so they do not have to outsource this. In the primary school, teachers are supposed to teach 'PE' which leads to the time being used sub-optimally. Private schools tend to have a specialist at the primary level, leading to graduates being better equipped by the time they reach secondary.

Rather than naming the department which teaches these practical sciences 'the sports department', one should term it the department of etiquette (*kulliyyat al-adab*, not the literature department!), or the department of character (*akhlaq*) or chivalry (*futuwwah*), as advocated by Shaykh Ibrahim Ose-Efe.

You might not have a horse trainer, but you need a male and female teacher of swimming.

You will need someone with enough training in two or three of the said disciplines to teach them in a primary school.

Developing and balancing character

The benefits listed above are the reasons these disciplines were revealed to the best of creation, upon him and his family be peace and blessings, who was sent to refine the best of character traits. And he brought ways empowering us to imitate him. He is amazing, but how do we follow him? Here is a method: get on the mat, aim arrows, be with a horse. Other sports are good, but they were not good enough to be revealed to the best of creation, may Allah bless him and send peace upon him.

In this vein, there is a tradition of balancing the disciplines: hard and soft. Archery, for instance, should be paired with calligraphy.

4.2.6 HISTORY & CULTURAL STUDIES

a. What?

This subject is a keystone to the rest of the curriculum: it shows how the subjects fit together to make the individual personality and the wider culture. It addresses ideals, as well as the drama of how it can go wrong, how wrongs can be righted, and how to live in an imperfect society. The elephant in the room is that children live in modernity which by now affects even the most isolated places such as Tinbuktu—which until recently only had dial up internet! While imperfect societies have always existed, it is an obligation to protect children from the corruption of the end times.

In this context, what you teach children needs to balance two poles. First is their concrete, lived experience. Second, following Ibn Khaldun, is to teach them the inner aspect of history: the nature of individual cultures. In particular, they need to know what is required for a healthy culture. This knowledge, if successfully taught, should enable their insight to penetrate the realities in front of them such that, without any illusions whatsoever, they are able to judge existing cultures. A matter of contemporary urgency is to understand modernity and its relation to what is described as the end times, as believers are warned of it in order to protect themselves from elements of its corruption.

In this manner, culture is taught historically, and its end, like that of other subjects, is to perfect the human being. It is different in that it is positioned to step back and see healthy culture as a unity and bring its intellectual form before the eye of students. The parts of culture are the parts of subjects as they map out the human personality and, from another angle, a cosmology. (As in the 'Introduction', the subjects *are* wisdom, while at the same time they are the bringing out of the potential of the personality and completion of the human being.)

These parts are reflected in the curriculum:

- The theoretical worlds of God, the angels, mathematical realities, and nature.
- The practical world of human acts where we practice virtue: the self, the home, and wider society.
- The liberal arts, the trivium (the so-called 'Lost Tools of Learning'), and the instrumental sciences which connect everything and prevent over-specialisation from divisions between secular/sacred and natural science/the humanities, etc.

Some might ask, should there not be a social studies programme for primary school. The approach outlined here contains an implicit answer: the social sciences are riddled with relativism or, worse, pure subjectivism. Our approach gives a way out that is capitalised on most in our secondary curriculum, which is to offer an alternative and realist notion of what culture is. It has three parts. The first is concrete expressions found in writing, art, and architecture. Second, it is the habits of mind and character (including the capacity to produce) of human beings studied collectively. Third, it is the ideals of a given culture. Whether we know it or not, these three are already 'judged' through the real ideals of culture. Namely, culture is the collective and social aspect of a particular group of humans. The aim of human existence is to worship God, know God, and complete the human being. (As the 'Introduction' explains, Allah most high says, {I created human- and jinnkind only to worship Me,} said on authority to mean, 'to know Me'.) So, cultures are good in terms of how well they facilitate these aims. Seeing the drama of culture and human existence from this perspective empowers students to live their lives as something other than a missed opportunity.

To accomplish what we have outlined, in Section 'c. *Why?*' you will find three approaches that aim to pivot from the concrete experience of the child towards the ideals necessary to understand culture and benefit from it towards completing their own souls. The reality is that most adults enter the world without the understanding needed to navigate it and see that 'what is' is not 'the only way it could have been'. Human culture was someone's choice. That choice was contested by figures we mention. We should not feel comfortable entering someone else's home and living their history (and culture).

b. Why?

Perfecting one's human nature requires knowing ideals contained in a healthy culture. And it requires knowing how to navigate an imperfect culture. Without this, learning religion, ethics, and ideals in general can lead to cognitive dissonance.

A healthy culture contains at least the following:

- Unity and integration, not a set of unrelated specialisations.

- A symbolism which is sacred and unified, not merely political ideological symbols designed to produce citizens of a state. (This may be expressed in literature and a culture's other expressions. The height of literature, if it may be called that, is revelation. The only revelation which has been preserved with certainty is the Islamic revelation, i.e., the Quran. The Quran itself and imagery of Arab culture spread to Persian and other high cultures, including places as far afield as Spain and Malaysia and Indonesia.)

- A broad set of theoretical subjects that map reality and the human personality.

- A set of practical subjects which are connected to the theoretical and aim directly to perfect the human practical faculty. (It is said by the great Indian scholar 'Ali al-Tahanawi that these subjects were largely replaced by the branches of fiqh. But from another viewpoint, the root of human acts is character trait of the heart, and these are taught in manuals of hadith and tazkiyah, including topics as practical as 'marriage', 'friendship', 'good treatment of neighbours', and 'seeking an ethical living'. One also finds ethical modes of production in the works of Muhammad al-Shaybani, al-Mawardi, al-Raghib al-Isfahani, al-Ghazali, and Ibn Khaldun.)

- A set of liberal arts and instrumental sciences which free human potential and connect the other subjects such that they are not mere specialisations studied for mere utilitarian and vocational ends.

Additionally, there are points that must be understood about how to live in a culture which is imperfect (i.e., not the virtuous society.) The combination of these two are required to empower a child to one day navigate the world according to the aims of creation and their existence: to work towards completing themselves while in the thick of life. Educators themselves need to understand this to avoid producing a hidden curriculum of cognitive dissonance in developing students.

c. How?

There are three approaches for teaching history in the elementary years. In summary:

Approach 1 is to follow a historical backbone with unit descriptions. Teachers will need to be confident enough to turn a lesson description into a lesson, and in some cases to order existing, printed resources ahead of time to plan and execute units. At the end of units, there is time for following the interests of children (who may feel just as soon as they found their favourite periods and heroes, they have to lockstep into another topic). Also, in both a school and homeschool, there is no statutory requirements to lockstep. So, you can also finish the material in a unit and decide to extend it, if you keep the aims of history to mind.

Approach 2 is to teach themes which examine tradition and modernity and set out what is a healthy culture (encouraging true human flourishing) and its opposite.

Approach 3 resembles a Robinson Curriculum approach in which one works through a list of books, ideally great books, either on the topic or biographies from the period. (See, 'Approach 3', below.)

APPROACH 1: HISTORICAL BACKBONE

The first is constructed as a backbone stretching from the beginning of historical human experience to contemporary times. This requires the confidence to construct units, because such a history which represents a scholarly take on what has occurred does not currently exist. There are units which may be used as an important resource produced by Noura Durkee or the Tasheel Series. Better yet, there are books in 'General Resources' below which would give a parent the confidence to guide these units.

How to construct units

We have provided a list of possible individual lesson topics. However, be empowered to use our formula and generate your own. In general, punctuate lessons with texts including biographies which convey the highest of morals in a true literary value. Always begin by locating the topic on a timeline and a map. Link this with other dates the children know until their knowledge begins to fill in. Spend the first two to three lessons laying down basic, unquestioned facts and grabbing the attention through either well-known, world changing, or personally significant occurrences or historical figures. In the first two to three years, provide not only biographies, but dress up and craft activities. Focus on the moral and let them imagine both what it was like to live and make decisions in that atmosphere. Begin introducing core ideas related to history of religion, society, and economics. 'How did people handle corruption and social disagreements? How did leaders and scholars avoid the temptation of corruption? How did land laws effect the need to survive and earn a living? How did people balance between the worldly and afterlife in their affairs? What was family life like? What were the means of production, largely in the hands of craftsmen before the invention of machines?'

One element of Approach 1 that is shared with the other approaches is to introduce the emergence of the modern world and the interaction between Europe and Islam and other religions in the last three to four years of elementary school (depending on how mature your students are). Introduce the disorder in ideas, then in society, then in politics, then in economics. Show them the positive ways Christians and spiritual and social reformers addressed the issues of their day. Be balanced about the results. At this age, after learning the basics on a topic, attempt to provide resources in which they can research and also develop their budding writing skills. (If they are more verbal or visual, allow them to sometimes present orally or focus on maps or drawings of people, places and artefacts.) To give purpose to this study, an ethical element, and development towards the difficult task of finding good work in the modern world address the question of why one would work hard to change the world if they know that we are in the End Times.

First of all, though many of the signs of the End Times can be academically demonstrated to have occurred, we do not know how long they will last. It could be thousands of years. We also do not know which communities will be hit hardest either with loss of property or life, or much worse, with loss of faith. So, every person, family, and community has a great reason to work. We also have many reasons to be positive towards many Western communities. Those who are just, ethical, believe in the sacred, hold on to tradition and religion need to cooperate most. European Christians know how to understand, critique, and reform modernity, because it came out of their neighbourhood. Muslim statements are often vague. Late primary students can be briefly introduced to how Afro-Americans stood up to oppression and how reformers such as John Ruskin and William Cobbett worked tirelessly to form a sane social movement that went against the widespread assumptions of their day. Gandhi did both, and his thinking was shaped by his early experience in Muslim communities. Though it is hard to identify a late-Malcolm X, Gandhi or William Cobbett (or C. S. Lewis, J. R. R. Tolkien, Jacques Maritain, T. S. Elliot, Abd al-Qadir al-Jaza'iri, or Mustafa Sabri Effendi, the last Shaykh al-Islam of the Ottoman Empire) today, nonetheless, many people are working to preserve the local, the organic, the sacred and to use technology right (whether this is minimalistically or towards one's own aims). One figure that all can respect is Shaykh Ahmad al-Tayyib, who has attempted to reform al-Azhar by bringing back traditional texts and restoring the basic methodologies of Islamic practice, scholarship, and spirituality. Otherwise, we must look for micro-heroes—of which there are of course many. Some who are worth mentioning are Alistair MacIntyre, Wendell Berry, the founders of the Radical Orthodoxy movement (with caveats regarding some opinions of one of its co-founders: John Millbank), S. H. Nasr (with caveats regarding his perennialism), and Imam Zaid Shakir. A recently past generation includes Malcolm X, Shaykh Abd al-Rahman al-Shaghuri, Dr. Ramadan al-Buti (whose debates with Damascene Marxist intellectuals prevented droves from becoming communist), Nelson Mandela, but also lesser-known figures such as David Kindersley, Stratford Caldecott, several of those listed above including who passed away in the 20th Century.

A hero cannot be a sport star who is indecent, a wife-beater or a murderer, or a tycoon with a reductionist idea of how to reshape the planet, even if they claim to be philanthropists. It is curious that it is harder and harder to find heroes without major problems, and it is mentioned in a hadith of the Prophet—on him and family be peace and blessings—that in the End Times, knowledge will be lifted back to Allah not through taking from the breasts of men, but by plucking scholars, and their lives ending. Unfortunately, the institutions for producing proper scholars have been destroyed in all except small backwaters, this being the case as far back as the so-called Indian Mutiny and the official closing of Ottoman madrasas in the early 20th Century. In the West, it must be said that the modern education and university system will never produce the likes of the past without reform.

The leading thinkers of the 19th Century, such as Hegel, Marx, Nietzsche, and Freud were all classically educated, and their assessment of their time was in terms of classical man and society. Their minds were greater than what our current, dominant education system is designed to produce; though there was obviously something wrong with their education, classical education is a necessary condition for some, but not a sufficient condition. Perhaps another reason it is difficult to find heroes and scholars is because we live in the age of the academic committee or because we live in a time in which Allah's chosen scholars and saints are not allowed to manifest, and so many have passed away as predicted in the Prophet's ﷺ hadith.

YEARS 1-5: HISTORY BACKBONE

Year 1: Anbiya' (Prophets)

A1: Adam (upon him peace), Hawa (Eve) (upon her peace), and Shaytan, Garden of Eden (Aden), Makkah

A2: Nuh (upon him peace), Mesopotamia

Sp1: Ibrahim (upon him peace), Mesopotamia to Canaan (Palestine) and Makkah

Sp2: Yaqub and Yusuf (upon them peace), Palestine to Egypt

S1: Musa and Harun (upon them peace), Egypt to Palestine

S2: 'Isa, Maryam, Yahya, and Zakariyya' (the Family of 'Imran) (upon them peace), Rome and Palestine

Year 2

A1: The Prophet ﷺ as a Child

A2: The Cave of Hira and Ta'if

Sp1: Year of Sadness, Isra', Mi'raj, and Persecution

Sp2: Hijrah and Arrival at Yathrib

S1: Yathrib to Madina: Internal Governing

S2: The Battle of the Trench, *Fath* Makkah, and *Hajj Wada'*

Year 3

A1: Adam (upon him peace), Hawa (upon her peace), and Shaytan, Garden of Eden (Aden), Makkah

A2: Nuh (upon him peace), Mesopotamia

Sp1: Ibrahim (upon him peace), Mesopotamia to Canaan (Palestine) and Makkah

Sp2: Yaqub and Yusuf (upon them peace), Palestine to Egypt

S1: Musa and Harun (upon them peace), Egypt to Palestine

S2: 'Isa, Maryam, Yahya, and Zakariyya' (the Family of 'Imran) (upon them peace), Rome and Palestine

Year 4

A1: Sirah

A2: Khulafa' and Sahabah (spread of Islam: Amr ibn al-'As, Khalid bin Walid, Mu'awiyah, etc.)

Sp1: Umayyads (Damascus, Kufa, Basra and the righteous forebears)

Sp2: Anglo Saxons and King Arthur (Ivanhoe and the many invaders of British Isles)

S1: Abbassids to Seljuks (Baghdad: nominal caliph, from tabi'in to Sufi paths, schools of law, guilds, then first university, al-Nizamiyyah named after Nizam al-Mulk; and madrasa as a guild)

S2: Moorish Spain and Early Medieval Europe (and Reconquista and Crusades with reference to Robin Hood, Salah al-Din, Richard the Lionheart)

Year 5

A1: Central Asia (Khurasan; Bukhari and Muslim, Mongols, rise of Turks, post-Ghazalian Persian scholarship; Razi, Samarqandi, Iji, Taftazani and Jurjani who set madrasa curriculum to our day, decentralised but universalised Islam)

A2: Mughals (Dars-i Nizami, Persian and local-language poetry, Sultan Bahu, Nizam al-Din Awliya' and service of poor, Taj Mahal and classical, Shah Wali Allah)

Sp1: Ottomans and Byzantium (Sultan Fatih and calling to court Persian scholars and Sufis; Astronomer 'Ali Qushju and Sufi Mulla 'Abd al-Rahman Jami)

Sp2: High Medieval Europe: Monastic life, Guilds, and Early Universities with hierarchical knowledge and balanced synthesis of reason and revelation, then breakdown with nominalist theologians. Project: Read Dr Coulton's *Medieval Panorama*. Attempt to set out the major elements of medieval life and reflect on their nature: production of food and other products, education, government, family, addressing social and personal problems, charity, and of course, the religious life (not just the monastery), etc.

S1: Renaissance, Reformation and Tutors (Bacon, Galileo, Luther, Calvin, Elizabeth and Akbar, Henry VIII: impact on piety and architecture, St. Thomas Moore, Shakespeare: eclecticism in knowledge, anti-intellectualism and anti-mysticism, turn from timeless Greek knowledge to material and quantitative change)

S2: Enlightenment and the 'Long Century' (1685-1815) (Abandonment of speculative inquiry and rebuilding sciences and politics on new grounds; Locke and liberalism, Rousseau and Revolution, Newton balancing the speculative and empirical methods in spite of those before and after him following a purely experimental method, French Revolution and Three Musketeers.)

YEAR 6: MODERN PERIOD (TOPICS)

How to become a contemporary Muslim, not a modern Muslim

- See through narrative of progress, with all it entails: that medieval ages (involving religion) were dark ages, that the Reformation and Protestantism, liberalism were peaceful or neutral (for instance Protestants burned unitarians at the state, liberals continued to persecute Catholics, Jews limited the rights of women for most of their history). That religion has led to more deaths than any other ideology (actually, Communism and atheism did), see that liberal capitalistic democracy and communism are two sides of the same coin

- Individualism and the rise of tycoons and robber barons

- Nationalism (qawmiyyah/jahiliyyah), human rights, racism, increasing usurpation of basics of life by state and corporations, and how this effects Islam: Increasingly, imams and muftis lack independence from the state (even though the mufti is valid if they fulfil the conditions set out in usul al-fiqh books).

- Project: 'It All Goes Together': Introduce children to the notion of the third type of Euro-American man: the modern celebrity/tycoon. Since certain fundamentals changed in ethics (like leaving detachment (zuhd) and turn to Protestant Work Ethic and then the third, modern person who is either a celebrity or tycoon) certain changes have occurred to society. Let them explore this through guided research. [This will lead them to topics such as waste (in food and clothing industries), industrialisation of food, etc. Let them follow this root wherever it goes, till they map out the tree roots and where they came from. How does it change the family, the approach to knowledge and subjects like poetry and liberal arts ('I ain't got time, but I do have time for TV and sports'), vacation and leisure (sitting on a beach staying in a European or American hotel).].

- Project: Link up al-Nubdhah al-sughra on the End Times with modern history. Students study the book and modern history and attempt to see who exemplifies what elements of corruption described in the book.
- Emergence of usury (the world can live without it).
- New science is neutral and merely progress.
- The Re-emergence of Greek atomism.
- Individualism, subjectivism come out of an empty notion of autonomy so important to Enlightenment thinkers.
- Positivism, Comte, Three Levels of Subjects.
- Phenomenalism.
- Generation of everyday life.

For resources, see the resources listed after approach 3.

APPROACH 2: CULTURAL & ETHICAL THEMES (IN UNDERSTANDING THE DIFFERENCE BETWEEN CLASSICAL TRADITION & MODERNITY.)

Great and careful thinkers such as Alasdair MacIntyre have argued that industrialised modernity has made moral discourse impossible (and in the words of another thinker reduced it to feelings: 'I feel this is right',) but has also destroyed the possibility of critical thought through destroying the past. We rush along in the moment and a triumphalist view of science propagated in popular culture by scientists. The Muslim community is being hit hard by scientism and liberalism, the latter being most harmful because it makes people feel alien to their own culture, while the premises of liberalism are everywhere assumed. There is no way out of this but understanding, for Muslims to hold on to traditional practices, and reform a sacred cosmology. Within history, the focus should be to poke some breathing holes into the cultural assumptions and see that no culture can succeed when it attempts to replace all inherited sacred values and virtues with empirical or pragmatic findings. In fact, clinging to scripture while holding on to these misbeliefs will only help temporarily, falling apart in the future just as Protestantism fell apart after a few hundred years in Europe's liberal climate: no religion was liberal enough to survive the revolution.

In approach number three, students learn the stories of the prophets and his biography (sirah) with a special focus on the moral lessons and the ways of life, not just religious rights or countering arguments for paganism. Then, when learning about medieval Europe, they identify the wholistic ways that religion and life were integrated with each other and examine matters such as land laws. Then in the last two (or three) years (because some Year 4 students are quite mature), they research themes in between classical/religious tradition and modernity, the pre-modern world and the modern. What were the changes of mindset that allowed for industrialisation. This is the key. This is not a purely theoretical exploration, but teachers should encourage students to begin thinking about community (like being dropped off at nursery or left for long hours at school) and making money and work. How can one find good work with the growing ownership and intense competition from cut-throat corporations? It is too late to start thinking about these matters the year before graduation.

Provide students with a short narrative developing the hadith from *Musnad Ahmad*, the characteristics of the End Times from a scholarly resource (such as *al-Nubdhah al-sughra* of Habib Abu Bakr al-Mashhur). Then on how land-laws (from early to late medieval to early modern to contemporary) and other matters have made a simple, independent, sustainable subsistence more and not less difficult. The core changes listed throughout this entry on primary history should be used to select themes (set out above or below). Guide students to find biographies where people spoke out against the change of land laws in England, the displacements of American Indians and Australian Aborigines, or the current nation-state's pushing of migrant farmers off their ancestral lands in order to increase registered GDP.

It is possible to blend methods 1, 2, and 3. The challenge in all is in finding resources, as most of the printed matter in English (and increasingly so in Arabic) pushes a Hollywood/Disney history of the world in which the medieval and religious centuries were dark, and modern times enlightened. Obviously, the problem with this is that it is expected that more and more Muslims will 'get with it', wake up, and leave the oppression of their religion, especially through freedom in the West, or through freedom being 'imposed' on the leaders of their own countries.

LIFE HISTORY, APPROACH 3:
ROBINSON CURRICULUM OR A READER

In this method, the parent does their best to follow a historical backbone but does not force it. Rather, one allows children to read age-appropriate books, hopefully with sufficient quality to justify their presence both for their literary quality and their historical content, and perhaps their historical writing. However, the story of the classics and tradition is now a minority story, that way of life was largely defeated, and history is written by the victors. So, in many cases, parents will need to present books which are not ideal, or they will be forced to summarise topics in their own words (or writing) and to choose sections from books which are not age-appropriate. The prose of John Ruskin is some of the best literature in English, and he dealt with so many topics that the world would be a vastly different place simply were his thought and message understood.

Resources for approaches 1-3

Note: Resources which discuss key historical junctures for children are easy enough to come by. Those which present traditional values for primary students are, by contrast, practically non-existent. So, for the time-being, parents may draw on resources which are relatively traditional and complement them with a) a timeline of Islamic history, so they know where to jump off and look for key Islamic events and cultures to at least complement these resources and b) readings in the below resources for orienting adults. Until LIFE produces a mini-course on the contours of history, educators will need to be confident or select carefully from the orienting resources. (Note that in almost all cases, lectures exist online which may give the heart of the author's message and greatly ease subsequent reading of their books.)

Child-friendly resources which may be read, studied the educator, or drawn on by the educator

Susan Douglas, *Islamic Social Studies* (The title does not necessarily indicate the author supports the social studies as a method overtaking the humanities and religion.)

Abiva and Durkee, *History of Muslim Civilization*

Durkee, Noura, *Stories of the Sahaba*, 5 vols

The Story of the World, Susan Wise Bauer (This is *The Well-Trained Mind*'s history resource for primary. As noted above, students may study this with the educator. At a slightly later age, they may read it themselves as per the Robinson curriculum. In both cases, we recommend using the timeline: *A Journey Through Islamic History* as noted just above.)

A Charlotte Mason inspired approach:

Middle Ages, Renaissance, Reformation & Epistles

Early Modern & Epistles

Modern Times & Epistles, Revelation

These three titles a) have lesson plans and b) recommend several books for children to read which are related to the historical period they study. The lists of books could be drawn on and used according to the approach one choses.

V M Hillyer, *A Child's History of the World*

Teresa Chris, *The Kingfisher History Encyclopaedia*, Kingfisher, London, 2012

Resources on individual figures or times

Note that numerous titles mentioned in literature are suitable for history. These include:

Ibn Kathir (tr. Gemeiah, ed. Mischler), *Stories of the Prophets*, Islamic Book Service, New Delhi, 2004

Leila Azzam, *Lives of the Prophets*, Hud Hud Books, Cambridge, 1995

James Rumford, *Traveling Man: The Journey of Ibn Battuta*, Houghton Mifflin, Boston, 2001

Noura Durkee, *Yunus and the Whale*, Tahrike Tarsile Quran Inc., Elmhurst, New York, 1999

Elma Ruth Harder *Yusuf and His Brothers*

James Baldwin, *Fifty Famous Stories Retold* (This collection includes stories from the lives of numerous historical figures from the ancient Greeks to late-modern history.)

Abdul Wahid Hamid, *Companions of the Prophet: 1, 2 & 3*, MELS, London, 1985. (This series could be spread over 2 or even 3 years.)

Denys Johnson-Davies, *Stories of the Caliphs: The Early rulers of Islam*, Bloomsbury Qatar Foundation Publishing, 2010

Tales from Syria, Denys Johnson-Davies, Dar el-Shorouk, Cairo, 2003 (also: Sunflower Books)

The Alleyways of Cairo, Johnson-Davies, Dar el-Shorouk, Cairo, 2005 (also: Sunflower Books)

Diane Stanley, *Saladin: Noble Prince of Islam*, HarperCollins Publishers, New York, 2002

Hood Hood Heroes of the East Series:

- *Rumi*: *Poet and Sage*
- *Saladin*
- *Razia*: *Warrior Queen of India*
- *Mehmet*: *The Conqueror*
- *Ibn Sina*: *(Avicenna) Prince of Physicians*
- *Cheng Ho*: *(Mao Sambao) Admiral of the East*

Gwen Gross, *Knights of the Round Table,* Stepping Stone series, Random House, New York, 1985

T. H. White, *The Sword in the Stone*

Howard Pyle, *The Merry Adventures of Robin Hood*

Charles and Mary Lamb, *Tales from Shakespeare,* Kibworth Books, Leicester, England, 1999 (Several of these stories are about historical figures.)

Robinson Crusoe, Daniel DeFoe, Bucknell University Press, Lewisburg, 2020 (Compare to *Hayy Ibn Yaqzan* which it borrowed from. You may read various sizes of abridgements, reflecting on why modern publishers generally remove religious discussions from the book.)

Hoodhood Treasures of the East: Shah Jehan and the Story of the Taj Mahal

George Orwell, *Animal Farm,* Macmillan, London, 1985 (Offers insights into communism and modern politics.)

Abdulla El-Tayib, *Changing Customs of the Sudan,* The Trust for Printing and Distributing the Works of Abdulla ElTayib, New Life Printing Press, 2nd ed., 2017 (Part of the *Finding Felicity* resource packet.)

Biographies: Enoch (Idris, from *Stories of the Prophets,* Ibn Kathir), Pythagoras, Homer, Plato, Aristotle

Harold Lamb, *Cyrus the Great,* Doubleday, Garden City, New York, 1960

Reza Nazari, *Cyrus the Great: The Inspiring Story of a Genius,* Effortless Math Education, 2024 (Cyrus the Great is said to be '2nd Messiah' in Old Testament and some Muslim scholars claim he is the real figure behind the title 'Dhul-Qarnayn'.)

Harold Lamb, *Tamerlane: The Earth Shaker,* Garden City Publishing Company, Garden City, New York, 1928

See also:

G. G. Coulton, *Medieval Panorama, Medieval panorama: the English scene from conquest to Reformation,* Noonday Press, New York, 1955

Harold Lamb, *Suleiman the Magnificent: Sultan of the East,* Pinnacle Books, 1978 (Lamb has many other titles one may consider.)

Resources for orienting adults

Ibn Khaldun, *al-Muqaddimah* (tr. by Rosenthal as *The Muqaddima: An Introduction to History*)

Muhsin Mahdi, *Ibn Khaldun's Philosophy of History*, University of Chicago Press, Chicago (The best book known to us on the topic of Ibn Khaldun's theory of culture.)

'Genealogies of Modernity' (which gives crucial nuance to the periodisation of history such as the term 'modern')

Tarikh al-Tashri' (which shows how the Islamic sciences unfolded based on Quran and Sunnah and links to positions of the Companions and early scholars)

Louis Massignon, *The Passion of al-Hallaj: Mystic and Martyr of Islam*, tr. by Herbert Mason (A one-volume abridgement also exists. This work historically documents the social life in early Baghdad, including ascetics (*zuhhad*) and Sufis.)

Habib Abu Bakr al-Mashhur (tr. by Shaykh Ahmad Saad al-Azhari), *Al-Nubdha al-Sughra: Introductory Synopsis to the Fourth Component of the Islamic Religion & Its Major, Minor and Middle Signs*

Ahmed Keeler, *Rethinking Islam & the West: A New Narrative for the Age of Crises* (This is an important work for the very important topic of 'getting the narrative right'. For instance, it addresses that any notion of a 'golden age' is not the age of al-Farabi and Ibn Sina, but later when the sciences of reason and revelation were synthesised. As such, the '1001 Inventions' narrative directs one to the wrong period, the wrong spirit, and an age at a historical time removed from us such that there is no living transmission possible.)

Khaled El-Rouayheb, *Islamic Intellectual History in the Seventeenth Century: Scholarly Currents in the Ottoman Empire and the Maghreb*

Peter Redpath, *From Twilight to Dawn: The Cultural Vision of Jacques Maritain*

Christopher Dawson, numerous books, including *The Crisis of Education*

Etienne Gilson, *The Unity of Philosophical Experience* (An incredible book. Explains such matters as how mathematics became the queen of the sciences.)

Alisdair MacIntyre, *After Virtue* and other works on modernity

Charles Taylor, *Sources of Self, Secular Age*, and other writings on modernity.

Brad Gregory, *The Unintended Reformation: How a religious revolution secularised society*

Alan Jacobs, *The Year of Our Lord 1943: Christian Humanism in an Age of Crisis*

Histories of philosophy which do more justice to ancient and medieval thought than others:

- Johannes Hirschberger, *The History of Philosophy*, 2 vols and *A Short*

History of Western Philosophy

- Sir Anthony Kenny, *A New History of Western Philosophy*, 4 vols
- Henri de Lubac, *The Drama of Atheist Humanism*
- Russel Kirk, *The Conservative Mind*

Orienting history & cultural studies at the primary level

As was noted at the beginning of Section 4 (on the weekly subjects), each weekly subject shifts from the child's environment (home & kitchen, garden, wider family and neighbourhood) towards understanding the world outside the home. History and cultural studies address the drama of the sciences and arts that make up our culture. For a child, these matters are initially abstract and removed from their immediate environment. Yet, it is crucial to prepare children for the world in which they will spend most of their lives. Children may begin to live differently in the immediate institutions serving as the environment of their lives: the home, the wider family, and the neighbourhood (and perhaps the school). One's garden and workshop and kitchen are, in a sense, institutions which need to be practically run right—and they are microcosms about how to go out and integrate.

The reality is that most enter the world of work or our adult lives without knowing the different directions our culture and the subjects that inform it went or could have gone if matters turned out differently. There is a temptation to take culture and history for granted, as though the contemporary world is the only world that could have been. Even worse is when Muslims or others whose ancestral origins are outside the West feel compelled to adopt contemporary culture in order to avoid being labelled as 'backwards'. The term 'backwards' itself presumes a metaphysical narrative about history: that the future is always better; a doctrine called 'progress' or 'progressivism'. There are a few ironies here. First, most who use the terms 'progress' and 'backwards' do not believe in metaphysics. So it is contradictory to hold a metaphysical doctrine of progress with religious zeal and sway it over the heads of others. Another is to contrast this with the saying of the Prophet Muhammad ﷺ, 'The best generation is my generation, then that which follows, then that which follows.' This results in living someone else's history, wearing someone else's clothes, living in someone else's house. (And Plato whispers: 'The unexamined life is not worth living.')

History is written, they say, by the victor. One who digs below the surface in Western history finds what Philip Sherrard referred to as a 'second Europe'. In other words, there are or were dozens of thinkers, or rather groups of thinkers, who wanted history to go a different direction. Scholars such as Charles Taylor refer to the direction taken as 'disenchantment', following sociologist Max Weber. History itself has been disenchanted. But aside from the subject 'history' itself, one needs to learn to negotiate the historical arguments that impinge one on a daily basis. One needs to understand how the subjects were formed and on what assumptions. One needs to be able to determine if one lives in a virtuous society or not. Then if one is not in a virtuous society, what is the advice of the prophets and sages on how to thrive and work towards the common good in a society whose image of 'the good' is misguided. There is no other way to navigate 'this' world, which through the destiny and decree of God, we were born into.

All major subjects have a historical element: the natural world, the human world, and religion, etc. But the nature of history and how to teach it is surprisingly contentious and debated by both Islamic and Western scholars. LIFE's wider approach to history is to go beyond the mere skills of determining the historical validity of facts, beyond citizenship production, and to address Islamic and wider sacred culture. There is a coherence and unity and meaning lacking in modern culture; without addressing this, the subject of history will follow suit and become a series of disconnect facts and events.

Younger children need a narrative to grasp their imagination, and culture can be examined in history via the lens of a narrative, examining cause and effect unfolding in the world (according to rules which transcend the world, lying with Allah and His Names and His destiny and decree which He makes descend through the heavens). Thus, towards education's aim of rearing the perfect person, LIFE's approach is to start with children in a paradisiacal cocoon, showing how the history of the world should be, etching sacred values in their minds through biographies in their historical setting. (Do not get us wrong. The most perfect people in the best circumstances were surrounded by enemies and challenges. The point is that their hearts and vision were clear, and their religion was whole and wholesome.) As children come out of this cocoon into the real world, the single greatest benefit as a budding adult is to be able to navigate a complicated, secularised world in a sacred manner. Eventually, the need to free themselves from illusions without becoming disillusioned. Even if things really are bad, they are not purely bad. There is goodness and Divine gentleness (*lutf*), improvement in certain areas of life in certain historical periods, and good examples of reformers who accomplished some degree of positive change.

History can verge into economics, politics, ethics, and religion, because history is human history. Also, the benefit of history is to gain experience from previous events and the actions and lives of previous people in order to get things right. In our times, the hardest things to get right are human things like finding good work, seeking knowledge when respectable 'knowledge' excludes the humanities and religion, preventing the destruction of nature and good sources of pure food and water, avoiding a de-humanising centralisation of knowledge which makes people dependent for their basics on apps and corporations which gather information profiles to drive politics, and the rise of the political far-right, just to name some of the most important. These issues mean that young people need to be smart just to be in charge of their identities, lives, families, and communities. Ideally, to do so much in so little time, such a scheme would be handcrafted. Until that is done, we give schematic guidance as seen below.

Most classical and Protestant home-schoolers are happy for history to be part of literature; literature is where the values—or to use the less secular term: virtues—of a given civilisation are taught. This was done through the writings of Cicero and Virgil and works devoted to the lives of great men (often titled 'Lives', and unfortunately only listed a few great women). Religious educators taught works entitled Lives of the Saints. Muslims have this to say about history:

> "It is the knowledge of the conditions of social groups (tawa'if), their lands, their protocol and habits, the contributions of their individuals and their lineages, their obituaries, etc. Its subject is: the conditions of individuals of the past, including prophets, saints, scholars, philosophers, poets, kings, sultans, etc. Its aim is to understand the conditions of the past. Its benefit is to take reflective lessons ('ibrah) from those conditions and derive advice from them and to obtain the disposition of experience (through reflecting on the experience of others) and to understand how times change to avoid what has been transmitted to us of harmful events, and to elicit the like of the benefits which came about for ourselves. As has been said, this science is like another life for those who inquire into it and obtain the (experience) of the traveller in one's own town."
>
>   - *Taskoprulu Zadeh*, Miftah al-Sa'ada

Thus, the study of social groups (including scholars) and nations are reflected on to improve one's life and decisions. Notice there is no mention here of determining the truth of historical reports (or historiography). There is a hint of Ibn Khaldun of this: one learns the nature of civilisations in part because it allows one to rule out reports which are unlikely or impossible based on the nature and character of given civilisations. For Ibn Khaldun, history has an outward and inward aspect. Outwardly, it is reports of events. Inwardly, it tells us about the being in which those events occur: a given civilisation.

Here I use 'civilisation' only as a general term to include communities, kingdoms, caliphates, city-states, without favouring one or the other.) Civilisations or polities have a life of their own, and reading into historical events can allow us to deduce the rules by which they originate (or rise), live healthily, and die (or decline).

The principles of our approach to teaching history and cultural studies drawn from the previous reflections are as follows. History has a contemplative element which is to watch the unfolding of a Divine plan, and to contemplate the intelligible form of things such as humans, communities, and their interaction with the environment. Classical politics was about the health of the polity, but the polity took as its end the production of the perfect person. In other words, the polity produces the basic and less basic needs of the human being to use these resources to gain the virtues of character and contemplation, which are the two core perfections of the human being. This in turn informs their practical study of history, in that it informs their actions. Before the modern world, it was enough to go to school (the *kuttab*, the guild, and the madrasa and tekke) to learn an integrated manner of making the human and polity thrive. Now, the school inducts one into a system which is harmful to all of these ends, even if society makes us feel that school is 'the only way to get a job'.

In this context, we need re-education about a number of core topics without which humans cannot thrive or even survive:

- true balanced religion

- sustainable production which does not destroy human health and the environment (including the earth's soil which is itself directly responsible for human health)

- the family and the community which are attacked by communism and capitalism alike

- true education which—as part of cultural studies forms the keystone holding a society together (while an emphasis on specialisation and vocational training pulls it apart), and

- a connection to nature, soil, and human communities which grounds the fitrah, rather than destroying it and replacing our interactions with dancing lights on a screen.

These matters will be discussed more at the secondary stage, and further in a theoretical version of the *Perfected Muslim*. But even at the primary stage, they provide a purpose which is real and motivating and to which we all need to be dedicated. Some children may not continue homeschooling and so need the main message by the end of Year 6. Then, they may repeat the journey through history at the secondary level. But let us turn to how to make an age-appropriate history scheme.

Certain aspects of modernity

The modern world is a specific bag. Whether it was medieval nominalism or the fideism of Protestantism which lead to the breakdown of the balanced synthesis of reason and revelation; or whether it was mechanism and the rise of mathematics as the new queen of the sciences which lead to the monarchy of quantity; or whether it was the religious in-fighting of Christianity which gave birth to positivism, the point is that not all Europeans appreciated the way things went. But those who win write the history books, so our heroes are Galileo and a partially-understood Newton who was an alchemist and persecuted for being a true monotheist. Though Newton was wiser than to accept it, by his time the empirical and speculative methods split from each other, and the speculative dried and withered in an England inspired by the actually ineffective scientific new method (*Novum Organum*) of Francis Bacon and his New Atlantis. By Newton's time, the Royal Society would only allow scientific theories to speak about the phenomenal appearances, not the realities of things. Liberalism as a way of governing based on the will of people rather than the intellect was developed by John Locke and J. S. Mill who, with Rousseau, helped construct the modern political and ethical self which actively rejected and attempted to replace all forms of traditional thinking, Greek or religious. Neither a classical education nor a religious education, the only two ways out of the modern mass instruction, can accept the premises of modernity, nor post-modernity. (Some try to make a messy mix between spirituality and post-modernism. Good luck.)

Rather than moan about the ugly and impossible situation, let us remember those who remembered a sacred reality and dealt with the situation in a healthy way. Healthy means they were reformers of thought and politics, like a pre-modern Mustafa Sabri or Charles Taylor. Healthy means they were reformers without being preachy. They were passionate, but not angry, and never frustrated nor bitter, the signs of spiritual rot. So, when it comes to Western history, let us remember Suarez and the relatively sane modern philosophers: Thomas Reid and Leibniz, Pugin, and Ruskin (the enlightened and almost saintly supporter of workers without being socialist), his avid reader Gandhi, Romanticists who were free from a merely transcendental, private spirituality or merely new age spirituality (especially the pantheistic spirituality influenced by Spinoza). Without Ruskin, we do not see the traditional English ways of life—farming and seafaring—being destroyed alongside the other main form of pre-modern education (or apprenticeship): guild training in the crafts that fulfilled the other needs of human society. Who better than Ruskin to challenge that science is only the empirical and that ethics is not a science. And five sane mainstream figures studied in Jacobs' study of 20th Century Christian Humanism: a) C. S. Lewis, b) T. S. Elliot, c) Jacques Maritain, d) Auden, and e) Simone Weil, and of course J. R. R. Tolkien These are all subtle, tasteful, and passionate reformers who served as a Socratic gadfly in a world which has made some wrong turns.

LIFE's approach to history is thus to start with prophets, the Prophet (our beloved, Sayyidina Muhammad, upon him blessings and peace), pious personalities from stages of history (including non-Muslims). To some point, this is an innocent world. However, before they are influenced by mass culture, they need to know how to protect their own dignity and the pure soul given to them, even though historically speaking there is no doubt that we are in the End Times (*akhir al-zaman*). While Muslims (like Tashkoprulu Zadeh) often include history in literature, it would overload literature and take too us far from the aims of history to load it with the aims of history.

In our current context, the aims of history need to be to equip budding adults with knowledge of their times and how to successfully navigate them. This will necessarily include topics such as economics which should also be touched on in fiqh lessons, as well as in arts and crafts (which are about goodly production). This will open up topics such as the community (or, unfortunately, the lack of one) and technology. One of the central topics in the minds of Muslims living in the West is the relationship between Islam and the West. (Do not forget that in the coming fifty years, this will be an outmoded investigation. Instead, the question will be, 'Islam and the East'. Of course, most of the East will be affected to a degree by Western values and institutions, so the question will not exactly 'go away'.) This subtle topic must be gotten right, and the conversation cannot be driven by either fear or anger, nor by unilateral policy production, nor by either extreme of politicising or secularising Islam. Muslims need a sophisticated narrative of their own history which connects them to what remains of their living tradition.

Muslim students also need a narrative of the West which is just *true*. This is difficult to find because knowledge production over the last two-hundred years has been dominated by Western universities. (This includes most universities in the 'East', as they are Western in spirit. But within the West, there is what we referred to earlier as 'A Second Europe'. These thinkers have written cogently on aspects of the West we might distinguish as modernity.) A science of the West from a global or truly religious point of view might be termed 'Occidentalism'. But if one moves beyond particularism with our Islam to a real understanding of religion, we will see that critics of secularism and the twists and turns which produced modern history have been carefully written, often by people who share most of our religious and ethical values. The only way to have the right relationship with the West is to deserve their respect; and of course there is a general civilisational bias.

So, winning their respect can only be done by holding up a mirror: you are so proud of scientism and liberalism that you believe Muslims should mass convert, or at least secularise. Turn the mirror around and see that we all have lots of work to do. Is this a waste of time for Muslims? Let us reality check: most children in the West learn Western history. Most discussions of history are guided by citizenship policies designed to develop better citizens on a purely secular model (which many Westerners themselves find inadequate). Also, we live up to our necks in a built environment which is not just a manifestation of progress, but which is built on modern principles which can be discerned and which, for Christian or Muslim, make it a challenge to be a morally autonomous agent with meaningful actions and to live a sacred life, especially in the so-called public sphere.

Modern built spaces of apartments (key syllabus being 'apart') and malls and high-rise buildings, highways and secular architecture separate us from particular locations, from the earth and nature and from extended family. Modern construction is one of the biggest implicit arguments for the modern way of life: 'Look, it works.' It depends on interest (or usury, *riba*) and wasteful and harmful materials (shipped long distances, not repelling heat and cold, and which are difficult to dispose of in spite of modern buildings having a short half-life compared to traditional buildings). It makes a sacred and traditional life of all sorts difficult and snuffs out sacred notions of space, time, and life. So, investing in being able to navigate this requires intelligence and the ability to research (which evades being driven by adverts and search engines pouring you back into mainstream), a good heart, and a moral compass, and better yet historical detail and a good, balanced critique. Some of the best literature is that written by conservative reformers John Ruskin (a great influence on Gandhi) and William Cobbett. These English gentlemen who fought against slavery will debunk the invention of the term 'science', show the injustice in modern labour (and let one see how the change came about), and reveal how to live, produce (and consume), and build in a sacred manner.

4.3 Curriculum Summary

For seeing certain core aspects of the LIFE curriculum at a glance and to visualise the relations between different subjects and stages of development, we have included three tables expressing the backbone of certain key elements of that curriculum. These are:

Table 4.3.1 (Quran, Arabic liberal arts and literature, and religious instruction),

Table 4.3.2 (Pre-Logic, Logic and Research Methodology), and

Table 4.3.3 (Local language (English) liberal arts).

Quran, Arabic liberal arts and literature, and religious instruction

CURRICULUM SUMMARY

Year	Quran	Arabic liberal arts and literature	Religious Instruction
Preschool: Age 3+	Informal learning: Orally memorise from *al-Fatihah* to *al-Fajr*.	Informal learning: 1. Introduction to the Arabic Alphabet through play 2. Learn basic vocabulary orally (and label objects in home/classroom, incorporating Tarim *Hadanah* levels 1-5, organising around tawhid), 3. Memorise songs about alphabet, numbers, etc.	Learn through play: 1. Fiqh: prayer & ablution, 2. Etiquettes and invocations, 3. Tawhid: Learn and memorise from the 99 Names, 4. Stories of the Prophets (read-aloud)
Reception (4-5) KG (5-6)	1. Phonics (tajwid): Complete 1 introductory book (*al-Qaʿida nuraniyyah* or *al-baghdadiyyah*, or Malaysian book: Iqra). 2. Complete preschool curriculum (to *al-Fajr*), then carry on in Juzʾ ʿAmma	1. (Overlap with Quran: Phonics.) 2. Learn basic vocabulary through labelling, games, and flashcards. (Draw on vocabulary lists integrated with tawhid from Year 1.)	1. Fiqh: start Level 3 from Tarim *Hadanah* curriculum, 2. Etiquettes and invocations, 3. Tawhid: Learn and memorise from the 99 Names, 4. Stories of the Prophets (read-aloud)

CURRICULUM SUMMARY

Year 1 (5-7)	1. Complete khatam / nazirah of juz' 'Amma 2. Continue to memorise orally (talqin) until confident in reading from Quran. 3. Memorize at own pace (complete Juz' 'Amma and some students may memorize Juz' Tabaruk). 4. *Understanding and translation:* Apply Arabic lesson to simple verses (grammar and morphology). Learn Quranic vocabulary and begin to translate	1. *Arabic 1 Textbook:* Stages 1-5. Stage 1 is spoken Arabic. Stages 2-5 draws on introductory classical texts in *sarf*, grammar, and high-frequency vocabulary. [Some students may take this more slowly, reading in 2 years instead of 1. This and other options explained inside this manual (PWTM).] 2. *Qasas al-nabiyyin:* Begin reading and use supplementary resources designed to consolidate vocabulary.	1. *Qasas al-nabiyyin* (selections) 2. A comprehensive, introductory manual on Islam, iman, and ihsan (according to *madhhab*)	
Year 2 (6-8)	1. Memorize at own pace (complete Juz' Tabaruk and some students may work towards Juz' Qad Sami'a). 2. *Understanding and translation:* Apply Arabic lesson to simple verses (grammar and morphology). Learn Quranic vocabulary and begin to translate from Quran. 3. Begin simple grammatical analysis (*i'rab*; parsing.)	1. Grammar: LIFE's *Commentary on Nahu Mir* in English or *al-Tuhfah al-saniyyah*, completing its exercises. 2. Morphology: *Bina' al-af'al* or *Imdad al-sarf* 3. *Qasas al-nabiyyin* (cont.)	1. Hadith: *al-Araba'in al-hawawiyyah*, 2. Fiqh: an introductory text devoted to fiqh (the first studied in its respective school of fiqh), 3. 'aqidah: select from list of texts for children, 4. Stories from Quran, 5. Stories from righteous and *awliya'*	

301

CURRICULUM SUMMARY

Year			
Year 3 (7-9)	1. Memorize at own pace (complete Juz' Qad Sami'a and some students may begin Juz' 1 & 2). 2. *Understanding and translation:* Learn Quranic vocabulary and translate from Quran. 3. Grammatical analysis (*i'rab; parsing*).	1. Grammar: *Sharh Mi'at 'amil li-Jurjani*, learning and memorising the parsing of the text 2. *Qasas al-nabiyyin* (cont.) Optional: see full curriculum for optional *sarf* texts	1. Hadith: selections from *Mishkat al-masabih* or *Mukhtasar Riyad al-salihin* or *al-Silsila al-dhahabiyyah* (in full; 200 hadiths drawn from *al-Mudawwanah*). 2. Fiqh: the first half of an intermediate text (as per one's fiqh school)
Year 4 (8-10)	1. Memorize at own pace (recommended: complete Juz' 1 & 2 and some students may begin Juz' 3 & 4). 2. *Understanding and translation:* Learn Quranic vocabulary and translate from the Quran. 3. Grammatical analysis (*i'rab; parsing*)	1. Grammar: Start with *Tasheel al-Nahw*, then read *Hidayat al-Nahu* With English Q & A in remainder of Years 5 & 6 2. Morphology: *al-'Izzi* 3. *Qasas al-nabiyyin* (cont.) 4. Vocabulary: Learn the vocabulary of *al-Burdah* and memorise	1. 'aqidah: *al-Jawahir al-kalamiyyah*, 2. Fiqh: the second half of an intermediate text (as per one's fiqh school)
Year 5 (9-11)	1. Memorize at own pace (recommended: complete Juz' 3 & 4 and some students may begin Juz' 5 & 6). 2. *Understanding and translation:* Learn Quranic vocabulary and translate from the Quran. 3. Grammatical analysis (*i'rab; parsing*).	Literature: Selections of poetry and prose (e.g. from Diwans of 'Abbasids (al-Shafi'i, Abu al-'Atahiyah and al-Mutanabbi), Ibn Zaydun (Andalusia) and Ibn al-Farid (Ayyubid)) and some students begin *al-Bayan wa -l-tabyin*, al-Jahiz	1. 'aqidah/kalam: *Qawa'id al-'aqa'id* (al- Ghazali) and brief commentary on *Jawharat al-tawhid* or *Bad' al-amali* (study and memorise

CURRICULUM SUMMARY

| Year 6 (10-12) | 1. Memorize at own pace (recommended: complete Juz' 5 & 6 and some students may begin Juz' 7 & 8).
2. *Understanding and translation*: Learn Quranic vocabulary and translate from the Quran.
3. Grammatical analysis (*i'rab*; parsing).
4. Complete a *khatam/nazirah* of Quran before completing primary | Literature options:
1. *al-Bayan wa-l-tabyin*, al-Jahiz (stories and other selections)
2. *al-Mawahib al-ladunniyyah* (studying *al-Shifa'* in the years after it is completed)
3. al-Ghazali, *Kitab Riyadat al-nafs* from the *Ihya'* (Islamic ethics: faculties of the soul and cardinal virtues) | 1. Sirah (options): a. *al-Mawahib al-ladunniyyah* or b. *Fiqh al-Sunnah* of Dr. al-Buti, for those not studying in Arabic.
Then *al-Shifa'* in the after *Mawahib* completed,
2. Tazkiyah (options): a. *al-Arab'in fi usul al-din* (al-Ghazali) or b. *Kitab al-Ma'unah* (*The Book of Assistance*) |

Table 4.3.1

CURRICULUM SUMMARY

Pre-Logic & Logic (Years 2-6)

Year	Pre-logic	Logic
Year 2 (6-8)	Optional: *Primary Logic: Grades 2-4*, by Judy Leimback, Dandy Lion Publications, 1986 *Bond Starter Papers in Verbal Reasoning*: 6-7 Years Optional: *Primary Logic: Grades 2-4* (cont.) *Bond 11+*: Verbal Reasoning Assessment Papers: 7-8 Years	N/A
Year 3 (7-9)	Problem Solving: Logic-Based Activities (Grade 3; Mead)	N/A
Year 4 (8-10)	*Primary Logic: Grades 2-4* (cont.)	N/A
Year 5 (9-11)	N/A	Informal logic: *Fallacy Detective* or *The Art of Argument: An Introduction to the Informal Fallacies* Introduce logic:
Year 6 (10-12)	N/A	1. Define terms from *al-Isaghuji* and give examples from Quran using *al-Qistas al-mustaqim and Logic, Rhetoric, and Legal Reasoning in the Qur'an: God's arguments*), Optional: Introduce logic in English through a. *FSTU Logic*, Shaykh Hashim Mohamed or b. *Minhaj al-Mantiq: A Primer to Classical Logic*, Yusuf Sulaiman

Table 4.3.2

CURRICULUM SUMMARY

Local language (English) liberal arts

Year	Literature	Grammar	Writing (& pre-rhetoric)
Ages 0 to 3	See, '3.3.6 Read-aloud books for the very young'	N/A	N/A
Preschool: Age 3+	1. Engage children's interest through child-friendly topics 2. Informal read-aloud of English stories of the prophets (upon them peace)	N/A	N/A
Reception (4-5)/ KG (5-6)	See, '3.6', Subject 3: English: 1. Phonics: *McGuffy's Eclectic Primer* or *Jolly Phonics* 2. Review of phonics and spelling: *Spelling Workout K* and start *Spelling Workout A* 3. McGuffy's *First Reader* (first thirty lessons are very simple) 4. Read-aloud and discuss board books and picture books (listed in this section)	'Grammar in Rhyme' (a poem on the parts of speech provided in General Resources)	Pre-handwriting skills

CURRICULUM SUMMARY

Year				
Year 1 (5-7)	1. Eclectic Bk 2 (Applying analysis, imitation, and summarisation simplified from *progymnasmata*) Optional: 2. Eclectic Bk 3 (begin)	1. First Language Lessons (Parts of speech) 2. Introduce basic parts of sentence: subject, predicate (including verbs), object (direct and indirect), and modifiers (adjectives, articles, adverbs, and prepositions; and the conjunctions relating them). 3. *Rex Barks* (sentence diagramming, mirrored in Arabic learning)	1. Copy work from famous sayings (including *The Content of Character Copybook* (Kinza Press) 2. Begin writing letters to family and friends. 3. Then introduce other simple genres such as stories.	
Year 2 (6-8)	1. Eclectic Bk 3 (' ') Optional: 2. Eclectic Bk 4 (begin)	1. Begin Harvey's English grammar (apply to sentences read in literature syllabus) or Charles Dickens (recommended)	Introduce copy-work (leading on to dictation when ready) of classical writings, including from *Aesop's Fables*.	
Year 3 (7-9)	1. Eclectic Bk 4 (' ') Optional: 2. Eclectic Bk 5 (begin)	Grammar of Adverbs and complex constructions: 1. Gwynne's English Grammar 2. Advanced English Grammar, Kitridge and Farley	Dictation in classic writings	

CURRICULUM SUMMARY

Year			
Year 4 (8-10)	1. Eclectic Bk 5 (' ') Optional: 2. Eclectic Bk 5 (begin)	N/A	Rhetoric: *Classical Composition I: Fable*, James Selby [From Year 4 on, writing skills now addressed via exercises in the literature and rhetoric strands.]
Year 5 (9-11)	1. Eclectic Bk 6 (' ')	N/A	Rhetoric: *Classical Composition II: Narrative Stage*, James Selby [' ']
Year 6 (10-12)	1. *Junior Great Books Series 6*	N/A	Rhetoric: *Classical Composition III: Chreia/Maxim Stage*, James Selby [' ']

Table 4.3.3

5

CONCLUDING WORD

5.1 THE COMPLETE MUSLIM MANUAL & ITS MODEL

In this book, we have offered the reader a complete manual for primary education including a comprehensive theoretical section and a detailed practical section. The theoretical section illustrates the classical model of Islamic education which forms the backbone of the practical section on curriculum. We took time to inform educators what is an Islamic philosophy of education and how it translates into practice, as we have observed how this model is missing from contemporary discussions on curriculum.[171]

We explained the LIFE model of the 'complete Muslim' on the paradigm of the Prophet Muhammad, upon him and his family peace and blessings. We chose this model because it is a true model of education designed to bring out the latent perfections of the human being, including moving from distance from God to closeness and knowledge of Him, {And I did not create man- and jinn-kind except to worship me},[172] which the companion 'Abd Allah ibn 'Abbas said means to 'know Allah'.[173]

We showed how this model is a comprehensive and integrated model of human development, not merely instruction designed for economic development. This model has much to say about how 'curriculum subjects' should be wisdom. Wisdom is defined by al-Tahanawi in his *Kashshaf* as that which accords with ultimate realities, including the Sunnah and traditional sciences. The latter is most especially wisdom when it has been filtered by the prior. The Quran was not revealed to teach us Euclidean geometry, but such treatments of mathematics, natural, science and ethics are the 'lost property'

---

171 And for those interested, we offered this philosophy of education more expansively in our Introduction to Islamic Education course as a live intensive and intend to offer this course as an online course in the near future.

172 Quran 51:56.

173 *Tafsir*s such as those of al-Baghawi and al-Qurtubi cite Ibn Jurayj and Mujahid elucidate on this point as well.

of the believer. The subjects in the LIFE model are our late, classical tradition. This integration is not found in 'Abbasid thinkers, so we should not refer to the 'Abbasid age as our golden age. Through this integration, these subjects have the capacity to perfect the human individual and, miraculously, the same subjects are those needed to inform a healthy community and society.

Some educators seeking wisdom and human development have opted for classical alternative curricula, or trivium-based education. But as Sheikh Amin Kholwadia has noted we need to move from trivium-based education to quadrivium: grammar, logic, and rhetoric, plus education in the sharia. The sharia is composed of theoretical and practical rulings. The theoretical sciences embodying the theoretical rulings are needed to complete wisdom, and in fact are its head and crown. The theoretical sciences —most specifically metaphysical *kalam* theology— also serve as a sound basis for the practical sciences. (This is the significance of the term *uṣūl al-dīn*: the root principles of religion.) The 'practical sciences' teach and inculcate virtues that purify the heart and soul, and are integrated with the prophetic Sunnah. These points are grasped by the polymaths of the Islamic tradition such as Ibn Khaldun, one of the scholars we build on. Pedagogy cannot merely be a technique, but must be integrated with subjects and their methods. For this reason, we believe that this model is the *sine qua non* of sound education, even if one uses Montessori or other techniques to facilitate teaching and learning, or to soften the educational experience, or to increase internal motivation.

The introduction set out the highest aim of real education: the complete person or human *(insan kamil)*. This is education according to what we all share: humanity. The complete Muslim receives the grace of the revelation of the crowning Abrahamic faith, integrating God's will expressed in His final dispensation. Thus, it builds on a foundation of individually obligatory knowledge, as indicated by the like of the famous hadith, {My servant draws close to Me through nothing more beloved to Me than that which I have made obligatory *(iftaradtuhu)* upon him.}[174]

Our model serves the complete human through serving its three capacities: the productive, practical, and the contemplative, which may be termed the speculative or theoretical capacity. Forming firm dispositions is universal across the three said capacities. Beginning with the speculative or theoretical capacity, Ibn Khaldūn specifically states that its true perfection inculcating firm dispositions *(malakat)*, not merely transient understanding *(fahm)*. Contrast this with the model of exam-based education—better termed instruction: successful students are generally sparky, rapidly forming hyper links in their minds, and capable of performing well under pressure in examinations

---

174 *Al-Bukhari* 6502. This hadith is also found in al-Nawawi's collection of forty hadith and receives a priceless commentary by the likes of Ibn Rajab al-Hanbali.

and interviews. After examinations, there is little encouragement to retain information as it is not seen as developmental wisdom. As for the practical faculty, the first step is to learn Islamic law and ethics in order to know good and virtue from bad and vice. After knowing what should and should not be done, one must vigilantly observe one's acts and repeat good actions until they become second nature. In the case of children, this must be facilitated for. Educators must learn to focus on firm dispositions (whose reality is better captured by its Latin root *habitus*). As Charlotte Mason states the precept: make a habit of making habits. In the end, this becomes easy for you as the educator, and in the end, teaching the child becomes a joy, rather the collection of bad or ill-formed habits in the student being a constant source of chafing for you. For these reasons, we contest the dominant model of instruction in which behaviour is policed and controlled. We advocate for the transformation into real nurture and human development (tarbiya). Children cannot do this alone and depend on you the educator to learn to be a *murabbi* (a pedagogue of character traits and the heart.) Achieving these high ideals requires an integrated system, which we offer in our practical guide comprising the bulk of the manual in your hands. LIFE has produced policy titled 'Tarbiya Policy' which is offered as part of its training courses and which should be integrated into the primary curriculum by educators.

The theoretical introduction was followed by a guide containing detailed instructions for those wishing to pursue true education. These instructions include timetables and recommended resources that are designed to fit several models of delivery: homeschooling, tutoring, co-ops, and schools of various sorts. For each subject, we offered a sub-section addressing what, why, and how. The what section attempts to slice through the confusion of the modern world to identify the subject in a manner that conveys wisdom and true knowledge of the world, perfects the soul, and informs society to pursue true felicity. In the why section, we spell out what this subject contributes towards human perfection, exploring what dispositions are developed and in which faculty. What knowledge, character or practical capacities does it develop in the soul? How will these virtues contribute to the formation of a virtuous society (*madina*)? How will these capacities empower one to contribute towards the wider society? The how section addresses the resources and proper pedagogy needed to teach this subject in order to get the benefits, internal and external. This section explains how to turn each subject into an education plan. This includes recommended 'high roads' and alternative 'low roads' for those unable for whatever reason to implement the high road. (Undoubtedly, learning *in* Arabic is the high road for Islamic instruction. But for many reasons there are significant barriers to this in practice.)

The general timetable then gives an example of how the subjects may be brought together into an education plan. In the FAQs below, we address how to prioritise if unable to implement all the recommended subjects and other questions needed to help you start moving or to keep moving towards true education. (Some particular tricks are of course mentioned inside the subjects, such as how to decrease the burden of daily mathematics teaching and learning without 'falling behind'.)

5.2 Frequently Asked Questions

The present frequently asked questions are intended to be supplemented with an updated list and accompanying discussions on our website: www.livinginsights.org.uk

- *What should I focus on during the primary years?*

As we indicated in charts in the theoretical introduction, children begin with exposure to language, playing with other children, and nature. Parents should try to expose children to spoken Arabic from a young age, such as having an Arabic friend who can speak to them or conducting some of their play in Arabic. When capable of rote memorisation, begin gently with the pre-school curriculum, including oral memorisation of Quran. The rest of the primary years should focus on: a) language acquisition, including writing and—dare we say— some grammar and b) gaining their obligatory Islamic learning and immersing them in Quranic virtues. Of course, one cannot afford to fall behind in mathematics as it is a 'discipline' in the true sense of the word. It requires continual practice and may be forgotten easily.

These are the best years to memorise Quran and other Arabic or English texts, best if these are in poetry. Ensure that at the very least children can parse sentences representing the major topics of grammar such as prepositions, adverbs, and direct and indirect objects before they graduate to the secondary. This lays the foundations for logic. Grammar identifies the subject and predicate, and then its qualifiers. This prepares the mind to see the logical propositions behind language, and to start to think about evidence and proof by which alone one moves from imitation to knowledge. Grammar also lays the foundations for rhetoric. The practice of rhetorical writing depends on knowing the impact of the different ways a sentence may be formed, and these ways must be valid. The basic validity of sentences is the subject matter of grammar. So, it all begins with the complete sentence. Some grammars focus on words, spending months or years teaching the parts of speech and the attributes of words such as singular, plural, masculine, feminine, etc. This is abstract, because the natural unit of meaning is the sentence. In addition to focus on whole sentences, we prefer that children have a robust experience of the world before they enter the world of language. Thus when they are pressed to define things and think what they really are, they are comparing words to their rich experience of nature, not merely the circular process of comparing words to words. They should pay attention to nature until it reveals its subtle behaviours. They should watch for symbiotic relationships between insects. They should learn how to win the trust of bee hives through being calm. They should snorkel till they learn from hermit crabs, star fish, and sand dollars. When older, they can snorkel over shallow coral reefs and silently watch till new species appear and they find cleaner shrimp entering the narrow homes of fish, operating on their injuries, or cleaning food from between their teeth. Then when they move to logic, they have the materials to define species and classify genera, and book knowledge will be like living flesh instead of dead ashes.

- *At what age should I start teaching my child and what if I am not sure they are ready for the recommended materials for their age?*

We have based the materials in our curriculum on our experience that many ordinary children in ordinary families have learned according to the ages we have recommended for subjects and activities. This does not entail that your own child is ready or not. For instance, if your child is in a home speaking two languages, their early language-development may 'lag' a full year behind others. Also, their preparedness for our curriculum relates to attending pre- school or other factors that may make them forward or behind in certain subjects. It is thus the responsibility of the parents to expose their children to good English, via speaking and reading to them, and as much Arabic as they may manage, and to take them into nature and stimulate them without screens. Otherwise, it would be unfair to expect them to be equivalent to how they would receive teaching if they do.

To put it another way, our strategy is to avoid what has been called 'dumbing down' in part through the process of lowest common denominator. We have recommended what many children can do and therefore need to do to reach their full potential.

So, pay attention to your child and take the time to lay down foundational experiences. As noted below, in addressing children starting learning in the middle a year, for instance, you not only can but should delay matters until you see preparedness and provide time to lay foundations. So our aim is to structure what is reasonably possible on the premise that parents took care of their child in certain ways. This allows a well-trodden path *(muwatta')* to emerge which others may contribute to and individualise to their needs.

- *How should I proceed if starting in the middle of the curriculum or a specific subject?*

As mentioned above, the focus of primary years learning is obligatory basic Islamic learning, language acquisition (English and Arabic), and competency in grammar to open doors for logic in secondary, and a steady stream of Quranic and related memorisation.

If you wish to start a full year later or only now are able to start your child's education and you are past the recommended age, start from the beginning in September if your child is not eight by September. It is good to keep some shape to the year in case you need or want to put your children back into local schools in the future.

If starting more than two years late, each subject will need some thought. Presuming the child has received some learning in language and maths, look at the year before the year which is age-appropriate, or even the year before that, and test the child to see if they can understand the material and lessons. When one finds material they do not understand easily, determine whether the material can be covered quickly to fill the gap. If not, then teach it at a normal speed, but look for topics that will repeat later to skip or other ways to get studies closer to the age-appropriate year / materials. (You are free to go at your own pace at home, but this can have repercussions if their educator or caretaker falls ill and they are forced into a school.)

In general, maths spirals through and repeats topics, but if one misses several years then one can completely miss a topic such as geometry or algebra, and this will cause problems later. Try to consult with an experienced primary teacher who can review your decisions of what to skim, skim, or review. You may know someone at your local primary school, have a relative, use LIFE's consultation process, or join an online forum for Muslim homeschoolers. In language—in this case English, a bit of cleverness on the part of the educator should allow them to select items such as grammar and vocabulary which are needed for a level and summarise them sufficiently for a child to quickly cover materials they may have missed from earlier years. 'Holes' will repair themselves more naturally than in mathematics.

As for Arabic, start with Year 1 materials, but you may be able to proceed faster than if taught at the age of Year 1 students. The same for Islamic instruction, except that one should look out for repetition which is not needed. For instance, one may be able to read the first fiqh quickly or not at all if the next text covers the same materials in more depth. An example of this is that at a certain age, Maliki students may study Ibn 'Ashir and skip al- 'Ashmawi. As for Quran, it must be memorised in order and at one's pace, whatever that is. For instance, always start with the final, thirtieth juz'/ *separa*, even if starting at a later age.

Some of the principles for starting in the middle overlap with the the following discussion on prioritisation, but we plan to expand on this topic on our website mentioned at the head of this section.

- *How should I prioritise if I am unable to teach the full set of recommended subjects?*

Obviously in the early years the lessons are shorter, so there are gaps between them or one can finish the day earlier. There is no need to put yourself or child under undue pressure, but there are passionate people would say, 'You need this much liberal arts. You need this much Quran. You need this much Islamic instruction. You need this much time in nature, this much art, this much maths, this much physical education. You need to learn handwriting well before using computers, and so on.' While subject specialists typically are over-passionate for their pet subject, our curriculum is not driven by mere subject specialists. Nonetheless, there are often very good reasons for ensuring a subject is taught properly. If you are going to drop things, prioritise and do not lose the heart. The reality is that many educators drop what is difficult for them to teach, not based on consideration of the learning.

Then what is the heart? It starts with what is individually obligatory, which does not include memorising the Quran, besides the *fatihah*. This individually obligatory knowledge and practice should be roots, branches, and fruit: iman, Islam and ihsan, respectively. Dry memorisation is like seeds with no water. When memorisation is not explained through stories, made significant and meaningful, and integrated as soon as possible into one's understanding and practice, it is dry memorisation. One way to water the seeds of memorisation is through practice, righteous company, singing, and following the Sunnah. We may swear that anything related to the Prophet Muhammad and his family and his Sunnah will have more *baraka* than that which is not. Whatever is approached as his practice will be easier to maintain joyfully. You can approach the whole religion through him, upon him and his family blessings and peace, and when you do you will find love. Remember the extraordinary verse, {Say if you would love Allah, then follow me, and Allah will love you and forgive for you your sins. And Allah is All Forgiving, Most Merciful.}[175]

Inside the practical curriculum's treatment of individual subject, we mentioned matters such as using Kumon practice to decrease the burden of teaching and timetabling daily mathematics lessons. Another reason to reduce mathematics teaching time is to make room for teaching Euclid which many, many people have done in late primary education. This book has a history of being the spark that sets thinkers off into a state of inspiration.

You should consider prioritising Arabic for a time, intending to make a breakthrough so that you can teach Arabic texts. Because the teaching thereafter is a form of reinforcement, there is less reason to worry about regressing.

If you wish to focus on Quran memorisation, we encourage you do the following. Give the student's mind a chance to gradually build up to a schedule which allows or nearly allows their minds to focus completely on memorisation for a period. This should feel like a clarity of mind and laser-

---

175 Quran 3:31.

sharp focus, rather than suffocation. The child has to be up to the challenge and generally motivated. Some may wish to keep this up till the Quran is memorised. We would not advocate leaving off English, mathematics, and physical exercise and getting into nature. It also seems sad to neglect Arabic and the discussion of meaning in such as process. This is a large topic, but suffice to cite examples of *hafizes* who do not understand what they have memorised, many of who cannot carry on the burden of review and eventually forget. So we prefer to temporarily limit the curriculum to a few subjects, then once the muscle is developed and focus obtained, slowly put a wider curriculum back onto the schedule.

The intention to prioritise may tempt you to cherry-pick. For example, grammar schools in the United Kingdom cherry-pick from traditional grammar school education and the classics such as Latin and Greek, and classical literature translated into English. They do not except in the rarest of exceptions teach a full classical education. Muslims may be tempted to cherry-pick subjects that transform and open the heart immediately such as sirah and Sufi stories. Sirah is highly inspirational and kindles love of Allah's Beloved, *upon him and his pure family peace and blessings*, but it is not a structural subject as it is generally taught. (Some teachers such as the late Dr Ramadan al-Buti could teach everything through the sirah, but that is exceptional.) When we say it is not a structural subject, what we mean is that it does not spell out the practical and theoretical parts of the syllabus. It does not cover a subject area normally taught (and thereby ensure that we have covered it in an Islamic manner.) It is added to the subjects on a palette model.

The same may be said for Quran and hadith studies: they are sometimes thought of sources rather than subjects, because we derive subjects from them. (Of course our curriculum includes daily Quran and several hadith texts. And there is no way to deny the intense *baraka* of studying texts such as al-Bukhari or *al-Muwaṭṭa'* of Imam Malik.) If the curriculum becomes too heavy with sirah, Quran, and hadith, we argue that it will not be clear to students how it integrates with life, especially in the modern world. We strive especially in the secondary curriculum to make it clear to students how religion is integrated into knowledge, in spite of living in a secular world even in Muslim countries. But the primary curriculum is a stepping stone to the secondary. So, if you neglect Arabic, you will learn always in English. If you neglect grammar, you cannot study pre-rhetoric in primary nor logic in secondary. If you neglect logic, you cannot understand the transformations by which natural science became 'science', nor how how the practical sciences became the social sciences. If none of this is understood and we cherry-pick the curriculum for instant inspiration, we produce modern Muslims rather than contemporary Muslims. They will unable to think traditionally across the curriculum and without knowing it they will be moving down the conveyer belt of secularisation. As greater thinkers have stated, theology alone does not counter secularisation. It sits as a specialisation in the humanities department where it can be ignored and where it has no implications for the other subjects. The university speeds along, adding business schools and science and technology departments, and eventually the university forgets why it started in the first place.

- *What if I have more than one child to teach?*

If you have multiple children to teach that are not the same age, you need to be creative and draw on the experience of others. This might motivate you to start a co-op. This option aside, if your children are one to three years apart, consider teaching them together. You can do what contemporary teachers term 'differentiating by outcome'. In other words, you teach the same lesson and generally have the same activity, but expect different results. Older children will be more capable and confident. You can use this to your advantage by having the older child model things orally for the younger child. (Children often learn better from children than from adults.)

If the children are more than three years apart, consider a version of the Robinson technique. This technique is named after a professor whose wife passed away, leaving him to raise and educate them. He chose books that do not require teaching and which are designed to develop independence in children. You still need to check their work, keep them on track in general, and answer questions when they are stumped. You will find that many subjects, Robinson-friendly or otherwise, do not require your continual presence. So, you could schedule language arts for both children and get into a routine where you explain points and set activities first to a younger child and get them working. Then you do the same for the older child who is more likely not to unravel while waiting, and who may benefit or even be used by you to motivate the younger child by answering some questions about their lesson.

We have all heard stories of a lesson where a baby takes off their nappy and drags it behind the piano while you try to teach your seven-year-old. This question and its like are best addressed elsewhere, and one can find blogs and online 'communities' where practical solutions are offered for questions such as how to feed children quickly and healthily so that you can focus on teaching and preparation.

- *What if my child is unmotivated due to addiction to their phone and social media or cannot focus on matters that do not involve a screen?*

Removing harm always has precedence over adding good. And relatedly, *takhliya* (divestment) must precede *tahliya* (adornment). And this is for a good reason. If your child loses interest in the world, people, activities, and things, how will you teach them and help them grow? The videos on phones and other screens are addictive; the child becomes like an addict looking forward to the next dose, often zombie-like when not on the screen. In the words of Jonathan Haidt, the author of *The Anxious Generation* and currently the leading expert on social media and children states, three to four companies now own childhood. They have vastly more influence on children than parents do. In the final practical section of his book, Haidt wants to drive home four norms:[176]

1. No smartphones before high school
2. No social media before 16
3. No phones in schools [or homeschools]
4. More free, independent play

Even before they start learning, parents need to battle to engage them in and encourage them to enjoy activities (not 'passivities' like starring at a screen). Those activities should be consumer free as well; they should not be part of a commodified product or experience. Take culture into your own hands away from corporations and governments. Why? Consumption feeds into the same passivity and sloth as the phone. Rather than perfect ourselves, we entertain ourselves. Soon enough, we feel depressed if we do not watch just the right videos.

That is a form of addiction. The designers of many major applications and platforms know the psychology of dopamine and the effect of every greater doses on the motivation centre of the brain. (Even if Muslims believe the brain is characterised by neural plasticity, the soul is spiritual, and Allah is in control of the universe, this does not mean the data collected on the psychological impact of screens, video, and social media is not true, if interpreted correctly.)

Addiction to doom scrolling of amazing or startling one-minute videos destroys the capacity to focus for extended periods. The links in social media direct too many people to a related but worse addiction we must confront in order to avoid: pornography. The mechanism is the same: higher and higher doses of dopamine triggered by more and more extreme content. In the end, the normal world does not motivate one nor capture one's attention, let alone interest. Many youth fail to engage, wanting only to sit in a room and scroll or chat.

What should one do to avoid these obvious and prevalent harms? First, take this as seriously as you would the information that your home or country are being invaded. Second, implement Haidt's list and discuss this matter with successful parents and teachers. The norm, 'No smart phones

---

176 https://theconnectedfamily.substack.com/p/the-anxious-generation-4-norms-to

before high school', affords your child the opportunity to develop and to have something to offer to the world before they pick up a phone. Third, if you are part of a school or co-op, make parents sign a contract that they will implement these or a similar set of norms. Without this, the whole ship will sink. Some schools fully aware the harms of phones and social media allow up to three hours of total screen time on weekends.

One has to set exact days and hours, and include notes such as that watching while visiting friends and the wider family counts towards their three hours. Obviously, media which is allowed must be approved and filtered to avoid profanity and nudity, and some schools include violence. Prohibited violence here does not mean bullies throwing a nerd into a trash dumpster, but rather normalisation of killing, murder, and gore.

It is true that smart phones are increasingly necessary for doctors and other professions. But these people have a skill set and their training has forced them to learn useful services and develop the capacity to interact with people. Youth on phones have nothing to offer and have not developed the capacity to do things. So the passivity of the phone is more crippling. The absurdity of their communication with their peers is more obvious. The social pressure is more paralysing.

Like any addiction, begin to reduce it slowly but firmly. Children need to lose the expectation of using the phone, and reintegrate their motivation and attention systems with the world and people. Think of the phone as something harmful, which it is. If your child cried and threw a tantrum, would you succumb to letting them play with knife? Start by setting times and sitting with them and selecting videos made when the window of activation was lower and screen shots and images moved much more slowly. Look for videos made through stop-motion, claymation or through filming the books themselves such as Beatrix Potter stories or *Wind in Willows* recorded in the 1980s if English-speaking. If Arabic-speaking or working seriously on Arabic, then Yahya al-Fakhrani's stories from the Quran. Limit these to the point that they are not expected and ultimately are forgotten.

Additionally, *The Complete Muslim* lists many early childhood and craft activities, as well as martial arts and encourages growing plants and raising animals. Young children can make figures from classical literature and Islamic history from cardboard or play dough. They can make backdrops and act out scenes. (Boys may favour fight scenes, but fight scenes are better than screens.)

www.ingramcontent.com/pod-product-compliance
Lightning Source LLC
Chambersburg PA
CBHW032302300426
44110CB00033B/278